HOWARD COSELL

THE CONTROVERSY, THE OUTRAGE, THE ACCLAIM

"MANY TARGETS, MANY DIRECT HITS...He is unique among his television sports contemporaries in that he has been certifiably both the most liked and the most disliked personality in his field. Howard Cosell doesn't roll in on little cat's feet. He huffs and he puffs and he blows your house down."
—Tony Kornheiser, *The Washington Post*

"There's nothing great one can say about Howard Cosell that he hasn't already said much better. He never played the game."
—Woody Allen

"Cosell steps on some toes when he takes his ego for a stroll...With apologies to Muhammad Ali, the book's subtitle should be *I Am The Greatest*."
—Bob Fowler, *The Orlando Sentinel*

"Fascinating...This is the kind of writing you look forward to when you pick up a book. It tells you things you can believe, and you feel that if you quote from this book, you'll be absolutely correct. Howard Cosell, above many, is a man who is in search of the truth and wants to let us in on it."
—Bill Cosby

HOWARD COSELL
THE CONTROVERSY, THE OUTRAGE, THE ACCLAIM

"If you believe as I do that no one has had a greater impact on television sports journalism in the last twenty years than Howard Cosell, then you won't want to miss this book. *I NEVER PLAYED THE GAME* is going to have the same kind of impact on sports readership."

—George Steinbrenner

"What Cosell says is almost invalidated by his outsized ego, bordering on the monstrous...And yet *I NEVER PLAYED THE GAME* is not just a diatribe, full of venomous air. It has punch and vitality...and he deserves high marks for bringing journalistic integrity to much of what he does."

—Larry Williams,
The Commercial Appeal

"The One and Only puts it down on paper and tells it like it is. If you don't like this book, you don't like finding out the truth about sports and having fun learning it."

—Dan Jenkins, author of
Semi-Tough and *Life Its Own Self*

HOWARD COSELL
THE CONTROVERSY, THE OUTRAGE, THE ACCLAIM

"It is fascinating to read Cosell's criticisms of the Monday Night crew: Gifford bows to the almighty god NFL and makes dumb mistakes... Meredith sings a silly song because he has nothing to say... Simpson is simply hopeless. So the reviewers have savaged Cosell for disloyalty and insensitivity, never bothering to say, 'Y'know, the guy's right, and, yeah, I'd have ripped him for lying if he said only good things about those clowns.'"

—Dave Kindred, *The Atlanta Constitution*

"THERE'S NEVER A DULL MOMENT!"
Publishers Weekly

"When I got the book, I was expecting '60 Minutes.' Instead, I got 'Dynasty,' 'Dallas,' and a daytime soap opera."

—O. J. Simpson

"An honest, courageous reporter, Howard Cosell speaks his mind in the hope that sports doesn't really have to be the way it is. If anyone could turn me into a sports fan, it's Howard Cosell."

—Mayor Edward I. Koch

HOWARD COSELL

WITH PETER BONVENTRE

I NEVER PLAYED THE GAME

AVON
PUBLISHERS OF BARD, CAMELOT, DISCUS AND FLARE BOOKS

"One Step Backward Taken" from *The Poetry of Robert Frost*, edited by
Edward Connery Lathem. Copyright 1947, © 1969 by Holt, Rinehart and
Winston. Copyright © 1975 by Lesley Frost Ballantine. Reprinted by
permission of Holt, Rinehart and Winston, Publishers.

Cover Photograph © 1983 Arnold Newman
Courtesy *Sports Illustrated*

AVON BOOKS
A division of
The Hearst Corporation
1790 Broadway
New York, New York 10019

The William Morrow edition contains the following Library of Congress
Cataloging in Publication Data:

Cosell, Howard, 1918–
  I never played the game.

  1. Cosell, Howard, 1918–   2. Sportscasters—United States—Biography.
3. Sports—United States. I. Bonventre, Peter. II. Title.
GV742.42.C67A35 1985   070.4'49796'0924 [B]   85-11548

First Avon Printing: November 1986

AVON TRADEMARK REG. U.S. PAT. OFF. AND IN OTHER COUNTRIES, MARCA
REGISTRADA, HECHO EN U.S.A.

Printed in the U.S.A.

K-R 10 9 8 7 6 5 4 3 2 1

For my beloved family: Emmy, my bride of forty-one years; my daughters, Jill and Hilary, and my four grandchildren, Justin, Jared, Caitlen, and Colin. Also, for Leonard Goldenson, the man who built ABC and who has been a surrogate father to me during my thirty-two years with the company; and for Roone Arledge, who, despite the vicissitudes in our personal relationship, gave me the opportunity to forge my career and supported me when it counted most.

Contents

I Never Played the Game

Prologue

I am writing this book because I am convinced that sports are out of whack in the American society; that the emphasis placed upon sports distorts the real values of life and often produces mass behavior patterns that are downright frightening; and that the frequently touted uplifting benefits of sports have become a murky blur in the morass of hypocrisy and contradiction that I call the Sports Syndrome.

I did not always feel this way.

I have spent the past thirty-two years of my life in sports journalism. Educated and trained at law, I ventured into broadcasting and sports quite by accident, and the manner in which I became a broadcaster of sports is a tired and often told story. In the beginning, like most people in America, I had romantic ideas about sports. I found beauty in the contests, and I really believed that the public needed the surcease that spectator sports provided from the daily travail of life. But the past fifteen years have developed vast changes in my thinking and have caused me to reach the conclusion set forth at the top of this prologue.

In that time, I have walked away from professional boxing, and I have come to have grave doubts about amateur boxing. I have walked away from professional football because of family pressures and because I no longer believed morally or ethically in the actions of the National Football League. By doing this, I gave up, literally, millions of dollars, and yet I suffered tremendous vilification in print for my actions.

In that time, I came to realize, however reluctantly, that there was an inexorable force working against revelations of truth about sports in America. That force exists in the form of an unholy alliance between the three television networks and the sports print medium. It is the fundamental purpose of both, for their own reasons, to exalt sports, to regale the games, the fights, the races, whatever, to the point where these contests are indoctrinated into the public mind as virtual religious rituals.

Only rarely does one ever read or hear about how sports in the current era inextricably intertwine with the law, the politics, the sociology, the education, and the medical care of the society. It is common practice now for sports franchise owners to rip off great cities in financial distress either by franchise removal or threat of franchise removal. I have seen the emphasis upon sports corrupt our higher educational process, and to at least some degree, our secondary educational system. The Olympic Games have long been little more than a political forum, yet there are those who still scream simplistically that sports and politics do not mix. I have heard U.S. Olympic officials cry out for "athletes' rights," yet I bore personal witness to an utter indifference to such rights by these same people in Mexico City, Munich, and Montreal. I have heard arguments made that an athlete should have the right to controvert the national interest, as if foreign policy should be established by a hurdler, a sprinter, a water polo player, or a gymnast. I have seen a heavyweight champion deprived of two constitutional guarantees, with the implicit—and, in many cases, the explicit—support of an overwhelming majority of the media. And yet, incredibly, I have seen the President of the United States call upon this champion, invest him with diplomatic robes, and have him roam the nations of Africa as an emissary of the United States.

I have witnessed the reputations of athletes ruined by innuendo in the name of freedom of the press. I have observed the disgusting extent to which television will go in order to get a rating. I have watched the ugly and continuing growth of a phenomenon known as fan violence. I have covered the development of labor unions in sports, lockouts in sports, special-purpose legislation passed by the Congress for sports. And I have seen the birth of a curious new stratum in the society, which Robert Lipsyte brilliantly entitled "the Jockocracy." In short, a vastly different world of sports from what it had seemed to be during my formative years in Brooklyn.

The world of sports today is endlessly complex, an ever-spinning spiral of deceit, immorality, absence of ethics, and defiance of the public interest. Yet, somewhere within all that, there continues to lurk the valid notion that there *is* good in sports and that the games themselves provide a necessary respite from the ills and frustrations of life itself.

It is in this latter notion that the bulk of the American public believes, although the number of such believers decreases almost daily. They believe as they do because they have been taught to do so virtually from birth. They are taught in their homes and by the sports media people. Hammerstein's *South Pacific* lyrics are curiously apt here:

You've got to be taught to love and to hate. . . .
You've got to be taught before it's too late.

And in America we are taught. We are taught a series of postulates, each of which can serve as a natural concomitant for any of the others, and which, in totality, constitute the Sports Syndrome.

They are:

1. The game is sacrosanct—a physical and almost religious ritual of beauty and art.

2. Only those who have played the game can understand and communicate its beauty.

3. All athletes are heroes, to the point where some are cast as surrogate parents in the American home.

4. Winning isn't everything . . . it's the *only* thing! (Something Vincent T. Lombardi *never* said!)

5. Sport is Camelot. It is not a place for truth—only for escape, for refuge from life.

6. The fan is sacred, even as sports are. He pays the freight, thus he is an entitled being. The media people tell him this

every day. Therefore, once within the arena, his emotions whetted by the Sports Syndrome, the fan adopts what John Stewart Mill found to be the classic confusion in the American thought process, the confusion between Liberty and License—a natural and probable consequence of which is fan violence.

In the course of this book, you will see these postulates used repeatedly. Sometimes they will be used by sports commissioners, sometimes by the sports operators, sometimes by so-called intellectuals when they turn their attention to sports, and sometimes by television and print journalists. The essential point is that sports are no longer fun and games, that they are everywhere—in people's minds, in conversation, in the importance we attach to it—and that they can affect the basics of our lives (to wit, the part of our taxes that may be directed to supporting a sports franchise, without our ever knowing it). Once I bought the Jimmy Cannon dictum that "Sports is the Toy Department of life." I don't now and never will again.

The task then, as I see it, is to get a fix on sports and put it in its place, in balance with the mainstream of life, and to dispel romantic ideas about sports—ideas that exist only in a fantasy world. The task is difficult to accomplish, so deeply ingrained is the Sports Syndrome in the average person's psyche. And yet I have noticed a change in public attitudes toward sports in the past twenty years—particularly in the young people of the 1960s and early 1970s. They grew up at a terrible time: the unwanted war, the three assassinations, the pill, the drug culture, the shoot-down at Kent State, the betrayal of the presidency, the FBI and CIA disclosures. These young people had much to be cynical about and too much to cope with. They were not disposed to walk through a looking-glass and find a panacea in a cubicle world, separate and apart from life, called sports. Rather, they selected an antihero in whom they felt they found truth—Muhammad Ali. And truth, not fiction, was what they wanted, even in sports.

So there now exists a nucleus for the public acceptance of reality in sports; as physical science dictates, "For every action, there is an equal and opposite reaction." And because, in the words of Chayefsky, "I am closer to the end than the beginning," it seems to me that this is the time for this book.

I have entitled the book *I Never Played the Game*. It is a title deliberately chosen for its shading and meanings. I have worked very hard in the past thirty-two years fighting for what I believed in, risking my career because many of my actions seemed on the surface adverse to the interests of my company. But I have been fortunate enough to have, on the whole, succeeded. I never played the game with advertisers, with my own company, or with the sports operators. And, of course, I never played the game as a professional athlete. The connections I made, the access I developed, the ability to break and explore stories, derived from a mutuality of respect developed by pounding the sports beat for more than three decades and reaching into the highest levels of sports, education, and government. Have I made compromises? Yes, because I am human; but I know in my heart and mind that I never forfeited a major principle during my whole career. So in this book I hope to take you inside the world of sports so you can perceive why in the year 1985 very often the least significant things that happen in sports are those things that occur within the arena rather than without it.

I never played the game.

1

"Everything's Coming Up Roses"

Man marks the earth with ruin—his control
Stops with the shore.

—Lord Byron, *Childe Harold's Pilgrimage*

On Labor Day weekend, 1970, funeral services for Vincent T. Lombardi were held, appropriately enough, in St. Patrick's Cathedral in New York. It was a High Mass, dignified and majestic, conducted by the late Terence Cardinal Cooke, and no one who was there will ever forget the somber farewell to the legendary coach of the Green Bay Packers and the Washington Redskins.

I sat with my wife, thinking of all the years I had known Lombardi, all the way back to Brooklyn, where we had each grown up. And then he went on to Fordham, and I ended up at his school's archrival, New York University. I thought, too, about his devotion to his God, his family, his craft, and the men who played for him, and how his simple and singular virtues were often twisted and misrepresented by the media.

In the hush of the great cathedral, you could hear people weeping, people from all walks of life—statesmen and soldiers, priests and politicians, athletes and owners. And it seemed that the bigger they were, the harder they cried, especially the men who knew him best, the men with names such as Robustelli and Gifford and Rote, Hornung and Kramer and Starr and Jurgensen.

Sitting directly in front of me was Larry Brown, then one of the finest running backs in professional football. He had been a failed player until Lombardi came to Washington, but the great coach had discovered that Brown was hard of hearing and had had a hearing aid implanted in his helmet. Almost overnight, Brown achieved stardom. That day, he could not contain his emotions, and he wept like a child who had just lost his father.

When the funeral service finally ended, we all solemnly spilled out onto Fifth Avenue, our eyes red from tears, and then many of us proceeded to the cemetery. It was a memorable tribute to Lombardi, and now when I think back on it, a memorable day in the life of the National Football League.

Nine years later, there was another service, this one for Carroll Rosenbloom, the owner of the Los Angeles Rams. In attendance were singers and actors. There were comedians and stale jokes, and there was the widow who arrived late for her own husband's farewell.

Think about it. A funeral as half-time entertainment. Across a single decade, these two services seemed to me to mark a transformation from dignity and majesty to vulgarity and burlesque—and to serve as a metaphor for the decline of the National Football League.

• • •

Carroll Rosenbloom drowned in a riptide off the Florida coast in April 1979, in the kind of unsettling circumstances he had known and sometimes encouraged all of his years. He died as he had lived—obstinate, embattled, quick to embrace a challenge. Too quick.

The waters of the Atlantic were rough that day, and warning flags were hoisted. Rosenbloom, in his seventies, ignored them. He had maintained a home on exclusive Golden Beach for five years and thought he knew the waters. Rosenbloom was not exactly ridden with self-doubt.

Despite his years, he was an almost passionately physical man who exercised methodically every day of his life, started to play tennis while in his sixties, and prided himself an excellent swimmer. He did all these things even though he had undergone a heart bypass operation a few years earlier. The football bug had bitten him when he was a kid, and he became a fair halfback for the University of Pennsylvania.

Rosenbloom was a complex and brilliant man, especially in business and finance. As executor of his father's estate, he was a mover, made deals that produced a fortune for the other children in the family, and wound up a multimillionaire himself, with large-scale interests in oil and communications. On top of all this, he owned the Los Angeles Rams, a team he acquired, believe it or not, in a tax-free exchange for the Baltimore Colts, of which he had been the longtime owner.

Rosenbloom was tanned, lean, with a carefully groomed white hairpiece that fell over his forehead in the style of a Roman senator. He would not have been out of place at Caesar's court. He was all things to all people: ruthless, kind, generous, tough, spiteful, forgiving, honest, and conniving. Cross him once, and he could be endlessly vindictive. He spoke in a soft, slow, measured voice that only thinly disguised the underlayer of steel that was the inner man. He used people and loved to manipulate them. When he wanted to achieve something with his fellow owners, he could be utterly ingratiating, testing them, confiding in them, gradually wooing their support. He would get to Chicago by way of Shanghai.

His inconsistencies were many. He helped make an unknown named Alvin (Pete) Rozelle the NFL commissioner. Some years later, he tried to get Rozelle's neck, and it required the dispatch of a committee of owners, headed by oil magnate Leon Hess of the New York Jets, to keep the peace.

Once Rosenbloom explained to me why Arthur Modell of the Cleveland Browns was a model owner: "Good for the game, good for the league. Bright, young, energetic. He did it *my* way." Weeks later, he and Modell were not speaking, and Rosenbloom denounced him as one who had grown too big for his britches. Why the change? An argument between the two over an assistant coach.

Before Rosenbloom died, he had, at one time or another, fought with virtually every owner in the league. It almost seemed as though his constitution demanded battle—yet, curiously, at the time of his death he was more at peace with them (and with himself) than at any time in the twenty-five years I had known him. The basic reason was clear: Under his ministrations and league rules, the removal of the Rams from Los Angeles to Anaheim was assured. As part and parcel of the deal, Rosenbloom would reap one of the lushest harvests in the history of sports and, cunningly, he had done it the Rosenbloom way. In his view, he had played the role of "The Godfather," a role he cherished, a higher figure who stayed behind the scenes but who, in fact, constituted a form of invisible government over the league.

The other owners knew the chain of problems that would be created by the Rams' removal: the outcry from Los Angeles, the possibility of legal action, and the consequent desire of another owner to fill the vacancy in L.A. But no matter. Rosenbloom had achieved his purpose.

I thought of all this on that April day in 1979 as I sat in the garden of his estate on Bellagio Drive in Bel Air, waiting for the funeral services to begin. Six hundred people were there, including a roll call of Hollywood greats, some of whom may actually have met the deceased. In life, Rosenbloom had relished the part of social lion, his tennis court a mecca for nearly everybody who was anybody. Now, as I looked around, there were Cary Grant, Jimmy Stewart, Greer Garson, Warren Beatty, Diane Keaton, Ricardo Montalban, and scores of others. The funeral service was not exactly . . . well, funereal. In questionable taste, it was conducted as a celebration, presided over by comedian Jonathan Winters, who used the occasion to draw upon many of his rejected routines of the past.

Winters stood there at the lectern, an incongruous, almost grotesque figure garbed in what might have been called his gardening suit. He wore a pair of brown, baggy, disheveled pants; a soiled, wrinkled, red turtleneck sweater; and a brown, stained sport jacket with leather patches on the elbows. Otherwise, he was the soul of physical dignity.

Winters told jokes at which the audience uneasily laughed, brought on a couple of Carroll's favorite singers and a guitar player, and called upon a mix of Rosenbloom's friends to speak—as though it were a roast and toast.

My wife, Emmy, and Sonny Werblin, once of the New York Jets and the New Jersey Meadowlands, then the chief operating officer of Madison Square Garden, were beside me. And beside themselves. We had arrived at 2:30 P.M., a half hour early. Somewhere a band was playing, festively, "Everything's Coming Up Roses." As we entered the house, I was corraled by Don Klosterman, the Rams' general manager, and Irv Cowan, a longtime friend of Rosenbloom's who ran the Diplomat Hotel in Hollywood, Florida. "You've got a choice," they said. "You can either be the emcee or make the final speech."

I was flabbergasted on at least two counts: First, I had no idea I was expected to speak; and second, I had never heard of a master of ceremonies in the conduct of a funeral service. I expressed both of my misgivings, said it was inappropriate for me to be involved, and made the obvious point that Pete Rozelle should be the key speaker. I was told that Pete had been asked but had refused. I went to Pete, and he held firm. Rosenbloom was dead now. One sensed that Rozelle harbored old wounds, and there was no longer a political need to court a difficult man. I thought that attitude was beneath him, but in fairness to Pete, he also felt that the tenor of the occasion was unseemly. For that and lesser reasons, he would not participate. I went to Klosterman and Cowan and said I would deliver the final eulogy.

Emmy and Sonny found their seats, along with Jack Kent Cooke, the principal owner of the Washington Redskins. Cooke had been Rosenbloom's neighbor in Bel Air. He also had been the father-in-law of Carrie Rozelle, Pete's second wife. The two men had strong feelings about each other—not warm and friendly, one can be sure.

Three o'clock came and went, but Georgia, the deceased owner's oft-married second wife, had not appeared. Then three-thirty. Now three forty-five. Some guests had to leave, among them a sheepish Jack Kent Cooke. Cooke had to meet with his attorneys, and those of Dr. Jerry Buss, to close the sale that day of his Los Angeles interests: the Forum, the Lakers, the Kings. As he tried to make an inconspicuous exit, head down as he climbed the terrace steps, he bumped into the widow of Rosenbloom, who was coming the other way.

It was three fifty-five. Now, nearly an hour late, the program could begin. Only later did I learn that Georgia, who fancies herself a vocalist, had wanted to sing but had been talked out of it.

One has to try to understand Georgia. She will be a blond

bombshell when she is eighty-five. All of her life she has had to fight for acceptance—in the social orbit as Rosenbloom's wife, and as his widow and inheritor of his team. She had a modest career in television as a weather girl, talk-show hostess, and occasional member of the Dave Garroway cast on the early *Today* show. Rosenbloom married Georgia in 1966, after a nine-year courtship that produced two children. Those who resented her, for reasons real or imagined, found her an easy target.

So Georgia would not let her husband slip quietly into the dark. There was music and there was comedy, some of it intentional. Oakland's Al Davis spoke, and seriously, as did Modell. Despite the ups and downs both had known with Rosenbloom, neither was disposed to treat this occasion with less than the deep respect they honestly felt for this mercurial figure.

Finally I spoke. I looked at Georgia and told her I understood how she felt—she wanted his friends to celebrate Carroll's life, not mourn his death—but I had known Carroll Rosenbloom too long and too well. I then detailed much of the things written here, about his battles with the other owners and the beguiling charm that healed most of those wounds.

I closed by quoting Lord Byron's *Apostrophe to the Ocean:*
". . . Roll on thou deep and dark blue ocean . . ."

And so the ocean took him.

So bewildering was that scene, I am unable to this day to judge it unemotionally. I am not entirely comfortable with having been a party to it, but Wellington Mara of the Giants, who cannot be characterized as a friend of mine, and Ethel Kennedy, whose courage I admire, both thanked me for lending some dignity to the proceedings.

Mercifully, the strange day was over—or so I thought. Many of us repaired to the upper level from the garden, where there is a patio adjacent to the pool. On one side, under a canopy, a long table filled with food had been laid out for the guests. Suddenly, from under a clump of bushes right next to that table, we heard ghastly sounds: a dog growling fiercely; the sobbing and moaning of a man. It was the Rosenbloom's houseman fighting with a huge German shepherd, an animal that had been notably troublesome in the neighborhood for some time. We stood there horrified as suddenly the poor man escaped and fled into the house, wailing, his right hand bloody from the bites of the dog, who scurried through bushes and around trees into the abutting property.

Emmy and I were standing with Leonard Tose, the Philadelphia Eagles' owner, and his lady. We agreed that the entire afternoon had been an excursion into unreality. We wanted to leave as quickly as possible but felt bound to find Sonny Werblin and take him with us.

Just then, the Minnesota Vikings' owner, Max Winter, charged up to me and blurted: "Howard, you cost me my new domed stadium! I hope to hell you're satisfied." Tose stood there transfixed. "Not now, Max," he said with a hiss. "Not here."

I knew what Winter meant. A few weeks earlier, I had been in the Twin Cities with a group of ABC personalities to welcome a new station affiliate into the network lineup. The Vikings were seeking a covered stadium in downtown Minneapolis, utilizing public funds. They threatened to move if the voters denied them. Where to? Los Angeles. That great city would welcome them because of the Rams' impending move to Anaheim.

While in Minneapolis, I was interviewed on this matter and had suggested that the order of urban priorities, in this day and age, argued against the public expenditures for a domed stadium. This was what had angered Max Winter.

I told Max to cool down—I like him personally—and assured him that the power of the Sports Syndrome would work in his favor. And, I added, this was no place to bring up the matter. Shortly thereafter, by the way, Winter's domed stadium was approved. Today, we are even better friends. One of the hardest lessons in sports is not to take seriously what anyone says in anger.

Forgetting about Werblin, Emmy and I and Tose decided to flee that zoo as quickly as possible. We drove to the Beverly Wilshire Hotel and tried to drown the whole depressing affair in martinis. They didn't help. I could still clearly see Rosenbloom in my mind's eye. Impeccable as always, half smiling and causing me to wonder if, in fact, he hadn't overseen the events of the day with a sardonic amusement. He always believed that without his presence to run things, chaos was inevitable. In his lifetime, there had been four things he loved: money; power; Georgia; and his players, for whom he'd do anything. Unquestionably, he was the most generous, supportive owner in my years in sports.

As for Georgia, the best evidence of Carroll's devotion lay in the disposition of his estate. Shortly before his death, he had executed a codicil to his will that gave her nearly everything, including the Rams. Only 5 percent of the club went to Steve, his son by his first marriage, who had grown up on football in the Colts' and Rams' front offices.

The decision may have been dictated in part by tax considerations—there is a 50 percent widow's exemption in California. But Rosenbloom had to know, I reasoned, that Georgia and Steve would never get along. After all, Rosenbloom well knew that Georgia disliked Steve's wife, Renee, and the feeling was mutual. It was Renee whose tart description summed up what many had felt about her father-in-law's last rites: "It was the only funeral I ever saw that could have played eight weeks in Las Vegas."

Georgia soon fired her stepson, Steve, who went to New Orleans and lasted less than a year as general manager. She negotiated a large New York bank loan to buy out the club's shares held by Steve and the other Rosenbloom children. One by one, she purged the franchise of people hired by or loyal to her husband. If turbulence had been Rosenbloom's mission in life, Georgia carried on his work.

It is an endless and fascinating study of the he-she relationship, against a football backdrop. Georgia has reestablished the reputation she wanted so long to avoid, or live down, that of the flashy and irrepressible blonde. She is the only owner in pro football who has been photographed kissing Bert Jones, or attempting a place-kick for a national sports magazine. Those who had known the Rosenblooms socially were not entirely prepared for the change in Georgia, because Rosenbloom kept her subdued, almost demure. While he lived, the Rams' offices were off limits to her.

Ironically, in Georgia's first season as leader of the team, the Rams managed to make the Super Bowl, an achievement that had long eluded her husband for all his scheming and mischief. Several months later, on July 21, 1980, Georgia Rosenbloom married her lyricist, Dominic Frontiere. According to news reports, the marriage was her eighth, and around Los Angeles, bumper stickers bore the message, "Honk if you've been married to Georgia."

And so the Rams played their first season in Anaheim under a woman named Frontiere, not a man named Rosenbloom, and since then the team's fortunes have deteriorated and she has become easy prey for football critics and gossip columnists. Some of the thinking has grown twisted, but even Steve Rosenbloom is compelled to give her credit on one point: "There was no competition between us for the favor of my father. That's crap. My father and I had a close and loving relationship, made more so by our working together. Georgia made him happy for twenty years, and I don't forget that."

Because everyone knew C.R. was a terrific swimmer and, on the face of it, would not have been foolhardy enough to risk his life, rumors began to circulate that indeed Rosenbloom was the victim of a foul act. Such an act, some whispered maliciously, was engineered by Georgia, the inheritor of her husband's fortune. Others focused on Rosenbloom's fondness for the heavy wager and theorized about alleged debts to the mob.

PBS, in an ugly documentary, took these rumors and gave them a whole new life. It was a distasteful stew of innuendo and disputed testimony: a witness who warned Carroll of the water's roughness; another who saw a "murky shadow" below the surface, presumably an underwater diver in a wet suit bent on murder.

To this day, no one, including the state authorities of Florida and California, has been able to uncover any real evidence that Rosenbloom indeed was murdered.

Interestingly, and sadly, sinister little jokes have been made in the inner chambers of the National Football League.

Carroll Rosenbloom did not live to see the Rams' relocation in Anaheim, nor the invasion of the Raiders, resulting in no less than eight lawsuits and a widening, nearly hysterical resentment between two great cities in the same state.

If chaos was Carroll Rosenbloom's legacy, I can't help feeling that he would have enjoyed it—most of it, anyway.

So, in the passage of one decade, I had been witness to two services, Lombardi's and Rosenbloom's, two vastly different memorials with vastly different values—moral, ethical, and spiritual. Lombardi's values dominated the NFL at the start of the decade, Rosenbloom's at the end, and the decline of the NFL could be seen in power, greed, arrogance, complacency, and disregard for the public. Money, from whatever source, had taken over the league. The old heroes were becoming memories, the games would become a stereotype, the athletes curiously faceless, and the public would grow to miss the spirit, the fervor of the competition it had loved and thrilled to. There would be a growing public indifference, and you will learn why in succeeding chapters.

On the day of Rosenbloom's service—that final, dreadful day—the last unseen-to detail was who would carry his ashes back to Baltimore, the city where he had made his name. The family asked a Baltimorean, an old friend named Sig Hyman, to do it. Rosenbloom had paved the way for Hyman to establish and administer the NFL pension fund, a move that placed the security of the players in able hands and made Hyman a rich man.

Hyman could not bring himself to take the ashes with him. I don't know who did.

I do know that as we all left, each of us was given a three-by-five glossy of Carroll holding up a tennis cup that he had presumably won somewhere. It was the last straw.

2

The Low
Road to Anaheim

Oh, what a tangled web we weave,
When first we practice to deceive!

—Sir Walter Scott, *Marmion*

There was a day when I stood in the office of Max Winter, the owner of the Minnesota Vikings, at the Vikings' plush new training complex on the outskirts of Minneapolis. Winter pointed to the wall behind his desk, a wall filled with many pictures. One was of Carroll Rosenbloom. And he shook his finger at Rosenbloom, saying, "That's the man who's responsible for all of our troubles!"

"It's not that simple, Max," I said. "It all began with Walter O'Malley, and the torch was passed to Wellington Mara. But I will say this: Nobody put more forces in motion—legally, morally, ethically, economically, and politically—more quickly than Carroll did when he took the low road to Anaheim."

We were talking, of course, about franchise removals, and I was expressing my views about the way O'Malley had moved the Dodgers from Brooklyn to Los Angeles and Mara had moved the football Giants from New York to New Jersey.

Major league baseball had its last franchise removal in 1971. In the years that followed, however, the National Football League had several teams that skipped from one location to another, creating a bewildering maze of intertwining issues and personalities—and turning the league itself into a Byzantine empire of political intrigue, corporate skulduggery, and legal manipulations.

The public may think the games are sacred—but in reality, they are merely a cloak behind which the sports operators can masquerade.

• • •

In the flow of time that has elapsed since the day of the Rosenbloom funeral, I have thought often about Carroll and about my friendship with him. As I attempted to get a grip on the complex, behind-closed-doors machinations of the NFL, I couldn't help but harken back to a day in May 1978, not quite a year before Rosenbloom's death. It was then that I received a call from the owner of the Rams.

I was in Los Angeles on assignment. He asked if I could pop over to his house; there was something important he needed to discuss with me. I sensed instantly that it was about the removal of the Rams to Anaheim, the city that was built by a mouse named Mickey.

Rosenbloom was waiting for me by the pool in a lounge chair, the perfect advertisement for the town and country gentleman—custom-made gray silk, open-necked sport shirt; tailored blue gabardine slacks carefully hugging the hips; and gray suede loafers over bare feet.

He got right to the point: "What position would you take, on the air, if I were to move the team to Anaheim?"

I had no reason to hesitate. "You know my position, Carroll. At least three times I have testified before congressional committees on sports franchise removals. Since sports has always adopted the posture before the Congress that it is a unique business, quasipublic in nature, and has gotten special purpose legislation enacted as a result"—e.g., the pooling of NFL television monies; freeing the pro football merger from the antitrust laws—"the only legitimate ground for removal is economic distress. You can't establish that, Carroll."

Rosenbloom listened patiently, a thin smile on his lips. He was a good listener. "But O'Malley couldn't prove economic distress when he left Brooklyn," he said. "And Mara couldn't prove it when he left New York."

"You're right," I replied. "But what they did was a moral and ethical disgrace. Carpetbagging franchises have become the trademark of professional sports. You guys"—my voice was rising now—"cloak yourselves in the guise of public servants, and then you abruptly desert for the next land grab. It's a Cimarron operation; open a territory, take the land. The hell with the public you leave behind, and the hell with the ripple effect upon the city you've left behind."

Carroll's smile grew wider. His eyes began to glow.

"Yet you all get away with it," I went on. "The game is sacrosanct. It is all that matters. And sport is the necessary refuge from life, a haven where truth is not welcome nor wanted. It's what the public has been taught from the beginning. I'm sick of it.

"This is exactly why I urged the establishment of a Federal Sports Commission. The public has to be protected despite itself. I think any attempt to move a franchise should be subject to that commission's approval, said approval not to be unreasonably withheld . . . as we say at law."

Rosenbloom cocked his head and looked at me with open amusement. Obviously he had expected me to say everything I had said. "What about legality?" he asked. "Can they stop me?"

"Call Ed Hookstratten," I snapped. "He's your lawyer."

What Rosenbloom was doing was trying me on for media size. There is little doubt in my mind that he felt he had everything else under control, professionally and legally.

For one thing, Rosenbloom was sure he could coax and cajole his fellow owners into approving his move to Anaheim. And as a matter of law, he was well aware how the city of Los Angeles had itself lured other teams from other cities, and by Rosenbloom's own precepts, it couldn't go into a court of equity to stop him.

I had known Rosenbloom since the 1950s, but only in 1970, with the advent of *Monday Night Football*, did we become close. Well, not really close. One could never be sure about Rosenbloom. But we saw each other often.

Socially, he was a delight to be with, but his wit could be

roguish. An incorrigible gossip, he would casually drop delicious morsels of inside information about almost anybody in the league. Then he would sit back, chuckle maliciously, and feast upon the reaction among his listeners.

I suffered the same swings in our relationship as everyone else. Once, Emmy and I had just arrived in Los Angeles after a Monday night game in Chicago. During the telecast, I had remarked that Jim Finks, then the Chicago Bears' general manager, had been instrumental in forging the Minnesota powerhouse teams and, indeed, might well be the best at his job in the game.

As we entered our suite in the Beverly Wilshire Hotel, the phone was ringing. It was Doug Krikorian of the *Los Angeles Herald-Examiner*, asking me to comment on Rosenbloom's remarks about me. I didn't know what the hell he was talking about. He read me a series of quotes from his article that day, in which Rosenbloom denounced me as an egomaniac who thought he was running the league. Anyone who knew football, he was quoted as saying, knew that his general manager, Don Klosterman, was the best in the business.

Immediately, I understood. Rosenbloom thought of himself as his own general manager. He had taken my comments as a slap at himself.

Emmy was furious and vowed that she would never speak to Rosenbloom again. By coincidence, we had been invited to a dinner party the next week at the home of Pete Rozelle, in Harrison, New York. The Rams would be in town to play the Jets, and the Cowboys were coming in to meet the Giants. The Rosenblooms and the Tex Schramms (Tex Schramm was president of the Cowboys) would attend. Emmy swore that we would not go. Then Rozelle sent word that Carroll wanted to offer a personal apology at the dinner. It would have been graceless not to accept. So we went.

Rosenbloom was seated next to Emmy. Butter wouldn't melt in his mouth as he greeted her. Georgia sat next to me. As drinks were served, he tapped a glass, stood up, and apologized to both of us. "A moment of hotheadedness," he said. Then he sat down, patted Emmy on the hand, and said, purring, "I'm really sorry, baby. You know me. . . ."

Emmy looked at him coolly and said, "Yes, I do, Carroll, and I know you meant every word you said!"

So the conversation at poolside, I knew, was a typical Rosenbloom production—a masquerade. Long before he ever called, his mind was closed, the plans laid. The Rams would move to Anaheim.

On July 25, 1978, the Rams held a press conference to announce their owner's intentions.

"Is this decision final?" Rosenbloom was asked.

"Nothing is ever final until it is done," he replied. "I have learned that much in business."

Translation: The decision was final.

Rosenbloom made it clear that Anaheim was just down the road from Los Angeles—forty-five minutes on the freeway. And echoing the words of Mara when he transplanted his Giants from Yankee Stadium to the Meadowlands, Rosenbloom emphasized that the move was for the benefit of the fans.

"It is a better facility than the Los Angeles Coliseum," he said. "The fans will have better viewing angles for the games and much more comfort than the Coliseum offers."

There were some things that Rosenbloom did *not* emphasize at that press conference. One, that he was to receive ninety-five acres adjacent to Anaheim Stadium, choice land that would be commercially developed by a realty group—in which Rosenbloom was a principal. And two, that the city of Anaheim would enclose the stadium in bowl fashion, enlarging seating capacity to seventy-six thousand. A third omission concerned the building of some 110 season loges, the gross proceeds from the sale of which would be apportioned 70 percent to Rosenbloom, 30 percent to Anaheim. You stand back to admire the artistry of the magician's sleight of hand. Anaheim would build the season loges but would be repaid by 30 percent gross proceeds from the sale thereof.

The Rams and their owner would realize over $2 million a year from this source, and the beauty of it was that such monies do not have to be shared with the visiting teams. After the home team takes 15 percent off the top for rent, it keeps 60 percent of the attendance gross, the visiting team 40 percent, but this applies only to the gate. Season loge revenues are a pure bonanza, based on the theory that the home team contributes to the capital improvement of the stadium in the construction of season loges and is therefore entitled to the proceeds. Obviously, more theory than fact.

The Rams were prepared to desert Los Angeles, a city that had given them its passionate support since 1946, and there was nothing anybody could do about it. Irony had reared its ugly head. This was the city that had invented the sports franchise rip-off and patented the land grab, and now it was time for Los Angeles to pay the price.

When the Dodgers made the western trek, they were the most profitable franchise in the National League—and the most colorful and traditional. But how could the late Walter O'Malley resist? Los Angeles offered *him* 295 acres in the Chavez Ravine section of the city. This was choice land. How choice is evidenced in the stark fact that it is a shorter distance from the beautiful new Bonaventure Hotel in downtown L.A. to Dodger Stadium than it is from Times Square in New York City to Central Park.

The hell with what it costs the L.A. taxpayers! The taxpayers wouldn't know or care. The hell with tenants who would be dispossessed so the land could become available for the construction of a ball park. River City was going to have a band! Los Angeles would be *big league!* They would get the Dodgers! They would get the games! And the hell with Brooklyn!

O'Malley got away with it. How could he be stopped? He patiently explained that this was a free-enterprise country and, therefore, he had a right to move his business anywhere he wanted.

This is true, except for one thing. O'Malley himself had testified before the Congress that sport was a unique business, "tinged with and affected by the public interest." It was on this basis that baseball's odious reserve system had been exempted from the antitrust laws for so long (the reserve system in baseball bound a player in perpetuity to whatever team held his contract, with or without his consent).

Thus it was with consummate hypocrisy that O'Malley established the precedent for the land grab as the motivation for franchise removal. He could not have done it without the aid and support of the city of Los Angeles.

Carroll Rosenbloom was intimately familiar with the O'Malley story and adopted it as his model. In fairness to him, originally he had not wanted to leave Los Angeles. He had sought an $8 million to $9 million package from the Memorial Coliseum

Commission to include the enclosure of the stadium, the renovation and modernization of the facilities and concessions and, finally, the creation of season loges, the revenues from which would help pay off the construction costs. The one other item that Rosenbloom felt the Rams must have was a practice facility, conveniently located, either adjacent to the Coliseum or in a city-owned park across the street from the Rams' executive offices on Pico Boulevard. Both the Coliseum Commission and the city of Los Angeles said "no"—and "no" was not a word Rosenbloom liked to hear.

But he had one more idea: Dodger Stadium. He went to see O'Malley, who would not lease the facility. Rosenbloom then offered him $75 million for the Dodgers and deluded himself into believing O'Malley would accept. O'Malley never had any such intention.

Spurned by O'Malley, Rosenbloom decided to play his trump card: Anaheim. Even though his lease with the Coliseum Commission would soon expire, he had to wonder about the possibility of a suit. Could the city take him to court and prevent him from leaving Los Angeles? Not likely, and Rosenbloom knew it. Los Angeles was a city hoist on its own petard: The record shows it had lured the Rams from Cleveland, the Lakers from Minneapolis, and the Dodgers from Brooklyn. By being party to these episodes, it was imprisoned by its own past misconduct. At law, Rosenbloom had *stare decisis* on his side—the law of precedents.

In my mind, Rosenbloom knew something else. The city's one direct recourse was to go into a court of equity for a restraining order to *estop* the Rams from removing. Equity courts exist where there is no adequate remedy at common law. But the fundamental precept of the law of equity is that he who would go into a court of equity must have *clean hands*. L.A.'s municipal hands were dirty, having seduced other teams away from other cities.

Thus, on strictly legal grounds, Rosenbloom felt secure. As for his fellow owners, how could they possibly stop him? Just several years earlier, they had allowed the Giants to abandon Yankee Stadium and settle in the Meadowlands complex in East Rutherford, New Jersey—a relocation to another state!

This was accomplished, very neatly, within the framework of

league bylaws, under a provision commonly called the seventy-five-mile rule. For all practical purposes, the league had no problems with a team moving within seventy-five miles of its present location. "Suburban relocation" is what the NFL calls it. And since Anaheim is well within seventy-five miles of Los Angeles, then Rosenbloom had nothing to worry about.

Wrong!

There was a hook in the rule, and Rosenbloom was determined not to hang on it. Publicly, he had already announced his intention to relocate, and nobody was going to stop him. Certainly not his colleagues. Through the years, he had collected and stored in the recesses of his brain enough damaging information to threaten or ruin men much mightier than his fellow owners. They were simply no match for this Machiavellian schemer, and he would have to be placated.

In taking the low road to Anaheim, however, Rosenbloom triggered a series of actions that would plunge into turmoil the structure of the National Football League—particularly those actions taken by a renegade named Al Davis.

3

Al Davis: I Love L.A.

Let me have men about me that are fat,
Sleek-headed men, and such as sleep a-nights.
Yond Cassius has a lean and hungry look.
He thinks too much. Such men are dangerous.

—William Shakespeare, *Julius Caesar*

The mavericks of sport are my kind of people. They always have been. Maybe it's because I'm a maverick myself, or maybe it's because they simply make for better stories. Through the years, they have included the likes of Jackie Robinson and Leo Durocher, Pancho Gonzales and Bobby Layne, Muhammad Ali and Joe Willie Namath, George Steinbrenner and John McEnroe.

And, of course, Al Davis, managing general partner of the Los Angeles Raiders. Yond Cassius!

Possessed of a brilliant organizational mind, Davis turned the Raiders into the winningest team in professional sports, first in Oakland, then in Los Angeles. And he's done this while maintaining an adversarial relationship with the rest of the NFL, including the commissioner's office.

Dressed in silver and black, the Raiders strike fear in the hearts of their opponents by fielding a weird assortment of oddballs and renegades, and their mystique is symbolized by their insignia—a man in a helmet, wearing an eyepatch, with crossed swords behind him. It's a mystique that Davis relishes.

Davis likes to play a little game with his companions in an effort to size them up. Of the following—love, power, glory, achievement, money—which is most important to you? he will ask. Davis himself never hesitates; he chooses power. Power to make his own rules. Power to control his own destiny.

So when Davis defied the NFL and moved his Raiders from Oakland to Los Angeles, it seemed totally in character.

As a matter of law, there was never any doubt in my mind that Davis would win his own notorious antitrust suit against the NFL, and I predicted his victory on the record. Morally, that was another matter. I told him so, and I said so on the air. Nonetheless, we have continued to enjoy a long and cordial relationship, and it's a measure of the man that he never let my questioning and my criticism interfere with our friendship.

My position on the Raiders' move was clear. A team like the Raiders isn't IBM. A team thrives on its fans' love and devotion, as well as their money. And there is something grubby about owners of teams jumping rivers, jumping state boundaries, and jumping coasts to get a better deal.

Thinking people must find answers to perplexing questions that simply won't go away. What is the responsibility of a sports franchise to a city? Should the law step in? What about the fans and their rights? Do they even know what their rights are? And if they don't, then whose fault is it?

• • •

Political intrigue and greed and defiance of the public interest—just a few of the things I associate with a never fully disclosed gathering of NFL owners in Chicago on October 4 and 5, 1978.

That meeting was prompted by two basic motivations:

1. To establish a league defense against an antitrust suit that had recently been filed by the Los Angeles Memorial Coliseum Commission.
2. To grease the wheels for Carroll Rosenbloom's removal from Los Angeles to Anaheim.

Knowing it couldn't stop Rosenbloom from moving, the Coliseum Commission had hoped at least to get a sympathetic hearing from NFL commissioner Pete Rozelle. What it wanted was an expansion franchise. No way, Rozelle said. The territory was much too valuable, and he seemed determined to hold on to it until he could auction it off for a king's ransom and fill the NFL's coffers to overflowing.

And neither was the Coliseum Commission going to get an existing NFL franchise, a practically impossible dream because of the league's so-called seventy-five mile rule. That rule prompted the Coliseum Commission's antitrust suit, just as it had the extraordinary meeting in Chicago.

Follow carefully, because this is really what sports is all about in America.

To sanitize Rosenbloom's relocation, the owners had to change the seventy-five mile rule, in actuality a bylaw of the NFL constitution, Section 4.3, under Article IV, "Territorial Rights," which said in part:

> ... Any transfer of an existing franchise to a location within the home territory of any other club shall only be effective if approved by unanimous vote; any other transfer shall only be effective if approved by the affirmative vote of not less than three-fourths, or 20, whichever is greater, of the member clubs of the league.

Historically, the NFL has never had any real problems with an owner who wanted to move his team within seventy-five miles of its present location. But according to Section 4.3, if that move impinges on the home territory of another team, he would need unanimous approval.

Guess what? Rosenbloom's relocation in Anaheim constituted an invasion of San Diego's territory.

Even a man as powerful as Rosenbloom can't always assure himself of the unanimous approval of his peers. And if he were denied it, he just might move anyway, and damn the NFL! Now, three-fourths approval, that was something Rosenbloom could live with—and most assuredly obtain.

As for the league, here was an opportunity to avoid a potential battle with this willful, headstrong owner and preserve its image.

What about the Coliseum Commission's antitrust suit? The Coliseum Commission knew that, for all practical purposes, the

Rams were gone, that the owners would knuckle under to Rosenbloom's demands. And to get an existing NFL franchise somewhere down the road, it would need the unanimous approval of the owners.

Why? Because with the Rams in Anaheim, a franchise brought into Los Angeles would impinge on Rosenbloom's new home territory!

On the advice of their attorneys, every owner in the league was well aware that a unanimous-approval rule was per se a violation of this country's antitrust laws. That's because any one owner could arbitrarily and capriciously deny another owner from pursuing a valid attempt to move. By changing the rule, they figured, not only can we help Rosenbloom to move, but we can also protect ourselves in case the Coliseum Commission manages to get us into a court of law.

Around the table where these men had assembled to rearrange their universe, several owners and their attorneys committed fragments of their thoughts to paper, scribbling notes for future reference. Some of those notes were unguarded, revelatory, potentially damaging; in their stark economy, they reveal sophisticated men who are at times surprised by their own capacity to ignore the law, logic, and even their own self-interests.

In attendance was Bob Schulman, an attorney for the Washington Redskins. A partner in Edward Bennett Williams' law firm, he has a brilliant and tenacious mind and is a mover and shaker in tax law. From reading Schulman's notes of that October meeting, one gains a sense of the conflicting currents:

> Coliseum suit vs NFL against unanimous consent to move into franchise area—allege violation S1, S2 Sherman Act—*No defense for such a suit* [emphasis mine]

> Rozelle feels strong—3/4 would be less offensive than unanimous vote.
> Coliseum wants to knock out territorial exclusivity.

> C. R. Proposal:
> Definition of home territory—population, geographical, area, stadium suitability, economy, travel, demographics, TV market, coverage, owners qualification.

Davis said Oakland lease is up.

His attys say even 3/4ths vote can't be defended. Suppose anyone who wanted, could move with no vote—NFL would not approve.

Argues 21 votes is too much & would still lose the lawsuit—

Irsay flatly opposes going to 3/4th vote—believes some owners could get 3/4 vote but other owners (like Irsay) could not—wants to hear from his own attys.

Alternatives
(1) fight lawsuit
(2) concede 3/4 voluntarily
(3) negotiate with Coliseum
(4) move another team to L.A.
(5) grant a new expansion franchise to L.A.

Robbie thinks L.A. will keep pressure on, even if NFL goes to 3/4 vote—& until L.A. gets another franchise—either keep Rams in L.A. or move another franchise to L.A.

The next morning, on October 5, the owners held another executive session, starting at nine forty-five. Schulman's notes provide a telegraphic account of the preceedings:

21 out of 28 votes, instead of 20, to approve move—Al Davis on record as not accepting any right to approval of a move

Al Davis reserves rights—

27 yes, 1 pass

Rozelle states flatly everyone has right to upset new by-law

acknowledges we all have the same rights as Oakland has—at specific request of San Diego and Washington

L.A. to move to Anaheim subject to satisfaction of arrangements with Anaheim. Approved 26, 2 absent.

Okay, let's examine exactly what Schulman's notes reveal about the meeting. Seeking to blunt the Coliseum Commission's case—and simultaneously solve the Rosenbloom problem—Rozelle and his attorneys reasoned that a three-fourths approval for one team to move into another team's territory was less offensive than a unanimous vote, but at least three owners disagreed.

Joe Robbie of Miami wanted Los Angeles to have a team. He was fearful that the Coliseum Commission would go all the way with its antitrust suit—and unsure of what might happen in a court of law.

Al Davis of Oakland argued that three-fourths approval was still too high—and predicted the NFL would lose the suit.

It was Baltimore's Robert Irsay, however, who was most expressive, noting that some owners were less popular than others—and perhaps those owners couldn't even get three-fourths approval. Without saying it directly, Irsay's words, like Davis's, got right to the heart of the matter: Even with three-fourths approval, Section 4.3 might still be interpreted as being arbitrary and capricious—and thus violative of antitrust laws.

The next day's notes reveal that Section 4.3 is changed from unanimous to three-fourths approval—and Rosenbloom has his colleagues' blessings to settle in Anaheim. But even more noteworthy is Davis's posture: He abstained, saying that the Raiders reserved their rights.

At this point, according to one insider, the voting "degenerated into a comedy of errors."

Untrusting of Davis, always worried that the Oakland owner had a new trick up his sleeve, Gene Klein, then of the San Diego Chargers, voted yes—but strenuously insisted that the Chargers were reserving the same rights as the Raiders. Schulman also voted yes—and said that the Redskins were reserving the same rights as the Chargers.

To assuage any feelings of uncertainty, Rozelle then stated flatly that every team has the same rights as the Raiders do.

This may sound hard to believe, but not a single person in that room had any idea exactly what rights they were talking about!

It gets better—or worse, depending on your point of view.

The vote was 27–0–1, with Davis the lone abstention. Robbie and Irsay, despite their objections, went along with the others.

Rosenbloom had won.

Oh, really?

There is a clause in the NFL constitution that requires a unanimous vote to *change* the rule. Considering Davis's abstention, the vote obviously wasn't unanimous—and yet Rozelle simply went ahead and declared the rule changed to three-fourths approval!

Lamar Hunt of Kansas City seemed dumbfounded by what had taken place. In a note handed to one of his aides, he wrote, "Don't ask me how that kind of vote can pass it, but it did."

Carroll Rosenbloom had his ticket to ride, but the quasisecret meeting in Chicago would haunt the NFL for years to come, for it was behind those closed doors that Davis laid the foundation for his own great escape. And then there were those scribbled notes. Those notes were entered as evidence in the seemingly endless courtroom struggles between Davis and the NFL. They were, in fact, the most convincing evidence against the NFL in the entire case.

My intention here is not to document the agonizing legal maze that accompanied the Raiders' exodus from Oakland to Los Angeles. What interests me is the human dimension of this story—how the spirit of countless people is dashed and their loyalty subverted by wealthy owners who skip town to become even wealthier, and how the mere threat of franchise removal continues to bring great cities to their knees as they scramble to mollify owners with new stadiums and other expensive perquisites and maintain their big-league image. In almost every case, it's the fans who get ripped off. Either they lose their home team to another city, or they end up paying additional taxes that keep an owner in limousines and Acapulco vacations.

If you want to know what sports has become in our time, then follow this sad and bewildering course of events:

The Coliseum Commission had filed its antitrust suit on September 12, 1978, accusing the NFL of impeding its search for a team to replace the Rams. Remember, as previously explained, the unanimous-consent controversy. The court found that such a claim was only hypothetical, and that the Coliseum Commission had no basis for its suit until it had a prospective tenant with whom the NFL was interfering.

Enter Al Davis. In late 1979, the Raiders became such a prospective tenant. Once Davis and the Coliseum Commission agreed on terms, the Raiders became part of the lawsuit because they, too, were eventually restrained by the NFL. In point of legal fact, the essential battle was between the L.A. Coliseum Commission and the NFL, triggered by the evacuation of the Rams to Anaheim. But it was Davis who would capture the imagination of the public and the media, and the simmering feud between Rozelle and Davis would boil into an obsession, perhaps finding its parallel only in literature—say, Captain Ahab and his great white whale.

It is an unassailable geometric truth that the shortest distance between two points is a straight line. On the map, Oakland and Los Angeles are 345 miles apart. For the NFL, however, the distance represented a journey of several thousand miles, a winding, tortuous road through such way stations as Baltimore, Jacksonville, Memphis, Minneapolis-St. Paul, and Phoenix; and only after these cities came into play did the Oakland Raiders reach the L.A. Coliseum.

The trip began when the Coliseum Commission realized it was going to lose the Rams and then was denied an expansion franchise by Rozelle. Shortly after its antitrust suit was filed, the hunt was on as the Coliseum Commission openly and notoriously courted other franchises in the league.

The first act of this sordid drama was played out on a *Monday Night Football* game in Los Angeles during the 1978 season. At one point in the telecast, as an ABC camera panned the crowd, I made the on-air observation that, in all likelihood, by 1981 the Rams would be playing in Anaheim—and there was nothing the people of Los Angeles could do about it. They were, after all, getting a taste of their own medicine.

Here's where William Robertson made his entrance. In its efforts to lure another NFL franchise into Los Angeles, the Coliseum Commission had designated Robertson as chief negotiator, and he called me after the telecast. He wanted equal time to respond to my statements about his city's concupiscence for fun and games.

"I think your remarks were unfair," he said, "and not really relevant."

"Not relevant!?" I shot back. "Explain to me your city's piracy of the Brooklyn Dodgers and how you enticed O'Malley with all that land. And as a result of that piracy, can't you see how Los Angeles set a precedent for Anaheim to give away the store to obtain the Rams?"

"That happened twenty years ago, Howard, and it doesn't matter anymore."

"That's terrific! You don't even intend to give a single thought to the harsh realities of the situation, do you? You're distressed and your fans are upset, and you want to rectify matters by stealing another team from another city and the hell with their fans. That really makes a lot of sense."

"Why blame me? The NFL won't give us an expansion franchise, so I don't see what other choice I have."

Armed with that attitude, Robertson first contacted Colts' owner Robert Irsay in Baltimore. Irsay was publicly disenchanted with Baltimore, primarily because of an antiquated stadium and the absence of an adequate practice facility. And so he was prepared to shop around. Like most sports operators, he had no compunctions about using a city, any city, for his own purposes. Why not Los Angeles?

Irsay visited Los Angeles to meet with the Coliseum authorities and examine the facility. The visit was trumpeted by a witting ally of the Coliseum Commission, the *Los Angeles Herald-Examiner*. In a travesty of journalism, a *Herald-Examiner* sportswriter named Doug Krikorian wrote a story headlined: "Twelve Reasons Why the Colts Belong in Los Angeles." The story would have been humorous had it not been so sadly unprofessional. But during the ensuing weeks, more such stories would appear in the same newspaper—stories about why the Miami Dolphins belonged in Los Angeles and why the Minnesota Vikings belonged in Los Angeles.

Irsay probably knew from the start that he could not get approval from the owners to move out of Baltimore. But his was the cruelest rip-off of all—getting everything he wanted just by the mere threat of leaving. His shopping expedition in other cities was cleverly designed to coerce Baltimore into seeing things his way. And he succeeded handsomely in this ploy. Once again, I became embroiled in the battle.

During a *Monday Night Baseball* game in Baltimore, in the summer of 1979, I opened the telecast by stating that Baltimore was a city under sports siege, noting that the famed Washington criminal attorney, Edward Bennett Williams, whose clients ranged from Jimmy Hoffa to John Connally, had purchased the Orioles. On the Potomac, the newspapers were filled with stories that the Birds might move to Washington. At the same time, I pointed out, Irsay had recently visited Jacksonville, and fifty thousand people in the Gator Bowl had chanted, "WE WANT THE COLTS!" It seemed to me a sickening thing that was happening to this city on the rebound.

You can imagine my feelings when I got the following letter from Jake Godbold, the Mayor of Jacksonville, Florida, who quite apparently had misunderstood the tenor of my comments:

Mr. Howard Cosell
American Broadcasting Company
1330 Avenue of the Americas
New York, N.Y. 10019

Dear Mr. Cosell:

You did a great thing for Jacksonville on Monday night when you chronicled our glorious night of delirium in the Gator Bowl last Wednesday night.

I believe the citizens of Jacksonville shouted "WE WANT THE COLTS" loud enough for the entire world to hear, especially those 28 individuals who own teams in the National Football League. We know we may not get the Colts to move from Baltimore to Jacksonville, but we also know that this city moved itself closer to the big-time and NFL football. We know that owners other than Mr. Irsay are looking for new homes, and I am not hesitating to move in their directions, also.

I have named a successful local businessman and sports promoter, Mr. Ted Johnson, to coordinate the entire effort for me, working with the Mayor's office and the Chamber of Commerce. We intend to meet Mr. Irsay's demand of a "Bankable commitment" of $8 million a year in ticket sales. In fact, we are gearing up now for our sales effort. But even before we could begin, Prudential Insurance notified us it wanted 1,000 season tickets a year for 10 years. That will be announced Sunday and should set off a chain reaction since Jacksonville is an insurance and banking center.

We intend to fix the Gator Bowl up to Mr. Irsay's standards, whether the Colts move here or not, and will probably use Cleveland's stadium as a model.

Our people are ready and we are proud that individuals like you on the national level recognize what we have accomplished and what we plan to do in the future.

Amazing, isn't it?

But it didn't stop there.

Mastering the art of community blackmail, Irsay wrapped his beefy arms around Memphis, sending a clear signal to the folks back home: If his demands for massive renovations and luxury boxes for Memorial Stadium weren't met, then there might be the Jacksonville Colts. Or the Memphis Colts. Or the Los Angeles Colts. Or the Phoenix Colts.

He would stop at nothing.

The result: a new Baltimore offer for $24 million in stadium improvements and a short-term lease that left open Irsay's options to leave—which, of course, he did five years later, sneaking to Indianapolis in the dead of night.

At the time, Jacksonville and Memphis—and later Phoenix—were left hanging in midair. But not Los Angeles. That city wanted action. Thus Robertson quickly forgot about Baltimore and sought his quarry elsewhere. He took a brief fling at Joe Robbie and his Miami Dolphins.

Robbie is a smart man with a deep political background in the Democratic Party and wise in the ways of inner-circle maneuverings. He knew he could not muster the votes to leave Miami, a thriving football market, so he made only perfunctory noises about moving. Knowing Robbie, it may have been a smoke screen for his future efforts to get a stadium on the borderline of Dade and Broward counties in Florida.

Robertson had to know that the Dolphins were a long shot, and he didn't waste much time with Robbie. He who hesitates is lost. Like a hawk, Robertson swooped down on Minnesota and turned his attention to Vikings' owner Max Winter, who was an embattled man in his home city. Winter wanted a domed stadium in downtown Minneapolis, where both the Vikings and the baseball Twins could play without concern for the frigid, unpredictable weather.

Once again, the ominous headlines set the stage. Vikings' general manager Mike Lynn warned a subdued state senate that the club was facing financial doom, but he adamantly refused to open his books. "We're a private business," Lynn cried.

And then Commissioner Rozelle, that champion of loyal fans everywhere, buttressed Lynn's position, declaring, "I doubt we would force any business to operate in its present location if it were failing."

Still, no financial disclosure was forthcoming, and named as possible alternative sites for the allegedly struggling Vikings were Birmingham, Memphis, New York, even Montreal and Mexico City.

It was dome or doom. When word leaked that the minstrel Robertson had dangled Los Angeles before Winter, the forces opposing a domed stadium dissolved. In the fall of 1982, Winter's dream became a reality. A $55 million bond issue built the stadium, which included 115 luxury boxes priced to generate more than $3 million annually for the Vikings.

And that is how the long and winding road led at last from Oakland to Los Angeles. When Robertson started whispering in Davis's ear, Robertson touched a precept that the Raiders' owner holds most dear: survival of the fittest. And to be the fittest in the NFL, Davis believed he needed a few things he didn't have in Oakland-Alameda County Coliseum—mainly, twenty thousand more seats and those luxury boxes that today's owners covet so much. That kind of deal would gross Davis and his team an additional $5 million a year, not to mention the millions more should the NFL switch to pay or cable TV. Simple arithmetic: There's a helluva lot more people in Los Angeles than in Oakland.

Had the Coliseum Commission built luxury boxes for Rosenbloom, he might've stayed. But now panic had set in, and come hell or high water, the Coliseum Commission would have a team in Los Angeles.

Blocking Davis's path was Rozelle, who objected to the potential move on several levels. First, he pressed his view that it was wrong to vacate a city that had supported its team with twelve years of sellouts. He also held that no prospering team had ever really left its home community. If the Raiders split for Southern California, Rozelle contended, that would hardly qualify as a "suburban" move. (There's that seventy-five mile rule again, though it had been stretched, if not in distance then certainly in concept and substance, to allow the Rams to move into another team's territory in another county and the Giants to jump across a state line.)

But no matter how fervently Rozelle protested, Davis intended to defy that proposition.

And so the battle was drawn. Davis's argument was a familiar one: To compete, he said, a team had to have monies equivalent to the richer teams'. Even though his balance sheet stacked up with the best in the league, he claimed that his future income in Oakland was limited, that his profits would not endure—and that free agency was inevitable in pro football. If he had to bid against other teams for players, Davis said, he'd end up a loser.

Maybe, though I doubted it. It was a neat position to take, but brains almost always dominate money—in pro football, anyway. And nobody knows better than Al Davis that efficient, knowledgeable management is the key factor in producing a winning team.

The bottom line was greater profits, period—and the loyal fans of Oakland be damned!

The most fascinating sideshow of these complex proceedings, however, was the intensely personal struggle that developed between Rozelle and Davis. If anything, these two men share one trait in common: They are whiplash smart. But their styles clash, and clash dramatically, and the media were seduced into covering this suit like a prizefight, not a court case. Like Roberto Duran vs. Sugar Ray Leonard.

Of the two, Davis makes better copy. A marginal athlete in school, the hotshot kid from Brooklyn always had big dreams. After graduating from Syracuse University in 1950, he moved fast and traveled light, winding up as an assistant coach—at $6,000 a year—with the San Diego Chargers in the new American Football League. He was a loner—distant and different—and he needed a jungle with no rules. That's what he got as he immersed himself in the donnybrook between the NFL and the AFL. He sweet-talked college stars such as Lance Alworth and Ernie Ladd away from the NFL, and he loved every minute of it. Even today, he'll tell you that if he puts his mind to it, he can charm anyone. The former coach of the Cleveland Browns, Sam Rutigliano, once said, "He'll take your eyeballs and tell you you look better without them."

In 1963, Davis became head coach and general manager of the Oakland Raiders, a team with a lifetime record of 9–33. He turned them into instant winners. Then, when the AFL needed a set of shark's teeth to attack the NFL's jugular, it tabbed Davis as its commissioner. He bloodied the NFL by raiding its quarterbacks. The NFL cried "Uncle!" and the two leagues quickly merged into one. But Davis felt betrayed. He had won the battle, but Rozelle won the war—and was confirmed as commissioner of the newer and bigger operation.

Thus the seeds of enmity between the two men. Rozelle got a gleaming office high above Park Avenue, while Davis returned to his old team. Oakland welcomed Davis back like a conquering hero. Producing winner after winner, he gave Oakland's citizens a sense of pride and self-respect, put them on the map, and the city responded by building him a modern sports complex that included an indoor arena and the Oakland-Alameda County Coliseum. The stadium sat fifty-five thousand fans, and the Raiders were eventually joined by baseball's Kansas City A's.

In these times, however, the sports euphoria of a city is an ephemeral luxury, a momentary high. Oakland proved no exception. Davis watched the passing of the 1970s in terms of his own new personal horizons for the future. He wanted what fellow owners Rosenbloom and Mara had, and he figured he deserved it. He had built the winningest franchise in pro football in much the same way he had built his life—with power, speed, and daring. He likes being called a genius. When people label him cunning, shrewd, and devious, his eyes twinkle with delight. And he readily admits he's a sore loser.

Al Davis would not lose to Pete Rozelle—even if the good fans of Oakland ended up as victims. He really didn't care how mad Oakland got at him. He'd leave. He'd fight Rozelle in the alleys and on the streets. Put the pressure on. Take him inside. Use the head, the shoulders, the elbows, the arms. Lean on him. Muscle him. Crowd him. Wear him down.

Rozelle wears well. Cool and unflappable, casually puffing a cigarette. Tanned and impeccably groomed in dark suits and Gucci shoes. Jab and circle. Never reveal your emotions. Admit nothing, deny everything. This is corporate America, after all. Let the other guy make accusations about scalping Super Bowl tickets. Let the other guy plant stories in the press about nefarious deals. We choose our words carefully on Park Avenue. Precise. Slick. A moving target. Looking to win by a decision.

Roberto Duran vs. Sugar Ray Leonard. With a twist. Davis never heard of the words *no más*.

The battle reached a crucial juncture in March 1980, when the owners voted against Davis's move at a meeting in Rancho Mirage, California. The score: 20–0, with five abstentions. In truth, many of the owners who lined up against Davis had mixed or divided loyalties. Some were even sympathetic to his position. Let's face it: Strip away the palaver that so infects these owners, and what you've got in general is not a sportsman but a hard-core businessman who casts a loving eye toward profits, not the fans. Like Davis, they are all firm believers in the free-enterprise system, and it's not so crazy to think that one day they might want to move their teams, too. And wherever they choose to.

But vote against Davis they did, whether out of fear or greed is anybody's guess. I still believe that many of them had to know that their rule was in violation of antitrust laws—and that their defense in court was doomed to die. They also had to know that they couldn't step on Davis, smooth out the wrinkles, blend him in with the rest. You can't scare off Al Davis. Maybe they had a death wish. Or maybe they were mesmerized by Rozelle, who had his own ax to grind.

Whatever the case, Davis returned to Oakland, and the other owners still did business with him. They traded players, exchanged jokes, and even offered occasional discreet words of encouragement. Why not? The United States decries all that the Soviet Union stands for, but our ships unload tons of grain on Soviet docks.

This whole crazy affair wasn't without at least one memorably delicious irony. Playing the entire 1980 season in a city they were bent on abandoning, the Raiders went on to win the Super Bowl by trouncing the Philadelphia Eagles. Immediately after the game, most reporters in the New Orleans Superdome rushed to the locker room to see Rozelle hand Davis the Super Bowl trophy. What would Davis do? Laugh at Rozelle? Sneer at him? Punch him in the nose?

The setting was electric. The Raiders booed when Rozelle entered. But when Davis arrived, they chanted, "Genius! Genius!" One insider said the plan was for the Raiders actually to seize the commissioner and throw him out of the locker room. Right in front of the TV cameras. Raider offensive lineman Gene Upshaw later said: "We had a code worked out with Al. If Al's first words were, 'We'd like to thank the commissioner,' that meant he didn't want us to do anything."

Davis climbed the platform and listened to Rozelle's polite and gracious speech, then accepted the trophy. "We'd like to thank the commissioner," Davis purred, a canary feather seeming to flutter from his lips.

Several months later, in a federal district court in Los Angeles, the case was finally heard. The result: a hung jury—which, of course, necessitated a new trial.

Another year passed. Like orphans in a storm, the Raiders played the 1981 season in Oakland, but with far less success. Then, on May 7, 1982, after a five-week trial, a jury of six women found that the NFL had violated the Sherman Antitrust Act by trying to block the Raiders from moving to the Los Angeles Coliseum, specifically citing the restrictive voting procedures as stipulated in Section 4.3 of the NFL constitution. What's more, the verdict was a blow to the NFL's most persistent argument—that the league's twenty-eight teams comprised a unique, single entity, and they were not, as Davis had insisted, "separate and distinct businesses" and "vicious competitors."

Perhaps most interestingly, the jury also found the NFL guilty of bad faith in its dealings with Davis. As we shall see, that finding would resurface in yet another case involving the Raiders' removal to Los Angeles.

And finally: The NFL was ordered to pay the Raiders $34 million in treble damages, a figure that might ultimately exceed $50 million after lawyers' fees and interest payments are tacked on.

The Raiders moved to Los Angeles, and on February 28, 1984—a month after Davis's team had won yet another Super Bowl—the U.S. Court of Appeals for the Ninth Circuit voted to uphold the Raiders. In a 2–1 decision, the majority concluded that the lower court had correctly applied federal antitrust rules—and that Section 4.3 was in essence an agreement to control competition among NFL teams.

Aside from the legal issues, which were varied and complex and sometimes concealed, the relocation of the Raiders held a certain magnetic appeal for me because of the cast of characters. Not only Davis and Rozelle, but also Joseph Alioto, the former mayor of San Francisco and an exemplary antitrust lawyer. He was the lead attorney for Davis, even though he had strong ties to the establishment NFL. His second wife, Kathleen Sullivan, is the daughter of New England Patriots' owner Billy Sullivan, who helped found the old AFL. He had also previously represented Philadelphia Eagles' owner Leonard Tose, and had defended the NFL in a lawsuit brought by former Minnesota quarterback Joe Kapp testing the validity of the basic contract.

In essence, though, this particular legal battle degenerated into an unholy, depressing mess. You needed a scorecard to keep track of all the separate lawsuits. As many as eight suits were involved at one time, embracing as principals the Raiders, the NFL, the L.A. Coliseum Commission, and the city of Oakland.

Yes, even Oakland.

Encouraged by the NFL, Oakland filed an eminent-domain suit, seeking to condemn the Raiders and purchase them at the market price. Eminent domain is the power of government to take private property in furtherance of a legitimate public use. It is frequently used today for purposes of urban renewal—the condemning of slums, for example, to provide adequate housing for low-income families.

Judge Nat Agliano of Monterey County Superior Court ruled in favor of the Raiders. Seven months later, however, the state's Court of Appeals ruled in favor of Oakland, remanding the case to the lower court for a clearer ruling on the issue of public use.

Then, on July 17, 1984, Judge Agliano again turned down Oakland's bid to reclaim the Raiders. In a harshly worded twenty-five-page decision, he ruled that the city's purpose in acquiring the team was not for a public use, adding, "The use of eminent domain as another means to keep the Raiders in Oakland is arbitrary, capricious, a gross abuse of discretion, and devoid of the fundamental fairness element of due process."

The most striking portion of Judge Agliano's opinion, however, confirmed the findings of the federal district court in Los Angeles in the Davis antitrust case, to wit: The NFL was guilty of bad faith in its dealings with Davis and his team.

Judge Agliano noted that on January 22, 1980, an informal agreement was reached between the Raiders and a committee representing the Oakland-Alameda County Coliseum Commission. Then, Judge Agliano said, "According to the evidence, the Commission did not execute this proposed agreement because a member of the Commission phoned Mr. Rozelle and was assured by him that the NFL would not permit the Raiders to move from Oakland. This promised restraint was unlawful.

"Now feeling confident that the club could not move even if it wanted to, the Commission withdrew its proposal and presented the Raiders with a less favorable one. . . ."

On September 14, 1984, the NFL petitioned the U.S. Supreme Court to hear Davis's antitrust suit. In its *certiorari* petition, the league again pursued its basic argument: It is unrealistic to treat a sports league as if its members were a group of unrelated businesses charged in a price-fixing conspiracy; all the league was attempting to do was maintain a franchise in a city that had provided twelve straight seasons of sellouts.

The NFL seemed confident that the U.S. Supreme Court would hear the case, and the NFL stressed the necessity of clearing up the endless confusion over the application of antitrust laws to sports leagues.

Several weeks after filing its *certiorari* petition, the NFL held an owners' meeting in New Orleans. At one point, as is proper, Davis was asked to leave the room while his case was discussed. That discussion eventually degenerated into a shouting match between two NFL attorneys and several owners, led by Ralph Wilson of Buffalo.

According to my sources, one of the NFL attorneys, Paul Tagliabue, told the owners, "We can't predict anything with certainty, but we think the Supreme Court will hear the case."

Wilson shot to his feet, mad as hell. "You told us the Supreme Court *would* hear the case!" he yelled. "There was never any doubt about it!"

Another NFL attorney, Jay Moyer, tried to soothe Wilson, saying evenly, "There's a good chance they'll hear it, Ralph. We're very hopeful."

"Don't give me any of that shit!" Wilson boomed. "You told us they'd hear it!"

The NFL attorneys were wrong.

On the morning of November 5, I received a call from Nancy Dobi, secretary to Roone Arledge, the president of ABC Sports and News. Arledge had asked her to advise me that the Supreme Court had declined to review the antitrust case.

Davis had won.

I immediately called him at his home in Los Angeles to get his reaction. I woke him up.

"Congratulations," I said.

"Wise guy," Davis replied, his voice still thick from sleep. "Why are you doing this to me now? I know we can't play. We stink."

Davis was referring to his team's performance the previous day, a crushing 17–6 loss to the Chicago Bears. Having lost for the third time in ten games, the Raiders were in danger of missing the playoffs, and Davis was cranky.

"You're a jerk," I said. "I'm not talking about a lousy game. The Supreme Court of the United States has declined the NFL petition to review your antitrust victory."

"What?!?" he screamed. "Give me a couple of hours and I'll call you back. I've got to contact everybody!"

When Davis called back, I arranged to get him exclusively for an interview on *SportsBeat*. As for the NFL, it issued a brief statement noting that the appeals court in California had yet to reach a final judgment on the question of damages; when that was decided, it planned once more to petition the U.S. Supreme Court to hear the case.

In my opinion, taking into consideration the fact that the Supreme Court refused to hear the case without comment, the NFL's chances for success a second time around are slim indeed, even though Davis seemed so wary of the league's behind-the-scenes political clout that he kept insisting anything could happen.

What I found particularly disheartening about the NFL's reaction was its persistent refusal to come to grips with the implications of the Raiders' case. Even more annoying was the coverage of the Supreme Court's action in most newspapers across the country. This headline, which appeared in *The New York Times*, was typical:

HIGH COURT BARS
N.F.L. CONTROL OF
FRANCHISE SHIFTS

Not true. The lower-court decision that the Supreme Court let stand did not—repeat, did not—prevent the NFL or any other professional league from having a say in franchise relocation; it merely held that the NFL's Section 4.3, which requires three fourths of its twenty-eight members to approve the shift of a franchise, was in restraint of trade. The Supreme Court was telling the NFL to amend its rules to conform with what is known in antitrust law as the rule of reason. One solution: a simple majority approval of the owners for any franchise shifts.

With that kind of vote, an individual owner would have a tough time proving that his colleagues were acting on whim and caprice in foiling his wishes to move his team.

The lower-court decision also implied that the NFL would be on more solid legal ground if it established objective standards and guidelines to govern franchise relocation. These might include such factors as population, geographic balance, financial viability, quality of facilities, fan loyalty, and "location continuity."

Never once had the NFL made any good-faith efforts to adopt such standards and guidelines that might have passed judicial muster. And the blame for that must fall on the shoulders of Rozelle, who seemed more determined to beat Davis than to take the necessary measures that were best for his league. Swayed by his own arrogance and power, Rozelle went so far as to spend millions of NFL dollars seeking an antitrust exemption in Congress. Getting an exemption for the antitrust laws under which other businesses operate, Rozelle figured, would give him the leverage in returning the Raiders to Oakland.

It didn't work, and the NFL paid the price for Rozelle's personal feud with Davis.

Three days after his victory, Davis showed up at ABC's Los Angeles studio for his exclusive interview with me. The interview was the centerpiece of my *SportsBeat* show, and portions of it got picked up in newspapers across the country.

The highlights:

1. As far back as 1966, Davis revealed, NFL attorneys had expressed their concern about Section 4.3, noting that it was highly vulnerable to the antitrust laws of the United States. Twelve years later, at the now infamous October 1978 meeting in Chicago, Davis said that he himself had warned his fellow owners about Section 4.3.

"I told them, 'Let's put Section 4.3 in conformity with the antitrust laws,'" Davis said. "I urged them to adopt objective standards and guidelines that would allow a team to move. And if ever there was a dispute, we could go to an impartial tribunal.

"In other words, we would take the vote away from the owners, who, based on malice, whim, or caprice, could stop a team from moving without any justified reason."

2. According to Davis, Edward Bennett Williams, part owner of the Washington Redskins and one of this country's most eminent lawyers, often spoke at league meetings and told the owners that the NFL could not defend Section 4.3 in a court of law. "He told us we just couldn't do it," Davis said. "It would not hold up."

3. During the trial, Davis said, NFL attorneys signed a "stipulation" that they had repeatedly advised the league of Section 4.3's vulnerability to the antitrust laws. "This was submitted to the court," Davis said. "Rozelle knew it, but they decided to go ahead with it because they thought they could get away with a court case."

Why?

Davis said: "Because of their power, their law firms, and their large amounts of money."

4. In response to my question about damages, Davis predicted that the Raiders would end up with close to $50 million from the league. As for the L.A. Coliseum Commission, almost $25 million.

5. I then asked Davis if the Supreme Court action would imperil the position of Commissioner Rozelle. Davis noted that Rozelle had destroyed his negotiations with Oakland, spent countless millions on attorneys' fees, waged a lobbying effort in Congress to get an antitrust exemption, disregarded the advice of his own lawyers, and carried on a five-year feud with the Raiders.

"Had he channeled all those energies toward the growth of the National Football League," Davis said, "we would have a tremendous climate now. We would be on the upswing, instead of that little downswing that everybody has said that we are in."

In essence, though, Davis wasn't sure if his victory would cost Rozelle his job.

I closed the interview by saying, "Commissioner Pete Rozelle is always welcome to come before these cameras to respond to Mr. Davis's statements."

Rozelle never came.

On a personal level, as we shall see, Davis's various legal battles with the NFL and Oakland strained my relationship with Rozelle to the breaking point. I had covered the story as honestly and as diligently as I could, but Rozelle insisted that my reporting was biased in Davis's favor—and he steadfastly refused to recognize the difference between my moral and legal views of the Raiders' removal to Los Angeles.

Instead of worrying about me, Rozelle might have more closely examined his own motivations in the Rosenbloom affair and his enmity toward Davis. It was Rozelle's own machinations and the whims of his owners that thrust the league into disarray—and contributed mightily to the Raiders' abandonment of Oakland.

None of this is said to absolve Davis of any blame. After all, the citizens of Oakland were the real losers. They're the ones who gave all those years of loyal support and got ripped off for it. Who will protect others like them in the future? The courts? The league? The media?

Unfortunately, in the wake of these courtroom contretemps, one thing remained painfully clear: The sad history of franchise removal was doomed to repeat itself. The New York Jets would move to the New Jersey Meadowlands, and the Baltimore Colts would become the Indianapolis Colts. In addition, both the Philadelphia Eagles and the St. Louis Cardinals would make loud noises about moving to Phoenix.

4

Escape to New Jersey

The worst sin towards our fellow creatures is not to hate them, but to be indifferent to them: that's the essence of inhumanity.

—George Bernard Shaw, *The Devil's Disciple*

Some people argued that the departure of the Jets from Shea Stadium in New York to the Meadowlands in New Jersey, a few miles across the Hudson River, was of little consequence. We live in a McLuhanesque world, a global village, they said, and football stadiums have become in effect giant television studios. Which prompts the question: Is sports today nothing more than a television show?

I think not—not to millions upon millions of loyal enthusiasts who endure rain and snow and countless other indignities and who gladly spend a portion of their wages to root for the home team. That is the essence of this country's sporting history, a tradition that traces its roots to a yesterday when America was young—a tradition that seems lost on today's owners.

Why? Most of these men made their fortunes in other businesses. For many of them, these teams represent enormous tax shelters, toys that provide vicarious thrills, or an opportunity to see their names in headlines. But don't kid yourself: The bottom line still reigns supreme—which means that the boardroom is where the real action is, not the playing field.

Jets' owner Leon Hess and other owners make a small fortune in television fees even before they open the gates for a game. No matter. Sports today is deals, always deals. Tax abatements, luxury boxes, a bigger slice of the concessions pie, and land, lots of land, to facilitate increased revenue from parking and perhaps the construction of a glistening new training complex.

Cross an owner, deny him these goodies, and he'll skip town.

Is it good business? Sure, but let's not forget that these are the same men who often shroud themselves in the public interest, seeking antitrust immunity in Congress and in the courts when it suits their purposes. And yet they are just as quick to raise the protective umbrella of free enterprise when a sweeter deal awaits them down the road.

• • •

Every now and then, a journalist has a story dumped in his lap when he least expects it. For me, the relocation of the Jets from Shea Stadium in New York to the Meadowlands in New Jersey was such a story.

It happened in March 1982, while flying to Phoenix for a party that ABC was throwing for the NFL owners. Sitting next to me on the plane was an attractive young woman, and I couldn't help but notice that the papers she was shuffling contained the Jets' logo. As it turned out, she was employed by an advertising agency, the same agency that had Jets' owner Leon Hess for a client.

With hardly any prodding, she said, "The Jets are moving to New Jersey, and we're preparing the ad campaign."

I concealed my surprise, striking an effectively dispassionate pose, and said, "Oh, I've heard about that. When is it supposed to happen?"

"In a couple of years, I think."

The young woman knew who I was, and I'm not really sure why she had spoken so casually and openly. Maybe she assumed I was privy to such information. Or maybe, in her naïveté, she thought it was common knowledge among those who covered pro football.

At any rate, I stored her words in the back of my head, ready to pounce on the story when the time was right.

The next night, I saw Hess and his wife, Norma, at the party. My older daughter, Jill, who was in Phoenix visiting friends, had accompanied me, and we accepted an invitation to dine with the Hesses.

"We're meeting tomorrow, and we're going to tell [Al] Davis he's got to drop his suit," Hess told me at dinner. "He can't move. He can't defy the other owners. It'll kill the league, and I'm going to tell him so."

"Regardless of my feelings about Al abandoning Oakland, Leon, I really don't think it'll kill the league. You're being a little dramatic."

"That city needs the Raiders. And besides, Howard, it reflects on the whole league when somebody like Davis can snub his nose at the fans who supported him so loyally for so many years. It's a disgrace."

"I have great sympathy for the citizens of Oakland," I said, mightily resisting the temptation to tell Hess what I knew about his impending desertion of New York.

The next day, I left for home, where I got a call from Davis. "Howard, am I hurting the Jews by moving to Los Angeles?" he asked.

I broke up laughing. "What the hell are you talking about, Al?"

"I met with Leon, and he says I can't move. I'll cause a wave of anti-Semitism in northern California."

"I really don't see the relevancy," I said. "You move, you move. Others have done it before you. Nobody started a campaign against the Roman Catholic Church when O'Malley left Brooklyn."

"Yeah, well, I'm moving anyway."

"That's your business, Al, not mine. You know my position."

"At least you're consistent, Howard. These other guys, what the hell other reasons are they going to come up with?"

Again, I stopped myself from saying what I knew about Hess's future plans for the Jets. And knowing what I knew, you can imagine my bemusement several days later when I found out what Hess had to say at the owners' meeting. The owner of the Cincinnati Bengals, Paul Brown, had raised the possibility of reaching some sort of compromise with Davis and the Los Angeles Coliseum Commission to avoid going to court. Hess wouldn't hear of it.

"We must not settle for anything less than victory!" he thundered. "It's a test of our manhood!"

To appreciate fully the story behind the relocation of the Jets, it is necessary to have an historical fix on the changing fortunes of pro football in New York. And when that perspective is obtained, one man assumes center stage. His name is David A. (Sonny) Werblin. If it weren't for his feud with Hess, a former business partner, the Giants might still be playing in New York—and so, ironically, might the Jets.

Werblin is one of a kind. Some would say that making money is his greatest talent. Others talk about his persuasive powers over a negotiating table behind closed doors. Either way, he's a man who's earned enormous respect, not so much out of fear as out of admiration for his financial genius.

Solid and staunch, you always know where you stand with Werblin. I've never known him to lie about his intentions, and he isn't given to flying off in a wild-eyed, intemperate rage if you happen to disagree with him. Which isn't to say he won't try to fight back on his own terms. If he's pinned in a corner, he will counter by omission, not commission—i.e., he'll keep his mouth shut and cast a wary eye on developments.

A smile from Werblin can light up a room, and he travels with ease and grace through all levels of society. Gracious and charming, he thrives on being the center of attention, though not in a flamboyant way, and he'll never use ten words when five will suffice. He's a traditional, pinstriped businessman. I could never imagine Werblin leaving New York for Hollywood and switching to suede loafers, hip-hugging pants, and silk shirts, like Carroll Rosenbloom did.

Though his legal residence for political purposes is Rumsen, New Jersey, Werblin is a lock, stock, and barrel New Yorker, maintaining a suite in the Lombardy Hotel.

That said, however, there comes a time in the lives of a lot of men when retribution takes hold of their hearts and minds. They are powerless in its grip. Getting even becomes an intoxicating drug. Little thought is given to the consequences of their vengeance.

That's what happened to Werblin. And despite his profoundly affecting love for New York, that's why the greatest city in the world is today without a pro football team.

At this juncture, let me say that no sportsman—not O'Malley, not Rosenbloom, not Davis—ever dreamed of concocting a scenario like the creation of the Meadowlands in New Jersey. And even if they had, I don't believe they could have pulled it off. What Werblin engineered was the most extraordinary exercise in political manipulation ever conceived in the name of sports. First, he forged an unholy alliance with an old adversary, Wellington Mara of the New York Giants, and then he took the state of New Jersey and turned it into his own personal playground.

Here, then, as succinctly as I can, a brief backgrounder, the better to grasp the full sweep of the Jets' removal across the Hudson River:

Werblin has the finest promotional mind I have ever encountered in the field of fashionable diversions. That mind was developed in show business. As one of the three principals in the renowned Music Corporation of America, along with Lew Wasserman and the late Jules Stein, Werblin helped mold the careers of people such as Sinatra, Jackie Gleason, Andy Williams, Ozzie and Harriet, Ed Sullivan, and others—some of the greatest stars in entertainment. He carried that acumen into sports. He teamed up with his best friends—Hess and three now dead: socialite Townsend Martin, dress manufacturer Phil Iselin, and stockbroker Don Lillis—and they formed a partnership to buy Monmouth Park racetrack in New Jersey.

Together, these men also bought the bankrupt New York Titans in the old American Football League for less than $1 million, changed their name to the Jets, and moved the team into Shea Stadium.

The rest is history. Werblin changed the map of professional football. He did it in two simple ways. First, thanks to his friendship with Robert Sarnoff, who was running NBC, he was able to negotiate a $34 million contract with that network. That was in 1964, and those television proceeds, pooled among all AFL teams, gave them the financial power to bargain equally in the marketplace with the NFL. Second, he made the continuation of the war for players a form of economic suicide for both leagues by driving up salaries to what was then the point of no return.

Werblin accomplished that in 1965 when he signed quarterback Joe Willie Namath out of Alabama for more than $400,000. Thus Werblin became the unwitting catalyst for the merger of the two leagues—a merger he never wanted. Also, with that one act, he hastened the advent of the age of big-time sports as big-time entertainment—and the first superstar of that era was Joe Willie Namath.

Werblin's shrewd eye for talent was rarely more in evidence than on January 12, 1969, when Namath led the Jets to an astounding upset over the Baltimore Colts in Super Bowl III—and gave the merger between the leagues instant recognition and credibility.

By then, however, Werblin had had a falling out with his partners. They had grown jealous of the constant attention paid to Werblin and his place in the spotlight. Petty bickering escalated into boisterous quarreling. The final solution: The trio of Hess, Martin, and Iselin joined forces to buy Werblin out of the Jets and to buy him out of the Monmouth Park racetrack.

Werblin never forgave them. And when the team he helped assemble went on to stun the sports world in Super Bowl III, it was just too much for Werblin to bear. He devised an incredible scheme to strike back: He would take a stench-ridden bog just across the Hudson River in New Jersey and build a racetrack, a football stadium, and an indoor arena.

Sensible people laughed at the whole notion. They said it couldn't be done. It was unthinkable that in one of the most troubled urban areas of the country, money could be expended for such purposes. The city of Newark had recently laid off desperately needed policemen. Several towns in Bergen County didn't even have proper sewage facilities—the very county where Werblin wanted to build the Meadowlands. And what about the problems besetting Camden, Trenton, Jersey City, and Asbury Park? In the face of all this, one could forget the Meadowlands.

But not Werblin. Together with his old friend, then Governor William Cahill, he would make his dream come true.

The key to this Utopia was the racetrack. To finance its construction, a bond issue would have to be floated. To get the state legislature to pass the enabling act, a more popular and legitimate front for the track was required. Werblin decided that the front should be a National Football League franchise. So he romanced Giants' owner Mara in a way that Mara understood. MONEY!

The money would come from three primary sources: the gate from seventy-six thousand seats, almost $2 million in annual proceeds from sixty-eight season loges, and *all* concession monies from Giants' games played at that stadium. Mara and the Giants were there for the taking.

When it seemed clear that Mara was going to abandon New York City, I wrote an open letter to Werblin at the request of Kyle Rote, the former halfback who had started a Giants' weekly publication. The letter was soon picked up by the metropolitan dailies.

In the letter, I told Werblin I was writing as an old friend; that what he was doing was totally wrong. It was not as if the Giants were suffering economically. They were not. He was doing it, we both knew, to get back at his old partners.

Of more importance was the cost to the greatest city in the world, to its psyche and its spirit, a city that had lost two baseball teams to California. I recounted the revenue the city would lose, recalled how he had stolen the Giants' thunder with the Jets, and said it was wrong to buy off Mara now. If anybody was of New York and understood the pulsations of the city, it was Sonny Werblin.

The letter ended, as my messages to Werblin always did, with, "Emmy and I send our love to Leah Ray."

The next morning, my phone rang. It was Mrs. Sonny Werblin. "You've got him," said Leah Ray. "Sonny read the letter and said, 'Damnit, he's right. But I'll win, because I'll never answer him.' "

He never did. And it came to pass: The legislation was enacted, the racetrack and the stadium and the arena were built, and the Giants moved to New Jersey. Now the state could challenge New York for sports supremacy. Not only that, the racetrack would pay only .5 percent tax on the total handle. Monmouth Park and the other privately held tracks would continue to pay 9.5 percent tax on their total handle to the state. Werblin's racetrack was destined to make a fortune.

The privately owned tracks—Monmouth, Atlantic City, and Garden State—were not inclined to accept disaster passively.

They went to court, using the Fourteenth Amendment of the Constitution as their fulcrum, alleging violation of equal protection under the law. New Jersey's high court, by a 4–3 vote, found that the equal-protection clause had not been violated. The four judges who were the majority had been appointed, quite coincidentally, by Governor Cahill. The Supreme Court of the United States declined to entertain the case. Werblin's scheme was legally sanctioned. (As a factual aftermath, the state of New Jersey later had to come up with state aid for the privately owned tracks, a further burden on New Jersey taxpayers. Without such help, privately owned tracks would have been doomed.)

Today the bondholders are, in the main, New Jersey taxpayers. The debt-service charges on the bonds are paid by those taxpayers. The bonds were, as noted, used to underwrite construction of the Meadowlands arena and racetrack. The sixty-eight season loges in Giants Stadium, as it was called, are part of the capital structure. Thus, in net effect, the taxpayers are paying taxes on about $2 million a year that goes to the Mara family by way of proceeds from those season loges.

Drawn into this whole interweaving fabric were New York City and then Mayor John Lindsay. It seemed preposterous that the Giants would have the audacity to leave their birthplace. No pro football team had ever received greater support. Despite unendingly bad management by the Maras, the Giants had SRO crowds year in and year out.

New York was left in dismay. It was 1971, a time when the great city was stumbling headlong toward bankruptcy. Spirits were sagging, and it almost seemed as if the Giants' departure would be an augury of terrible things to come, not only in terms of money—the city and state were sure to lose millions in tax revenues—but in big-time image as well.

For months prior to the Giants' announcement of their jump to New Jersey, Mara and William Paley, then chairman of the board of CBS, which owned the Yankees, had been negotiating with Mayor Lindsay and the city for the renovation of Yankee Stadium. Lindsay, believing it critical to keep the Giants in his city, subordinated urban priorities to urban morale. He fought for the renovation at any and all costs—and did so with the belief that the Giants and Yankees would stay.

For verification of this background, one need only place a call to the distinguished dean of the New York University Law Center, Norman Redlich. Dean Redlich had been corporation counsel for the city of New York and had conducted the negotiations in good faith with Mara. It didn't matter. To combat Lindsay's campaign, Werblin chartered a helicopter, flew two New York sportswriters from the roof of the Pan Am Building in midtown Manhattan to the Meadowlands—and proclaimed the trip only six minutes longer than from that same spot to Yankee Stadium.

Of course it was. If you took a helicopter.

Only after Lindsay had all but won his battle with the City Council and the Board of Estimate, and the necessary monies were appropriated, did Mara announce his decision to move. That was in August 1971. Mara did not bargain in good faith. He *did* act legally. The city of New York, in effect, was raped. And would be raped again by the renovation of Yankee Stadium, which was supposed to cost $24 million but ended up costing between $75 million and $100 million, depending upon whose estimates you believed.

The Giants played the 1973 and 1974 seasons in Yale Bowl, and the 1975 season in Shea Stadium. The next year, they finally got to play their first game in their new stadium in East Rutherford, New Jersey, on October 10—and lost to the Dallas Cowboys, 24–14.

They are still called the New York Giants.

In the aftermath, as I reflect on it now, Werblin figured right on at least two counts. In removing the Giants, he'd be able to play the press like a violin, and indeed, the sports print medium was curiously quiescent about the departure of the Giants. Dave Anderson, Pulitzer Prize-winning columnist for *The New York Times,* and Dick Young, then of the *Daily News,* both supported the move on the grounds it would benefit the fans. A coincidence, perhaps, but both men live in New Jersey, not far from the Meadowlands. Only the late Red Smith, when he finally got a column at *The New York Times,* wrote a stinging, good-riddance-Giants epiphany as the departure was announced.

Werblin also knew he had his former partners where he wanted them—with both hands wrapped around their necks. Even with state aid to Monmouth Park, that racetrack has become a financial dud. It is simply unable to cope with the fact that the Meadowlands, based substantially on its tax break, can provide superior purses and better horses for far more important races than Monmouth can now produce.

Werblin had gotten even. And in so doing, he turned his attention elsewhere, severing his association with the Meadowlands. Indeed, it even became his adversary. He came back to New York, where he belongs, as the chief operating officer of Madison Square Garden, and found himself fighting to get the Garden a huge tax break by threatening to remove the Rangers to—of all places—the Meadowlands, and the Knicks to the Nassau Coliseum in Uniondale, Long Island.

The most ironic twist of all, however, was the eventual seduction of the Jets.

Werblin's grandiose design had come full circle: He had built the Meadowlands to get even with Hess—and ended up providing his old enemy with a lovely new home and the increased profits that come with it.

The Jets' departure had yet to be announced when I happened to get together with the Werblins. They were hosting a dinner on the occasion of my daughter Hilary's birthday at Le Cirque, a French restaurant near Park Avenue. At one point, Leah Ray said to me, "Don't turn around, Howard. Norma Hess is sitting right behind you."

Of course, I turned around. The Hesses were most cordial, and they greeted everybody at the table—everybody, that is, but the Werblins. When I resumed my conversation with them, Werblin hissed at me and quietly said, "If you keep talking to them, Howard, I'm leaving this table, and let's not forget I'm your host."

"Excuse me, but I'm in an awkward position," I told the Hesses. "I have to return to my host."

Werblin was already aware of Hess's intentions to move the Jets to New Jersey, and later that evening I asked Werblin how he felt about it. "I don't feel anything," he said evenly.

"Listen, Sonny, I know how deeply you resent Leon, and it's because of you, in the ultimate, he's got new digs for his team."

"So what?" Werblin said with a shrug. "It's part of my life that's behind me now."

Today the Jets' sole owner, Leon Hess is a septuagenarian oil tycoon with a mania for privacy and cleanliness. His desire to abandon city-owned Shea Stadium dates back to 1977, when he complained bitterly about the shortcomings of his lease. At the time, his primary complaint: The Jets weren't allowed to play any home games until the Mets finished their season in October.

City officials finally persuaded the Mets—the prime tenants of Shea Stadium with a sweetheart deal that always made Hess feel like a poor cousin—to allow the Jets to play home games in September. But bile lingered in the belly, and there were some who were convinced that Hess would never renew his lease when it expired after the 1983 season.

In the spring of that year, a resourceful cityside reporter for *The New York Times* named Maurice Carroll brought the possibility of the Jets' removal bubbling to the surface. City and Jets' officials were meeting, he wrote, and the negotiations were "exceptionally touchy." The city was ready to put up $40 million, with the help of the state, for the renovation of Shea Stadium, including a ten-thousand-seat expansion. There was also, Carroll wrote, "an air of urgency to the talks."

This story was mine, and now was the time to try to break it. But how? Who the hell was going to admit that the removal of the Jets was a *fait accompli*? Nobody was talking on the record, not Mayor Ed Koch, not city or Jets' officials, not politicians, and certainly not Hess himself. One man, however, was ready to say what he knew—Nelson Doubleday, the publishing magnate and owner of the Mets.

Doubleday laid out some of the maneuverings in an interview on my *SportsBeat* show of May 14, 1983. He revealed that Mayor Koch had recently made a $43 million offer to Hess, the price of twelve thousand additional seats to Shea Stadium, ninety-eight new loges, general renovations, and major concessions on parking and other revenues by the Mets, the primary tenant. On this subject, Doubleday was forthright. Of course he wanted the improvements to Shea Stadium. What he did not want was the Jets to leave. "One hand washes the other," he said. "There's more money to go around."

Doubleday went on to say that the last time he met face to face with Hess was about two years prior to our conversation. In the interim, according to Doubleday, Hess had ignored countless letters and phone calls to discuss the situation with the Mets.

The owner of the Mets also made these rather remarkable revelations:

COSELL:	"Have you discussed the Jets' potential removal with Commissioner Rozelle?"
DOUBLEDAY:	". . . He was very forceful. He said he'd do everything he could to keep the Jets in New York City. . . . His feeling is that New York deserves a National Football League franchise, and it's his intention to see that it has one."
COSELL:	". . . the history of the Jets talking about moving to New Jersey goes back to 1977. At that point in time, Mr. Hess made it clear that he wanted to move the Jets to the Meadowlands. Do you recollect that?"
DOUBLEDAY:	"Yes, I think he made a commitment. That's when the original commitment was made."
COSELL:	And you have information to the effect that he is probably committed now to go to the Meadowlands."
DOUBLEDAY:	"That's what we hear. . . ."

Then, almost as an aside, Doubleday made this astonishing statement: ". . . Leon, I know, is a very close friend of Mayor Koch's, and for a long time would not discuss this until Mayor Koch's reelection was behind him."

I had nailed down the story. The Jets were gone. That's all there was to it. But the story attracted little or no notice around the country. It was a "local" story. It always is—in the next city to be raped. Even more surprising was the New York press's failure to follow up on the story. You needed a magnifying glass to find the odd account here and there, usually a couple of paragraphs in length buried near the auto ads.

A few months later, though, the story started busting out all over. Things really heated up on September 15, 1983, when the *Daily News* carried a report that the city would consider building a domed stadium ". . . if that's what it takes to keep the Jets from moving to New Jersey."

Several days later, columnists Dave Anderson of *The New York Times* and Mike Lupica of the *Daily News* chimed in with their views. Both men conceded that, in all probability, the Jets were moving to New Jersey the following season. But there ended a similarity between the columns. It was hardly breathtaking that Anderson parroted the Jets' party line—after all, he took the same position when the Giants had skipped town. According to Anderson, New York City and northern New Jersey may be two separate states geographically, but in reality they are one state of mind. And, of course, the Jets' relocation to a better stadium was good for the fans. Nowhere did Anderson mention the tax revenues the city would lose. And neither did he have the grace to tell his readers that he was a New Jersey resident.

Lupica, younger, hipper, called Hess "a gutless carpetbagger," blasting him for deserting the people who supported the Jets through all their losing seasons and for his lack of feeling for history and tradition. He decried what sports has become, "a boardroom game . . . a television show . . . cosmopolitan blackmail . . . deals, always deals." He also alleged that the Jets' move was tied to another deal, a deal that would surely be revealed somewhere down the line.

I had given Lupica that last morsel of information, telling him to keep the specifics to himself. Here's the way the deal was going down:

Hess is not one to take a loss. Werblin's Meadowlands racetrack was rapidly eroding Monmouth Park's profits, and my sources were convinced that the New Jersey Sports and Exhibition Authority, the state-run operation that owns the Meadowlands complex, was going to purchase Monmouth Park to get Hess off the hook. The quid pro quo was the delivery of the Jets to the Meadowlands. These reports had reached Koch's office. One sly move begat another, and a mad scramble was on to figure out a way—mainly, money—for the city to keep its last pro football team from becoming the New Jersey Jets.

This quickly became one of the more fascinating stories I had ever covered, filled with contradiction and intrigue. From the outset, Hess had clamped a lid of secrecy on the Jets' negotiations with the city. He remained an elusive, reclusive figure, almost paranoiac about even being seen by the press. In his corner was the NFL commissioner, Pete Rozelle, who, in an early September appearance on *SportsBeat*, insisted that he had no idea what the Jets were going to do. So you had to dig hard and deep for whatever scraps of information you could unearth. A lot of questions went begging for answers. There were so many different sides of the issue, so many different maneuvers, so many different characters swinging in and out of the story.

The ebb and flow of events is perhaps best chronicled in tick-tock fashion:

September 21. I attended a luncheon at "21" Club for the syndicated television show *Legends of Sports.* Afterward, in the lobby of the restaurant, I bumped into former New York Governor Hugh Carey, who had recently been appointed by Koch to head the New York City Sports Commission. Carey's main responsibility was to try to keep the Jets in town. At least that's what the newspapers claimed. Carey indicated otherwise.

"Just the guy I've been thinking about," Carey said as we greeted each other. "Every time I have a meeting with Hess, he plays a tape of your interview with Doubleday. He screams at Doubleday on the screen, 'You sonuvabitch, you sonuvabitch!' "

"Hughie," I said, "Leon's taking the Jets to New Jersey, isn't he?"

"Yeah, he's gone. We're now laying the groundwork to get another team in here."

"So now you'll rape another city, just the way this town's being raped. What's the sense of that?"

"Look, Howard, all I know is that Leon's leaving. He's furious with Doubleday, and he's mad as hell about Shea Stadium. He's out of here."

"Well, he's got a lousy coach," I said with disgust, sick of all the lies and hypocrisy swirling around the Jets' departure. "They're not going to win anything, anyway."

"He knows that. Off the record, he's trying to get Don Shula from Miami."

That night, at my apartment, I got a call from Miami Dolphins' owner Joe Robbie, and I told him that there was no doubt about it: The Jets were moving to New Jersey. "I never thought he'd go through with it," Robbie sputtered. "I'm going to explode this whole goddamned league, and I'm going public with it. I'll do it on your show."

"Anything you want to talk about, anything you think you should reveal about the league, Joe, you can do it on my show."

I knew that Robbie was influenced by the heat of the moment. He'd never spill any secrets on the air, but I figured I'd extend the invitation, anyway.

"It just can't go on," Robbie said, fuming. "There should be one set of rules for everybody. I don't know what the hell is happening with this league. They'll let Hess leave without so much as a peep. But I make noises about leaving Miami and getting a better stadium and they jump down my throat. Well, from now on, I'm doing what the hell I want to."

"Listen, Joe, I can't reveal my source, but I hear that Hess is after Shula. Where do you stand with him?"

"We're supposed to have a meeting soon. As you know, his contract's up the end of the year, and there are certain things he wants that he can't have. But basically, as far as money is concerned, he's paid far more than any other coach in pro football. They're not going to steal my fucking coach from me!"

No sooner had I hung up with Robbie than the phone rang again. It was an official of the one-year-old United States Football League, informing me that Donald Trump, the brilliant real-estate impresario, had just purchased the New Jersey Generals, and that the announcement would be made tomorrow at a press conference at Trump Tower. I couldn't help but think that Trump probably had every intention of moving the Generals to New York. What with the Jets leaving, the timing was ideal. And besides, I thought, New York City is tailor-made for Trump. He's only thirty-seven, and he's already the face of the city—Trump Tower, Trump Plaza, the Grand Hyatt Hotel. He'll use that image. He'll bring that team here, and he'll take over this town.

September 22. In a two-paragraph story, the *Daily News* quoted a city official as saying that negotiations with the Jets had taken a "more positive" turn. Why, he wouldn't say. It was a lie, a sop for the public.

At 10:30 A.M., in the Trump Tower, hard by a marble waterfall that served as a dazzling backdrop, Trump announced his purchase of the Generals, hinting that coach Chuck Fairbanks' job was in jeopardy—and insisting that his team would stay in New Jersey. After the press conference, he asked me to meet with him privately in his office atop Fifth Avenue.

Dressed in a no-nonsense blue suit, Trump wasted no words. "Do you think I can get Shula?"

I told him I didn't think so, but he'd might as well try. Everybody else was. "And that includes the New Jersey Jets," I said.

"Are you sure they're gone?"

"Positive," I responded. "Do you know about the Monmouth deal?"

"Is that true? That the state will take the racetrack off his hands if he delivers the Jets?"

"That's what I hear. So when are you moving into New York? It's all yours."

Trump smiled, then chose his words carefully. "I'm staying in New Jersey—for the time being. If I wanted to, though, I could move the team tomorrow. I have an out in my lease. I'd have to pay a penalty, which is fair, but not much. The important thing is, I've got a lock on this territory. No other USFL team can move into New York without my approval. That was a key point for me in the deal."

Then Trump offered to sell me a piece of the team. I told him I'd think about it, knowing full well that I couldn't, not while I was still a working journalist. I left Trump's office convinced that he would one day bring the Generals to New York.

As it happened, I ended up having dinner that night with Trump and our wives at a French restaurant on the East Side. Somebody sent a bottle of Dom Perignon champagne to the table. It was Hess! He was having dinner with his wife, and they later stopped by our table to chat.

We exchanged pleasantries. I didn't ask him about the Jets. It was a social occasion, our wives were there and happy to see each other, and I felt it simply wasn't the time or place to put him on the spot. But before Hess departed, he first said to Trump, "I wish you luck, Donald. Any help you need, just give me a call."

Then he turned to me: "I consider us good friends, Howard, and I hope we always will be. I do want to talk with you at some point regarding the Jets."

"Are you going to be in town this week?" I asked.

"Yes, and I will return your call. I promise."

September 23. I placed a call to Hess. It wasn't returned.

September 24. The New York Times carried a one-paragraph item that Hess was to meet with Koch and other city officials on Monday. The story noted that Hess had met only once with city officials in the six months since the city's $43 million offer to improve Shea Stadium.

September 26. Hess finally returned my call. This was prior to his meeting with city officials. I invited him to appear on *SportsBeat,* but he declined. "I can't now, Howard," he said. "The negotiations are very delicate, and I still hope to work things out with the city. But I'll tell you this, Howard: I'll only stay if they build me a new and separate football stadium."

September 27. Not a word in the newspapers about the Hess-Koch meeting the day before—but the *Daily News* did print a story that quoted Shula as saying he was tentatively offered $1 million a year to coach the Generals. Nobody was denying the story, but a team official stressed that Trump himself had not yet spoken personally to Shula.

Later that morning, I happened to get a call from an administrative aide to Governor Mario Cuomo of New York. He said that Cuomo would be attending the *Monday Night Football* game between the Jets and the Bills in Buffalo and wanted to drop by the booth to say hello. That was fine with me, I said, but he should be prepared to answer a few questions about the Jets' impending relocation. "That might be moot by then," the aide told me. "I understand that yesterday's meeting with Koch degenerated into a shouting match. You didn't hear this from me, but I'm fairly certain that Koch is ready to announce that the Jets are leaving. Probably tonight or tomorrow morning."

September 28. Sure enough, Koch held a press conference at City Hall to announce that talks with the Jets had broken down, and beginning next year, they'd be playing their home games at Giants Stadium in the Meadowlands. Finally, after all the lies and petty subterfuges, the truth was out.

Koch accused Hess of being neither fair nor candid in his dealings with the city. Not only had Hess rejected the city's $43 million offer to refurbish Shea Stadium, said Koch, but Hess also for the first time demanded a wholly new stadium. Koch then revealed that the city intended to make every effort to lure another NFL franchise—main candidates, Miami and Baltimore—to New York.

I guess nobody ever told the mayor that two wrongs don't make a right.

Werblin called me.

"You started the whole thing, you son-of-a-bitch," I joked. Chuckling with self-satisfaction, he replied, "I did, didn't I?"

"What about the deal for Monmouth Park?"

"That's very shaky," Werblin said. "Most of the shareholders down there don't want to sell, and since Hess controls only fifty percent of the stock, he can't make a move. He's fighting like hell to sell it, but so far, nothing doing."

"What about the Jets? Does that mean they stay in New York?"

"Oh, no. Leon's gone. The Meadowlands are glad to have him. And besides, he'll still keep fighting to sell them the track somewhere down the road."

September 29. The Jets' potential relocation to New Jersey was now front-page news in New York, and each and every newspaper noted that Hess was, as always, unavailable for comment. That morning, though, Hess called me again. He was upset—extremely emotional, in fact—and several times in the course of our half-hour conversation, I advised him to calm down.

Hess was furious with Koch and Doubleday, calling them liars and scoundrels in trying to paint him as the villain. His position was no secret to Koch, hadn't been for a long while, he said, and he would go public with it only after he had a chance to present his case at a meeting of team owners in New York in another week.

Over the phone, however, Hess complained that he was sick and tired of being a second-class citizen at Shea Stadium and contended he'd always be one as long as he stayed there. "I'm a New Yorker," he said in a quaking voice. "I pay my taxes here, I live here, and I'll die here. Even dying here will cost me a fortune, but I won't move to another state. My heart is in this city, and nobody knows that better than Ed Koch. God knows, I've given millions in his support.

"I told Ed from the beginning the kind of stadium to build. Not a domed stadium, like he's been talking about. It's too expensive and unnecessary. A single-purpose football stadium is what this city needs. Shea Stadium is a piece of shit! The bathrooms stink, the roof leaks, the winds are awful, and their proposal to fix it is ludicrous. Forty-three million dollars?!? It will cost twice that!"

On that point, I agreed with Hess, remembering as I did the

Yankee Stadium fiasco. He then told me how he hoped things would work out:

First, Hess said, he'd go to Trenton and ask Governor Thomas Kean for his support in getting a two-year lease in the Meadowlands. In return, he'd put up as much as $10 million to purchase bonds still outstanding on the Meadowlands complex. Then he'd ask the city of New York to float a bond issue for the building of a single-purpose football stadium—probably on the World's Fair site near Shea Stadium. Considering the city unions, he placed the cost for such a stadium at between $60 million and $80 million.

"To show my good faith," he said, "I'd put up money to retire a portion of those bonds. And I'm not talking about a million dollars. I'm talking real money—ten, twelve, twenty million dollars, whatever it takes, and I'd come back when the stadium is completed. We're not a New Jersey team, Howard. We're a New York team."

I told Hess that he had made some persuasive arguments, but in the main, his potential exodus to New Jersey was wrong. "Regardless of my feelings on that subject, Leon, I must ask you if your move to New Jersey is tied to a deal to sell Monmouth."

Hess replied: "I was negotiating a sale to the Meadowlands until last July, but I've put it away forever. As long as I live, Monmouth Park will not be sold to the Meadowlands. I have no intention of tarnishing the Hess name."

"Are you after Don Shula?"

"I've never talked with Shula. I made Joe Walton the head coach, and he's going to get every chance to prove himself. I have no interest in Shula."

October 6. The *Daily News* headline—front page—read:
LINK JETS MOVE
TO TRACK DEAL

This report basically jibed with what I had known for several months. Of special interest to me, however, was a single paragraph in the middle of the story. It noted that the sale of Monmouth Park to the Meadowlands was indeed called off last July—by a group of stockholders who had blocked the deal.

Remember, Werblin had given me that same information the

week before. This made the tone and texture of Hess's remarks to me concerning Monmouth Park at least questionable: A stockholders' vote had voided the sale of the racetrack to the Meadowlands, not Hess's concern for his good name.

The *Daily News* story also quoted Rozelle, who said Hess had told the other team owners that "he had not completely decided" whether to move the Jets to Giants Stadium in 1984.

Oh, really? Who was kidding whom?

The newspapers also carried accounts of the owners' meeting in New York, reporting that Hess had outlined his problems with Shea Stadium in a twenty-minute address to his colleagues. Also reported was the position of Rozelle, who noted that if Hess decided to move his Jets, he could do so without a vote for approval by the other owners.

Rozelle: "The league's position on a possible Jets' move is that the Los Angeles court decision in the Raiders' case makes the league powerless to consider or vote on the Jets' move."

What wasn't reported was far more interesting. According to my sources, it was Davis who became the center of the drama behind those closed doors.

After Hess had spoken, Davis told the Jets' owner that he had his support, then asked: "Do you realize, Leon, that your words are almost the same as mine were when I told this group what had happened to me in Oakland?"

"Yes," Hess said, "there's a great similarity."

"What will happen to the NFL without a team in the greatest city in the world? What if another NFL team wants to move into this city? Will you object?"

"Don't try to pull the wool over my eyes, Al. You want to move the Raiders into New York."

"That's not true, Leon, and you know it," Davis said. "You offered me control of the Jets in 1979. You remember, in the reading room at Monmouth Park after Phil Iselin's funeral, and I turned you down."

(I was there and witnessed the offer. Hess said, "Do me a favor, Al? Come to New York and take over operating control of the Jets. Keep me out of it. Just call me when it's time to go to the Super Bowl."

"I need thirty days to think about it," Davis said.

Thirty days later, Davis called Hess. "I just can't leave Oakland right now, Leon, and the reasons are deeply personal."

"Who do you recommend?"

"One man. Don Shula.")

After reminding Hess of his offer, Davis then directed several questions at Rozelle. "What are your feelings on this matter, Pete? Should we allow the Jets to leave New York City without a team?"

"The question is moot," Rozelle said, "based on your court-room victory."

"That's wrong!" Davis snapped. "Why do you keep dancing around the truth? My courtroom victory was based on your lousy rule, Section 4.3, which per se violates this country's antitrust laws. And what about the precedents that you yourself set? You let the Giants leave New York for New Jersey, and it was okay for the Rams to split for Anaheim. That's why you can't stop the Jets from moving, even if you wanted to."

Rozelle remained silent. Davis pressed on. "Pete," he said, "I still want your personal view on the Jets. The owners deserve it. The league owes me thirty-four million dollars in damages, and interest mounts every day. They're the ones who have to pay it. Now what's your opinion of the Jets' move?"

Rozelle hesitated, his eyes darting around the room. Finally, he said: "I don't know. I haven't formed an opinion yet."

Hess eventually sent Koch a letter, informing the mayor that he had signed a five-year lease, running through 1988, to play in the Meadowlands. In the letter, Hess pledged to return to New York in 1989—if the city had a proper football stadium in place. Nowhere in that letter did Hess promise to aid in the financing of such a stadium with millions of his own, as he told me he was prepared to do. And remember, too, he had talked to me about a two-year lease, not one for five years.

Apparently Hess thought he could use me, gain my support in his bid to hold up the city for a new stadium. I didn't take the bait, though I was careful to give Hess fair treatment on *Sports-Beat* and in my daily radio commentaries. As always, my position was unwavering, and I was in wholehearted agreement with Koch's reply to Hess's letter. To wit: Forget about the taxpayers' hard-earned money, and build your own stadium.

And so, in 1984, Hess's team played its first season in the Meadowlands, still calling itself the New York Jets.

Item:

On April 10, 1985, the New Jersey Sports and Exposition Authority, which owns the Meadowlands, reached an agreement with Hess and others to purchase Monmouth Park, offering the race track's stockholders $58 a share. The deal infuriated Robert Brennan, a securities broker who had already bought Keystone Race Track near Philadelphia and reopened Garden State Park. As chairman of International Thoroughbred Breeders, Inc., Brennan claimed he had been trying to buy Monmouth Park for two years, and in his latest bid, had offered more money—$60 a share—than the sports authority. "It's been a very deceptive, disquieting couple of weeks with Monmouth," Brennan said, charging that certain Monmouth Park officials had leaked his bids to the sports authority to freeze him out of the purchase.

Brennan said he planned to fight the sale in court. "There will be many issues that we'll uncover in the discovery process of litigation that will be very troublesome for certain members of the Monmouth Park board and the sports authority," he said. "We'll get to the bottom of it."

A couple of weeks later, in a surprise agreement between ITB and the sports authority, Brennan said he would drop his challenge to the sale of Monmouth Park. Why? Because the sports authority promised to support a request by ITB to the New Jersey Racing Commission for more racing dates for Garden State Park.

Thus, Hess, who had sworn to me that he would never sell Monmouth Park to the Meadowlands, went ahead and did it anyway—under disturbing circumstances, to say the least.

5

Rozelle's Folly

*A prince being thus obliged to know well how to act as a
beast must imitate the fox and the lion, for the lion
cannot protect himself from traps, and the fox cannot
defend himself from wolves. One must therefore be a fox
to recognize traps, and a lion to frighten wolves.*

—Niccolò Machiavelli, *The Prince*

To survive as NFL commissioner for as long as he has, Pete
Rozelle had to learn the art of politics in the classic Machiavellian sense. And until only recently, it seemed to all the world
that he had learned his lessons exceedingly well.

Early on, the youthful Rozelle won the favor of the league's
First Families—the Maras in New York, the Halases in Chicago, the Rooneys in Pittsburgh, the Bidwells in St. Louis. Oh,
sure, he had his shaky moments, but these men were soon
amazed at the way Rozelle made them rich with ever-increasing
revenues from television. And being conservative men, loath to
rock the power structure of their league, they have stuck by him
and supported his office.

Later on, Rozelle added yet another layer of powerful new
friends who would stand behind him. The oil tycoon who owns
the New York Jets, Leon Hess, was one. Another was Hugh
Culverhouse, the owner in Tampa, and Culverhouse, in turn,
exerted tremendous influence in two other camps. (As the chief
executor of the late Carroll Rosenbloom's estate, Culverhouse
is close to Georgia Frontiere, Rosenbloom's remarried widow
and the owner of the Rams. Then there was his sway over Leon-

ard Tose, until early 1985 the owner of the Philadelphia Eagles, who once borrowed money from Culverhouse to settle gambling debts.)

And always in Rozelle's corner was Tex Schramm, the president of the Dallas Cowboys, who gave the commissioner his first job in pro football.

No wonder, then, that Rozelle roared like a lion when he wanted to, secure in the alliances he had forged. The dissidents within the league—Jack Kent Cooke in Washington, Joe Robbie in Miami, Ralph Wilson in Buffalo, among others—were wolves without teeth.

Rozelle then made a crucial mistake. Playing the lion so appealed to him that he came to lose the instincts of a fox that once were within him. When that happened, he failed to recognize the biggest trap of all, the trap that was set by Al Davis in Oakland. And in the end, Rozelle got snared, making him easy prey for the wolves who want a piece of his hide.

· · ·

"Whom would you rather have dinner with—Pete Rozelle or Al Davis?" If you had asked me that question several years ago, I wouldn't have hesitated. The answer is Rozelle. He is a charming, deferential man. He's got a sharp mind and an engaging sense of humor. The atmosphere is relaxed, the conversation convivial, and he embraces you with the kind of warmth and attention that makes you feel like a special friend.

Davis couldn't relax in a hot tub. He's always tense, charged up, his eyes working a room as if he were looking for snipers. And the talk is football, always football, whether it be on-the-field strategy, executive intrigue, or courtroom drama. The conversation is more often than not absorbing, but by the time the check is deposited on the table, you feel like you've just walked through the middle of Beirut during an air raid. You're shell-shocked. That's Davis's style.

Through the years, my wife and I had been guests many times at Rozelle's red-brick Tudor house in Westchester County, and he and his second wife, Carrie, were always gracious hosts.

I have never set foot in Al Davis's home.

And yet, today, I can no longer say that Rozelle and I are friends. Our relationship has cooled considerably. The reason: Al Davis and his antitrust suit against the NFL. And the irony is that Rozelle felt I opposed the NFL in its attempts to keep the Raiders in Oakland out of my fondness for Davis.

This is simply not true. Time and again, in my daily radio reports and on my weekly *SportsBeat* show, I expressed my opinion that the Raiders would win on the merits of the case. I also stated in no uncertain terms that while Davis was legally right in deserting Oakland and moving his Raiders to Los Angeles, he was morally wrong. My opinions are all a matter of public record. Rozelle, however, chose to see only black and white in this case. Legal and moral shadings be damned!

You were either with Rozelle or against him on this one, and I wouldn't play his stooge.

Funny, though, I never blamed Rozelle for not being happy with me. He had a job to do, and that was to serve the selfish interests of the NFL owners. But that wasn't my job. Sadly, he didn't understand that—or perhaps he simply refused to.

The wedge that now separates Rozelle and me, however, in no way changes my historical view of him as commissioner of the NFL. He is without doubt the most effective commissioner ever to govern any league in any sport. This is a man who made the best of every opportunity that came his way and his league's way, and he did it with consummate skill, verve, and panache.

Rozelle was raised in Lynwood, California, where his father lost a grocery store in the Depression. Rozelle went to high school with Brooklyn Dodger Hall of Famer Duke Snider, and they became close friends. It wasn't long before Rozelle would start displaying an uncanny knack for being in the right place at the right time. What he wanted to be then was a sportswriter. But when he got to Compton Junior College, he found himself working as a gofer for the Rams' publicity man. That was in the summer of 1946—the same summer that the Rams moved from Cleveland to Los Angeles and opened training headquarters in Compton.

Rozelle discovered he had a flair for PR. He accepted a job as an undergraduate PR man at the University of San Francisco and completed his education there. He was then a PR man for a brewery, then a PR man for the Rams, and then later the general manager of that team. Nobody ever accused Rozelle of having a brilliant football mind, and he labored in semi-anonymity. But, lucky for him, he had developed the proper social amenities. He was unfailingly polite to his superiors and never offended anybody. And so, on January 26, 1960, apparently in desperation on its twenty-third ballot, the NFL elected Rozelle as its commissioner.

Rozelle was only thirty-three, washing his hands in the men's room of a Miami Beach hotel when Carroll Rosenbloom, then the owner of the Baltimore Colts, came in to give him the news. "It would be ludicrous," Rozelle said, "to consider myself as anything but a compromise choice."

The young commissioner had fallen out of the sky, but he soon had his feet firmly planted on the ground. Two of the league's crusty old patriarchs—George Halas of the Chicago Bears and George Preston Marshall of the Washington Redskins—tried to bully Rozelle into seeing things their way, and they lost. Then, in 1963, he suspended two of the game's biggest stars—Paul Hornung of the Green Bay Packers and Alex Karras of the Detroit Lions—for betting on their own teams.

On the financial front, Rozelle was equally as bold. He persuaded owners such as Marshall and Rosenbloom, who had lucrative, private TV contracts, to give up their deals for a cooperative venture with CBS. This pooling of television money provided the fulcrum for the growth of the NFL, enabling Green Bay, for example, to compete against a glamorous city such as New York. Even more impressive than his sway over the owners was the way Rozelle wrapped the whole package up—by obtaining an antitrust waiver in Congress.

Several years later, in 1966, Rozelle was back in Washington, smoother than ever, winning friends and influencing legislators. He wanted another antitrust exemption, this time to merge with the American Football League. No sweat. He coddled and cajoled two powerful Louisianians—Senate Finance Committee chairman Russell Long and the late House Democratic whip, Hale Boggs—and the Congress approved the merger by slipping in a rider to an investment credit act. And guess what? The NFL awarded the next expansion franchise to New Orleans.

And the money continued to pour in.

The scope of Rozelle's accomplishments usually is measured in dollars, and it's hard to ignore. Under his direction, the NFL has grown from twelve to twenty-eight teams, and ten million more tickets a year are sold for a considerably higher price. Shortly after Rozelle was elected, the Cleveland Browns were purchased by Art Modell for $3.8 million, and the league operated out of the back room of a suburban Philadelphia bank. Today, an average franchise is worth as much as $50 million, and the commissioner and his staff have a scrubbed corporate image, with two floors of offices overlooking Park Avenue in the heart of Manhattan.

In 1962, Rozelle negotiated his first television contract, selling CBS the rights to televise a single season for $4.6 million. Exactly twenty years later, he sold those same rights to all three networks for $400 million a year.

There are those who will argue that Pete Rozelle is the architect of the greatest success story in the modern American entertainment industry.

Thus, thanks in the early years to his shrewd and decisive actions—and many other well-publicized but less important matters of leadership—the image of Pete Rozelle was cast. And thanks to his influence over the media, he has persevered, becoming in the process a sort of omniscient presence in the world of sports.

I have a different story to tell.

When Rozelle was working for the Rams, I was hardly the personality I would later become. ABC Television had acquired a special package of preseason games—Cleveland at Pittsburgh, and Chicago at Baltimore—and I was hired as the broadcaster. Rozelle and I would meet only fleetingly, and he was always gracious.

Rozelle's ascendancy to the job of commissioner caught me by surprise, as it did almost everybody else. At the time, I was covering the pro football beat for ABC, both on radio and local television in New York. As Rozelle started carving out a formidable reputation, I had many opportunities to interview him. He was not only accessible, but also direct in meeting all my questions.

This was especially true when Rozelle was faced with the

thorny problems of the Hornung and Karras cases. I'll never forget the press conference that Rozelle held when he finally announced his decision to suspend indefinitely each player from football for his gambling indiscretions. (The suspensions were lifted after a year.) Rozelle called me the next day and told me that Jim Kensil—then Rozelle's chief aide, now the president of the New York Jets—remarked on how I asked the best and most penetrating questions. It was a nice gesture, and there developed a great mutuality of respect between the two of us, which frankly pleased me.

Then came the merger, and I was impressed with the way Rozelle got the Congress to approve it. As soon as the bill was passed, he left Washington and appeared exclusively with me in New York on local television to discuss how the merger was certified and the ramifications of it. Our relationship continued to blossom in the late 1960s, and I regarded Rozelle with respect and even some affection.

I won't easily forget how supportive Rozelle was during the dawning of *Monday Night Football.* It was Rozelle's brainchild. ABC acquired the rights after CBS and NBC turned the idea down. This was in the spring of 1970. I was having lunch at Jimmy Weston's when I got paged to the phone. It was Roone Arledge, the president of ABC Sports. "I want you to come to my office immediately," he said. "I've got to talk to you."

Arledge told me he wanted me to do *Monday Night Football.* I later called Rozelle to talk it over with him, and it turned out that Rozelle had suggested me for the job. This is not to suggest that I wasn't Arledge's first choice, too. After all, Arledge was then the company's savior because of his brilliant pioneering efforts in television sports. ABC was far ahead of the other two networks in sports programming, largely due to the success of *Wide World of Sports.* And what was at the core of *Wide World of Sports?* Muhammad Ali and Howard Cosell.

It seemed logical that Arledge would tap me for the job, and I only mention the fact that Rozelle had suggested me because it is illustrative of the man's shrewd understanding of television. Pro football was entering the promised land of prime time, and Rozelle instinctively realized that *Monday Night Football* needed a different presentation. Why? It had to transcend sport. Prime time obviously required a larger audience than Sunday afternoon, which meant that *Monday Night Football* had to attract not only the casual fan but women as well. Survival would depend, in large measure, on the guys in the booth and the entertainment value of the show.

The first Monday night game was between the New York Jets and the Cleveland Browns, and I thought the telecast had gone well. A few kinks needed to be ironed out, but, hell, we had only just begun. I was living in the suburb of Pound Ridge, and *The New York Times* was delivered every morning to my home. Jack Gould was then that newspaper's television critic. He lived in Greenwich, and we'd often see each other on the commuter train on our way to work. I respected Gould enormously. He was one of the finest analysts of the television industry ever to appear in print, and we'd talk about the business during those long rides into Manhattan.

I was devastated by Gould's review of that first Monday night game. He scorched me. "Maybe his sport is boxing," he wrote. "It's certainly not football." I couldn't believe my eyes. It was so shattering that to this day I don't recall whether I phoned Rozelle or he got to me.

"Howard, you did extremely well, a helluva telecast," Rozelle said. "Sid Gilman, who knows more football than any man I've ever known, Lombardi included, said you did a helluva job."

I said, "Pete, didn't you read Jack Gould this morning?"

"No, not yet."

"He slaughtered me."

Rozelle told me not to worry. "What the hell does Jack Gould know about football, anyway?"

That wasn't the end of it. During the first year of *Monday Night Football*, I was the object of a terrible and unexpected assault in print. Nobody in my business should ever have to endure the unrelenting vilification that was heaped upon me. The newspaper reporters were like vultures, picking at my bones. It deeply affected me, and by the fifth game, I broke down. The scene was a hotel bar in Minneapolis. I ran into an NFL official named Don Weiss, and I ranted and raved: "This is crazy! I don't know why the press is doing this to me. I can't go on. I'm not going to take any more abuse. I want out!"

Weiss related the incident to Rozelle, who then invited himself over to my apartment in Manhattan for a drink. "You mustn't quit," Rozelle told me.

Rozelle also addressed my wife, Emmy. "Look," he said, "I

just wanted to come here as a friend and tell you that Howard is taking this thing much too seriously. He should have fun with the games. I think he has been, on the air, but deep inside apparently he's still being troubled. It's ridiculous. Howard"—and he turned to me—"just have fun with the games."

Rozelle's support meant a lot to me—and the rest is history. *Monday Night Football* became a national phenomenon, and I prospered beyond my wildest expectations. So did Rozelle. We remained friends—though not on the same level as his close, personal friendship with former players turned broadcasters such as Frank Gifford and Pat Summerall—and it was a pleasure revolving in Rozelle's social orbit.

The 1970s were halcyon years for Rozelle, even though he had his share of problems to contend with. The proliferating drug scandals involving NFL players had yet to cast their long shadows over the league, but disputes with the NFL Players' Association and a rising tide of antitrust suits demanded time and attention.

Beginning to flex its muscle, the players' union staged brief preseason strikes in 1970 and 1974, then received $16 million from the league to settle two lawsuits. Numerous other antitrust actions—initiated either by the players or outside parties—bedeviled the league, and its record in defending itself was abysmal. The league ended up losing millions in settlements and lawyers' fees.

Expressions of outrage followed each loss, and Rozelle sought to portray himself as a misunderstood minstrel of joy and peace, always looking out for the best interests of the NFL, the owners, the players, and even the public.

And just about everybody bought Rozelle's act.

Let's face it: Rozelle does have an engaging personality. People like him. Always tanned and impeccably groomed, he's like velvet to the touch. Loath to offend anyone, he's cool and patient. And those who know him best say he's a compassionate and decent man.

The word most often attached to Rozelle, however, is "slick." At heart, he is and always will be a PR man, and he admits as much. But he's somewhat uncomfortable with the label—"slick" has so many connotations. It can mean smooth or calculating, confident or conniving. When embodied in Rozelle, it probably means all those things. And as a result, most people find it practically impossible to paint a complete picture of the man. He closely guards his privacy, and there are precious few revealing anecdotes that bridge the gaps. But one thing I know for certain: Rozelle is a superb manipulator of people—and he's at his best when he's manipulating the media.

Never in my lifetime in sports has anyone commanded and controlled the media like Pete Rozelle.

Take, for example, his mass press conference a couple of days before each and every Super Bowl game. His performances at this annual event are legendary. The scene is always a hotel ballroom, and Rozelle stands at a podium, sometimes for as long as two hours, fielding questions from upward of fifteen hundred accredited reporters. He is utterly beguiling and mesmerizing as he calls on reporters by name, a technique that always scores points; his familiarity with members of the media goes a long way toward getting him the benefit of the doubt and stacks of glowing press notices.

But that is merely a clever ploy. His real talent comes into focus while answering a variety of questions on the state of the NFL. He is witty and graceful, his voice clear and authoritative. He never assumes a threatening posture but gives the impression that he firmly believes exactly what he's saying. And he has that rare quality of being elusive while all the while appearing candid.

Most sportswriters and TV reporters allow Rozelle to get away with this trick—either because they don't recognize the ploy, or because they want to be considered friends of the NFL. Whatever the reason, they always seem to play into Rozelle's hands, enabling him to solidify his control. As Frank Deford once wrote in *Sports Illustrated*, with considerable perspicacity: "It is revealing that while baseball's great resurgence of popularity has been well documented, none of the credit is ever given to [baseball commissioner Bowie] Kuhn—in the public mind he will forever remain just the dummy who goes to freezing cold baseball games in tropical worsteds—while the press and fans are quick to attribute even the most minor NFL advances to Rozelle."

I beg to differ only slightly with Deford's observation—i.e., if the fans do indeed adulate Rozelle, it's because the media have convinced them of his greatness. To buttress my argument, I give you Dave Anderson, a Pulitzer Prize winner who writes for *The New York Times*. His column is dated November 7, 1982. The headline over it reads: BASEBALL NEEDS PETE ROZELLE. The question is put to Rozelle if he'd accept an offer to be the new baseball commissioner. He answers, "I'm committed to the NFL. I'm going to stay in this job the rest of my working life. My contract has several years to run. And except for being a casual fan, I don't know much about baseball. Certainly not enough for me to have a feel for it, to be comfortable in it. You need that feel to be effective, to make decisions that you think are right."

Despite those words by Rozelle, Anderson closed his column with this paragraph: "But the first choice should be Pete Rozelle, despite his apparent disinterest. Let him turn it down officially before anybody else is considered."

Believe it or not, that column appeared in the midst of a long and debilitating strike by the NFL Players' Association, the first such strike in the history of the league.

Again, it is revealing to bring up baseball commissioner Kuhn. When baseball struggled through a two-month players' strike of its own in 1981, Kuhn was generally pilloried by the media for his alleged ineffectiveness in bringing about a settlement. But there was Rozelle, delegating responsibility for settling his own league's players' strike to a council of owners while he washed his hands of the dirty work, and a *New York Times* columnist is nominating him for baseball commissioner!

Perhaps the media are so deferential to Rozelle because his boyhood dream was to be a sportswriter, or so he says. The fact is, though, Rozelle would never allow himself to get too friendly with a journalist; ultimately, he doesn't trust the breed. From time to time, I had talked with Rozelle about Robert Lipsyte, a brilliant journalist who once wrote a sports column for *The New York Times*. Lipsyte was concerned about public-policy issues— violence, racism, drugs, unions, etc. He was perceptive and dead honest, unafraid to probe for the truth. Rozelle's opinion of him: "He's not a sportswriter, Howard. He doesn't write about the game."

To Rozelle, the game is sacrosanct, and when the problems that buffet the outside world intrude upon the game, he tends to get indignant about it. Stories that tarnish the image of the league are officially labeled as "exaggerated." And if you take a position that is in opposition to his point of view—which, needless to say, is also the league's—your relationship with him will suffer.

That's what happened to me.

In early March 1980, at Rancho Mirage in California, the NFL owners voted against Davis's moving his Raiders to Los Angeles. Shortly after those meetings, Davis filed his antitrust suit against the league. It was around this time that I invited Rozelle to be my guest at Yale, where I was teaching a course, "Big-Time Sports in Contemporary America." He graciously accepted my invitation, and my students were frankly excited about the opportunity to question the commissioner of the NFL.

These were intelligent young men and women, and they put Rozelle through the ropes. For the most part, their questions concerned the Davis affair in particular and franchise removal in general. How, they wondered, could the league justify keeping Davis and his Raiders out of Los Angeles when it had already allowed the Giants to move from the Bronx, New York, to East Rutherford, New Jersey; the Lions to move from Detroit to Pontiac; and the Rams to move from Los Angeles to Anaheim? He never did convince them of the viability of the league's position.

Later, driving home together, I told Rozelle that I thought his posture was untenable. "You mustn't go to court on this one, Pete. You will lose as a matter of law."

We stopped at Rozelle's home in Harrison, New York, for a couple of drinks, and as always, Rozelle stubbornly defended the league's pattern of suburban removal. Under league rules, a team was allowed to relocate within seventy-five miles of its present location. Moving a team from Oakland to Los Angeles was obviously a violation of that rule, and it was Davis's obligation to operate within the rules.

"Suburban relocation is a lot of crap," I told him.

"Come on, Howard," Rozelle said. "The Giants moved only a matter of miles away from Yankee Stadium."

"Yeah, into another state and another tax jurisdiction. And by the way, have you ever tried to get from Detroit to Pontiac? It's ridiculous. All I'm saying, Pete, is that these various moves have weakened your position. But even that's beside the point. As a matter of law, Davis must win."

Almost a year went by, and the trial was set to open on February 9. I called Rozelle. "I'd like to sit down with you, Pete. I know you're going to trial soon, and I was hoping to review the case with you and go over your position with you again."

I knew this would be perhaps the biggest story in sports, and I was concerned about being utterly fair in my coverage of the case. To my surprise, Rozelle said he'd come to my apartment. A dear friend, Jim Mahoney, was in from the West Coast, and we had planned to have dinner together. But when Rozelle arrived at my apartment with an attaché case full of documents, Jim and my wife, Emmy, repaired to another room, and our dinner was put on hold until Rozelle and I had discussed the case.

Several months later, the trial ended in a hung jury. A new trial was scheduled to start on March 15, 1982. The day before, I aired a report on the case on my *SportsBeat* show, paying careful attention not to take a position, concerned as I was about fairness and objectivity.

My opening remarks: ". . . the sole issue on which this case will be decided is Section 4.3 of the NFL constitution. This rule requires the approval of seventy-five percent of the team owners for a franchise to move from one city to another outside a seventy-five-mile radius. What must be decided is whether seventy-five percent is an unreasonable figure, or whether another figure—say, fifty percent—would be reasonable under the so-called rule of reason in antitrust law. There has been a previous trial, which resulted in a hung jury, with eight of the ten jurors voting in favor of Al Davis and the Los Angeles Memorial Coliseum Commission. This week, two breaking developments . . ."

I then detailed those developments. One, a meeting in Dallas between Rozelle and several members of the Coliseum Commission to discuss the possibility of an expansion franchise in Los Angeles; and two, the possibility of a settlement in the case. I noted how this represented a change in the NFL's hard-line position, and toward the end of the report, the following opinion was offered by Charles Maher, the legal columnist for the *Los Angeles Times*: ". . . I don't see how the NFL can win it . . . just looking at it from what I know of the law and of this case, I would say it would take a miracle for the NFL to pull it out."

I closed with these words: "Why is this case vital? Because it may affect the whole structure of American professional sports as we know it. Rozelle argues that if a man joins a league he agrees to abide by its rules; if he's allowed to break those rules, there'll be anarchy. In effect, a man could move at whim and caprice. In the meantime, all other sports commissioners agree with Rozelle.

"However, Davis says that a rule that is illegal is no rule at all. Let the rule of reason, as decided by the court, prevail. And you wouldn't have whim and caprice; you'd have obeyance of the law.

"It's a tremendous issue, the biggest in American sport today."

And so the second trial commenced. Davis was the principal witness for the plaintiffs, and Rozelle the principal witness for the defense. As I mentioned in a previous chapter, it was Duran vs. Leonard—and not only in styles but also in the hatred these two men harbored for each other. And believe me, hatred existed, regardless of how strenuously Rozelle denied that this suit had become a personal battle between Davis and him.

Davis rattled Rozelle, got under his skin, and on occasion, the normally unflappable Rozelle lost his cool, once going so far as to brand Davis an "outlaw." Davis's public posture was even more intemperate; he drew blood by accusing Rozelle of being involved in a Super Bowl ticket-scalping scam and using the league's security force to investigate owners and bolster his own personal power. "What the NFL has become," Davis said, "is a political theater. If you're not in the inner circle, you're exiled."

Davis wanted to turn these legal proceedings into a street fight between Rozelle and him, and he succeeded. During the course of the trial, Rozelle was hardly a model of grace under pressure. This case had obviously drained him, physically and emotionally, and his vaunted reputation for being well prepared might have seemed a sham to those who didn't know him well. On the stand, he too often answered opposing attorneys' questions with the phrase "I don't recall."

To be fair, Rozelle's performance had little impact on the jury's ultimate verdict in favor of Davis. The NFL's defense of Section 4.3 of its constitution was shaky at best. But it's also important to note that the jury found the league guilty of bad faith in its dealings with Davis. Basically, these: Rozelle had tried to take the Raiders away from Davis and put it in receivership; stacked a league committee investigating the Raiders' move against Davis; and had disseminated distorted information concerning the situation in Oakland and the removal to Los Angeles.

On May 9, 1982, two days after Davis's victory in court, Davis and his attorney, former San Francisco Mayor Joe Alioto, appeared with me exclusively on *SportsBeat.* At the top of the show, I emphasized that I was presenting Davis's and Alioto's side of the case; then I added: ". . . let's make this absolutely clear. This camera, these microphones will be offered to Alvin Pete Rozelle, the NFL commissioner, to grant him equal time for next week."

The interview proceeded as follows:

COSELL: "Al, Commissioner Rozelle says that if the verdict against the NFL on Friday past is sustained, the league will face anarchy, that owners will be able to move at whim and caprice, deserting loyal fandoms. What do you say?"

DAVIS: ". . . On the contrary, we're stronger than ever. This rule that the NFL lost on is an illegal rule. We've known it for fifteen years. It should be out of our constitution. It can be written in a way that's enforceable and made enforceable by the laws of our country, and we won't have any problems with it whatsoever."

Davis, of course, was referring to Section 4.3. He and his attorneys had always believed that a 75 percent approval of the twenty-eight NFL owners to move a franchise was illegal; that if Section 4.3 had called for a simple majority vote, they probably would not have had a case. As it turned out, according to the opinion of the court, they were right.

COSELL: "All right, Al, be that as it may, you did make money in Oakland. The fans supported you. Don't you have any feelings for them?"

DAVIS: "Oh, I have a great deal of empathy for the fans of Oakland and the community of Oakland, Howard, but only I can see what the future is in the 1980s in professional football. And the stadium we had was a stadium that was growing old. It wasn't going to give us the facilities that we need to be competitive in the 1980s in professional football. For example, not to complain, but in 1980 alone, the Los Angeles Rams in Anaheim made over five million dollars more than the Raiders did in Oakland. With that kind of disparity in wealth ... we're going to have to be competitive and not put an apologetic team on the football field. Our players are great ... they should be paid, and I intend to pay them. I want a facility that's competitive, where I can compete with these people in the 1980s."

COSELL: "Would you have stayed in Oakland if your original deal had been held up by the Oakland people?"

DAVIS: "I think that that's come through in the courtroom, that I certainly would have stayed in Oakland. But Rozelle came into that community and kind of told them that I was locked in, that I couldn't move, and therefore they repudiated their own negotiators. But, in any event, there's no reason to prevent me from moving to Los Angeles. In fact, the only reason that's come forward in the past three years is what Rozelle expressly stated in the courtroom, that the owners wanted this lucrative franchise to divvy up among themselves. They didn't want me to have it. And that, I thought, was unconscionable, and I think the jury ... thought that was unconscionable."

I then questioned Alioto about the legal and financial ramifications of the case, and wound up the interview by saying, "Al, don't look so discomfited. For the moment, at least, you're a winner."

"What do you mean 'for the moment,' Howard?" Davis shot back with typical brio. "I've been a winner all my life, and I'll continue to win."

The following week, I invited Rozelle to appear on *Sports-Beat* to give his side of the story, his views on Davis's victory. He was unable to appear.

The subject I featured that week was franchise removal. I opened the show by noting two recent developments: one, Davis's victory in court; and two, the granting of enormous tax concessions by the city of New York to Madison Square Garden to keep the Knicks and Rangers from moving elsewhere. "Those two stories," I said, "are but the latest chapters in a continuing saga that presents the nation's great cities with a prime dilemma. What to do when, one, a sports franchise deserts a city, or, two, a sports franchise merely threatens to desert. As the nation's cities struggle to find the money to provide vital services, local officials are busily trying to put together packages of concessions to prevent their teams from moving to cities making more attractive offers. . . ."

The story went on to document the various desertions of cities, and threatened desertions, by team owners, much as I have written here in previous chapters. I also mentioned a bill in the Congress—H.R. 823. That bill asked the Congress to declare that it is national policy to discourage relocation of professional sports teams that are consistently supported by their communities.

One of the key ingredients of the bill was the requirement to demonstrate a net financial loss for at least three consecutive years prior to notice of intent to move. Teams could neither move nor threaten to move at whim and fancy. I then commented, "Now, the intention here is not to attack the owners. The flow of events, as historically recited, speaks for itself. Nor is it to justify Al Davis's attempt to remove to Los Angeles, though he may have been helped in his case by these very past events. What we want to do is make you, the taxpayer, aware of the true cost of keeping and maintaining sports franchises.

"If one accepts the premise that professional sports teams are as essential to a city as such vital services as housing, public safety, education, health, and job opportunity, then the only way to protect against franchise removal or threat thereof may be through federal legislation of the type just set forth."

My position, I thought, was quite clear. Fairness and objectivity were my goals, and I think I achieved them. As a matter of law, Davis had to win; on moral grounds, he was wrong. That was my opinion. Furthermore, on national television, I came out in support of H.R. 823. If that bill had become law prior to 1979, Davis never could have deserted Oakland, and that would have set very well with me. The good citizens of Oakland deserved to keep the Raiders.

Rozelle heard only what he wanted to hear, a condition born of arrogance. If you don't agree totally with Rozelle and his colleagues, you are against them. Objectivity doesn't matter. Fairness doesn't matter. The right to express your own opinion doesn't matter. And what's worse, they deliberately distort what you say, in spite of the fact that what you've said reaches millions of people on the public airwaves and is a matter of public record.

I offer as evidence the following letter, dated the day after my story on franchise removal appeared on *SportsBeat* and written on official NFL stationery:

Mr. Howard Cosell
ABC Sports
1330 Avenue of the Americas
New York, N.Y. 10019

Dear Howard:

I regret that I was unable to honor your request to appear on *SportsBeat*, but after being gone for almost two months I felt obligated to fulfill a personal family commitment yesterday.

On the subject of the Oakland Raiders' efforts to move to the Los Angeles Coliseum, Howard, I have felt for the past 2½ years that your public position has been totally inconsistent with your previous position.

Your public posture on previous sports franchise shifts is well documented. You've voiced outrage at the move of the Brooklyn Dodgers to Los Angeles in 1958. You vehemently criticized the transfer of the Milwaukee Braves to Atlanta in 1965.

For several years you castigated the Mara family and the league for the move of the New York Giants to the Meadowlands—some eight miles from Times Square. You evidently overlooked the fact that ninety percent or more of the Giants fans continued to follow their team in the same manner as before—on television. That is true of all our other NFL suburban moves.

However, your posture on the Raiders' proposed shift to Los Angeles without an approving vote by the other NFL clubs has been contrary to your total outrage against earlier sports franchise moves. You have been totally silent regarding this move on television, radio and before congressional committees.

Obviously, you have every right to take whatever position you choose. I simply offer my view that it constitutes a glaring inconsistency.

It is my belief that the man who originated the term "telling it like it is" and who has been a constant critic of the so-called "carpetbagging" aspects of professional sports has stamped his personal imprimatur on the first franchise shift of an NFL team to a different metropolitan area in more than twenty years. I can only conclude that you have compelling reasons for your unprecedented position due to your close personal relationship and contact with Al Davis.

Should you wish to discuss this with me on a private basis, I would be glad to do so.

Sincerely,

PETE ROZELLE
Commissioner

The day after I received Rozelle's letter, I responded to his charges in a letter of my own. I then called him and took him up on his invitation to discuss the matter on a private basis. We agreed to have drinks at five o'clock at the Laurent in the Lombardy Hotel on East Fifty-sixth Street.

When we met, I handed Rozelle the letter I had written. "Before we talk," I told him, "I think you should read this." Rozelle read the letter. It follows here:

Commissioner Pete Rozelle
National Football League
410 Park Avenue
New York, New York

May 28, 1982

Dear Pete,

Thank you for your candid letter of May 17, 1982. I feel compelled to reply because I respectfully disagree with you as to my alleged inconsistencies of position. I honestly believe that the inconsistencies are yours.

You are quite correct about my outrage at the move of

the Brooklyn Dodgers to Los Angeles, and the transfer of the Milwaukee Braves to Atlanta. Indeed, Bowie Kuhn has privately admitted to me that the Braves move should never have taken place; but as the attorney for the National League in that case, he was bound to represent the Braves to the fullest.

I do not believe that the Giants' removal is remotely related to the distance from Times Square to the Meadowlands. The issue there is complex because it involved the emotional and spiritual loss to New York City at the worst possible time in the city's history; it had a major negative ripple effect on the economics of the city at the worst possible time. And, as Sonny Werblin has admitted to me frequently, the enticement of the Giants to New Jersey—a new and different tax jurisdiction—was to provide a front for a race track that enjoys huge tax advantages over the privately owned tracks in the state of New Jersey.

The Giants' removal was what Sonny needed to get the enabling legislation for the building of the track, so that he could avenge himself against the owners of the Jets, who also owned Monmouth Park. All of this, Sonny will tell you, is why I fought the Meadowlands so vigorously, even as did the owners of Monmouth Park and the Jets. Sonny never took me on publicly because he knew I was right. Yet we have remained warm friends because he respected my right to my position and my obligation to my company to do my job as a journalist.

With regard to the Oakland Raiders, my position on their removal has never changed. In principle, it is my view that no profit-making franchise should ever remove unless there is abridgement of the lease by the landlord. The Raiders are no different. On March 30, 1972, when Marlow Cook introduced his bill for a Federal Sports Commission, I supported that bill because of my concern about franchise removals. In fact, the then Senator Marlow Cook of Kentucky drew upon my name in introducing the bill. This is on page 11065 of the Congressional Record. Then, last summer, as you are well aware, I testified before the Rodino committee. In that testimony, I supported two House bills: 1) H.R. 823 that, in essence, would prohibit franchise removal unless the franchise could show at least three continuous years of economic loss, and 2) H.R. 3287, a bill to abolish baseball's exemption from the antitrust laws. I consider baseball's exemption from the antitrust laws an anomaly at law and utterly out of touch with the conditions of the baseball business in contemporary society. Again, Mr. Kuhn knows my position and respects it.

Having read the transcripts of both trials it is my private view, and I do have legal background, that Davis won his case on the basis of rule 4.3, and the league has always had a legitimate concern over the legality of that rule; plus the notes of Bob Schulman and others concerning the October 1978 league meeting; plus the actions of Carroll Rosenbloom, the Maras, and the threatened removals of other owners.

I think you know that, in point of fact, Emmy and I have been far more at ease and congenial socially with you and Carrie than we have ever been with Al Davis. My respect for Davis is as a football man. My concern as a journalist remains where it has always been—with the taxpaying public.

In sum, I respect your personal opinion and your advocacy of the league's case. Beyond question, you have been the finest commissioner in the history of professional sport, and the position of the National Football League in the sports spectrum of this country is vivid testimony of your achievements. Nobody knows that better than I do. But I must adhere to my own basic tenets, and I trust that you can understand that.

Sincerely,

Howard Cosell

Rozelle folded the letter and put it back into its envelope. "First, yes, Giants Stadium was tied in with the racetrack," he said. "But that doesn't change the fact that the Giants moved only eight miles away."

"Pete, we're beating a dead horse here," I said. "My letter speaks for itself."

"Okay, Howard, but as far as Davis is concerned, I stick to

my position. You have supported him, and that's inconsistent with the stands you've taken in the past."

" 'Support' is the wrong word," I replied. "I simply predicted Davis would win as a matter of law. Morally, he was wrong to move. I don't understand why you think that deviates from previous positions I've taken."

"I disagree. You've been on Davis's side."

"All I can say, Pete, is that my position is a matter of public record. My radio reports, *SportsBeat*, my testimonies before Congress, it's all a matter of public record. There's no doubt in my mind I've been fair and consistent."

Before we got up to leave, Rozelle said, "I do want to say this to you, Howard. What Gene Klein said was terribly, terribly wrong, and I want you to know how I feel about that."

Rozelle was referring to an incident that occurred a couple of months earlier. I was in Phoenix for an ABC function that was connected to the annual NFL owners' meetings. My first night there, at a restaurant with my daughter Jill, who was in Phoenix visiting friends, I spotted Klein, the owner of the San Diego Chargers, and his wife, Joyce, at another table and walked over to say hello. We had always been on friendly terms, and so I was totally unprepared for Klein's outburst. "Don't come near here!" he bellowed. "You're a goddamned whore. You're Davis's whore!"

"I'm shocked," I said. "What the hell are you talking about?"

"You're with Davis, aren't you?"

"No, I'm not, Gene, and that's it. Never again."

I walked away.

Klein wanted me to be a whore for the NFL. That would've been fine. But because I had taken a position that was in keeping with my obligations as a journalist, then I was necessarily a whore for the other side. That's the kind of tunnel vision that besets some NFL owners.

The next night, Klein attended the ABC party, at which I served as the host at the door. Jill was with me. I told Klein that I regretted his outburst the night before; then I introduced him to my daughter. He swung around, gave her a hug, and couldn't have been more of a gentleman. You figure it out.

At any rate, I thanked Rozelle for his concern with regard to the Klein incident and added, "I'll never forget what Gene Klein said. Never."

Rozelle and I then parted company with an apparently friendly disagreement based upon the two letters, and I told him, "I'm glad we had this talk openly and honestly."

In my heart and mind, however, I knew that we would never be friendly again—and the breach widened in the months ahead. One reason: Rozelle's oft-stated position that an antitrust exemption was clearly the NFL's top priority for the 1980s. To accomplish that, the NFL was in the process of waging a huge and expensive lobbying effort to win such approval in the Congress.

Rozelle knew exactly where I stood on that issue. I agreed wholeheartedly with an editorial that had appeared in the April 5, 1982, issue of *Business Week* magazine and said so on the air. The editorial questioned the wisdom of the U.S. Supreme Court in granting antitrust exemption to baseball so many years ago— and characterized pro football's similar request as "ridiculous." Why should a sports league, I agreed, be treated any differently from any other business? Why should a sports league have the right and privilege to carry on whatever monopolistic practice it wants to carry on?

In August 1982, the NFL's lobbying force was in high gear. I explored the subject on *SportsBeat*, detailing the fact that the NFL had hired two prestigious lobbyists—former Senator Marlow Cook of Kentucky and former Democratic Party Chairman Robert Strauss—to help the league influence legislators in favor of a bill sponsored by Senator Dennis DeConcini of Arizona. That bill—S. 2784—covered basketball, hockey, and soccer as well, and it was designed to grant a sports league sole power in deciding whether a team may move. The bill would be retroactive, thus in effect negating the Raiders' right to move to Los Angeles.

At the same time, another bill—S. 2821—was being sponsored by Senator Arlen Specter of Pennsylvania, and it differed radically from DeConcini's bill. Specter's bill established rigid criteria under which a team had to document economic distress or other compelling reasons for moving. It *could* be retroactive, too.

Both bills were being considered by the powerful Senate Judiciary Committee, and as part of the *SportsBeat* report, I aired some of Rozelle's key testimony before that committee. Rozelle favored DeConcini's bill and thought that the setting of criteria for a team to move, as outlined in Specter's bill, was unworkable. For example, Rozelle noted, if you had financial guidelines, a team might juggle its books and "arrange its figures in a way to show losses for several straight years."

Rozelle had been quoted as saying that unless the NFL was granted antitrust immunity, the league would not grant any new expansion franchises. The chairman of the committee, Senator Strom Thurmond of South Carolina, asked Rozelle if that quote was accurate. Rozelle answered "yes," then explained: ". . . the league cannot consider expansion in this uncertain climate . . . we would have no assurance that the team would stay in that city with this ruling of the antitrust court in Los Angeles. They could just move. . . ."

Another witness before the committee, Ed Garvey, then the executive director of the NFL Players' Association, made an appearance on the show. He had testified against the DeConcini bill. He said, in part: ". . . it gives the NFL monopoly even more power over the cities. . . . It sets no standards.

"The Specter bill makes sense. . . . Pete Rozelle's answer to that was the most incredible statement I've heard before a congressional committee in my life. He couldn't accept [guidelines for relocation] because owners would simply juggle the books or put family members on the payroll to show that they lost money for three years. Well, how should we then turn around and trust the monopoly to protect the fans if they're going to juggle their books or make other kinds of arrangements to justify a move?

"So I think Senator Specter is finally hitting the real issue—that is, how do you protect these cities from NFL teams or baseball teams that threaten the cities with a move unless they build a dome stadium?"

My last guest was Senator Specter. I asked him whether his bill, like Senator DeConcini's bill, would be retroactive. He replied: "Howard, it hasn't been resolved with finality. My own sense at the moment is that it ought to apply to the Raider controversy, although as a general rule I am opposed to retroactive application. But, as I said when I introduced the bill, I think we ought to have hearings on it, examine it from every aspect, before making a final decision on retroactivity or application to the Raiders' case."

What about the fans of Los Angeles, I wondered, who have

already purchased fifty-five thousand season tickets? What about their rights? Specter answered, in part: "The romance in Los Angeles is just getting started. The marriage in Oakland is of long standing."

"My problem is," I said, "with the Constitution of this land and retroactivity. I say that what Davis did was morally wrong . . . you're right, stop it in the future, which your bill does, but don't render it retroactive."

"Well, Howard, we had slavery in this country for many years and we finally changed it with the Thirteenth Amendment. Now, you certainly wouldn't say that once you've passed the Thirteenth Amendment that it would apply only to all black people born in the future. . . ."

I then asked Specter about stories that had appeared, earlier in the year, in the *Memphis Commercial Appeal* and in Phoenix newspapers. These stories had suggested that the NFL had dangled expansion franchises for those cities before Senator Howard Baker of Tennessee and Senator DeConcini to get a favorable vote on antitrust exemption.

Specter answered: "I am absolutely convinced that there are no deals that involve Senator Baker or Senator DeConcini to bring NFL franchises to Memphis and to Phoenix. . . . I am convinced there is no skulduggery here in any way, shape, or form."

I closed with these words: ". . . briefly reviewing, one, the real issue is the protection of the cities and you, the taxpayer. Two, the thorny issue that arises is the question of retroactivity and the uncertainty as to its constitutionality. Three, a collateral issue is the basic difference between the DeConcini and Specter bills and the question of whether the league should have the sole power to decide on franchise removals or whether the Congress should establish specific criteria. Four, personally I believe the Specter bill is good because it will protect cities in the future under clearly defined and strict guidelines for any future franchise removal. And that way, you, the people, will be protected assuredly."

Several days went by and I got a call from Specter's chief counsel, Bruce Cohen, who asked me to testify before the committee. I told Cohen I'd be happy to, giving no thought to ABC's approval because I had testified before congressional committees many times before without any repercussions or objections from my company. Cohen mentioned a date—September 16—but I couldn't appear because I had to work a Thursday night game in Buffalo. We then agreed on September 29.

Out of a clear, blue sky, I got a call from Roone Arledge, ABC's president of News and Sports. "Pete called me," Arledge said, referring to Rozelle, "and he's concerned about your testimony."

"Oh, come on, Roone," I snapped. "I'm tired of this shit. He's monitoring my shows, and he—"

Arledge interrupted. "Hold on, Howard. Pete agrees that your show on the two bills was perfectly fair, and so do I. He's worried about the date of your testimony, and I think he's got a legitimate point. If you wait until the twenty-ninth, Congress will adjourn before his bill has a chance to get out of committee, and that could kill it. And I don't feel that you, as an ABC commentator, should be put in that position."

"Wait a minute, Roone. I don't set the dates. Specter's aide, a fellow named Bruce Cohen, wanted me to appear on the sixteenth, but we've got a game that night in Buffalo."

"Look, Howard, whatever the reasons, I don't want our commentators testifying before the Congress."

"Why not? I've testified on numerous occasions, and you've never said anything."

"But now I'm the president of News, and I don't like it. But, for the moment anyway, if you'll testify on Thursday the sixteenth, I'll provide the transportation."

"Fine," I said, "but I want to make one thing clear, Roone. I intend to testify because I'm going to do what's right. Nobody's going to impinge on my principles."

"That's not my intention, Howard, but I'll be honest with you. I'm going to contact Specter's office and let them know that as a matter of policy, I don't like your testifying."

"I can't stop you from doing that, Roone. It may be that we've come to a parting of the ways, but I must be faithful to my principles in this matter."

Arledge contacted Specter's office and talked with Cohen. As a result of that conversation, Cohen sent the following letter to Arledge:

September 8, 1982

Mr. Roone Arledge
President
ABC News and Sports
1330 Avenue of the Americas
New York, NY 10019

Dear Mr. Arledge:

When we spoke on September 2, you raised two potential barriers to Howard Cosell testifying before the Senate Committee on the Judiciary on S.2784 and S.2821.

At your suggestion I inquired into the possibility of Mr. Cosell testifying September 16 instead of September 29, as originally scheduled. The Committee will be able to accommodate this change in scheduling and looks forward to hearing from Mr. Cosell on September 16, 1982, at 10:30 a.m., in room 2228 of the Dirksen Senate Office Building, Washington, D.C.

You also asked whether I knew of other instances in which journalists testified. Besides Mr. Cosell's testimony in 1972 and last year on related subjects, I mentioned to you the testimony of Chuck Stone, Senior Editor and Columnist for the *Philadelphia Daily News*, who testified before the Senate Subcommittee on Juvenile Justice last year on S.1688, S.1689 and S.1690. In addition, Dotson Rader, feature writer for *Parade*, testified at a July 22, 1982, hearing of the Senate Subcommittee on which he had written a cover story in February for *Parade* and on which he had just finished research for his follow-up cover story published last Sunday, September 5, in *Parade*.

I took a brief look through past hearings and found that many other well-known journalists had testified. For example, Howard K. Smith in October, 1977, testified before the Senate Committee on Commerce, Science, and Transportation on amateur athletics; Walter Cronkite testified in March, 1976, before the Select Committee on Missing Persons in Southeast Asia and in September, 1977, before the Senate Subcommittee on the Constitution on freedom of the press; David Brinkley testified in October, 1971, before the Senate Subcommittee on Constitutional Rights on freedom of the press; James J. Kilpatrick testified in 1965 before

Senate and House committees on the Voting Rights Act, in April, 1967, before the House Select Subcommittee on Education on obscenity and pornography, in February, 1973, before the Subcommittee on Constitutional Rights on newsmen's privilege legislation; George Will testified in April, 1979, before the Senate Subcommittee on the Constitution on a proposed constitutional amendment to provide for direct popular election of the President and Vice President; Carl Rowan testified in June, 1977, before the House Subcommittee on International Operations on international communications and broadcasting; and in December, 1970, before the Subcommittee on Africa on U.S. policy toward Africa; and finally, Hugh Sidey, Martin Agronsky and Jack Anderson all testified in September, 1975, before the House Subcommittee on Future Foreign Policy Research and Development on foreign policy and how the relationship between government and the press affects it.

I hope that these arrangements and references will suffice to reassure you of the propriety of Mr. Cosell's appearance. I trust that the rescheduling of Mr. Cosell to testify on September 16 in accommodation of your expressed concern that no one be able to accuse Howard Cosell or ABC of delaying Senate consideration of these matters is acceptable to you. As I assured you in our conversation, a series of at least three hearings on these matters, including scheduling of a hearing on the morning of September 29, were all arrangements made even before Mr. Cosell was invited to testify. The Committee has still to hear from several interested parties before the hearings may be concluded.

I attempted to telephone you on September 8, to report back in accordance with our earlier discussion, but understand that you were unavailable. I write in order to convey without additional delay this information concerning the adjustments in scheduling we have been able to make.

Yours truly,

Bruce A. Cohen

Cohen's letter was copied blindly to me. To this day, I can't say for certain whether Arledge is aware that I received a copy. At any rate, without hearing again from Arledge, I appeared before the Senate Judiciary Committee on September 16, and Arledge had a plane waiting to take me to Buffalo.

In my opening remarks, I noted that I had testified before various Senate and House committees several times before, dating back to 1972, when I gave my support to a projected federal sports act being sponsored by then Senator Marlow Cook of Kentucky.

I also gave a brief backgrounder on the history of franchise removal, beginning with the Dodgers' exodus from Brooklyn in 1958. Then, in the course of answering questions posed by the senators, I made my positions on the salient issues very clear:

1. Once and for all, baseball's exemption from the antitrust laws should be wiped away. Neither pro football nor any other sport should be granted antitrust immunity. Like every other business, professional sports should act in open competition—and take the consequences if they do not meet the laws of the land.

2. Al Davis's action in moving his Raiders from Oakland to Los Angeles was morally wrong. His was a legal victory, based largely on the NFL's flagrant abuse of the antitrust laws.

3. I favored Senator Specter's proposed bill, not Senator DeConcini's, because the former contained guidelines that coincided with my personal views. To wit: No team may desert a city unless it could prove economic distress over a continuing period of time—say, three years.

During my testimony, while noting that I supported Senator Specter's bill, I added, "The bill does not address itself to the thorny issue of retroactivity, which, in my mind, produces questions. . . . However, on *SportsBeat* on August 22, Senator Specter, whom I know to be a distinguished and even brilliant lawyer, was very clear about the fact that he has not finalized his position on retroactivity. Indeed, one of the purposes of these hearings was to hear more about it, and only after the hearings finalize his decision in that regard.

"Is that a fair statement, Senator Specter?"

Senator Specter answered, "Unusual as it is to respond to

questions, the answer is, 'yes.' I had thought that, contrary to *SportsBeat*, this would be an occasion where I might ask the questions."

"You will have your opportunity, Senator," I responded, a smile on my lips.

"Thank you, Mr. Chairman," the senator said—and the other members of the committee thoroughly enjoyed the repartee.

I mention that exchange because when I next saw Arledge, at a party in honor of former New York Yankee President Mike Burke, Arledge told me that he had caught my testimony on public television. "I thought your testimony went very well," he said. "And I really enjoyed the way you handled Specter."

Arledge made that comment with a smile. He was in high spirits and seemed genuinely impressed with my performance before the committee.

Neither Arledge nor I ever spoke again about my testimony—or about his original objections to my testifying.

I never heard from Rozelle, either.

Rozelle was well aware of my testimony, just as he was of my daily radio commentaries and weekly *SportsBeat* shows, and he knew exactly where I stood on the NFL's massive lobbying efforts to win antitrust immunity. And when the NFL failed to get the legislation it wanted, there is little doubt in my mind that Rozelle blamed me—or at least figured that I shared a large part of the blame. This was fine with me. I had simply been doing my job as a journalist, and I was proud of the stand I had taken.

The strike, drug abuse, the Davis case, and other matters had combined to make 1982 a particularly horrendous year for the NFL and an oppressive experience for Rozelle. For the first time in his long career as commissioner, Rozelle was buffeted by forces that shook him from his perch on Mount Olympus, and he seemed to be losing his heralded ability to control and manipulate everything and everyone around him. He had even begun to avoid the media, granting precious few interviews, especially to network reporters.

My first *SportsBeat* show of the 1983 season was scheduled to air on January 28, the day before the Super Bowl game between the Washington Redskins and Miami Dolphins. And since Rozelle had been relatively silent on the recent problems besetting his league, I decided to invite him to appear on the show and thought perhaps even to devote the entire half hour to an interview with him.

I called him ten days before the Super Bowl and left a message with his secretary. Considering the deterioration in our relationship, I wasn't at all sure whether he'd call back—but he did. We had a brief but cordial chat, and I was mildly surprised when he seemed on the verge of accepting. He asked if he could think about it over the weekend, and I told him that I'd be awaiting his call in my office on Monday morning.

Rozelle declined to appear. Naturally, I asked why.

"Your continuing support of Al Davis," he said.

"I thought we'd been all through that, Pete. My position on that matter is clear, and I object to your using the word 'support.'"

"I don't see it that way, Howard. As recently as several weeks ago, on one of your radio reports, you praised Davis's victory, and there was an implicit attack on the NFL and its policies."

Rozelle was referring to a radio report I had done in late December, from Key Biscayne, Florida, where I had spent the Christmas holidays with my family. The report gave my professional opinion of the year's biggest story—Davis's courtroom victory over the NFL. It was by no means an attack on the NFL, and again I repeated my conviction that Davis was morally wrong in deserting Oakland but legally on solid ground.

I am positive that Rozelle was informed of the report by Joe Browne, the NFL's director of information. The NFL, you see, monitors and collects just about everything that is written about it in newspapers and magazines and said about it on radio and television. Apparently, Browne and his troops go so far as to tape my twice-daily radio reports, which I find a particularly frightening aspect of the NFL's never-ending quest to dominate the media.

Like the CIA and the FBI, the NFL has its own enemies list—and I got the distinct impression that I was at the top of it.

Be that as it may, months went by, and not a word passed between Rozelle and me. Then, toward the end of the summer of 1983, I called Rozelle. For some reason—call it a journalist's instinct—I had a funny feeling that Rozelle might be ready and willing to sit for an interview.

By his normal standards, he was still keeping a relatively low profile, and there was still a broad range of issues that needed airing.

As I suspected, Rozelle agreed to appear on *SportsBeat*, though we never discussed exactly why he had his change of heart. The interview was conducted at the NFL headquarters on Park Avenue, and it took up the entire half hour of the show, serving as a preview of the upcoming season.

We treated each other in a thoroughly businesslike manner, and there was no hint of any rift between us. In the beginning, Rozelle did not seem his usual unflappable self. He was hesitant, groping for the right words, but as the interview progressed, he warmed up, becoming the Rozelle of old, smooth and self-assured.

The interview was remarkable in the number of subjects that were discussed—labor relations, drug abuse, gambling, the new United States Football League, franchise removal, expansion, political intrigue, the college eligibility rule. It was a typical Rozelle performance, embodying the spectrum of his virtues and faults—candid, crafty, sincere, evasive, and vulnerable. In fielding my questions, he was, at one time or another, all those things, and I pursued him diligently. Sure, he dodged some questions, but he had to work at it.

On balance, I think, it was a helluva interview.

Rozelle admitted that drug abuse among NFL players was a serious and disconcerting problem, though it wasn't as widespread as the media would have the public believe. On the other hand, he refused to concede that the NFL was derelict in recognizing the problem earlier than it had, insisting that the league was historically vigilant in checking for drugs and educating its players.

Rozelle defended baseball commissioner Kuhn's $54,000 fine against Los Angeles Dodgers' pitcher Steve Howe for his repeated use of cocaine, then defended himself for suspending four players for four regular-season games for their involvement with drugs.

We also talked about Art Schlichter, the Baltimore Colts' quarterback whom Rozelle had recently suspended indefinitely for gambling. (Schlichter was reinstated for the 1984 season.)

"How much do you think that problem exists in the league?"

I asked. "Do you think players other than Schlichter are gambling?"

"I don't think so," Rozelle said. "I think it's a very isolated case . . . the boy had a compulsive gambling problem." Then he added, "The players know that it strikes at the integrity of the game, and I don't think there's gambling in the National Football League."

I questioned Rozelle about the apparent disparity in his meting out of punishment. Why is Schlichter suspended indefinitely, while convicted felons who are involved with drugs receive only a four-game penalty?

ROZELLE: "Well, they're both major problems, of course, drugs and gambling. But gambling goes right to the heart of our sport's integrity. In the case of Art Schlichter . . . he had gotten into serious trouble with gambling. Now he's going to psychiatrists that specialize in gambling compulsion. In that case, it's just difficult to accept the fact that while he has that problem, he can play in the National Football League."

COSELL: "But what about drug users? Carl Eller of Minnesota went bankrupt because of drugs. When a man gets into fiscal trouble because of the use of drugs, doesn't that, too, go right to the integrity of the game?"

ROZELLE: "It could, it could. And it's a serious problem. I'm not attempting to play down the problem of drugs. I'm merely saying what gambling does directly, rather than indirectly, to the integrity of the game. And that's why it's such a problem for us, and a lot of players know that we will not tolerate it."

On a previous *SportsBeat* show, Nelson Doubleday, the owner of the New York Mets, had said that Rozelle told him he didn't want the New York Jets to move to New Jersey. I asked Rozelle if that was accurate.

"I think Nelson paraphrased what I told him," Rozelle said. "He told me of the plans to improve Shea Stadium, and he said he thought he'd need the Jets playing there to get them accomplished. I said, 'Well, I wish you luck.' But I didn't take a position on the actual move because it wasn't viable at that time, and it still isn't. I don't know what they're going to do."

"You honestly don't?"

"Not for sure, no," Rozelle said. "I know it's being considered . . . but I don't believe a decision has been made."

Rozelle had to know a decision had been made. I knew, and so did other people. But Rozelle wasn't going to budge, so I attacked the issue from another angle.

"If the Jets do move to New Jersey," I said, "that would leave the National Football League without a franchise in the largest city in this country—and, in many respects, the most important. Would you state your view on that?"

ROZELLE: ". . . the Giants' move to the Meadowlands, across the river to New Jersey, was a move of six or seven miles from Times Square. . . . I don't think there's any question that the Giants are getting the same support that they got from New Yorkers. They're on the same television channel in New York, and I don't think it makes that much difference if you're moving to a better facility in the suburbs. . . ."

COSELL: "It makes a big difference to the people of this city. It makes a big difference in the restaurant business and the hotel business. It makes a big difference in taxes, and it comes at a time of continuing urban distress in this nation. And so I ask you again—do you really feel that a Jets' move to New Jersey would be justified?"

ROZELLE: "I think that a suburban move by any of our clubs, such as we've had in the past . . . is justified. I realize the city may be concerned, but I'm saying the Jets' fans will be serviced as they have been in the past on the same television station—if they were to move."

I then asked Rozelle about a story that had appeared in the *Memphis Commercial Appeal.* It alleged that at a meeting between Rozelle and Senator Howard Baker, Rozelle promised to grant Memphis an NFL franchise—if Senator Baker would help the league in its fight for antitrust immunity.

Was that report true?

"There was no commitment made, and there was no inference of a commitment," Rozelle said. "It's totally untrue. Totally untrue. I simply told Senator Baker and others representing Memphis at that time that we would give consideration to Memphis for expansion. We think it's a good city, just as we think four or five other cities are strong candidates. But there was no commitment. . . ."

"There are no plans for expansion," Rozelle continued. "The owners aren't thinking about it or talking about it. I think they want to see the Raiders' case finally concluded. Someday, I imagine, we might add two more. But I don't see large expansion in the National Football League in the near future."

We then talked about the United States Football League, which had recently completed its first season of operation. Since the USFL conducted its games in the spring, Rozelle conceded that year-round football was not healthy for the NFL, and he took a wait-and-see attitude on the potential dangers of oversaturation.

Rozelle was reluctant to call the NFL-USFL competition for college players a bidding war, but he did express concern over escalating players' salaries. He was quick to point out, though, that escalating salaries were a two-edged sword—and that the NFL was better able to handle the financial burden than the USFL.

I brought up the days of the American Football League, which went head to head with the NFL and eventually forced merger.

"Aside from the fact that the USFL plays in the spring, do you see any similarity between the USFL and the old American Football League?"

"I really don't," Rozelle said. "When it merged with the NFL, the AFL brought many new markets that we were not then in. And, of course, that made pro football bigger than it had ever been before. . . . As for the USFL, I don't think it will be able to hold out for its owners the carrot of merger because we're at twenty-eight teams already—and many cities that don't have NFL football are now seeking it.

"I think ten of the twelve USFL cities are cities in which the NFL has home teams. So I don't see the correlation with the American Football League merger."

Considering the scope of the NFL's travails in the past year, I asked Rozelle if he had ever become dispirited.

"Oh, sure, you get down at times," he said, "but it hasn't been just recently. People forget that in '74 and '75 we had three antitrust suits going in different parts of the country, in Washington, Minneapolis, and Los Angeles. We had a players' strike of preseason games. We had the World Football League competing against us.

"Certainly, in the last ten years, sports has been filled with problems, but that's the way society goes, too. I get depressed, sure, but there are a lot more highs than lows. And I enjoy pro football, and I enjoy my job."

Portions of the interview were picked up by the wire services and publicized widely, and I'm sure Rozelle was pleased with the way it turned out.

Over the next several months, we had no contact with each other, but I knew it was a most difficult period for Rozelle. I had been receiving an almost constant stream of phone calls from various owners bitching and moaning about Rozelle's heavy-handed leadership, and some predicted that Rozelle was close to being dethroned.

Of course, their comments were off the record, and little by little these same disgruntled owners started leaking anonymous quotes to the press. Their biggest gripe, according to printed accounts, was the way the league was conducting itself financially. League expenses, they claimed, were skyrocketing, and there were threats to hire an independent accounting firm to audit the league's books.

Those reports indeed had some validity, but the real genesis of the owners' mounting disaffection with Rozelle was his handling of the Davis case. Although many owners had condoned his conduct, Rozelle's bitter and obstinate pursuit of Davis had not only caused the league an embarrassing loss in the courts but also a whopping $34 million in treble damages—a figure that almost surely would exceed $50 million once interest and lawyers' fees were tagged on as Rozelle dragged the case through various courts of appeal.

And how was that money to be paid? Out of the pockets of the twenty-seven other owners, that's how.

The 1984 league meetings were scheduled for the week of March 18 in Hawaii, but the week before, an extraordinary gathering of owners was convened in Chicago. Ostensibly, these men were there to discuss the situation in Baltimore and to ascertain what Robert Irsay planned to do with his Colts—move them to Phoenix or Indianapolis, or keep them in Baltimore.

The real reason for the meeting, however, concerned Rozelle.

The owners were called together at the urging of Leon Hess of the New York Jets. An ardent supporter of Rozelle, he knew that the anti-Rozelle faction was growing stronger, and he was looking to stem the tide against the commissioner.

To the best of my knowledge, the anti-Rozelle faction included Davis, Ralph Wilson of Buffalo, Paul Brown of Cincinnati, Joe Robbie of Miami, John Mecom of New Orleans, and William Clay Ford of Detroit. Their leader was Jack Kent Cooke of Washington.

Beside league politics, Cooke had personal reasons for disliking Rozelle. Cooke's son was once married to Rozelle's second wife, Carrie, and Carrie had supported her former mother-in-law in her notorious divorce against Cooke—which cost the Redskins' owner $41 million.

Cooke did not make the trip to Chicago, making Hess's task a lot easier. Hess wanted to blunt any criticism of Rozelle and rally the owners around their commissioner. In addition, he wanted to show his own faith in Rozelle by revealing the terms of Rozelle's new contract, which Hess had drawn up as the head of the NFL Finance Committee.

After Irsay was heard from, Hess cleared the room of everyone but owners, then detailed Rozelle's income from the league. Including perquisities, Rozelle was making in the neighborhood of $1 million a year—and his contract extended to 1990.

"Now you've heard the facts," Hess said. "Does anybody have any questions?"

Davis got up. "How can you sign Rozelle to a new contract without the approval of the owners?" he asked.

"I did have approval," Hess replied, referring to an owners' meeting that Davis did not attend.

Lamar Hunt of Kansas City questioned the length of the contract. "Isn't it a little long?" he wondered.

At that point, Ford of Detroit laughed loudly in open derision—but Rozelle got his contract with hardly a peep and escaped with nary a scratch.

As for Irsay, a little less than three weeks later, he showed what kind of man he is. Under cover of night, Irsay had the Colts' equipment loaded onto a fleet of moving vans and stole away to Indianapolis.

And what about the people of Baltimore, the people who had given their hearts and souls, not to mention their hard-earned money, to the Colts' franchise for thirty-one years? Well, without so much as waving good-bye, Irsay said, "This is my team. I own it, and I'll do whatever I want with it."

The Colts' departure caught Baltimore's mayor, William Donald Schaefer, by surprise. A good and decent man who worked a miracle in turning Baltimore into a model of urban renewal, Schaefer had spent countless hours negotiating with Irsay. Schaefer's final offer included a continuing program to improve stadium facilities, a guarantee of forty-three thousand season tickets, and a $15 million loan at 8 percent interest.

That wasn't good enough for Irsay. He was supposed to get back to Schaefer on the offer, but Schaefer said he never did.

On the night the moving vans left for Indianapolis, Schaefer couldn't sleep and happened to turn on the radio. That's how he learned his beloved city had lost the Colts!

In an exclusive interview on *SportsBeat*, Schaefer expressed his hurt and anger, saying, "All of the memorabilia of the old Colts is gone, all taken out of that building that night and dumped into a van ... Buddy Young's shoes, five-and-a-half inches, the little bitty shoes he wore when he was great ... Unitas's jersey ... all those things that mean nothing to any other city but us."

"The final humiliation to a city" is how Schaefer described Irsay's taking of the memorabilia. "Why couldn't he just leave it? It doesn't mean anything to him. It doesn't mean anything to anybody but us. We'd like to have it. But I have a little pride left. I won't ask for it—but I'd like it to come home where it belongs."

Irsay's sly midnight removal of the Colts outraged just about every segment of society, sparking numerous newspaper and television editorials. The reaction went so far and deep, in fact, that a bill sponsored by Senator Slade Gorton of Washington cleared the Commerce Committee.

Gorton's bill would require the NFL to create two expansion teams by 1987 and place one of them in Baltimore. In addition, a baseball, football, basketball, hockey, or soccer league could not approve a franchise shift before it considered a variety of factors, including a team's profitability, playing facilities, and fan support. A league decision to allow a franchise shift would then have to be approved by a board composed of a league representative, a person from the community threatened with the franchise loss, and a neutral member appointed by the American Arbitration Association.

Gorton's bill faced an uncertain fate in Congress, but it's important to note that it got farther than either Specter's or DiConcini's bill—an indication that such legislation just might be an idea whose time has come.

Rozelle, of course, vehemently opposed Gorton's bill, uttering the same excuse he made when the Jets left for New Jersey. The league was powerless to prevent any franchise shifts, he said, because of Davis's courtroom victory in Los Angeles. What's more, he insisted, the league itself could preserve franchise stability if it were granted the proper tools by the Congress—i.e., immunity from the antitrust laws.

Rozelle was wrong, and it was shocking how he adamantly refused to recognize the realities of the Raiders' case. He could have listened to his attorneys and changed Section 4.3 to a simple majority vote, but he didn't. He could have established objective standards and guidelines to govern franchise relocation, but he didn't. And let's not forget how Rozelle destroyed Davis's deal with the Oakland-Alameda County Coliseum Commission when he told a member of that commission that the NFL would never permit the Raiders to leave Oakland.

These were the major factors that contributed to Davis's victory, and it was simply untrue to say that the lower-court ruling prevented the NFL from exerting any control over franchise relocation.

In fact, if Section 4.3 had required a simple majority vote, and if objective standards and guidelines were in place, it is entirely possible that the NFL could have stopped Davis from abandoning Oakland—just as it could have stopped Irsay from sneaking out of Baltimore.

The futility of Rozelle's conduct was never more apparent than on November 5, 1984. That morning, the U.S. Supreme Court declined without comment to hear the NFL's appeal of a lower-court ruling that the league had violated antitrust law in its dealings with Davis and his Raiders. Davis had won, and Rozelle had suffered his most bitter defeat.

Subsequently, when Davis appeared on *SportsBeat*, we had a lengthy chat.

"I knew you'd win as a matter of law," I told him, "but I still feel sorry for the people of Oakland."

"So do I," Davis said. "Hey, let me tell you something: When people get into the guts of this case, I think Oakland can sue Rozelle's ass. When they discover all the things he did behind my back, they're going to be awfully upset."

"I don't think the damages are going to be mitigated one bit, Al, and you could end up with fifty million dollars. What happens then to the National Football League?"

"Nothing. They have the money."

"The owners are going to pony it up?"

"They'll have to," Davis said.

"What happens to Pete Rozelle?"

"They're scared of him, Howard."

"Why?" I wondered. "At this point in time, why are they still afraid of him when he's led them into this terrible trap?"

"I can't explain it," Davis said. "They think they'll just pay me out of the television money. Maybe they think my case was just a freak thing. Some of the guys are pissed at Rozelle. That I know."

"Who are they?"

"Max Winter in Minnesota. He kept telling Rozelle to get out of that suit. And Leonard Tose in Philadelphia. When Tose read about what Rozelle had done to me, he wanted to sue him. You know, Howard, until we went to court, a lot of the owners had no idea how Rozelle had destroyed my negotiations to stay in Oakland."

"Then how the hell does he survive?"

"Hess is the key," Davis said, referring to the owner of the

Jets. "He's in Rozelle's pocket, and I don't know why. And for one reason or other, Hess is in bed with a group of owners who listen to him and always back Rozelle."

"It's beyond me."

"One of the big problems, Howard, is they don't have anyone else to replace Rozelle. There's one guy lurking around that they think is pretty good. You're going to laugh, but it's Jack Donlan."

Donlan is the labor negotiator for the owners, the guy who deals with the NFL Players' Association, and I had heard he was pushing for the job.

What Donlan's chances are is anybody's guess. But one thing is certain: Rozelle's obsession with Davis has seriously thrown into question what was once his greatest asset—leadership. What's worse, two different courts had found him guilty of dealing in bad faith with one of his league's owners, further tarnishing his reputation.

Poor Pete. The repercussions of the Davis case continued to haunt him into 1985. First, in early December 1984, Leonard Tose seemed on the verge of moving his Philadelphia Eagles to Phoenix. Buffeted by debts estimated as high as $40 million—a huge chunk of which was lost playing gin, blackjack, and other games—Tose reportedly agreed to sell 25 percent of the Eagles to a buyer named James Monaghan, a Canadian businessman with a home in Phoenix. The price: $30 million. And as part of the deal, Monaghan could move the team to Phoenix.

The people of Philadelphia rose up in anger. The Eagles were *their* team, as much a part of Philadelphia as the Liberty Bell and cheese-steak sandwiches, and they had given their team fifty-one years of loyalty through thick and thin, mostly thin. This was a profitable franchise. This was unfair. This was unthinkable.

Mayor W. Wilson Goode entered the breach. After three days of intensive negotiations with various civic leaders and the Eagles' owner, Goode was able to assemble a consortium of several banks and insurance companies that agreed to lend Tose up to $42 million to ease his financial burden. In return, these people demanded certain controls in managing the team. Tose balked.

Meanwhile, the crisis in Philadelphia had sent shock waves through the NFL. Tose's conduct played havoc with the league's image. Not only that, he also was situated in the fourth-largest TV market. The league sued to keep the Eagles from moving to Phoenix. Then Mayor Goode said he was prepared to go to court to force the Eagles to abide by their lease with Veterans Stadium, which ran until 2001.

There it was, another unholy mess dumped in Rozelle's lap, and it was his own damned fault.

On December 15, I devoted an entire *SportsBeat* show to the subject, first presenting a lengthy history of franchise carpetbagging, then an interview with Goode and Senator Specter, who happened to be a former district attorney of Philadelphia. Goode was optimistic, noting that he believed he was close to working out an arrangement with Tose that would keep the Eagles in Philadelphia. Specter addressed himself to the larger issue at hand: whether the NFL was or was not powerless to stop the Eagles from moving to Phoenix.

According to just about every newspaper you picked up, the NFL *was* powerless to prevent a team from moving from one city to another because of the decision in the Davis case. This was palpably wrong. A brilliant attorney with solid experience in antitrust law, Specter noted that he had carefully read the federal court decisions in the Davis case. First, he said, the NFL must change Section 4.3 to a simple majority vote. Next, the league has to establish objective standards and guidelines governing franchise removals. From a legal point of view, he said, "It is plain that the National Football League has the power to have reasonable restraints on franchise movements. They can stop a franchise from moving if it doesn't have a good reason to do so."

Obviously, the Eagles had no reason to move. They had the loyalty of the fans, they were making money, they played in a modern stadium, and nobody was seeking to break their lease agreement with Veterans Stadium.

Specter also revealed that, two days earlier, he had sent a letter to Rozelle urging him to change Section 4.3 and establish objective standards and guidelines—such as fan support, the profitability of the team, the condition of the stadium, and similar factors—to govern franchise shifts. In his letter, Specter assured Rozelle, "... it is my thinking that such an NFL rule would be interpreted by the courts not to violate antitrust laws. In any event, I do believe there would be a strong sentiment in the Congress to remove any doubt that such a rule does not violate antitrust laws, which could be accomplished by a relatively simple amendment to the antitrust laws. . . ."

Specter said he was confident that the NFL would not get an antitrust exemption in the Congress, which would give the league sole discretionary power to determine which teams could move and which could not. "The ramifications and implications of that are so broad that no one can predict where they would go," he said, adding, "The NFL ought to put its own house in order." If it didn't, Specter warned, there was a growing sentiment in the Congress to pass such legislation itself.

What was Rozelle's problem? Why was he steadfastly refusing to change Section 4.3 to comply with the federal court decisions in the Davis case? Why was he ignoring words of wisdom from the likes of Senator Specter? Since the press was either unwilling or unable to comprehend the fallout of the Davis case, since it constantly misreported and misrepresented the decisions of the federal courts, did Rozelle think he could go on fooling the public? Was he trying to blackmail the Congress into granting the NFL an antitrust exemption?

Well, I finally had the opportunity to question him directly. In preparing my show about the Eagles, I placed a call to Rozelle, wishing to invite him to appear with Goode and Specter to get the NFL's reaction. Ten minutes later, he called me and declined to appear.

"I really can't, Howard," he said. "I've called a meeting of the owners in several days, and on advice of our counsel, I am obligated to discuss the issue with them first."

"I understand your position, Pete," I said, "and it's a fair one. But let me ask you, Pete: Why haven't you changed Section four point three? Why won't you conform to the decisions in the Davis case?"

"Our counsel advises me that the opinions in that case are mere dicta, Howard. And that's the position we're taking." (At law, dictum is a judicial opinion on a point other than the precise issue involved in determining a case.)

"I don't agree with you, Pete. I think the ruling of the lower court was very clear, and what's more, it was backed up by the Ninth Circuit Court of Appeals. Based on that opinion, the NBA changed its rules to a simple majority vote and inserted guidelines into its constitution regarding the movement of teams. What have you got to lose?"

"Our counsel insists it's mere dicta, and we think the NBA, even with its new rules, will lose the Clippers case. (In June 1984, the NBA sued the Clippers for moving from San Diego to Los Angeles without league approval.)

"In my opinion, Pete, you can talk about dictum all you want. The fact is, a rule that is declared illegal is no rule at all."

As it turned out, several hours after our *SportsBeat* show, Goode and Tose reached an agreement to keep the Eagles in Philadelphia. Goode came up with a package of concessions designed to increase the Eagles' profits. Among them, the Eagles would be allowed to defer rent on Veterans Stadium, estimated at $800,000 a year, for ten years—with the rent due in a lump sum along with only 9 percent interest. In addition, the city promised to build a new practice field for the team and make certain stadium improvements, including fifty luxury boxes. According to some, these concessions will cost Philadelphia about $20 million over the next two decades.

The deal was contingent on Tose's ability to refinance the team and extricate himself from his financial problems. And where was he going to get the money? From the NFL, of course. Rozelle formed a committee of owners to examine the matter, saying there was "considerable support for doing something for Leonard Tose" that would allow him to retain control of the team.

I ask you: How sick is that? Tose gambles his fortune away, mismanages his team, and what happens? He's rewarded with a sweetheart deal from Philadelphia, and the NFL steps in to try to bail him out. You're going to tell me that Philadelphia doesn't have better uses for its money, like improving its police force, its fire department, its school system, its roads and transit system, its public hospitals? What a sham!

In the aftermath of the Eagles' debacle, U.S. senators and congressmen were falling all over each other proposing legislation to put restraints on franchise shifts. Both Specter and Gorton once again sought laws to protect the cities from conniving NFL owners, and I think 1985, or shortly thereafter, just might be the time when such legislation might come to fruition. It's still hard for me to understand Rozelle's posture in all of this. In the days before the Super Bowl between San Francisco and Miami, two teams served notice—the St. Louis Cardinals and the New Orleans Saints—that they were considering moving to other cities—and that they were reserving such rights to relocate under federal court decisions in the Davis case.

And what was Rozelle's reaction? He sent his owners a memorandum that contained his own list of criteria to govern franchise shifts, then stated publicly that such criteria were only voluntary. According to Rozelle, an owner bent on leaving a city could still challenge the NFL in a court of law and win. Of course he could, because the NFL constitution—specifically Section 4.3—was still in violation of the antitrust laws in that it required a three-quarters vote rather than a simple majority. Rozelle could implement as many criteria as he wished, but until those criteria are embraced within the NFL constitution along with a change in the voting procedures, that constitution will continue to violate the rule of reason and the federal laws.

Rozelle was still playing games. Then, at his Super Bowl press conference, he said ' . . . I haven't heard anyone say, 'Fine, now I indemnify you against further legal action.' We need some guidelines from the courts or Congress."

The media faithfully printed Rozelle's words as if they were etched in stone. Nobody challenged him. In his letter to Rozelle, Specter practically guaranteed him that objective standards and guidelines governing franchise moves would pass antitrust muster in the courts and in the Congress. But Rozelle chose to ignore Specter's advice and continued to push for an antitrust exemption. For example, he backed a bill cosponsored by Missouri's two senators—Republican John Danforth and Democrat Thomas Eagleton—who were obviously concerned about the possibility of the Cardinals' leaving St. Louis. In simplest terms, the Danforth-Eagleton bill gave the NFL a limited antitrust exemption in the matter of franchise relocation. It also contained various guidelines and a timetable that had to be taken into consideration, but the final decision on whether a team could or could not move rested with the NFL and the NFL alone.

The NFL-supported bill was approved by the Commerce Committee, but faced a protracted struggle to reach the Senate floor. Critics of the bill said it served the interests of the league, not the fans, and it seemed to have little hope of becoming law.

Deep inside Rozelle, in my opinion, he considers the Davis case an aberration. He really believes the NFL is all-powerful and will ultimately prevail. He's dead wrong. He can't go on hoodwinking the public and the press much longer. How is the NFL going to look if both the Cardinals and the Saints indeed abandon their cities? As Specter warned, unless the NFL gets its own house in order, the Congress will step in. And when that happens, Rozelle must know his time has come. He failed to exercise leadership just when his league needed it the most.

All of which raises this question: How much longer can Rozelle survive as commissioner of the NFL?

The answer is indefinitely. As of this writing, Rozelle is fifty-eight, and he will most likely continue in office until he chooses to retire in his midsixties. Why? Because his power is as firm as ever despite repeated expressions of unhappiness and dire warnings of a palace coup by some dissident owners. That power is based not only on his alliances with various blocks of owners but also on the partnership he has forged for his league with the three networks, which in effect constitutes a monopoly in broadcasting—and places severe strains on a potential competitor such as the fledgling United States Football League. In addition, Rozelle still exerts a mesmerizing, almost ironclad control over the print medium. He can count on pro football writers and sports columnists across the country to denigrate everyone and everything that the NFL might perceive as a threat to its dominance. For example, you can bet the mortgage that you will continue to read stories mocking the USFL but praising the NFL and its commissioner.

To this day, Rozelle maintains the essential skills that made him a superb PR man. And even though close observers notice him slipping, he has still managed to divert public attention from the corruption within the league and the confusion at the top that I have detailed in previous chapters. Further evidence of that was provided at an owners' meeting in New Orleans in late October 1984.

At that meeting, one of the main topics of discussion was the USFL's $1.32 billion antitrust suit, which was filed against the NFL on October 17, 1984. In its suit, the USFL alleges that the NFL is guilty of antitrust violations in the areas of player contracts, television deals with the networks, stadium availability, scheduling conflicts and media relations. Representing the USFL was Roy Cohn, the powerful New York attorney.

Two NFL attorneys, Paul Tagliabue and Jay Moyer, were present in New Orleans, and they told the owners that they didn't put much credibility in the USFL suit. Ralph Wilson of Buffalo summed up the feelings of a lot of NFL owners when he got up and said, "Listen, I'm told so many things around here, I don't know who to believe. I do know that Cohn is smart, he's dangerous and tricky, and he's got a lot of political clout. I don't want Covington & Burling to represent us."

Covington & Burling is a law firm in Washington, D.C., that has a long association with the NFL.

"We're looking at four or five lawyers in New York," Rozelle said, "and we'll come up with a cocounsel for Covington & Burling."

Tose then stood up. "Why do we need Covington & Burling at all?" he asked.

"They've got twenty-five years of experience with us," Rozelle said, "and I think we should keep them."

Davis wasn't so sure. "They had twenty-five years of experience in my case, Pete, and they didn't know what the hell they were talking about," Davis said. "Look, I don't know what you're up to. I know the Raiders are totally clear in this goddamned case. We've done nothing to harm that other league, and there's no way I intend to stand by and have you pick the counsel."

A couple of owners then suggested that the NFL hire Joe Alioto, who represented Davis in his suit. Davis smiled wickedly, while Rozelle turned beet red. The meeting then turned into a shouting match, and nothing was resolved.

Rozelle wasn't used to that kind of treatment, but he'll weather whatever storm he has to. He loves the job. If things get really hot, he'll fight like hell to keep it—and few in sports are more tenacious.

6

Monday Night Blues

Two may talk and one may hear, but three cannot take part in a conversation of the most sincere and searching sort.

—Ralph Waldo Emerson, *Essays: First Series. Friendship*

From a broadcasting standpoint, the best *Monday Night Football* telecasts were the ones that Frank Gifford and I worked alone. Gifford knew it, too, and he enjoyed those games the most. One instance in particular comes to mind: an exciting contest between Houston and Miami during the 1978 season. Earl Campbell rushed for 198 yards and led Houston to a 35–30 victory, and Bob Griese, the Miami quarterback, was brilliant in defeat. I'll never forget how his coach, Don Shula, put his arm around him and hugged him after the game. It was one of the most moving scenes I'd ever witnessed in professional sports.

Gifford and I were marvelously in tune that night, and we pulled off a helluva show. Even NFL Commissioner Pete Rozelle was impressed enough to contact Roone Arledge, the president of ABC Sports. "I've always told you, Roone," he said, "you don't need three men in the booth. Howard and Frank are a terrific team."

Gifford was ecstatic. "We're a hit, Howard!" he said. "We're much better alone!"

And he really meant it, despite his close friendship with Don Meredith.

Gifford was right, and so was Rozelle. The director of *Monday Night Football*, Chet Forte, also believed that two broadcasters in the booth were more effective than three.

Arledge never bought it, and only he was ordained with the power to make that kind of decision. When Arledge initiated *Monday Night Football* with three broadcasters, the sports television critics—the vast majority of whom know nothing about my business—eventually got around to seeing things Arledge's way and wrote about the chemistry in the booth. They hailed Arledge as a genius, and he wasn't about to tinker with a successful package even though he had the opportunity to improve the telecasts.

That's right. I truly believe that two men in the booth could have made *Monday Night Football* just as hot, maybe even hotter. You don't need three people in the damn booth. It's sometimes confusing and often cluttering. It's restrictive. It's absurd. If Arledge had paired one of the ex-jocks with me—preferably Gifford—we'd still have scaled new heights of popularity. After all, I was the key ingredient, and Arledge always knew it. No way he could've employed two ex-jocks alone in the booth, spouting the same old football garbage, not if he wanted to attract a prime-time audience. Hell, anybody with any intelligence knows that it would have been impossible to create an institution on the level of *Monday Night Football* with a lot of insipid drivel about the 4–3 defense.

If Gifford and Meredith were left to their own devices, they could've seriously damaged the package. I constantly had to adapt and adjust, using my knowledge of the medium and my gifts as a performer to try to inject some entertainment value into the telecasts. I realized early on that it was up to me to interact with the millions of women and casual fans who were tuning in and get a reaction out of them. *Monday Night Football* very quickly managed to transcend the game of football. The game became less important than the act of watching it on television. The locus shifted to the living room, and there was a greater need than ever to communicate with all those viewers. And if I'm nothing else, I'm one helluva communicator.

Working with two ex-jocks, I had to pick my spots, knowing when to make observations and editorial comments with maximum impact, and rescue the viewers from being bored to tears with an endless stream of nonsensical football jargon. One way I accomplished that was by humanizing the players and the coaches, relating stories that brought them to life, and giving the viewers a chance to empathize with them.

If I had had only one jock to cope with, I could've changed the nature of the telecasts, elevated them by providing more information beyond what was happening on the field, more enterprising journalism, and a more entertaining approach to the games. Why not? Who's kidding whom? Who the hell made *Monday Night Football* unlike any other sports program on the air?

If you want the plain truth, I did.

• • •

My reasons for leaving *Monday Night Football* were numerous and complex.

When I walked away from professional boxing, my decision was based on a clear and simple set of principles. I could no longer be connected with it on moral grounds, and I had despaired of ever seeing legislation achieved that would provide some reasonable and improved administration of the sport.

In contrast, my departure from *Monday Night Football* was accompanied by a kaleidoscope of emotions. In broadest terms, I'll not deny that for a number of years I enjoyed covering pro football. Doing those telecasts gave me a tremendous ego gratification in a career sense. My association with Muhammad Ali had made me a national celebrity, but *Monday Night Football*, with its weekly prime-time exposure, vastly multiplied that celebrity status. After a while, though, you come to realize just how synthetic fame can be and how fleeting its pleasures. People tend to regard you as public property, and everybody wants a piece of you. I began to hunger for privacy, which was impossible to obtain when we took the show on the road—and I was once again thrust into the glare of the spotlight.

Intellectually, looking back on it, my work on *Monday Night Football* is a matter of monumental indifference to me. I'm a man of causes, and I never had a cause. My real fulfillment in broadcasting has always come from crusading journalism, fighting for the rights of people such as Jackie Robinson, Muhammad Ali, and Curt Flood, and obviously there was none of that on *Monday Night Football*.

Physically and emotionally, it was debilitating. All the years of criticism in the press had begun to eat away at me. No matter how expertly I performed on a telecast, I rarely was allowed the luxury of enjoying it because the next day somebody would knock me. How could I get high on my work when I knew in my heart that I was a cinch to be picked on by critics and sportswriters who had no knowledge of my medium? It's hard to describe the rage and frustration you feel, both personally and professionally, when you are vilified in a manner that would make Richard Nixon look like a beloved humanitarian. You can't imagine what it does to a person until you've experienced it yourself, especially when you know that the criticism is essentially unfair.

Coupled with my heavy responsibilities on *Monday Night Football*, this constant source of aggravation led me more than ever to ponder my mortality. In 1983, my last season with the show, I was sixty-five, and at that age, you begin to wonder about how many more years you've got on this earth. My father was a traveling auditor, and he died on the road, far from his home and his family, and I resolved not to endure the same kind of passing. Whatever time was left me, I wanted to spend it with my wife and my children and their children.

Specifically, that was my primary reason for quitting *Monday Night Football*. In the early years of the show, my wife, Emmy, traveled to every game with me, and I was sustained by having her alongside me. There developed a mystique about *Monday Night Football*, and it had become a civic event. The pace was grueling. In every city, I was expected either to host or speak at a huge luncheon on the day of a game. Then I had to rush to the stadium, getting there earlier than almost everybody else to take care of the halftime highlights. That finished, it was off to an ABC party to mingle with the sponsors, a responsibility that both Gifford and Meredith usually shirked. And once the game started, of course, I had to be the catalyst in the booth, buttressing Gifford and Meredith.

There were other duties as well. I covered the breaking news stories on the telecasts, even those not related to football. That entailed restructuring the halftime highlights, researching the story, and interviewing the subject by way of the split-screen technique. During those telecasts, I reported on everything from labor strife to drug abuse, and I interviewed a host of newsmaking personalities ranging from baseball Commissioner Bowie Kuhn to boxer Sugar Ray Leonard. At least, for me, the steady flow of sports journalism on the telecasts was exhilarating, but even I have limits.

And nobody knew that better than Emmy.

Emmy had watched how hard I worked, and she worried, too, about the impact of the crowds on me, the insatiable desire for autographs, for my presence, for my attention. It was slowly chewing me up alive. Emmy was convinced I wasn't going to survive much longer, and she had no intention of witnessing me keel over in front of her. It reached the point where she adamantly refused to live through another *Monday Night Football* season. She wanted me to give it up. If necessary, she said, she'd get a house for the season in Key West, Florida, and live there by herself. And my two daughters totally agreed with her. They also wanted me to quit the package and stay home. My family had always come first in my life, and so I finally acquiesced to their wishes.

Three other reasons also played a part in my leaving *Monday Night Football*: my own sense of morality, the overwhelming boredom, and my relationship with my two longtime colleagues, Gifford and Meredith.

First, the moral problem I had with the NFL. I no longer believed in the league, and I became increasingly disillusioned with what I felt was a deception of the American public. Thanks to *Monday Night Football*, the NFL took off in the 1970s, becoming the most powerful, prestigious, and glamorous organization in professional sports. At the same time, however, what was happening off the field began to sicken me. As I have related in previous chapters, power eventually corrupted a lot of the owners and the men who run the league. Greed and political chicanery became normal business practices. Their arrogance knew no bounds. They thought they had a license to do exactly as they pleased, particularly with regard to carpetbagging franchises—or threatening to carpetbag franchises if the cities in which they played didn't come through with bigger stadiums, better tax breaks, and other concessions.

The NFL got away with such outrageous behavior for two reasons: one, its partnership with the three networks; and two, its almost all-encompassing influence over the sportswriters, who could be counted on to parrot the party line. It was disgraceful, and I wanted no part of it.

This doesn't mean that I came to dislike and disrespect every owner. Some, in fact, I still count as friends. But it does mean that as a group, under the leadership of Commissioner Pete Rozelle, their conduct was in my view in defiance of the public interest.

And God forbid you disagreed with them, or criticized them, or as a working journalist exposed their duplicity. They circled the wagons, even tried to discredit you by distorting what you had reported. Evidence of that is contained in the preceding chapter in the exchange of letters between Rozelle and me. If you'll recall, Rozelle had steadfastly insisted that I was in support of Al Davis moving his Raiders from Oakland to Los Angeles, in spite of the fact that my words to the contrary were a matter of public record.

If you weren't a whore for the NFL, then you were a pariah. I wasn't going to shill for the league, and Rozelle's letter made me realize where I stood. That's life.

And that's the way it remains today. Nothing has changed.

I've mentioned that the game had become an utter bore. One week collided into another, and I got the distinct impression that I was watching a rerun of a game I had seen before. It was like a form of Chinese water torture. I became convinced that every team in the league was using the same playbook. Hell, you could have photocopied the first game of the season and played it for sixteen straight weeks, and nobody would have known the difference. Where were the so-called brilliant football minds? Why was there such a dearth of creative action to heighten one's enthusiasm?

Came December, and there were still more than twenty teams in contention for the playoffs, and it was difficult distinguishing one team from another. Teams lacked an identity, and they were populated by nameless, faceless players incapable of arousing the imagination as so many before them—such as Joe Namath and Gale Sayers, Kenny Stabler and Mean Joe Green,

Johnny Unitas and Dick Butkus and on and on and on. Where had they all gone? And what had happened to the great teams—such as the Packers and the Colts and the Steelers—who seemed to play as a single personality with an easily definable flair and style?

Many theories were postulated for the NFL's malaise, and many solutions were offered—which I will get into later. At that point, however, I couldn't have cared less. What's more—and this relates to my boredom with the game—I had grown disgusted with television's continuing reliance on former athletes. It had reached outlandish proportions. Every time I turned around, another ex-jock had found his way into broadcasting. The result: Their presentation of a game had begun to sound like a broken record—and for my own money, not only had I tired of working the games, but also I couldn't even view them in my living room without either falling asleep or grinding my teeth at the inadequacy of the ex-jocks and the ineptitude of the telecasts.

Now, it is no secret that I have long held deep feelings about television's proclivity for hiring former athletes, thus creating a powerful wing of a whole new stratum in our society that author Robert Lipsyte so insightfully tagged "the Jockocracy." However, let me make it clear that I have never objected to the hiring of a former athlete in broadcasting simply because he or she is a former athlete. The late Paul Christman, for example, was dry and sardonic, and above all, he was the first ex-jock to take to the air with literacy and a willingness to criticize.

Like Christman, such other ex-jocks as Pat Summerall, Joe Garagiola, and Bob Uecker—and newcomer Ahmad Rashad has potential—have indeed applied themselves and worked hard over a long period of years. But, generally speaking, these alleged analysts and colormen serve a limited role—and they rarely proved themselves capable of bridging the gap between entertainment and journalism. The bottom line: They are not communicators.

How many times must the viewing public be subjected to the same old worn-out bromides?

"To beat this zone, folks, the tight end has to shoot the seam underneath the safety and behind the linebackers."

"Turnovers will kill you."

"He read the blitzing safety, checked off the line, then dumped the pass to the halfback in the flat."

"Dropped passes will kill you."

"It's a mismatch, fans. They've isolated the setback one-on-one against the linebacker, and you can't let them get away with that."

"Missed tackles will kill you."

"He came to play."

"They dodged a bullet on that play."

"They dodged a major bullet on that play."

"What moves!"

Oh, boy.

Put an ex-jock in the booth, and their cliché-ridden presentation of a game is the least of their sins. As a result of their lack of training, most of them are blessedly lost when trying to establish a story line for a telecast—i.e., detecting trends, keying on the personality and experiences of a player as they relate to his performance on the field, knowing his strengths and weaknesses, recalling the flow of events from earlier in the game and from other games in other years. Thus they tend to view a game as a series of plays rather than as a contest, and often they are ignorant of the human perspective.

What the ex-jocks had perpetrated on my medium was bad enough, but then I had to read know-nothing sports television critics praising them for their supposed insights. What a joke! Listen to the ex-jocks, they wrote, and you'll get the inside of the game. Inside? Come on.

Anybody over the age of two knows that football is basically a sport without any mysteries. The late Vince Lombardi once told me, "There's no magic to it, Howard. If you block better, if you tackle better, if you run better, if you pass better, you win."

I knew that growing up in Brooklyn when we played football at Manhattan Beach. You try to match a tall guy against a short guy, a big guy against a small guy, a fast guy against a slow guy. You try to obtain an advantage. That takes real brains, right? That's insight, right? That's the inside of the game, right? And, of course, you've got to be an ex-jock to grasp the complexities of the game, right?

Sure.

As far as *Monday Night Football* is concerned, what these myopic critics never fully understood or appreciated was the necessity to attract the largest possible audience. This was prime time, not Sunday afternoon. On Sunday afternoon, a network is satisfied to get the hard-core fan, essentially male, to buy its sponsor's beer or tires. In contrast, prime time is a teeming marketplace—men, women, teenagers, casual fans, as well as football aficionados—and *Monday Night Football* had to offer more than a mere game to get and hold a mass audience. On Sunday afternoon, an audience of perhaps twenty million is cause for celebration; in a weekly prime-time format, a game must draw between forty million and fifty million viewers to justify itself.

That was my mission on *Monday Night Football*, and I was painfully aware that the inane blathering of ex-jocks wasn't going to make it. By standing parallel to the game and owing nothing to it, by demystifying it, by bullying it and not being bullied by it—by regarding the game as primarily an entertainment, though realizing also the social forces that impacted on it—I was able to turn *Monday Night Football* into an Event—and I do mean to use the capital E. Now it is part of American pop culture, and if it sounds like my ego is churning on overdrive for taking the lion's share of credit for it, then I'll take the mane.

At this point, once and for all, I'd like to set the record straight about *Monday Night Football*'s presentation on radio. The games are carried on CBS Radio. I think that the announcers, Jack Buck and Hank Stram, the former head coach of the Kansas City Chiefs and the New Orleans Saints, do a fine job, and I'm personally fond of both men. They get a good audience. Why shouldn't they? It's *Monday Night Football*.

Have either Buck or Stram ever had the impact on this country that I had on the *Monday Night Football* telecasts? Come on. And yet how many times have words to this effect—"It's no secret that many viewers turn the TV sound off and the radio on because they dislike Howard Cosell"—appeared in print? More times than I can count. Now, let me ask you this: How often have you heard football fans in saloons or office hallways talk about what Buck and Stram had said on the air the night before? How many people do you know who actually turn off the sound of their television sets and turn on the radio when they watch *Monday Night Football*?

It's lunacy. And nobody knows better than the sponsors, who must make hard business decisions about how and where to spend millions of dollars in advertising. As an example, here's a copy of a letter I received at the end of the 1978 season from

Mike Roarty, the vice president of marketing for Budweiser beer. The original was sent to the managing editor of *Sports Illustrated.*

Dear Sir:

Re: "The Monday Night Alternative," a TV-Radio section article by William Oscar Johnson in *Sports Illustrated,* December 11. Commercial time on the 1978 ABC telecasts was unavailable to Budweiser, so we purchased the CBS radio package. Anxious to promote CBS radio listenership, and thus increase the reach of our commercials, the brand team made an announcement at the outset of the season emphasizing the excellence of the Jack Buck-Hank Stram broadcast team.

However, for reasons we do not completely understand, our announcement struck the fancy of certain journalists, including one at *Sports Illustrated.* As a result, Anheuser-Busch and Budweiser were positioned as at least implicitly impugning the quality and character of the ABC-TV play-by-play team.

While Buck and Stram have been excellent on the radio broadcasts all season long, any suggestion that the ABC team is anything less than outstanding to us is both regrettable and untrue.

Let's face it: ABC-TV made Monday Night Football the American institution it has become, and the trio of men in their broadcast booth deserve the lion's share of the credit. Perhaps more to the point, were commercial time on the ABC telecasts available to us, we would execute the buy without hesitation.

By my fourteenth and final season on the show, *Monday Night Football* had become the longest-running prime-time hit on television, outlasting such rivals as *M*A*S*H, Rhoda, The Doris Day Show, I Love Lucy, I Spy,* and *Lou Grant.*

All of which leads me to my colleagues. Right here and now,

let me say that Gifford is a friend of mine. Meredith is an engaging fellow. I am quite fond of O. J. Simpson, and he of me. Working with them, however, had finally taken its toll. As my tolerance for the pervasiveness of the Jockocracy sunk lower and lower, it became almost impossible for me to find any satisfaction or contentment in my role on *Monday Night Football*. Through all those years, I had to restrain myself for their benefit, and I got sick and tired of it. The fact is, there were many times when I had to subjugate myself on the telecasts, doing it *their* way instead of *my* way to help them for the good of the show.

Nobody understood that better than the genuine professionals in this business. As NBC's Dick Enberg told Tony Kornheiser of *The Washington Post*: "People don't appreciate how well Howard has featured those with whom he has worked. When he likes you, he can make you look great on the air. That's an art. He *made* Meredith. Last year, time and again he set up O.J. perfectly. I'll really miss his balance on those games. Taking away nothing from the other guys, when Howard said something, you *listened*. Isn't that why we're here?"

If my colleagues on *Monday Night Football* had really appreciated what I had done, they rarely showed it.

I give you an impromptu meeting at the Beverly Wilshire Hotel in Beverly Hills. It was the middle of November 1979, and I had stuck around out there to speak at a dinner honoring David Wolper, the brilliant producer who masterminded such blockbuster hits as *Roots* and *The Thorn Birds*.

In attendance at that meeting were Gifford, Meredith, and me, along with the president of ABC Sports, Roone Arledge, and the director of *Monday Night Football*, Chet Forte. We were there because of Meredith, who had been making unhappy noises about his position on the show. Until we had all gathered together, I really had no idea what the hell was going on.

Urged by Forte to speak up and clear the air, Meredith complained about me, and Gifford backed him up. In a nutshell, this was what each had to say:

MEREDITH: "I have things to say, points to make, and Howard keeps getting in my way."

GIFFORD: "Howard seems to be angry in the booth, and he's making us uncomfortable."

They had teamed up against me, and I was outraged. I had given my life's blood to the package. I was still the object of vicious attacks in the press, and here they were with their petty complaints that I simply did not deserve, complaints that had no basis in fact. Every study ever taken of the *Monday Night Football* telecasts had revealed that nobody talked more than Gifford and that Meredith made his most valid contributions when he played off me.

I needed that, right? I had busted my ass for them, and for what? So they could turn on me?

My blood boiled. I kept pressing Meredith, "Can you please be more specific, Don? What is it that you want to do that you're not doing now?"

Meredith had no specifics to offer, merely babbling on about having things to say. Like what, he never articulated.

As usual, Forte walked a tightrope. Having worked the telecasts from the beginning, he knew what I meant to the package, and he thought that my colleagues' complaints were ludicrous. At the same time, however, he worked for Arledge, and he had been around long enough to sense that Arledge wanted to appease both Gifford, whom he was close to, personally and socially, and Meredith, who was Gifford's best friend. Forte was too self-serving to rock the boat and express his true feelings about what was being said against me. He played both sides of the street while privately giving me my due and trying to keep me cool.

As for Arledge, he essentially said nothing, which was always his tactic at such confrontational meetings. Later that night, however, I invited Arledge and his then wife, Ann, to accompany me home on a private plane provided by Wolper. Since others were along for the ride, we didn't get an opportunity to talk much, but I did tell Arledge that I thought the meeting was a shabby exhibition of opportunism and ingratitude.

"I think you misunderstood their intentions," Arledge said.

"I didn't misunderstand anything, Roone," I said.

"They meant well."

"Come on. They want me out of the booth, and you know it. Don quit the package for three years because he wanted to be the star of the show, and he couldn't. He still wants it, and so does Gifford, and they think the only way they can get it is with me out of the way. Fine. They can have it."

"Howard, just keep doing what you're doing, and everything will work itself out."

My contract was up in a matter of weeks. Still seething after that meeting in Los Angeles, I began to have serious doubts about staying with *Monday Night Football*. I contacted my attorney, Bob Schulman, and told him about my misgivings. Schulman then called Fred Pierce, then the company's executive vice president and top aide to ABC President Elton Rule. They arranged to meet in Pierce's office. Pierce was surprised to see me show up with Schulman, but I felt compelled to be there.

I informed Pierce about the meeting and Gifford's and Meredith's whining and how hurt and angry I was over their attitude toward me. It was time for me to quit the package, I said to Pierce, and concentrate on other duties. I wanted out, and I told Pierce we should think of restructuring my new contract accordingly.

"You mean too much to too many people," Pierce said. "I'd hate to see you leave *Monday Night Football*. Let's face it, Howard: You are *Monday Night Football*."

I thanked Pierce for his gracious words, but considering how I felt, it was small consolation.

Pierce then summoned Arledge to join us, and he was told of my dissatisfaction and what I thought was best for my future. "What you're telling me you want to do isn't enough for you, Howard," Arledge said. "*Monday Night Football* is a part of you, and you need that forum. On a personal and a professional level, you won't be satisfied without it. Besides, Howard, think of the company. *Monday Night Football* is of utmost importance to ABC, and the company needs you there. Radio is nice, and so are horse racing and boxing and baseball. But they don't compare to *Monday Night Football*."

Over the next few days, I searched my heart. There was a lot of truth to what Arledge had said, though I was still upset with him for not backing me in Los Angeles. And what the hell? I'll admit it: No other show was going to pay me more than *Monday Night Football*, and I wanted the money for myself, my wife, my children, and my grandchildren. Like any doting grandfather, I wanted the best for the newest members of my family, and I was determined that they should never want for a thing, that they'd be well taken care of long after I was gone.

Schulman got word to Arledge that I would stay with *Mon-

day Night Football. Schulman was prepared to work out a new deal for me as quickly as possible, and Arledge agreed to get to it. Instead, he dragged his feet. Phone calls from my attorney weren't returned, and it annoyed the hell out of me.

Finally, a few days before Christmas, I got a call from Herb Granath, a good friend and then the assistant to Rule. Granath wanted to know at what time I planned to show up at the Christmas party being thrown by ABC's Entertainment Division. I was supposed to play Santa Claus. No kidding. White beard, red suit, the whole shmear. "This isn't going to be easy, Herbie," I said. "I'm not exactly imbued with the holiday spirit."

"What's wrong?" Granath asked.

"Arledge still hasn't approved my deal. I've been jerked around for too long, and I'm furious about it."

"Nothing's been done? Seriously?"

I assured Granath that I was.

"You come to the party, Howard," Granath said. "The contract will be there. Signed."

Pierce arrived at the party with my contract, and it was signed by him personally, not Arledge. I got everything I had asked for, and when we shook hands, Pierce said, "Here's to a whole new beginning."

Pierce's whole new beginning wasn't exactly that. More precisely, it was the beginning of the end for me with *Monday Night Football.* I had already begun to experience the intellectual, emotional, and physical turmoil that I mentioned earlier. The meeting in Los Angeles served to deepen those feelings, and I knew that my relationship with Gifford and Meredith would never be quite the same again. Sure, we had had our disagreements in the past, just as others who have worked so closely together for so many years sometimes find themselves at odds with their colleagues. And all those countless newspaper stories that claimed I didn't like Meredith or that Gifford hated me were simply untrue. Considering how much time we spent together and how much pressure we had to cope with, we got along damned well. But there was something about our confrontation in the Beverly Wilshire Hotel—call it tone or attitude or spirit— that seared my soul.

Not that we were the greatest friends in the world. Friends, yes, but certainly not inseparable. Gifford and I go back a long way; my younger daughter Hilary, when she was an infant, once tinkled on Gifford's lap. And when Hilary grew up and took a job with KABC-TV in Los Angeles, Meredith and his wife were unfailingly kind to her, and she saw them frequently. Both Gifford and Meredith and their wives were guests at Hilary's wedding, and Emmy and I were delighted to have them celebrate the occasion with us.

When Gifford and Meredith were around, I enjoyed their companionship, and we shared many happy moments together. There were more laughs than heartaches. The fact is, though, on all the trips through all the years, rarely did I spend much time with Gifford and Meredith—other than at production meetings—until we got into the booth. Occasionally, they showed up at a luncheon or a sponsor's party, where we'd indulge in some good-natured repartee. In the main, however, we went our separate ways. I'd often have dinner with a coach, a general manager, an owner, or friends outside the business, while Gifford and Meredith were content to share each other's company.

That was fine with me. They were the best of friends and had a lot in common. I came from a vastly different background—geographically, ethnically, socially, educationally, professionally—and I was older than they. Obviously, we had different tastes and interests, and the only thing that really mattered was our working relationship. Drive a wedge in that, and there wasn't much to sustain us except memories.

That meeting in Los Angeles was the wedge, and it became increasingly difficult for me to dismiss those differences between us and pretend I could go on as before.

I will forever have ambivalent feelings about Frank Gifford. Somewhere inside me, if you go deep enough, I consider him a friend. And if you go deep enough inside Gifford, he considers me a friend. There were times when he touched me with his warmth and caring. I was always impressed with his commitment to the Special Olympics for mentally handicapped kids. And when his first wife, Maxine, whom Emmy and I love dearly, contracted multiple sclerosis, Frank started an MS chapter in New York. It was because of Gifford—along with former Notre Dame football coach Ara Parseghian—that I served as national chairman of MS for four years, and together we set new records for fund raising.

When I left *Monday Night Football*, I received a letter from Frank's estranged second wife, Astrid, wishing me well—and saying how much Frank respected me and depended on me on the show.

That said, I'm well aware that Frank Gifford represents motherhood and apple pie and that a great many men would like their sons to grow up to be just like him—a handsome football hero and a glamorous media personality. Frank has led a charmed life, but in all fairness, he has worked diligently to achieve everything he has. And he has inspired in many people a sense of being a loyal and dependable friend in times of trouble.

What I have to say about Frank is based largely on my views as a professional broadcaster and journalist. You will get opinions, and you will get facts. In no way should this be misconstrued as a personal attack against Frank. It's as measured and forthright an assessment as I can make about somebody with whom I've worked for almost half my ABC career.

To begin, Gifford's greatest talent is not in broadcasting. He is what he is, a physically attractive man with a matchless ability to charm almost everybody he meets. One adjective often used to describe Gifford is "nice." That he is. Maybe too nice. He's also easy—easy to like, easy to humor, easy to interview. Maybe too easy. He is a master at masking his emotions, as evidenced by his bravery in dealing with Maxine's multiple sclerosis. After so many years of playing the role of hero—first at USC, then with the New York Giants and *Monday Night Football*—he has grown so accustomed to the part that he often seems more concerned about preserving his image than expressing his true feelings. Believe me, I know full well the personal storms that Gifford has weathered, and there is pain and bitterness within him that he suppresses for the sake of remaining everybody's All-American.

As a result, there is nothing controversial about Frank. Like President Reagan, he is a Teflon man; no matter how many mistakes he makes during a telecast, no matter how glaring his weaknesses as a performer, nothing sticks to him. The sports television critics, wooed by his smooth off-camera personality, generally rave about him, rarely taking him to task on purely objective standards. And since Gifford is one of Arledge's closest friends in life, Gifford will always have security at ABC.

In the wake of my departure from *Monday Night Football*, Gifford responded to my widely quoted barbs about the Jockocracy with some published comments of his own. For one thing, he said that he got his start in broadcasting before I had, referring to some limited experience he had gained during his playing days.

Oh, yeah?

How absurd.

I remember a day before the third Floyd Patterson-Ingemar Johansson match, in early 1961; Patterson was training at Glenrock Country Club in Rockland County, New York, and I went there to interview the champ. A young, handsome football player arrived later on, hoping to get a few words with Patterson. He knew little about either boxing or Patterson, and to make things worse, his tape recorder broke down. I lent him mine and even gave him some questions to ask. He was effusively grateful.

That football player was Frank Gifford.

I would also hope that Frank hasn't forgotten how I gave him one of his first breaks on television. In the late 1950s, I had a nightly network show called *Sports Focus*, and I used Gifford as an alleged correspondent to interview other football players. It wasn't much, but Gifford got a taste of the business. Just because he was a jock didn't mean that he didn't deserve a chance, and I gave it to him.

When I quit, Gifford lauded me as a thorough professional—but also said that my decision to leave would not harm the continued success of *Monday Night Football*. "We are as good as the game," he said. "If the game remains strong, then you can have Attila the Hun in the booth."

Gifford is entitled to his opinion, though I have never agreed wholeheartedly with the theory that the game is all-important and the announcers have little sway over the viewing public. Hell, I was able to arouse a reaction even when the games were lousy, and we got terrific ratings. But, you see, the game means everything to Gifford. He thinks the NFL was ordained from Mount Sinai by Moses to be above all else. For Gifford, all Ten Commandments can be reduced to one: The NFL shall prevail.

Is it any wonder, then, that Gifford was much too respectful on the air? He was an apologist, constantly making excuses for players who fumbled or dropped passes, and coaches who made rotten decisions. You never heard Frank say, "He blew that one, didn't he, Howard? The receiver was wide open. All he had to do was throw it in his vicinity. Easiest thing in the world, if you're a pro quarterback. I wonder how he's going to explain that one to his coach."

Instead, Frank might say, "Oh, what a shame! You know, Howard, I heard that he twisted his thumb a couple of weeks ago, and it's probably still bothering him."

Thus, while Meredith often relished my bursts of irreverence, Gifford refused to participate in any repartee that might smack of portraying his beloved NFL in a less than glorious light. My criticisms of players, coaches, owners, and the league itself irritated Frank, and he'd often try to deflect what I said by contradicting me and hoping to enlist Meredith's support. All Meredith really cared about was getting off a good line. If he could by agreeing with Gifford, he'd take me on. If not, he'd mumble some innocuous comment and leave Frank hanging.

Gifford never jumped all over me when I expressed my opinions, and we rarely argued over our contrasting perceptions of the game and the people who played it and coached it. Quite frankly, he had too much respect for me as a broadcaster. He admired my command of the language, my ability to communicate, and he was shrewd enough not to engage me in a debate. He had to know he couldn't win.

I'll give Frank this: Few people in this business are more industrious. He works as hard as he can for as long as he can. To watch him prepare for a game was almost excruciating. On the day of a telecast, he'd lock himself up in his hotel room and pore over scores of little index cards that contained the names, numbers, positions, and brief biographies of every player on each team. He'd try to commit this information to memory as best he could, then bring the cards to the booth with him, constantly referring to them during the course of a game.

Those damned cards only served to confuse Frank. What with his play-by-play duties and his responsibility to bring Meredith and me into the telecast with our observations, he had his hands full. At some point in the late 1970s, however, Arledge gradually altered the texture and tone of the telecasts, giving Gifford carte blanche to interweave color commentary—such as players' backgrounds and statistics and personal observations—into his call of a game, and it hurt the presentation.

In my opinion, Gifford simply couldn't handle such a heavy load, and he ended up making mistake after mistake. He already had a central role in the telecast—setting the plays, calling the action, recording the results—and any additional tasks were too much for him to handle. I told Arledge that, but it didn't matter to him. Neither did it matter to Gifford, who relished his expanded role and actually thought he was doing a helluva job.

I was determined to act as a professional and continue to support the telecasts, even though it meant subjugating myself to another performer. If that's the way Arledge wanted it, that's the way he was going to have it. It was useless to complain too loudly or too strenuously. Arledge and Gifford are dear friends, and Arledge is protective of him. Whether their friendship influences Arledge's opinion is a matter of conjecture, but he's told me that he thinks Frank is the best play-by-play announcer in television. And he's always felt that way. The year after he hired Gifford away from CBS for *Monday Night Football*, he put Frank on basketball, in a glaring misuse of talent, at the 1972 Olympic Games in Munich; this despite the fact that Keith Jackson had been covering pro basketball for the network and was widely regarded as the voice of the NBA.

Jackson came to me in distress, complaining about Arledge's decision. So, too, did Bill Fleming, a veteran broadcaster. "How can Arledge do this?" Fleming asked, fuming. "I've been calling Big Ten basketball games for years, and you know what he's got me doing? White-water canoeing!"

What could I tell him? "Bill, stay calm," I said. "It's a beautiful scene. You'll love it."

Thus, as you can see, there was no sense arguing with Arledge about the merits of expanding Frank's duties on *Monday Night Football*. And, hell, it was Arledge's show.

For my money, however, Gifford is far from your classic play-by-play man. He is not in the same league with NBC's Dick Enberg or CBS's Pat Summerall, once his teammate on the Giants. Gifford's voice is thin and monotonic, and he is incapable of using it with rhythm and pace for dramatic effect. In addition, he stumbles over words, and it's not uncommon for him to lose his train of thought.

In his first few years with the show, his propensity for error was embarrassing. He was—and still is—very sensitive about his reputation for fluffing calls. He tried hard to overcome his weaknesses, improved a little, and then developed an arrogance about himself as a performer. It's inexplicable. He's not a natural performer, never was, never will be. And to this day, he still mispronounces names, forgets which teams are playing, gets the yard lines wrong, and lacks the know-how to establish a story line and give the game perspective.

In spite of my problems with Frank as a performer and a colleague, it's only fair to mention that when his sincerity shone through, he was engaging company, respectful and deferential. And there were times when he could be charming and self-effacing in very awkward situations. For example, I remember once when Frank, Emmy, and I were waiting for our luggage in the Kansas City airport. An attractive young woman spotted us and asked for our autographs. I gave her mine, and then she handed the slip of paper to Frank.

"Sign it to Bob, please," she said. "That's B-O-B."

Without missing a beat, and smiling broadly, Gifford replied, "I know how to spell Bob. I can spell Tom, too. T-O-M. Three-letter names I can handle."

Emmy and I broke up. The young woman was a bit embarrassed, but Frank put her at ease. As we walked away, still laughing over the incident, Frank said to Emmy, "I guess she doesn't think I'm very bright."

I know that what I have said about Frank will prompt people to charge that I am envious and resentful of him. That's simply not true. I feel it's my obligation to express my opinions about Frank in as honest a manner as I know how. Perhaps now it's pertinent to repeat that I will always have ambivalent feelings about the man. And such feelings are also lodged within my wife. Emmy has often said, "If Howard were to die, and if I had some problem to deal with, I wouldn't hesitate to go to Frank for help, and I'm sure he'd go out of his way for me. That may sound strange, but that's how I feel."

I do not understand Don Meredith, and I never will. In the beginning, I loved the guy. He was terribly insecure about his performance in the booth, and I'd often counsel him to stick with it and assure him that he'd prevail. Eventually, he ended up winning an Emmy. I was genuinely pleased for him, in spite of the fact that I realized he had won a popularity contest. What the hell. At least his philosophical approach to football and his job appealed to me. I mean, I had to react favorably to a guy who'd sit high above the game and say, "There's got to be more to life than what's going on down there."

I respected Meredith for that, and I believe he truly meant it.

On the other hand, Meredith rarely prepared for a telecast in the manner of a professional broadcaster. Putting the games in their proper perspective is one thing, but he often showed no interest at all. He'd try to compensate for his lack of knowledgeability by singing a song or talking to his imaginary alter ego, Harley Smydlapp, and everybody would write about how funny and irrepressible he was. Meredith's lackadaisical attitude never bothered me as much as it did Gifford, who always worried about his friend's state of mind and how cooperative he'd be during a telecast. As far as I was concerned, Meredith could play the part of my foil *ad infinitum*, and I'd set him up with one-liners—even if they occasionally zinged me—as long as he wasn't hurting the telecast.

And besides, Arledge loved Meredith's act and felt he added immeasurably to the proper admixture of football savvy, humor, and entertainment that was the essence of the package. I sometimes wondered if Arledge really knew what was going on in the booth and how difficult it could be trying to keep Meredith on an even keel and aware of what was happening in a game. It got to the point where Forte used to tell the press that Meredith was at his best when he didn't even know who was playing. Easy for him to say.

Of course, the press lapped it up. One of Meredith's greatest attributes was supposed to be his unpredictability. Well, few people ever knew it, but Meredith's unpredictability wasn't necessarily a matter of his performing style. I think Don wrestles with life. I'm not sure if he's ever known what he really wants to be or what he's really capable of accomplishing. He's uncertain about himself, and it produces a behavior pattern that I call "Texas Cruel." There's a mean streak within him, and it was hard to figure out just when it would manifest itself. He groused and grumbled, snapped at people, and he could be contrary in the extreme. On those occasions, he was hardly the lovable ol' cowboy with the homespun view of the world that was so ingratiating. Not in the least.

Meredith was most ornery during the last half of the 1973

season, when he had determined in his own mind that he wanted out of the package. It was at that time that I traveled to Bermuda to run a sales effort for ABC, and most of the company brass was there. No sooner had I arrived than I received a phone call from an old friend in Los Angeles, a public-relations whiz named Jim Mahoney. His first words to me were, "You've got to get off that fucking show."

Then Mahoney read me some words by a *Los Angeles Times* columnist named John Hall. In essence, Hall wrote that in a recent telecast Meredith had stripped me nude, torn me apart, exposed me as an ignorant fool who didn't know the game. How ludicrous! Naturally, in his desire to get at me, Hall totally misread what was going on and failed to understand the substance of Meredith's remarks, none of which smacked of brave new insights into pro football. In a foul mood, Meredith was openly cruel, constantly contradicting me and trying to ridicule practically everything I said. I was tempted to tell him on the air, "Look, Don, you don't know what you're talking about. Don't start in because you don't stand a chance. Get into a duel of words with me, and I'll put you away."

As I say, I was tempted, and I experienced a similar temptation on numerous occasions. But I never let myself go. I stayed in control and conducted myself as a professional. Even after the telecast was over, I refused to say what I felt privately to him. It wasn't worth my time, and there was the possibility that it might've been counterproductive and disruptive. What's more, I knew how it would be the next morning after such telecasts. Meredith and I would run into each other—in the lobby of the hotel, or at breakfast, or later at the airport—and he'd be as charming as ever, as if nothing had happened. He'd never apologize, or try to explain himself. And I let it pass.

After talking to Mahoney from Los Angeles, I happened to be with Elton Rule, then the president of ABC. "I'd like to talk to you about the telecast the other night," he said.

"Please, Elton, I'd rather not."

"What the hell is going on with that imbecile?" Rule said, referring to Meredith and his treatment of me.

"Look, Elton, it's up to you and to Arledge to control Meredith. I'm doing the best that I can under the circumstances, but I don't know how much more I can take. Sometimes he's just impossible to deal with. What can I say? You heard him. Meredith is Arledge's guy. Talk to Roone about him, not me."

As far as I know, nothing was ever said to Meredith. At the end of the season, when Meredith's intentions to leave the package became obvious, Arledge spent days trying to talk him out of it. When all hope was gone of keeping Meredith, Arledge told me, "He's leaving, Howard, and that's that. Whatever I said was to no avail. In fact, Don was adversarial with me."

Without saying it in so many words, Arledge also indicated that I was one of the reasons for Meredith's unhappiness. The implication seemed to be that if Arledge had gotten rid of me, then Meredith might have considered staying on. Meredith wanted to be the unqualified star of the telecast. If he couldn't, bye-bye.

At first I thought, How do you like that? He had won an Emmy. I didn't. He had received raves from the press. I was pilloried day in and day out. Well, I figured, that's the way it is with jocks. How shallow can they get?

The more I dwelled on what Arledge had told me, however, the more I suspected that something was awry. Had Arledge really spoken the truth, the whole truth, and nothing but the truth? I wasn't so sure. This is not to suggest that Meredith didn't give Arledge some reason to believe that he was jealous of me. At bottom, what was going on here, I concluded, was Arledge spinning his little webs of intrigue. At the time, my first book was a big best seller, and my celebrity was skyrocketing. Making me aware of Meredith's uneasiness with me was part of Arledge's game plan to keep me in my place. Keep me insecure. It was a tack he had taken before and would take many times again in the future.

Whatever Meredith's true feelings about me—and I do believe that he indeed craved greater stardom—I had no intention of confronting him about them. He was leaving. We had shared a lot of good times together, and I wanted our parting as colleagues to be as friendly as possible. To that end, I decided to profile Meredith on my sports magazine show. It would be my good-bye gift to him. And so I went to his farm in Elephant, Pennsylvania, where I shot the piece. To close the show; I had Don walking with his wife and dog alongside the lake on his property. And as a final warming touch, in the background I played Bob Dylan's stirring "Forever Young"—"May your hands be always busy, may your feet be always swift, may you have a strong foundation . . ."

When Arledge saw the piece, he said to me, "Why'd you make such a hero out of the son-of-a-bitch?"

Three years later, the same man asked me, "Would you accept Meredith back on the package?"

"Sure," I said. "I have no objections."

Actually, I understood why Arledge wanted Meredith back. Fueled by the television critics, the public remained steadfast in its perception that Gifford and I along with Meredith composed the best possible combination in the booth. Arledge wanted to recapture the plaudits of the press, and bringing Meredith back was one way of assuring that. I never believed that the three of us were as wonderful as everybody thought, but I figured that Meredith's return just might reignite the excitement and mystique of *Monday Night Football*.

After Meredith left the package, I talked with Joe Namath about joining Frank and me in the booth. Still playing quarterback for the New York Jets, he had style and panache, and he was articulate and no stranger to performing. We even discussed it over drinks with Arledge on the terrace of my apartment. I know that Arledge had broached the subject with Namath's attorney, but nothing came of it.

Then I brought Dick Butkus to meet Arledge. A former All-Pro middle linebacker with the Chicago Bears, Butkus possessed an infectious personality, and I sensed that he was a helluva performer. Arledge didn't agree. I guess he didn't think Butkus was good-looking enough. At any rate, Arledge picked a former defensive back with the Kansas City Chiefs named Fred (The Hammer) Williamson to replace Meredith. History will record that Williamson was so palpably unsuited for broadcasting that he was unceremoniously fired after a few exhibition games.

And guess who took the heat for Williamson's demise? You've got it. Williamson had the gall to allege that I was anti-black. He gave interviews claiming that he was a better performer than I and that I was jealous of him. Thus I got him fired. Of course, the press ran with Williamson's charges, painting him as the poor victim of a monstrous ego. It was a total lie.

To replace Williamson, Arledge hired Alex Karras, the former mighty defensive tackle of the Detroit Lions. At the time, Karras was a good choice. He had a quick wit, and his increasing self-assurance as a performer was reflected in the fact that he was getting more roles in Hollywood. In addition, I liked Karras as a human being. He was a sensitive man. He was also a straight shooter, up front, and it was pleasant working with him because I didn't have to worry about two guys ganging up on me all the time. Karras was his own man, went his own way, and he didn't care whether his opinions jibed either with mine or Gifford's.

After a couple of years, though, Karras had lost interest in the package. Things were going very well for him in his acting career, and it was time for him to move on. Karras hung around another year—and then Arledge went out and rebagged Meredith.

Meredith had spent his three years away from *Monday Night Football* under contract to NBC, primarily hoping to make his mark as an actor. He thought he had the kind of talent that he didn't remotely possess, and he found the going tough. He was associated with one of the most expensive bombs in network history—an ill-fated prime-time series called *Supertrain*, which was the brainchild of then NBC President Fred Silverman. But let me stress that Meredith is blessed with an appealing personality, and I thought he turned in several credible performances on the *Police Story* anthology.

As far as sports was concerned, Meredith never really clicked with Curt Gowdy on NBC telecasts of AFL football. In my opinion, Gowdy was the best all-around play-by-play announcer who has yet lived, but he always played it straight—and Meredith was lost without having anybody to react to. Meredith had to play the part of a color man in the classic sense of the term, and his old problems with being unprepared were more obvious than ever.

When Meredith returned to *Monday Night Football*, I figured that he'd be somewhat chastened by his experience at NBC. However, I never noticed any perceptible change in Don. His buttress was Gifford, and before too long, the two of them were once again having a high old time together. What's more, Frank helped Meredith secure very profitable commercial work through Ross Johnson of Nabisco, and Meredith was properly appreciative. In the booth, he became increasingly subservient to Gifford, often complimenting Frank for even the most ordinary observations. Check the tapes. How often did you hear Meredith utter words to this effect: "Oh, that Frank. He's a smart one," or, "Nice going, fella. Frank really knows his stuff, don't he?"

And yet, in the booth, Meredith would nudge me and smirk every time Frank made a mistake. There were times, too, when, privately, along with me, he'd shake his head and say, "You know, the truth is, Frank isn't calling a good game."

It really didn't matter, though. When push came to shove, Gifford and Meredith were as thick as thieves. They would never take sides against each other, and somehow I always was cast as the bad guy. I could never really trust either one of them.

When I officially quit *Monday Night Football,* I never heard a word from Meredith, not a call, not a note. It wasn't until late December 1984 that he made contact with me. He and his wife sent Emmy and me a Christmas card. There was a personal note: "It's not the same without you. We miss you terribly."

As part of his new deal, Meredith had begged out of working a full schedule of games, which meant that Arledge needed to hire a fourth announcer to fill in during Meredith's absences. He chose Fran Tarkenton, the former scrambling quarterback of the Minnesota Vikings.

Fran and I liked each other. He often sought my advice, and I was glad to help. Before his first telecast, the Hall of Fame exhibition game, Tarkenton said, "Howard, I'll be lost. Please lead me, and I'll follow every lead you give me."

Which he did. I'd steer him away from spouting a lot of incomprehensible jock jargon by setting him up with questions that touched on his experience as a quarterback and enabled him to explain what was happening on the field in flesh-and-blood terms. For example: "Fran, what makes you think this kid can make it as a quarterback in the NFL? What are his assets?" Or, when a receiver dropped an easy pass, I'd ask him, "What do you think the quarterback will say to him in the huddle?"

These are hardly penetrating questions, but the point was to get Fran thinking about the viewers and giving them information they could readily grasp. As a result, he didn't get bogged down talking about X's and O's, and he came to appreciate what I was trying to do for him.

Fran and I got along so well, in fact, that he'd sometimes call me for advice on matters beyond the booth. He once asked me if he should accept a job as one of the regular hosts of a prime-time series called *That's Incredible*. Apparently, ABC Sports was pressuring him not to take it. "You tell them to go to hell," I said. "That's twenty thousand bucks a week. You take that job. It's a helluva lot better than working a handful of games each year."

As silly a show as it was, *That's Incredible* ended up a big ratings winner for four years, and Fran made a small fortune. He never forgot what I had told him.

After Fran got fired off the package, he'd call routinely, always expressing his gratitude and how much he enjoyed our association. He was better off. The last couple of years, he wasn't exactly thrilled about his working on the package, and now he had more time to devote to his vast and profitable business interests. Not long ago, Fran authored a how-to business book, and he called wondering if I'd interview him on my weekly radio show, *Speaking of Everything*. "The first day you're free," I told him, "pop over to the office, and it's done."

Fran spoke smoothly and confidently about his book. He always did have a knack for making money, and he was enthusiastic about telling what he knew. After the interview, we talked about *Monday Night Football*. He had to laugh at several newspaper stories that alleged we didn't like each other and that I was the one who finally got him fired. "What horseshit," he said. "We both know that you weren't the problem."

In truth, the one who didn't like working with Fran was Gifford. In my opinion, he resented Tarkenton, who was a contemporary player—and who basically dismissed Gifford's opinions because he thought Frank didn't know what he was talking about. In addition, Gifford was often impatient with him. Tarkenton had a habit of belaboring an observation, and there were times when Frank would cut him off by saying, "You've made your point, Fran."

On those occasions, Gifford would attempt to use a jocular tone, but it annoyed the hell out of Tarkenton. He viewed it as a snide and sneaky way of putting him down. He was probably right.

When the ax fell on Tarkenton, Arledge never consulted me concerning a replacement. He had already made up his mind to put O. J. Simpson on the package. At first I had no quarrel with his choice. For one thing, it wasn't of monumental significance to me because I knew I didn't want to work the games much longer. And besides, thanks to all the commercials Juice was getting, I thought his speech was improving, and he could handle the assignment. I was wrong. Once again, except in rare instances, it was a mistake to take a jock and put him on the air, and I ended up feeling sorry for the man.

My emotions concerning Simpson run deep. I got to know the Juice when he was a star at USC. And when he came to New York to accept the Heisman Trophy, he asked me to take him to Joe Namath's joint, Bachelor's III. *The New York Times'* sports columnist then, Robert Lipsyte, accompanied us, and we sat at a table in the back. The Juice was anxious to meet the famous New York quarterback. When Namath finally arrived, he hung out at the bar. I knew he had spotted us, but he refused to acknowledge our presence. After a half hour or so, I started to get up, saying, "This is ridiculous. I'm going to get that son-of-a-bitch and bring him back here."

The Juice touched my arm. "Howard," he said, "you can't rush the great ones. Let him play his little game."

The Juice finally got to meet Namath, but what I took away from that day was a lasting impression of Simpson. I remember thinking, this kid's got a lot on the ball. He's nobody's fool.

Midway through his pro career, Simpson got his first big break on television. Arledge used him as the Sunday host on *Wide World of Sports*. By then, the Juice and I had developed a close personal relationship. Sunday was my day off, but I'd catch a cab to the studio to be with Simpson. I'd play cards with him, shoot the breeze, give him a few pointers, try to relax him. Then, after the show, he'd usually wind up at my apartment for a few drinks with Emmy and me before heading for the airport. He was like a part of the family. "Howard," he used to say to me, "before my race is run, I've got to do *Monday Night Football* with you. It's the dream of my life."

Anyway, the Juice's first appearance on *Monday Night Football* came during an exhibition game in Washington. Not bad, I thought. He had made some excellent points, but there was still a lot of fine-tuning ahead of him. After the game, we had drinks together at the Watergate Hotel. I told him the following:

"What you must do is slow your speech. Your mind operates like a jackrabbit going down the road. It's ahead of itself, and you don't yet have the dictional capacity for your tongue to keep up with it in an understandable way. Don't worry about showing the public how much you know. Much of what you know they won't understand anyway. They won't care. Keep it simple. Measure your words.

"Tonight, when you noticed that it wasn't the running back who was responsible for the fumble but the quarterback who caused the loss of the ball, that stuff works. That's the kind of thing the public can understand. Then, when we replayed it and the viewers saw it, they probably said to themselves, 'Gee, the Juice was right.'

"That's the kind of thing you can do and do effectively. Just remember, though, slow down, get comfortable. I know it seems as though you've got a lot to say and so little time to say it, but you'll learn to economize. First, work on your speech."

Like any rookie, Juice had his ups and downs in 1983, but I began to doubt whether he'd ever conquer his locution problems. The fact that he didn't have to appear on the package every week was a blessing in disguise. While the sports television critics were generally kind to him—as they usually are with ex-jocks—the viewing public didn't get a chance to experience how familiarity can breed contempt. Simpson's enthusiasm often masked a lot of his weaknesses, and unlike Gifford, at least he was willing to criticize players and coaches. I worried, however, that the Juice was fighting a losing battle.

Nevertheless, as it turned out, my biggest disappointment was not with Juice as a broadcaster—but as a friend. As you shall see, if it weren't for all the years we had known each other, I don't think our friendship could have survived.

I can't pinpoint the date exactly, but it was during the 1981 season. If I ever had any doubts that Gifford and Meredith would be happier without me, they were dispelled that year. *Monday Night Football* was on its way toward achieving record ratings and profits. We were riding high—so high, in fact, that I could sense a newfound cockiness within Gifford. And whenever Gifford acted like he was at the top of his form, it usually infected Meredith—and reinforced his faith in Frank. They both beamed with self-esteem, strutting their stuff like a pair of roosters in a chicken coop.

Full of themselves, obviously convinced they could handle the telecasts as well without me as with me, Gifford and Meredith suggested that I might be happier staying home and working out of the New York studio. I could voice-over the half-time highlights from there, they said, and use the studio to interview pertinent guests and break news stories. At first I didn't take them seriously, thinking they were merely throwing ideas into the air in reaction to my bouts of weariness with the show. Then, however, their suggestion about staying in New York started coming more frequently, even during the weeks when my mood was mellow and spirits unflagging, even during the 1982 players' strike when briefly I was able to renew myself.

If that's what they want, I thought, they may get their wish sooner than they think.

With the summer of 1983 came the news that Simpson would be joining us in the booth. It was then that I started dropping broad hints about cutting back on my *Monday Night Football* schedule, or perhaps even leaving the show altogether. If I didn't quit soon, I theorized, they'd have to cart me into the booth in a wheelchair. It was time for me to take cognizance of my age and my health, and there was really nothing left for me to accomplish in broadcasting.

These feelings were first expressed in a *Sports Illustrated* cover story by Frank Deford, then in an article by the enormously talented Tom Shales, the television critic of *The Washington Post*.

Little did I know then that the very first regular-season game of the 1983 *Monday Night Football* schedule would crystallize my worst misgivings about remaining with the show—and intensify my desire to quit. In that game, between the Washington Redskins and the Dallas Cowboys, I happened to call Redskins' running back Alvin Garrett "a little monkey." Garrett is black, and at the time, I was praising his talent and relating how his coach, Joe Gibbs, appreciated having him around. No matter. That single, innocent remark caused a national sensation, fueled by the sportswriters and fanned by the Reverend Joseph Lowery of the Southern Christian Leadership Conference (see Chapter 12).

The furor over that crack lasted for what seemed like days on end. I was besieged by phone calls for interviews, letters of support from the black community, and a steady stream of commentary in the press. It was ludicrous. Considering my lifelong record with regard to race relations and my association with the likes of Jackie Robinson, Muhammad Ali, and Curt Flood, imagine how I felt being castigated in some quarters as a racist. And how absurd it was that I even needed defending.

The whole thing sickened me. I was riding an emotional roller coaster. My spirits were sorely taxed, and it even affected me physically. I felt awful. The very thought of going back into the booth depressed me. I did what I had to do, however, and three days later, I was in Minneapolis for a Thursday night game, grinding out another telecast and wondering how I could continue much longer.

Shortly afterward, while in Chicago to emcee a dinner, I gave an interview to an old friend, columnist Irv Kupcinet, mentioning my growing disaffection with *Monday Night Football* and predicting my imminent retirement.

The chairman of the board of ABC, Leonard Goldenson, saw the item and invited me to lunch in the company dining room. Goldenson and I have shared a long and close friendship, and he's very dear to me, like a father.

"You're not serious about leaving us, are you?" Goldenson asked.

"I'm not a kid anymore, Leonard," I said. "Every year gets tougher, and more and more I find myself wondering how much longer I can go on. Hell, there's a time to reap and a time to sow."

"In my opinion, Howard, you can't quit. Not yet. I've seen it happen too many times. Vigorous men who'd dedicated their lives to their work decide to retire and then they're gone, just like that. It would be the same with you. You quit, you die."

"I've always thought the same thing, Leonard, but I'm not so sure anymore."

"What does Emmy think?"

"She'd certainly like to see me cut back," I said. "I know she's fed up with me working *Monday Night Football*. That's got to end soon. On the other hand, if I started hanging around the apartment all the time, I think she'd throw me out."

Knowing Emmy as well as he did, Goldenson had to laugh. "You're probably right," he said. Then, on a more serious note, he said, "Please, Howard, give this thing careful thought. You know you're part of the family here, and we'll always want you with us."

"I appreciate that, Leonard, and I don't have to tell you what this company means to me. Look, I'll make you a personal commitment. I will surely see my contract through to its end. Then, after the Olympics in August, we'll sit down and thrash things out. I'll contact you first."

Just prior to working the World Series, I went to Buffalo for a game between the Bills and the New York Jets. This marked the Juice's turn in the spotlight, as he was returning to the city where he had spent his glory days as a pro. At a luncheon on the day of the game, he made several unfortunate remarks that got picked up in the press—and quite frankly infuriated me. What he did, in essence, was question my knowledge of football and promise to bring his own special brand of insights to the telecast.

I let it pass.

Simpson, however, wouldn't let up. While I was off doing the World Series, I continued to read how Simpson intended to teach me a thing or two about the game. Then, in a column in *Sports Illustrated,* he was quoted as saying, "To be honest, I've found I can tease him [Howard] a little more off-camera than I can on-camera."

Few know better than Simpson how much I relish arguing and exchanging barbs. What was his problem? Why was he rapping me? I finally came to understand his motivation. People had started talking about his deplorable diction, and in his insecurity, he lashed out at me in hopes of deflecting criticism that might be leveled at him. It's interesting to note that never once did he knock either Gifford or Meredith. The ex-jocks are members of the same fraternity, and they stick together.

The next time I saw Forte in the New York office, I told him, "Look, Chet, tell the Juice I've had it. Tell him to stop this crap once and for all. Who the hell does he think he is?"

"Howard, he's frightened," Forte said. "He's saying those things to protect himself."

"Don't you think I know that?" I said, my voice rising. "But I deserve better, damn it. All those years, all that help I gave him. Is this how I'm repaid?"

"What can I tell you, Howard?"

"Don't tell me anything. Tell Simpson!"

During the World Series, I had missed two *Monday Night Football* telecasts, and I dreaded returning to the package. It was perhaps the lowest point of my career. I was distraught. I didn't think I could face doing another football game.

I called Arledge, determined to quit the telecasts right then and there. Arledge was unavailable. Then I got to Tony Thomopolous, the president of the ABC Broadcast Group. "Tony, there's something urgent on my mind," I said. "I'd like to talk with you as soon as possible."

In a half an hour, we were having drinks at the Hampshire House bar on Central Park South.

"I can't go on any longer, Tony," I said. "I don't ever want to do another *Monday Night Football* game."

Thomopolous seemed shocked. "What's wrong?"

"It's an accumulation of so many factors," I said. "I'm tired of the traveling. I'm bored with the games. I hate the damned NFL. The press is always on my back. And I don't like what's happening in the booth. I could go on for hours."

Thomopolous listened intently as I aired my complaints, rarely interrupting.

"One thing's for certain, Tony. I'm not going to Dallas for the Sunday game against the Rams. I can't. It's not in me."

"Howard, believe me, I understand," he said. "If you're serious, I don't believe in Band-Aid procedures. Your emotional and physical health are more important than *Monday Night Football*, for Christ's sake. I'll make sure Arledge calls you, and we'll get this thing straightened out."

The next day, Arledge called, and we had a long lunch. I told him I couldn't hack it any longer, and I didn't want my professional life to end in unhappiness. After I enumerated in great detail all my reasons for wanting to quit the package, Arledge said, "I know exactly how you feel, Howard, I often feel the same way myself."

"Come on, Roone, let's cut the crap. Haven't you heard what I've been saying? I'm sick of the game. I'm sick of the jocks. And I'm sick of being the whipping boy of the press. They'll never write the truth about me. I want out!"

"All you need is a couple of weeks away," Arledge said, "and you'll come back refreshed. You'll see."

I told Arledge that I'd indeed take a brief vacation and then I'd get back to him. For the next several days, Emmy and I discussed my future. According to Emmy, the bottom line was this: "Go back and see the season through. You owe Arledge and the company that much. But after this year, no more. I've never been more serious in my life, Howard. You can renew your contract next year and stay on at ABC if you want—but absolutely no more *Monday Night Football*."

I spent my days working on my *SportsBeat* show and catching up on my reading and correspondence. The Sunday night I was scheduled to be in Dallas, I didn't even watch the game on television. I went to bed early and got a good night's sleep. It was bliss. I didn't care whether I was missed or not, though the next day I did find out that at least one person wished I had been there. That person was John Lazarus, then vice president in charge of sports sales. He was in charge of running the sponsors' party before the games. He sent me an interoffice memorandum that read: "Missed you in Dallas. As always, the jocks never showed up."

In the meantime, rumors of my quitting *Monday Night Football* began circulating around ABC and in the newspapers. When I didn't appear on the telecasts after the World Series, one press report went so far as to allege that Forte and I had a huge fight, and he had threatened to bolt the show unless I were fired. Naturally, ABC had no choice but to fire me. Can you believe that?

Then, one night, I got a call at my apartment from Simpson. He had heard the rumors, and he wondered if they were true. "You can't leave *Monday Night Football*, Howard," he said. "Without you, there is no *Monday Night Football*."

"Well, that's not what I've been reading in the newspapers."

"What're you talking about?"

"I don't know the game. You're the one who's going to bring fresh insights to the telecasts. Crap like that, all attributed to you."

"Come on, Howard. You know those fucking writers."

"No, Juice. The first time, maybe. But it's been happening too often for me to dismiss those stories as mere fantasy."

There was now desperation in Simpson's voice. "I was misquoted, Howard," he insisted. "I don't have to tell you about the writers. They twisted everything I said."

"You're no virgin, O.J. You've been dealing with the press since you were a kid."

"But Howard—"

"I don't want to talk to you, Juice. I was your friend. I always tried to help you, going back so many years. I can't believe the things you've been saying about me. I understand why you did it, but that's no excuse. It's over between us."

Simpson broke down and cried.

I handed the phone to Emmy. "You talk to him, dear," I said. "He's very upset."

When Emmy got on, Simpson said, "You know how much I love Howard and how much I love you. I never meant to hurt Howard. He's my dear friend."

Emmy kept saying, "Calm down, O.J. Calm down. Everything will work itself out."

Emmy really didn't know what else to say, and I got on again. I felt terrible. "We'll talk again when I see you, Juice," I said.

I eventually relented, and O.J. and I patched up our differences. He's basically a decent man. I'll always like him. We had come too far, I guess, not to remain friends.

On the last day of October, I returned to the telecast for a game in San Diego between the Chargers and the Redskins. It was a rather auspicious return, considering that the last time I called a Redskins' game I created a national furor. It gave me a weird feeling, and I hoped that the press wouldn't make a big deal out of it. The night before the game, I had a lovely chat with Garrett, who told me he had actually appreciated what I said about him on the air, and we laughed over the whole silly incident.

That game went smoothly. Despite my weariness with the show and my certitude about quitting at the end of the season, I was proud I hadn't let down. One of my greatest talents, I believe, is my unending ability to keep my energy level on a high plane, and I was able to mask my weariness and disaffection with the show by maintaining a spirited pace.

As the season wore on, however, I had to face yet another crisis, and even knowing that I was going to leave the package was small consolation.

That new crisis: declining ratings.

By the end of November, the ratings for *Monday Night Football* had dropped to 17.5, a decline of 19 percent from the record year of 1981. This represented a loss of about three million viewers, and sponsors were starting to demand "make goods"—more commercials on other programs—as compensation. Ratings for pro football telecasts were also down at CBS and NBC, but not as precipitously, and most stories focused on ABC.

Many factors were responsible for the decline in ratings: disillusionment with cocaine-snorting players, the lingering effects of the previous year's players' strike, the birth of the USFL and spring football, and the fractionalization of the marketplace—by that I mean the growth of cable and the surfeit of sports on television.

Some also pointed a finger at the multiplicity of dull games and a general malaise that had infected the NFL. And—you've guessed it—some even blamed me.

A column by Shirley Povich, an octogenarian columnist with *The Washington Post*, was typical. Climbing new heights of logic, Povich claimed that the viewers had put up with me for thirteen years, and they had finally had enough. Imagine the kind of twisted mind that would write that viewers suffered for thirteen years because of me. What about the record ratings all those years, Shirley? What was going on? Were fifty million people each week in the autumn suddenly gripped by a mass case of masochism?

As it happened, two days after Povich's column appeared, *Monday Night Football* featured a not-so-hot contest between the Detroit Lions and the Minnesota Vikings, and got a 21 rating with a 34 share, just like the old times. I guess the nation was into whips and chains that night. Right, Shirley?

In my heart, knowing all I knew about the television industry, I was convinced that *Monday Night Football* would never again achieve the ratings it had in 1981. It was practically impossible. The biggest single factors were the proliferation of cable and the growing popularity of VCR machines and video cassettes. The public was getting ever greater opportunities to choose the kind of home entertainment it wanted, and no longer would they be the captive audience of the three major networks.

But I had taken such a pounding from the press all my professional career that I began doubting myself. I began to wonder. Are they right? Am I really responsible for the decline in the ratings? Hell, you read criticism like that over and over again, and you begin to believe it yourself. That's the power of print.

The last game of the *Monday Night Football* season was scheduled for San Francisco. I didn't go. That was it. For the record, the last *Monday Night Football* game I worked was in Miami, the Dolphins against the Jets. It was a terrible game; Miami won easily. The Jets' coach, Joe Walton, had taken the best group of players in the NFL and reduced them to nothing. Another brilliant coaching mind.

At the start of 1984, I dedicated myself to a new season of my *SportsBeat* show, secure in my conviction never to work another *Monday Night Football* telecast. Arledge and the rest had been put on warning and knew how I felt. The next move was theirs. As for me, I would work through the Summer Olympics, then meet with Goldenson as I had promised and discuss my future. The members of the press could speculate all they wanted to. I'd fulfill my obligations to my company, then take it from there.

In early February, in a prime-time interview with Barbara Walters, she asked me: "Howard, earlier [in 1983] you decided you wanted to quit ABC. Realistically, you've got it all going for you. Why did you want to quit?"

"Because one reaches the point of boredom, no more challenges, and fatigue. Fatigue with travel, boredom with the contests. I don't care who wins or loses the game. I need challenge."

"It wasn't made public you wanted to quit. It was all hushed up, and you decided to stay until your contract is up in August."

"That's correct."

"But you said once, 'If I quit, I die.' "

"I suppose I did say that once, but times change, and anybody who adheres to a posture earlier enunciated when times change is a fool."

The next day, the newspaper guys started calling, wondering if my words on Barbara's show meant I was quitting *Monday Night Football*. I wasn't going to tell them anything until I had worked things out with Goldenson. The people in my company were protected. They knew where I stood, and that's all that really mattered to me.

At a charity dinner the following April, I ran into Meredith and his wife. "Are you really going to quit the show?" Meredith asked me.

"Believe me, Don, I'm gone."

"I'll be damned."

There were mixed emotions in Meredith's eyes and voice. Though he was hopeful that I'd really quit, I could sense that he also doubted I'd adhere to my decision. Won't he be surprised? I thought.

In July, I spoke before the National Press Club in Washington, then answered questions concerning my future, once again noting that I was sick and tired of football. This was just before my departure for Los Angeles to call the boxing at the Olympic Games. I hadn't spoken to Arledge for months. Several people in the company told me that he didn't believe I'd really leave *Monday Night Football*. I don't know how I could've been more forceful than I was at our last meeting. And besides, all Arledge had to do was sit down with me and say, "Okay, Howard, no more crap. I need to know now so that I can make my plans. Are you or are you not going to work *Monday Night Football*?"

I would've told him, "No, Roone—and you can take it to the bank."

As the months dwindled down toward the fall, I'm sure there were a lot of people at ABC who thought I'd have a change of heart, and they were probably telling Arledge, "Oh, it's only Howard making noises again. He entered the world with 'ABC' branded on his ass. It's his lifeblood."

In my opinion, this was Arledge's thinking: If Howard stays, fine. He's always reliable, and he's an integral part of *Monday Night Football*. If he goes, he goes. No sweat. The ratings will soar. Print will love Gifford, Meredith, and Simpson. I'm protected every way, and I'm rid of a guy who's always been a pain in the ass to me.

Still, I'm convinced that Arledge, down deep, never thought I'd leave the package.

Upon my return from the Olympic Games, where I had set a grueling pace, working day and night on the boxing, I took a week off to be with my family at our home in Westhampton Beach. It was then that I arranged to meet with Goldenson. We were joined by Pierce and Thomopolous. Arledge was not present; he had flown from Los Angeles to Dallas for the Republican Convention and then went on vacation.

We got right to it.

"Leonard, I made a commitment to you last year," I said, "and now it's time to keep it. I want to stay on with the company and continue working—radio, *SportsBeat*, some other things. However, I must leave *Monday Night Football*. You know all the reasons. I've talked it over again and again with Emmy, and it's what she wants, too. But if my remaining here is predicated on *Monday Night Football*, then I am prepared to leave altogether."

"I understand," Goldenson said, "but don't think you're leaving the company. We want you to stay. You're part of the family, and *Monday Night Football* has nothing to do with it."

"Anticipating this, Howard, I've already talked with Roone," Thomopolous said. "He agrees that considering what you've done for this company, you deserve to get what you want. You'll have to work out the details with him."

"I'll be happy to," I said.

"And we're happy you want to stay," Pierce said.

The day after my return to Westhampton Beach, I got a call from a sports television critic by the name of Larry Stewart, who writes for the *Los Angeles Times*. I had met Stewart at the Olympic Games but had no idea how he'd obtained my phone number.

"I understand that it's official, Howard," Stewart said. "You're not doing *Monday Night Football* anymore."

I assumed that ABC had issued a press release, and Stewart was following up. I patiently answered his questions, once again repeating my complaints about my boredom with the game and the pervasiveness of the Jockocracy and my concerns for my health and my family. The interview also touched on my meeting with Goldenson, Pierce, and Thomopolous and how they had agreed in principle to have me continue with *SportsBeat*, some baseball and tennis and horse racing broadcasts, and my national radio commentaries. "I'll work what I want to work," I told him. "When a man gets into his midsixties, it's time to cut back. As for *Monday Night Football*, it's the end of a chapter."

Stewart's story appeared the next day in Los Angeles—and then all hell broke loose. Without realizing it, I had given him a scoop. My company had yet to make any official announcement about my departure from *Monday Night Football*. How Stewart got his information is beyond me. Maybe he was just fishing, but it was certainly plausible for me to think that my company had already released my decision. At any rate, I was then inundated by countless requests for interviews to confirm Stewart's story. It was impossible to talk to everybody, but I handled the situation in as agreeable a manner as I could.

I thought it was over. It wasn't. Shortly after the story of my quitting *Monday Night Football* had appeared in newspapers all over the country, I got a call from Thomopolous.

"Have you heard from Arledge yet?" he asked.

I told him I hadn't.

"Well, I've got to level with you, he's pissed."

"I've got to level with you, Tony. Arledge can go shit in a hat. What the hell's the problem?"

"He feels that you've usurped his authority by going public with your decision to leave the package before telling him."

"Look, Tony, this is a lot of nonsense. I made my intentions known to the three top men in this company, and now I have to worry about Arledge? What are you telling me? If you want me, fine. If you don't want me, that's fine, too. Just tell me!"

"Howard, Howard, you know we want you. You know that. Now, Roone will simmer down. You'll get what was promised, but you have to work it out with Roone. It's company policy."

For the first time in my life, the majority of columns written about my leaving *Monday Night Football* were flattering. I received either letters or phone calls from almost every NFL owner, dozens of players, colleagues from within and without my company, and people from almost every walk of life, including the likes of Jesse Jackson, U.S. Senator Bill Bradley, and Kirk Douglas. It was extraordinary.

One letter in particular meant a lot to me. It was from Chuck Howard, a vice president of ABC Sports, a producer with whom I had worked closely for many years—and with whom I'd had my share of battles. Howard wrote: "*Monday Night Football* will 'endure' but it will not be the same. I am speaking not as a broadcaster but as a viewer when I say that your departure has caused a tremendous vacuum. You added a perspective and a dimension that will be sorely missed."

"I have always respected your professionalism and your decision to dance to your own tune, particularly in a year when we are televising the Super Bowl. It's simply another example of your character."

I never heard from Arledge. I had broken my back for him for thirteen years on *Monday Night Football*, and he never even called or dropped a line to say good-bye. What's more, it was impossible to make contact with him to discuss the terms of my new contract. Finally, on September 7, we happened to run into each other at the "21" Club. I was with Emmy, and she promptly asked Arledge about his separation from his second wife and wondered whom he was dating at the moment. Then she said, "Now, Roone, I want you to stop this nonsense with Howard. Get together with him and work out a new contract."

"Oh, Emmy, there's nothing to worry about. I have no problems with Howard."

I had overheard Emmy's conversation with Arledge as I was chatting with Helen Gurley Brown, the editor of *Cosmopolitan* magazine, and her husband, who were with Arledge for dinner. Arledge couldn't have been more ebullient with Emmy. As for Arledge and me, we simply greeted each other cordially but didn't converse. *Monday Night Football* never came up.

I didn't see or hear again from Arledge until almost two months later.

In the meantime, the ratings were falling precipitously, sending shock waves through ABC and Madison Avenue. After the third game of the season, the television sports critic of *USA Today*, Rudy Martzke, called my office to check out a rumor, to wit: The NFL was putting pressure on ABC to bring me back into the booth. I could neither confirm nor deny the rumor. I hadn't heard any such gossip, though I was told about a remark that passed between New York Jets' owner Leon Hess and Giants' owner Wellington Mara. Hess is a member of the ABC Board of Directors, and he assured Mara, "Don't worry about a thing. Howard's coming back for the telecasts."

Where Hess got his information, I'll never know.

At any rate, by the fourth prime-time telecast, a Sunday night game between the Denver Broncos and the Cleveland Browns, the ratings hit an all-time low of 9.5, which measures the percentage of homes with television sets. The next night, in a game between the Miami Dolphins and the Buffalo Bills, the telecast got a 14.9, inordinately low for a Monday night.

Panic set in. The following Monday night game, scheduled for September 24, was to match the defending Super Bowl champion Los Angeles Raiders and the San Diego Chargers—on paper, a terrific matchup. But the game was being played in the cavernous L.A. Coliseum, where the Raiders rarely sell out. That meant, under NFL rules, that the game would be blacked out in Los Angeles, the second largest television market in the country. ABC needed Los Angeles viewers to help boost its *Monday Night Football* ratings, and it tried desperately to get them.

How? I have it on good authority that an ABC officer called Raiders' owner Al Davis and offered him $200,000 if he'd voluntarily lift the blackout. Davis refused, realizing he'd make a helluva lot more money drawing fans who couldn't get the game on television.

The Raiders and the Chargers played one of the most exciting contests in the history of *Monday Night Football*. Trailing, 30–20, with nine minutes to go, the Raiders pulled out the game and won, 33–30. The ratings: a dismal 15.5.

The following week, the Cincinnati Bengals vs. the Pittsburgh Steelers got a 14.9, and then the San Francisco 49ers and the Giants reaped a pathetic 14.6—the lowest rating in 15 years of Monday night telecasts!

That night, NBC countered with a made-for-TV movie called *The Burning Bed*, starring Farrah Fawcett, which went through the ceiling with a 36.2 rating. To be sure, Farrah's movie was a good example of strong counterprogramming. But, hell, the other networks had always thrown their strongest stuff at us, and *Monday Night Football* had always prospered.

By the middle of the season, *Monday Night Football* ratings were down 9 percent over the previous year, and everybody was scurrying around trying to come up with reasons why. The 1982 players' strike was now two years in the past, and so that was beating a dead horse. Some of the factors that contributed to the decline of ratings in 1983 were still valid—such as boring contests, the signing of future stars by the USFL, and the proliferation of cable. It also didn't help that a recent U.S. Supreme Court ruling had left the colleges free to make their own television deals. This meant that on any given Saturday, viewers could watch what seemed like an endless supply of college football games. Everywhere you turned, there was football. Too much of it. Even CBS and NBC were experiencing sagging ratings on their pro football telecasts on Sunday.

As for *Monday Night Football*, an additional factor came into play: me!

I am sure that my absence had a negative effect on the ratings. Without me, the nature of the telecasts was entirely altered. I had commanded attention. I had palpable impact on the show, giving it a sense of moment, and now it seemed no different from an ordinary Sunday afternoon telecast. If that sounds like ego, what can I say? I'm telling it like it is.

And just about everybody in my company knew it. I can't tell you how many calls I got and how many conversations I had with members of the Board of Directors and others in positions of power, all of them asking me to return. The senior vice president of ABC Sports, Jim Spence, wanted me to appear as a guest commentator on a limited basis. I politely declined.

Several newspapers started conducting polls and surveys—and viewers voted overwhelmingly for my return. Even the sports television critics got into the act, running stories with headlines like, "Howie, Come Back!" and "Howard, the Guys Need You."

I had to laugh. These were the same guys who had blamed me for the drop in the 1983 ratings, and now they were eating crow. One sports television critic whose column I found particularly amusing was William Taaffe of *Sports Illustrated*. After the second month of the 1983 season, Taaffe wrote an encomium to Simpson. According to Taaffe, "Simpson comes across as warm, sincere and enthusiastic. He has an intensity and radiance about him that help compensate for his lack of language skill.

"Whenever O.J. appears with Frank Gifford and Danderoo—whenever Cosell disappears, that is—the crew's mood seems to improve. For a rookie in the booth, the Juice is unusually perceptive. . . ."

Fine. That's Taaffe's opinion. Then, however, Taaffe somehow managed to reach a conclusion that strained credulity. He said that Simpson was just the tonic that *Monday Night Football* needed to rescue it from its ratings doldrums. What?!?! For whatever reasons, the ratings didn't start declining until Simpson got into the booth, and there was Taaffe portraying him as a savior. The column was based on such a totally illogical premise that I wondered if *Sports Illustrated*'s editors had fallen asleep at their desks. Didn't anybody over there read the column before it got into the magazine?

A year later, Taaffe noted how the ratings were once again tumbling. But this time he wrote that "without Cosell the sense of wonder and drama is gone." Then he took out after Simpson, calling him repetitive, windy, and obscure, "in content if not location. Worse than that, he contradicts himself."

That's what I like about the sports television critics—their consistency.

Anyway, it was a pleasure having writers like Taaffe tripping over their own words. Hey, I'm only human. I'll not lie about it. Some small part of me, on a highly personal level, was gratified to witness the eroding ratings. I didn't want my company hurt, but if any performer tells you that he has terrible feelings about a show being less successful without him, don't believe it.

By the way, during all this time, I never heard from Arledge. He simply kept repeating in the press that it was too early to assess the impact of my absence on the ratings—and that all *Monday Night Football* really needed was a good game. What nonsense! Even the good games weren't drawing what they should have. The truth is that Arledge was loath to give me any credit. As I've said, I firmly believe that Arledge thought the ratings would soar with three jocks in the booth. He was wrong, and he wouldn't admit it.

As this disastrous trend continued, all sorts of solutions were offered to revitalize the game—and thus help goose the TV ratings. These included less obtrusive officiating, shortening the games, changing the scoring, more imaginative coaching, sprucing up the players' images, tighter screening of prospective owners to avoid more Bob Irsays coming into the league, and on and on and on.

Some of these ideas are constructive. On the other hand, the folks at the networks and the NFL must consider a larger and more disturbing question: Have people simply had their fill of football? In my opinion, they have. As I've said before, it's practically impossible for the networks ever to recapture its record ratings in 1981. The revolutionary changes in the industry—cable, home video machines—militate against it. This is not to suggest that the networks can't improve on 1984's depressing showing. They can, but they must also realign their expectations according to the new realities of the marketplace.

In the future, for example, it appears that ABC will have to be happy with, say, an average rating of 18 or 19 for *Monday Night Football*. The result: ABC must adjust its advertising rates, which in turn means that the NFL can no longer expect a financial windfall from the networks for the rights to its games. When the networks' five-year, $1.2 billion contract with the NFL is up after the 1986 season, it will be very interesting to see just how much the NFL demands for a new deal and how much the networks are willing to pay.

As far as *Monday Night Football* goes, if I were negotiating for ABC, I'd tell Rozelle flat out: Let's cut the crap. If you want the kind of money we're paying you, then you must give my company the right to pick the games it telecasts. The way the arrangement stands now, the NFL chooses the Monday night schedule in the preceding February, and there's nothing ABC can do about it. It's a terrible deal. *Monday Night Football* made the NFL the dominant professional sports league in America, and ABC deserves better. "Pete, forget about CBS and NBC," I'd say. "We're the guys who made you, and these are the games we want. After all, if *Monday Night Football* scores big, the impact is felt not only by the NFL but throughout the entire television industry as well."

On a number of occasions during the 1984 season, I received requests from sportswriters and television critics to watch a *Monday Night Football* telecast with me in my living room. I turned them all down. The fact is, I never watched an entire game. If I watched at all, I barely made it through the half-time highlights before falling asleep. I was through with *Monday Night Football*, and I was happy for it.

I watched enough to know, however, that the telecasts were dreadful. There was never a story line, only discussions of play upon play upon play. No perspective. No reportage beyond the game. No humanization of the players. Only feeble attempts at humor, trying to be funny and prove they could prosper without me. There wasn't a skilled performer among them.

Meredith was lost. He had nobody to react to. I didn't know whether he was a singer, a cowboy, a philosopher, a clown, or what. Unlike Meredith, at least the Juice had points to make, but he was ultimately miscast. He couldn't articulate spontaneously and thus wasn't understandable to the viewers.

As for Gifford, I got embarrassed listening to him make mistake after mistake. Funny, when you're in the booth, you tend to overlook a lot of Frank's mistakes because you're concentrating on your own job. That's impossible, however, when you're listening to him on television. And he came across like a male mannequin, his voice still too weak and undramatic to have any impact.

The half-time highlights were a joke. I had turned them into one of the most popular moments on television. My replacement, Jim Lampley, couldn't match my delivery. Okay, he had a tough act to follow, and there were times when I felt sorry for him. But, hell, the kid's no dope. He had to know he'd suffer by comparison. He never should have allowed himself to be placed in that position.

There was constant speculation as to who could replace me to enliven the telecasts. Two names kept popping up: John Madden and Brent Musberger, both of CBS.

In the weeks before Christmas, Arledge pursued Musberger, offering him many plum assignments, including baseball, the Olympic Games, and *Monday Night Football.* I thought Arledge was right to go after Musberger. He's glib, knowledgeable, and quick on his feet. I've certainly had my reservations about him. He's often a hype artist and only sometimes a journalist, but he's better than Gifford, Lampley, and Al Michaels. He'd be a plus for ABC.

But on *Monday Night Football?* Come on. Musberger is not a broad-based performer who can reach a huge, diverse, prime-time audience. He's perfect for weekend afternoons, which is the province of male sports fans. Those people like him—but he'd have limited appeal on *Monday Night Football.* He doesn't possess star quality. Here's a guy who was profiled in *Sports Illustrated,* and the thrust of the article concerned his relative anonymity, even though he appears countless hours on television each weekend. Some impact.

Madden has a higher recognition quotient than Musberger, but he's got other problems. On a personal level, he's an outstanding man. In 1978, while still coaching the then Oakland Raiders, one of his players, defensive back Jack Tatum, viciously tackled a New England Patriots' wide receiver named Darryl Stingley and knocked him out of the game. Later it was learned that Stingley had suffered severe spinal damage and would end up a quadriplegic, forever consigned to a wheelchair. Madden was at Stingley's bedside, stayed with him and prayed for him, and eventually organized benefits to help Stingley financially.

That's the kind of man Madden is. Unfortunately, as sensitive and interesting as he is, he's allowed himself to become an overblown parody of himself, a caricature bursting through a screen with a beer can in his hands. He's in danger of becoming a lot of sound and fury signifying nothing. He screams and bellows and waves his arms and talks about linebackers' eyes and arcane strategy. His chalkboard routine is a bore and a waste of time. ABC used the same technique in 1961—then abandoned it because it was no damned good. But the sports television critics love it, and they regale Madden as another Einstein. A chalkboard is a helluva way to communicate, isn't it?

In my opinion, Madden has already reached the peak of his popularity. He's beginning to turn off a lot of viewers who aren't rabid sports fans. For the most part, he is a creation of the sports print medium, and he's not remotely qualified to restore the luster of *Monday Night Football*. To call him a prime-time performer is to know nothing about television.

Which raises the question: Who *can* ABC use to boost *Monday Night Football*'s ratings?

ABC needs a star. Let's not forget that first and foremost *Monday Night Football* is prime-time entertainment. It must attract big numbers, women as well as men. Okay, how about someone like Bill Cosby? That's right, Bill Cosby. He'd really shake things up, make people take notice. A former college football player and an avid sports enthusiast, he knows what he's talking about. What's more, he's a brilliant communicator, and his performing skills are above reproach. In short, he's a prime-time dream, witty, knowledgeable, and vastly entertaining.

At the moment, Cosby's got a fantastically successful sitcom on NBC, and he's not available. Too bad for ABC—but that's the way the company should be thinking. Hiring another ex-jock just isn't going to hack it.

Early November was the next time I saw Arledge. We met at a party for Mike Burke, the former president of the Yankees, Knicks, and Rangers who had just published his autobiography. We posed for pictures with Mike. Then I talked with Arledge about his delay in working out a new contract with my lawyer.

"Look, Roone," I said, "I really don't know what your game is, but you have no problems with me. You know what I want. It's a simple matter."

"We're all set, Howard. In fact, I've arranged to have *Sports-Beat* follow David Brinkley on Sundays. It's where you wanted to be and where you belong. It's a much better spot."

"I'm appreciative, Roone, but let's conclude our deal. Okay?"

"No problem, Howard."

And that was that. Arledge never brought up the subject of *Monday Night Football* and the declining ratings. I think he was embarrassed. What's more, he had to know my feelings about the telecasts—I'm certain others in the company had told him—and he didn't want to get into a debate with me, opening up the possibility that he'd have to give me credit for what I had done for the show—and how lousy it was without me.

A month later, I was invited to attend a party thrown at the Four Seasons by Jets' owner Leon Hess for his son, who was soon getting married. Goldenson was there early, waiting for his wife, and Emmy and I had a long chat with him.

"Howard, would you consider doing the Super Bowl?" Goldenson asked me.

"Ask Emmy," I said.

"I'm sorry, Leonard, but we're through with the NFL. I really don't want Howard to be any part of it. And I'm sure he feels the same way."

"Emmy's right, Leonard. I just can't do it. It's not in me. I hope you understand."

"Of course, I do, Howard," Goldenson said, "but I thought I'd ask."

I then spoke freely, giving my unvarnished opinions of the *Monday Night Football* telecasts. Goldenson agreed with me and said he wanted changes made. The package simply couldn't go on in its present form, he said.

"The fact is, Leonard," I said, "Arledge thought the ratings would climb without me. He thought America would fall in love with three jocks in the booth."

"Howard, I must tell you, I never heard Roone say that. He never once even hinted at it. Everybody knows that you made

Monday Night Football, and I think Roone feels the same way. He never said anything to make me think otherwise."

Then it happened, just as I knew it would. The sports television critics had waited all season to prove that I wasn't responsible for the decline in the ratings—and they finally got their chance. It came during the last game of the year, Dallas vs. Miami, perhaps the most significant contest ever to appear on *Monday Night Football.* For all intents and purposes, Miami vs. Dallas was a playoff game, affecting the postseason aspirations of four cities. Two of those cities represented the biggest TV markets in the country, New York and Los Angeles. Millions of viewers had a genuine rooting interest in the outcome of the game.

The cards were stacked in ABC's favor, and the game ended up with a terrific 25.1 ratings and a 40 share, by far the most successful telecast of the year. In the wake of those numbers, take a guess as to what was written in the press. Naturally. See, fans, Cosell's absence really meant nothing after all. Give the fans a great game, and they'll tune in. Who cares about the announcers?

What a joke! In their minds, a single game—and one that had huge significance—wiped out an entire season of faulty ratings. ABC couldn't miss with that game, but no matter. How myopic!

There was no fooling the hierarchy at ABC, though. At a meeting between Pierce and Herb Granath, the president of ABC Video Enterprises, Pierce laughed off the stories in the newspapers. "How can they say one game makes the season?" he said. "One game proves we don't miss Howard, right?"

"Fred, there's no getting around it," Granath said. "A lot of the mystique is gone. And you know how you spell mystique?"

"C-O-S-E-L-L," he responded.

In the first week of 1985, after a full *Monday Night Football* season, I finally had the chance to go head to head with Arledge and let off some steam. He had jerked me and my lawyer around on my contract for almost four months, and we were at last drawing close to a settlement. The delay had infuriated me. Here I was, a loyal employee of ABC for thirty years, a guy who had busted his ass for the network and helped bring it recognition and profits, and I had to sit by while Arledge went after Musberger of CBS instead of taking care of me first. It was outrageous, and I think any devoted employee of any big company would have felt the same way.

Be that as it may, when Arledge and I met for lunch, I put that all behind me. We were joined by Dorrance Smith, the executive producer of *This Week with David Brinkley*. Smith was in the process of launching a Saturday edition of *World News Tonight*, and both he and Arledge wanted me to make regular appearances on the show. I refused.

"But it'll be good for you, Howard," Arledge said. "Think of the exposure."

"Don't talk to me about exposure," I snapped. "I'm long past that kind of crap. My celebration in this country is higher than it ever was. All I had to do was leave *Monday Night Football* and expose it for what it is with your damned jocks. I've had the greatest year of my life. I don't need exposure, I need privacy. I've gotten everything I ever wanted out of this industry and more. I've done some job for my company. Even you can't quarrel with that."

During the course of the lunch, Arledge told me he was thinking of replacing either Meredith or Simpson—or perhaps both—in the booth for the Super Bowl telecast. He wouldn't reveal more than that, and I didn't push him. "No big deal," I said. "You'll get a sensational rating anyway. Hell, Miami against San Francisco, it's perhaps the best matchup in the history of the Super Bowl. It doesn't matter whom you put on the air."

"Well, you know, Howard, the game's the thing. That's what's really important."

"Yeah, I've read that, and it's a lot of garbage. You can't have the Super Bowl every week. I had more awful games than I can count, and *Monday Night Football* continued to have a mystique. Why? I was the mystique, and nobody else."

"Why did you think you were there?" Arledge asked.

"To add guts and life to a damned football game! And for that, I had to subvert myself to a couple of jocks every week. That's a great way to live, right?"

"Howard, come on. When you felt it was time for you to leave, I didn't push you to stay."

"You're right, Roone. But let's lay it on the line. You thought you were safe with the jocks. You thought the ratings would skyrocket without me."

"That's wrong, Howard. It's ridiculous for you to think like that."

"I'll give you this, Roone: Leonard Goldenson backs you up. He did tell me that you had indicated you were worried over my loss on the package."

"That's true, Howard. Believe me."

Quite frankly, I didn't believe him. If Arledge had really believed he needed me, he would've come to me and told me so. He could've asked me to remain on *Monday Night Football*. He never did.

Several days after my lunch with Arledge, it was announced that the Washington Redskins' quarterback, Joe Theismann, would replace O. J. Simpson in the booth for the Super Bowl. I like Joe. He's an articulate young man. However, I think it's bad policy to have an active player in the booth. How can he really speak his mind? What kind of journalistic integrity can he possibly summon while commenting on a game? He's still tied to a team and tied to the league, and his loyalties are necessarily divided. During the course of a game, he most surely faces this dilemma: Do I inform the viewer with my critical analysis of what's just transpired—or should I keep my thoughts to myself so as not to offend a fellow player or coach who happen to be friends of mine?

Theismann's selection confirmed in my own mind Arledge's profound belief in the Jockocracy, no matter how strenuously he may deny it. What's more, he hired Dallas coach Tom Landry to be part of the telecast, yet another indication to me of the course he had set for ABC Sports.

The most disturbing aspect of the Super Bowl switch was the public humiliation of the Juice. It was wrong. The decision to replace the Juice was made on high. Certain members of the ABC hierarchy were disappointed in the Juice's performance during the season and wanted him out of the booth. Arledge was following orders. Why Arledge chose a replacement with far less experience than Simpson is his business, but he shouldn't take the blame for the Juice's demotion.

In the days following the announcement, the NAACP made numerous calls to ABC, protesting its treatment of Simpson, and the organization's displeasure was ultimately reported in the press. I felt sorry for Simpson. It must've come as a shock to him, but he handled the situation with dignity and grace, alleging that he was happy to participate in the pre- and postgame segments of the show.

At first I thought that Simpson's demotion meant that he would not return to *Monday Night Football* for the 1985 season. I may have been wrong. After the telecast, Simpson received laudatory reviews for predicting San Francisco's victory and running back Roger Craig's big day. Simpson had made a comeback. Whether his Super Bowl performance helps him survive remains to be seen, but he's got a good shot.

Actually, Simpson had a better day than his colleagues. In general, I thought the performers rated a C. In contrast to the technical merits of the telecast, the performers were lackluster, adding little to enhance the presentation of the game. Gifford was his usual one-note self, but he got hardly any help from Theismann or Meredith. Theismann had nothing to offer. I can't recall him making even one thought-provoking comment, and there were long stretches when he didn't even utter a single word. To be kind, I guess I could say that the normally talkative Theismann exercised commendable restraint. Then again, how much can I or anybody expect from someone who had appeared as a color analyst on only one other occasion before being thrown into the Super Bowl?

As for Meredith, again he wasn't prepared. By now, his disinterest in what he's doing must surely be apparent to anyone over the age of two. When Carl Monroe scored San Francisco's first touchdown, Meredith yelled, "Wendell!!!" as in Wendell Tyler. And he kept telling us that the 49ers were getting to Miami quarterback Dan Marino, but he didn't try to explain what was going wrong and how Marino might overcome the problems that were haunting him.

The Landry gimmick with the Telestrator was a waste of time. For one thing, Landry might be a brilliant football coach, but as a television personality, he's a national cure for insomnia. And why the hell was ABC using a gimmick that it had abandoned two decades before? A lot of people probably thought we were merely following CBS's lead. It made no sense.

As dull as I thought the telecast was—and in spite of the lopsided nature of the game—I was still convinced that ABC would score a record rating. After all, the game featured the two best teams and the two most glamorous quarterbacks in Marino and Joe Montana, and an Arctic chill that covered almost two thirds of the country seemed certain to keep people indoors and huddled around their television sets.

When the ratings were released, I was surprised. The game got a 46.4 rating and a 63 share, making it the fifth-highest-rated Super Bowl and tying the previous year's contest between the Redskins and the Raiders. Many in the company were bitterly disappointed. I couldn't blame them. The numbers were terrific, sure, but ABC was hoping for a record to end the desultory *Monday Night Football* season on a promising note. It wasn't to be.

In my opinion, Super Bowl ratings have peaked, just as they have for *Monday Night Football*. The changes in the industry that I have already mentioned are irreversible. The marriage between the NFL and the networks has entered a period of reevaluation and readjustment. Those halcyon days of yore are gone for good.

As you have read earlier, my distaste for the NFL and what it had come to stand for contributed to my quitting *Monday Night Football*. I truly wish it hadn't turned out that way, but I have no regrets about helping to popularize the league and its game. I simply did the best job I could. The huge success of *Monday Night Football* has always astounded me, and it's still hard for me to explain the electrifying impact it had on the public. The fame and recognition the show brought me will forever mystify me. But it's over now, and I'd like to leave the frustrations and heartaches behind me. I think I can. In quieter moments, when I think back on *Monday Night Football*, I'm starting to remember the good old days. And yes, Frank, Don, O.J., there's a smile on my face.

7

One Fight Too Many

These rites are a bit trying, but they simplify everything. Good and evil, the winner and the loser: At Corinth, two temples stood side by side—the Temple of Violence and the Temple of Necessity.

—Albert Camus, *Lyrical and Critical Essays*

Albert Camus was once an amateur boxer himself and remained a lifelong fight fan. The emotional satisfaction he got out of boxing was at odds with his intellectual opposition to violence and capital punishment, and it provoked ambivalent feelings within him.

I know exactly how he felt.

Boxing is drama on its grandest scale. No other athletic event is as electrifying as a championship fight. I continued to cover boxing perhaps longer than I should have because of my admiration for the fighters, their earthiness, and their honesty. Generally speaking, the ones who become champions spring from poverty; they work harder and sacrifice more than other athletes. Rarely do they make excuses. They have no teammates to lean on. They are out there all alone, exposed, vulnerable, valiantly summoning up reserves of courage in situations where a lot of other athletes would simply call it quits. There are no secrets in the ring, and they willingly accept the fears and the pain and the scars as part of their trade.

One need only climb into a ring to understand how terrifyingly small it is and what guts it takes to ascend those three or four little steps to engage in battle with another man. And always they must wonder, "How will it be when I come out?"

Early on, in the days when ABC was carrying the big fights on radio, I worked with the late undefeated heavyweight champion Rocky Marciano, and it was through him that I learned a lot about the inside of boxing. At the time, my interest was further inspired by a great writer named W. C. Heinz, and I became fascinated with fighters as people.

Few athletes were more captivating subjects than Floyd Patterson, who carried his emotional baggage like a huge stone on his shoulders, who used to sit alone and afraid in the subways beneath the Bedford-Stuyvesant section of Brooklyn. And then there was Patterson's eccentric manager, Cus D'Amato, a reporter's dream. His Freudian lectures on boxers and boxing made you feel like you were sitting in a musty old classroom in Vienna.

I called nearly all of Patterson's championship fights, and then after Patterson came Muhammad Ali, and we would become locked in the public's mind as an inseparable television team.

Joe Frazier and George Foreman were also favorites of mine, and soon thereafter came Sugar Ray Leonard—and I had the same kind of identification with him as I had had with Ali.

And so it was, until all my years of covering fights and fighters came crashing down around me, and I could no longer justify my association with the sport.

• • •

November 26, 1982. The Houston Astrodome. On that date, in that place, WBC heavyweight champion Larry Holmes beat up Randall (Tex) Cobb in as gross a mismatch as I have ever witnessed. In the ninth round alone, Holmes registered no fewer than twenty-six unanswered blows—and yet the referee would not stop the fight. Mercifully, the champion laid back in the fourteenth and fifteenth rounds so as not to inflict further damage upon Cobb, who was nothing more than a human punching bag with a tremendous capacity to absorb punishment.

During that fight, I made up my mind to walk away from professional boxing forever. At the time, it was perhaps the most significant decision of my career—and I stuck to it.

For almost a quarter of a century, I was ABC's boxing specialist, its most visible association with the sport, more durable than the fighters themselves. When ABC underwrote mismatches, I said so on the air, loudly and clearly. And when referees and judges rendered lousy decisions, I said so on the air, loudly and clearly. "Tell it like it is" is a phrase that people most likely identify with my coverage of boxing.

There is no denying it, however—my public persona helped revitalize boxing's once flagging popularity and boosted its TV ratings. And, of course, boxing gave me my first glimpse of media stardom, and I'd be less than honest if I didn't admit that I was gripped by a spellbinding attraction to the sport.

My disaffection with boxing, however, did not begin with the Holmes-Cobb mismatch. Ten years earlier, I had appeared before the Senate Commerce Subcommittee headed by then Senator Marlow Cook of Kentucky. I called for a federal sports commission with two purposes in mind: one, to regulate the movement of professional sports franchises from one city to another; and two, to regulate and control professional boxing.

It distressed me that the various state boxing commissions operated as independent fiefdoms and that there was no uniform code to deal with boxers' safety, records, and ratings. Such a lack of national uniformity led to many abuses; for example, a fighter denied a fight in one state could quickly obtain a license to fight in another state. And as the 1970s wore on, I was increasingly concerned about the power that was falling into the hands of promoters Don King and Robert Arum, the kind of power that the courts had ruled illegal years before.

King derives much of his power through his friendship with Jose Sulaiman, the president of the World Boxing Council. Arum's connections are lodged in the World Boxing Association. The WBC is based in Mexico City, the WBA in Panama, and each has often in the past handed down rulings that defy logic and arouse suspicions of political chicanery. These organizations play by their own rules and create their own champions—and unless a promoter or manager is part of one or the other's inner circle, he will have a helluva time getting proper recognition for his fighter.

For example: If either King or Arum has a fighter he wants to get a shot at a title, or needs an opponent for one of his champions—presto!—the fighter is suddenly ranked in the top ten of his division to legitimize the match.

The WBC and WBA are allowed to exist for two reasons: one, the willingness of the overwhelming majority of sportswriters to tolerate them and concentrate instead on the fights—with the notable exception of a crusading reporter named Jack Newfield of *The Village Voice*; and two, the financial support of the three American commercial television networks, which continue to televise phony title fights and egregious mismatches. In their consuming hunger for ratings, it's the networks that subsidize the WBC and WBA, and if they refused to recognize those two ruling bodies tomorrow and use some other independent source for ranking fighters, it could be a start toward cleaning up the sport.

Another factor in my growing disenchantment with boxing came in the winter of 1977, when ABC staged a tournament called the United States Boxing Championships. It seemed a dream come true for many faceless, hardworking fighters who toiled in backwater arenas for a couple of hundred bucks and the use of a locker. This was to be their opportunity for glory, and the tournament was universally praised in publications such as *The New York Times* and *Sports Illustrated*.

It was King who had persuaded Roone Arledge, the president of ABC Sports, to bankroll the tournament. To safeguard ABC's interests, Arledge got King to agree to two stipulations. He was to use Jim Farley, the chairman of the New York State Athletic Commission, as a consultant charged with selecting referees and judges for the matches. He was also to use *Ring* magazine as his source for fighters' records and rankings.

But soon the whispers of favoritism, kickbacks, falsified records, and rigged ratings began to threaten the integrity and the success of the tournament. When he first heard the whisperings of corruption, Arledge demanded affidavits from King and the editors of *Ring* that no favoritism and no kickbacks existed in the tournament. Then he started collecting affidavits from the fighters and their managers. After the sixth week of fights, Arledge pulled the tournament off the air.

I was a minor principal in the story. Once the deal for the tournament was sealed, I stepped in to call the fights, dishing out praise and criticism as each match warranted it. In doing my job, I was fair and impartial. In fact, when a heavyweight named Scott LeDoux lost a controversial decision to Johnny Boudreaux, I stayed on top of the story. After the fight, LeDoux went berserk in the ring, screaming, "Fix! Fix!" I insisted on interviewing Le-Doux, and he fully aired his accusations, condemning the tournament for favoring fighters handled by the late Paddy Flood and Al Braverman, a pair of managers who worked with King.

Nevertheless, as ABC's most visible on-air personality, I took a lot of the heat. One sportswriter went so far as to call me "the architect of a boxing scandal."

It was an unholy mess. To be sure, there were gross improprieties. King and his cronies had played fast and loose with ABC, and somehow I got caught in the middle. But let me say this: It was ABC that initiated its own investigation into the sordid affair and took the tournament off the air. Afterward, the Federal Communications Commission found that the tournament was unquestionably tainted, but investigations by the Congress, the FBI, the attorney general's office of the state of New York, and the U.S. District Court for New York State's Southern District (Manhattan) yielded not a single criminal indictment.

For me, however, that brought little solace. Through all the years, I wasn't naïve enough to think that I was covering a pristine sport. Corruption was all around, and I was trying to cope with it as best I could. But nothing was changing, no matter how hard I tried to expose the dirty underbelly of the sport, and my involvement in it served only to frustrate me more.

What was going on outside the ring was one thing. My attitudes toward the fights themselves were changing, too. Unlike any other sport, the objective in boxing is chillingly simple: One man purposefully endeavors to inflict bodily harm on another man. And I had seen Benny Paret die and Willie Classen die and Cleveland Denny die, and the dying slowly eats away at you. I had seen Earnie Shavers and Sugar Ray Leonard hurt their eyes, and I had seen Sugar Ray Seales receive permission to fight even though he was close to blindness. And I couldn't shake the gut-wrenching anguish of watching Ali in his twilight as one comeback after another stripped him of his dignity and stature.

You can't imagine how I felt when I ran into Ali shortly after his last fight. I was in Los Angeles attending a banquet. Ali was there. Though still a relatively young man, he was puffy, and he moved slowly, almost deliberately. Once a symphony of metaphors and rhymes, his speech was now thick, and he spoke in half-completed whisperings. Too many blows to the head and body had transformed him into somebody I no longer knew. He put his arm around me, and he said, "I'm gone, and you're still on top."

"Don't ever say that to me again, Muhammad," I said. "You're part of American history. You'll never be gone."

And so the horrible feelings were there, chipping away at my romance with boxing. Then those same feelings started to fester and sicken me. In the weeks preceding the Holmes-Cobb mismatch, a couple of events contributed to my ultimate disillusionment. First, Boom Boom Mancini defended his WBA lightweight title against a Korean named Duk Koo Kim—because the WBA somehow managed to rate Kim the No. 1 contender. There were much more worthy opponents—such as Howard Davis and Edwin Rosario—but Kim got the nod. By most reliable accounts, he did not even deserve to be ranked in the top ten. Mancini knocked Kim out, and later Kim lapsed into a coma and died.

In a display of chutzpah that was enraging, Arum solemnly called for a two-month moratorium in the wake of the fight that he himself had promoted. It happened that all the major fights in that two-month period belonged to Arum's archrival King.

Next was the fight between Aaron Pryor and Alexis Arguello for the junior welterweight title. A legitimate fight, yes, but that fact didn't ease my distress as I watched the proud and cunning Arguello succumb to a savage barrage of blows in the fourteenth round. Arguello lay unconscious in the ring for three or more minutes, and I feared for his life.

All through the week before the Holmes-Cobb fiasco, I had proclaimed the fight a travesty. I was even quoted to that effect in newspapers around the country. Why, then, did I go to Houston to cover it? Because I was contractually bound to work it, and I had not yet reached my breaking point. Nevertheless, I felt obliged as a journalist to give my opinion of the fight, and if potential viewers took it as a warning not to watch ABC that night, so be it. That was a risk I had taken within my company many times previously—and a risk I was prepared to take again.

On the day of the fight, my contempt for the parasites in boxing reached such a degree that to avoid the sleaze in the hotel lobby, I went to Holmes's room to play a set of gin rummy with him. Talk of the fight was obviously unavoidable. "Why do you keep knocking this fight, Howard?" Holmes asked me.

"Because it's a joke, and you know it. No way in the world this guy can beat you."

Holmes chuckled. "Unless I slip and bust my head."

"I don't really want to do this fight, Larry. It shouldn't take place."

"C'mon, Howard. Cobb's a big boy. He can take care of himself."

"Maybe. But with all that's happened this month in boxing, Duk Koo Kim and Arguello, and with boxing under such scrutiny, it's wrong."

"I'm just trying to make some money, that's all. Nothing wrong with that."

Holmes and I weren't getting anywhere, but I couldn't get terribly upset with him. I had liked Holmes from the beginning, when he was Ali's sparring partner. It's a temptation to say that he copied Ali's style and that he was a poor imitation of the self-proclaimed Greatest, but Holmes was indeed a helluva fighter. And I always said so. He was blessed with a marvelous left jab, pistonlike in its recurring power—bang, bang, bang, bang, bang; and that punch set up a nifty right hand, all of which were complemented by superb footwork. He often said to me, "Make me big, Howard. Make me big like you did Ali and Leonard."

There was in Holmes a great insecurity and a great longing for recognition. As Ali's successor, he suffered in comparison, and he blamed the sportswriters for denying him his due. I sympathized with his frustration and became increasingly supportive of him. Once, I had both Holmes and then WBA heavyweight champion Mike Weaver in a studio for separate interviews. I said to Weaver, "Mike, you have fought Larry Holmes. You had him, but he came back and knocked you out in the twelfth round. Do you feel that you're the real champion now, or is Holmes?

"No, Howard, I'm not," Weaver confessed. "Until I beat Holmes, he's the real champion."

Holmes was standing in the wings, watching the interview, and he was positively ecstatic.

Not long afterward, in June 1981 in Detroit, Holmes beat up Leon Spinks. While interviewing Holmes at ringside, I spotted Gerry Cooney, a future challenger for the title, and called him over. Holmes suddenly went berserk, screaming at Cooney on the air. Then he started shaking his fist and threw a punch in Cooney's direction—cutting my lip in the process. I closed the show by telling my wife, "Don't worry about a thing, Emmy. I'm fine, see you tomorrow."

The following morning, Holmes met me at the studio for a follow-up interview for *Wide World of Sports*. We showed that crazy scene and talked about it. Holmes was very upset by it. "I don't know what came over me, Howard," he said. "I apologize. You know how I feel about you and all you've done for me."

Holmes also invited my wife and me to Larry Holmes Day in his hometown of Easton, Pennsylvania, and we gladly accepted. I was called on to speak, and I praised Holmes's integrity. "I respect this man not only as a fighter but as a person," I said. "He could make millions for a fight in South Africa, but he will never accept. He will never fight in the land of apartheid because this man stands for what he believes in."

The crowd went wild, and Holmes got up and hugged me. Later he insisted that Emmy and I visit his home, and he and his wife were delightful hosts.

That respect between us would crack and crumble as a result of Holmes's fight with Cobb.

By the end of the fifth round, I figured that the referee—a man named Steve Crosson from Dallas—would shortly stop the fight. But no. Crosson let it continue, and I kept wondering on the air why he was permitting the debacle to go on. Sitting by my side was Don Chevrier, whom ABC was thinking of using as a substitute for me when the occasion warranted it. I was helping to break him in that night, and he thoroughly agreed with me.

The ninth round was an assault on the senses of any civilized human being. Twenty-six unanswered blows. Cobb's face looked like hamburger meat—but still Crosson failed to stop the fight. "Doesn't he know," I said, referring to the referee, "that he is constructing an advertisement for the abolition of boxing?!?!"

From then on, I did not comment at all on the fight strategy or tactics. There weren't any. The only intelligent and humane thing to do, I felt, was to keep calling for the referee to end the fight, which I did. I also repeatedly fixed the blame for this bloodbath on the referee, and to this day, I still contend it was as measured a performance as I've ever given.

I had no intention of insulting the audience with how-tough-Cobb-is anecdotes. And I had no intention of becoming a two-bit shill and telling the audience to stay tuned, because, you never know, Cobb might win the championship with one punch.

Moments after the judges awarded a unanimous decision to Holmes—what a surprise!—ABC's director of the telecast, Chet Forte, informed me from the truck that New York wanted me to jump into the ring and interview the referee. "Let Chevrier do it," I said disgustedly. "That man should have stopped the fight. He was unqualified, and I will not dignify him with an interview."

"I agree with you, Howard," said Alex Wallau, the producer. "You're absolutely right."

"I agree, too, Howard, but what the hell am I supposed to do?" Forte said. "They're ordering me."

Forte was referring to instructions that were coming out of New York from Jim Spence, vice president of ABC Sports. "You'd better say something," Forte urged. "They're all over me."

So I did. "I will not dignify this fight with any interviews," I said on the air. "I think what you have seen tonight speaks for itself."

It was sickening. As I was leaving the arena, people were shouting, "Hey, Howie, that Texan sure can take a punch, can't he?" And I thought, Good Lord, don't they realize what's happened here? Four days, four weeks, four months, four years from now that man is going to pay for the pounding he took.

I had had it.

The next morning at six o'clock, before catching a plane to Tampa for a *Monday Night Football* game, I called John Martin, vice president of ABC Sports, at his apartment in New York. "What a terrible experience," Martin said. "I felt sorry for you."

"John, I've made a decision," I said. "I am never going to call another professional fight."

"Come on, Howard, you can't take that position. What about your contract? You're bound to us for the championship fights at least."

"I realize that, John, but I'm not going to do them, and the company has a perfect right to fire me. It's that simple."

"What am I going to tell the media people?"

"That's up to you, because I will tell them my position if anybody should get to me and ask."

The following Monday night in Tampa, before going on air, I got a call from Martin. He wondered if, in light of our previous conversation, I wanted to call two important upcoming fights. He was merely following routine, and I appreciated that. Under the terms of my contract, I got first call on such fights. I told him, no, I was sticking to my position.

The next day I took a call from David Kindred, then with *The Washington Post*; he was a man I regarded as a truly forthright columnist. He told me that his editor, George Solomon, felt that I had gone too far in my denunciations of boxing during the Holmes-Cobb telecast, and he wanted a reaction.

"Solomon has a right to feel that way, David, but I'm sorry—I know a lot more about boxing and I've lived with boxing many more years than he has. I did what I had to do by my precepts. I've had it."

"Well, Howard, you made me think," Kindred said. "I'm wondering why I'm still covering boxing. I thought you delivered a superb polemic against the sport, and that's what I'm going to write. I'm not siding with my editor on this one, not at all."

"You do what you think is right, David," I said. "But I promise you this: I will never call another professional fight. I will call amateur fights, but never a professional one."

(My decision to stick with amateur boxing was based on my respect for the people who run the sport. They care about the fighters, and they take every precaution to ensure the safety of the young men in their charge. It was a joy to be around those fighters and trainers, and there were no greedy, scheming promoters to deal with.)

Two days later, Kindred's column appeared, expressing my thoughts on my decision to leave professional boxing. Kindred quoted my belief that the blame for boxing's sickness today fell on three groups. "First, the networks who make possible the continued existence of organizations such as the WBA and WBC, which exist only for the purpose of creating championships that the networks, including ABC-TV, can sell for top dollar.

"Second to blame are the ruthless, sleazy promoters. And third is the vast majority of the print-media members who are apologists for boxing."

Kindred also quoted me as saying, "If I were the networks, I would declare a moratorium on boxing until some form of legislation was passed to, 1: protect the men who fight with the strictest rules for safety and medical examinations, 2: create an honest system of ratings and records, and, 3: create one federal government group to administer boxing.

"The print media should support such legislation instead of, by saying the federal government has no business in sports, vilifying those who suggest it. There should be licensing of promoters, and there should be an accounting of money on every fight.

"It has to be in all 50 states under the administration of one group. Either that, or abolish the quote-sport-unquote."

When the column appeared, I was in Anaheim, California, for a Thursday night football game. Martin got me there. He had started to receive numerous inquiries from the press, and he said, "I'm telling them that you have every right to do what you want to do."

"How do you think it will go down upstairs?" I asked him. "There's still the matter of my contract."

"That's not for me to say, Howard. But for the time being, I would ask you one thing. Will you at least publicly, for the sake of the company, leave the door open for yourself to cover the Holmes-Cooney rematch?"

I considered that a fair request, and I agreed.

Later that day, I was in the lobby of the South Coast Plaza Hotel when I was paged and told that Roone Arledge was calling. I got to a phone, and Arledge's first words were, "Hi, how's everything?"

"Just great," I said. "How's everything with you?"

"Great. I understand you're not doing any more professional fights."

"That's right, Roone. I've had enough. I refuse to be identified with it any longer."

"You've read your contract recently?"

I said, "Yes, and I know I'm in breach of contract, Roone, and I understand that you have every right to dismiss me from the company."

"Are you crazy? I think you've done the right thing. Congratulations, and have a good game tonight."

"Thank you, Roone," I said, and he hung up.

8

Taking Off the Gloves

I sorrow'd at his captive state,
but minded
Not to be absent at that
spectacle.

—John Milton, *Samson Agonistes*

I was with him when his name was Cassius Clay, and I was with him when he changed it to Muhammad Ali. I was with him in 1964 when he beat Sonny Liston in Miami and won the heavyweight championship of the world for the first time. And I was with him when he was in exile from boxing and when he returned to the ring, when he traveled to far-flung arenas around the globe and when he broke my heart on a humid October night in Las Vegas.

That was in 1980, and Ali had convinced a lot of people that he could really whip Larry Holmes and win the heavyweight title for the fourth time. I wasn't one of them, and I told Ali so. There was no way Ali was going to beat Holmes, and he was a fool for trying. His speech was already slurred from the beatings he had taken through the years. He walked awkwardly. His hands seemed unsteady, and there was often a vacant look in his eyes.

Ali listened to only one voice, his own, and it sang a siren song.

It's hard to describe the terrible feelings I had covering that fight, watching Holmes reduce Ali to rubble. He *was* the Greatest, and what an awful thing it was to watch him slumped and battered in a humiliating defeat.

Thinking back on it now, I am certain that Ali's fight with Holmes exacerbated Ali's physical problems. In the years that followed, whenever we chanced to meet, it was practically impossible to carry on a cogent conversation with him. And that meant our once famous relationship as interviewer and subject was ended.

During the 1984 Olympic Games in Los Angeles, in fact, Ali often attended the boxing matches, which I was covering. On several occasions, a longtime friend of Ali's named Howard Bingham asked me to interview the champ. Each time, I told Bingham that it wasn't right, that Ali would only embarrass himself.

The following month, Ali made international headlines when he admitted himself into Columbia-Presbyterian Hospital in New York. His illness was diagnosed as Parkinson's syndrome, which was most likely connected to the pounding he took in the ring. During that time, I got a call from the producer of ABC's Nightline, saying that he had received permission to bring cameras into Ali's hospital room. He asked me to interview him.

"That isn't journalism," I said, "that's exploitation. I want no part of it."

Let me stress that I do not pity Ali. He has already experienced enough to fill several lifetimes, tasting the kind of fame and fortune that preciously few men will ever know. I am saddened, however, when I think what he might have accomplished had he remained whole.

The irony is that Ali has become a victim of the sport he saved—and now the sport is in trouble for having victimized him.

• • •

My decision to quit professional boxing elicited heartwarming support from just about everybody within my company, including ABC's chairman of the board, Leonard Goldenson, and other powerful Board members. ABC, of course, had every intention of continuing to spend millions for the "privilege" of televising fights. Like every other industry in this country, its primary concern is the bottom line, and what's more, I had no quarrel with ABC's commitment to cover a thriving, popular sport, just as I had no quarrel with sportswriters who continued to attend fights for their newspapers.

After all, professional boxing is legal in this country, and it is possessed of a long and colorful tradition. However grotesque boxing's ills may be, it wasn't my purpose to legislate morality. I was simply abiding by my own moral precepts, which is my right as a human being—or so I assumed.

The reaction among sportswriters, however, was akin to the vitriol usually reserved for murderers and child-molesters. They went off half-cocked, vilifying me with epithets such as "hypocrite," "shill," and "phony." One "journalist" in San Francisco, displaying an unmitigated contempt for the First Amendment, called me a "boxing pimp."

If these same sportswriters had had the intelligence and integrity to check, they would have learned of the countless physicians, lawyers, educators, and legislators who wrote to thank me for my stand.

Even Judge John Sirica of Watergate fame dropped me a note, recalling how he'd once been a boxer and was a longtime boxing fan, and said I was right to walk away from the sport because of what was happening to it. And as for those who criticized my supposedly harsh treatment of the referee that night in Houston, they might have had their eyes opened by a letter I received from Harry M. Covert, Jr., the commissioner of the Virginia Athletic Commission. "You were absolutely one hundred percent correct in your analysis," Covert wrote. "The referee ought to have stopped the fight. He should be suspended by the Texas Athletic Commission. And, too, the fight should never have been allowed to be scheduled."

At the time, I wasn't presumptuous enough to think that I could kill boxing by myself, nor was I sure that I wanted to. I was simply following my conscience. Obviously, though, many of my critics in the sportswriting fraternity were afraid of their myopic little world being imperiled, and they lashed out at me with a vengeance. None of them, by the way, dared mention that I was forfeiting between $500,000 and $1 million a year by walking away from boxing. Why not? Because it would have impugned their slurs against me as a hypocrite and shill. Their primary interest was in carrying on their hateful, twenty-five-year-old literary pogrom against me and the hell with examining the sordid situation that prompted my decision.

To further cloud the real issues behind my decisions, they even went so far as to enlist the aid of Holmes himself. And Holmes willingly fell in line. Here was a man who had invited me and my wife to his home, but he chose to ignore whatever personal warmth there was between us and greeted my decision with a strikingly crude and stupid diatribe.

Leaving aside the dirty names he hurled at me, Holmes said, "Howard Cosell don't know nothing about boxing. He don't know nothing about football. He don't know nothing about baseball."

Warming to the attack, Holmes made other twisted comments that defied belief. If you can imagine, he claimed that he and other fighters had been pleasant to me "because we were afraid of Howard Cosell. We have been afraid of the media. We are no longer afraid."

Brave man, that Larry Holmes, the heavyweight champion of the world.

And, of course, the sportswriters lapped it up.

One exception was George Vecsey, the columnist for *The New York Times*, who wrote a fair and balanced account and who had the guts to give me the benefit of the doubt. "He is open to the charge," Vecsey wrote, "of using the violent trilogy of Kim-Arguello-Cobb to lighten his workload and focus on his excellent 'SportsBeat' show. Cosell could also be accused of trying to come down on the right and/or popular side of a controversy. But isn't it also possible that Howard Cosell has had a change of heart about a business he has observed for 25 years?"

The day after Vecsey's column appeared, I got a call from

Stan Isaacs, the sports TV critic for *Newsday*, a suburban Long Island newspaper. Noting that I had stated my intention to call the Holmes-Cooney rematch, Isaacs said he was trying to understand my position because it appeared to him to be hypocritical.

I replied, "That was based on a promise I made to John Martin. He wanted me to give my company whatever protection I could, and I felt obligated to go along with him. This network has given me more than I could ever give back, and it's still in shock over what I have done.

"Stanley," I continued, "in all the time you've been writing your column, never once have you mentioned the horrible hypocrisy and conflicts of interest that are lodged in Ferdie Pacheco at NBC and Gil Clancy at CBS."

Clancy, a former trainer, was once the matchmaker for Madison Square Garden and reportedly retained a financial interest in several fighters while announcing fights for CBS. As for Pacheco, he held a dual role at NBC as both the network's matchmaker and on-air analyst. You'll rarely hear Pacheco knock a fight that he has put together. Then again, whether or not Pacheco criticizes a fight really shouldn't matter and misses the point. It is wrong for Pacheco to wear those two hats.

"In light of those facts," I asked Isaacs, "how in hell can you call me a hypocrite? I'm the man who took the risk and violated my contract. I'm the man who walked away from a small fortune. And when the hell did you not know me to call a fight for what it was even though my own network had paid for it?"

Isaacs knew I was right. It was a matter of public record. And it caused not inconsiderable consternation and disagreement within my own company. Take, as an example, Muhammad Ali's fight with a Spanish heavyweight named Alfredo Evangelista several years ago. The fight was a disgrace, and I called it a stinker on the air. Immediately after the fight, I grabbed a plane to Las Vegas, and when I got there, a message was waiting to call Elton Rule, then the president of the network. He said, "Leonard [Goldenson] and I just wanted to thank you for preserving the integrity of the company with your call of the fight."

Back in New York, I got a call from Vice President of Sports Jim Spence. He wasn't pleased. "I wish you'd knock it off, Howard," he said. "I'm sick and tired of you criticizing a match that we put on the air."

I never did yield to Spence's point of view, but it wasn't always easy maintaining my journalistic principles.

A little more than two weeks after the Holmes-Cobb mismatch, *The New York Times* weighed in with its official position. Extracting several quotes from Vecsey's column, the editorial went on to say, "Professional fighters used to win a special admiration from Mr. Cosell. He once praised boxing's ability to pull poor kids out of the ghetto. More, Mr. Cosell concedes that boxing helped to make him a rich man. Still, he says, 'I've had it.'

"So have many people, who are repelled by both the theory and practice of a sport whose central purpose is to hurt. The World Boxing Council's decision to limit fights to 12 rounds and invoke a mandatory count of eight for defenseless fighters changes nothing. State legislators ought to deliver boxing a knockout punch."

At about this time, I received a call from Representative James Florio of New Jersey, the chairman of the House Commerce Subcommittee. Moved to action by the Kim tragedy and the Holmes-Cobb debacle, Florio was determined to conduct hearings into safety in the ring and the ability of the various state boxing commissions to police the sport. Now was the time, Florio said, for deciding whether to sponsor legislation for the creation of a national commission to regulate boxing. Aware of my personal posture, Florio asked me to testify, and I agreed.

The tide was turning. The sportswriters' attacks on me were dying down, while responsible individuals from almost every walk of life started focusing on boxing's problems rather than going after me. Boxing came under a microscope in 1983, with my *SportsBeat* show leading the way—and the irony was that my involvement with the sport would end up being as intense as it ever was.

In January, things really started heating up. Two passionate editorials in the *Journal of the American Medical Association* (*JAMA*) called for the abolition of boxing—and made front-page news across the country. In that same issue, a Cleveland radiologist named Dr. Ronald J. Ross and several colleagues published a paper that arrived at this conclusion: the more fights, the worse a fighter's CAT scan. (The technical name for CAT scan is computerized axial tomography. Introduced in the 1970s, a CAT scan is a highly advanced form of X ray, enabling a physician to observe abnormalities.)

Accompanying the Ross study was a report by a scientific council formed by the AMA to summarize available information about brain injuries and deaths in boxing. The council did not recommend a ban on boxing but called for a national registry of boxers' records and medical histories, more training for ring personnel, and standardized safety regulations among state and local commissions.

By early February, the time was ripe for an in-depth look at the current state of boxing. I tackled the subject on my *Sports-Beat* show, interviewing several physicians and legislators, including Dr. George Lundberg, the editor of *JAMA* who had written one of the two scathing editorials against boxing. He called boxing an obscenity and said it should not be sanctioned by any civilized society. "I'm an editor," Lundberg said, "and so I live by words. When I was writing this editorial, I thought that obscenity would be a good word. I went to the dictionary . . . and obscene is defined as 'disgusting to the senses, repulsive, abhorrent to morality or virtue.' And I couldn't think of a better word to describe boxing in its current state."

Voices for reform were also heard, including Dr. Jack Battaglia, the chairman of the AMA's panel on brain injuries in boxing. "What is needed is better control of boxing," Dr. Battaglia said, "because you're not going to abolish it. People watch it and people are in it because they like it. It's a lot better to have it under good medical control rather than going back to the old days when they put on fights on a barge in the Mississippi River."

Various states, including New York and Nevada, were in the process of passing boxing reform bills designed to protect the fighters. And in Washington, Representative Florio was preparing to begin his hearings on boxing.

Those hearings interested me greatly, but I took pains to point out that such hearings were nothing new. Dating back to 1961, the late Senator Estes Kefauver of Tennessee, alarmed at the inroads made by organized crime, held hearings at which he called for the appointment of a federal boxing czar. No such commissioner was ever appointed, and the fight crowd was back in Washington in 1979 for hearings on a bill sponsored by Representative Edward Beard of Rhode Island. Its purpose: to establish a three-member federal boxing commission in the Department of Labor. Again the plan fizzled.

Cynics felt that the Florio hearings would come to a similar end, but Florio thought he had a different approach. He said: ". . . my committee, and hopefully the Congress, has come to the basic new realization that there is no system to fix up. If we start from the correct premise, that there is in existence a nonsystem for a multimillion-dollar industry and that that is not acceptable, we will feel the need to structure some sort of response."

Of particular concern to Florio was the shocking lack of uniform regulations and cooperation among the various state boxing commissions. His concern was best illustrated by the case of Mark Pacheco, a bantamweight whose story was unearthed by Mike Marley of my staff. On May 6, 1982, Pacheco was knocked out in one round in Portland, Oregon, and was handed a sixty-day suspension by Dr. Battaglia, who was also the chief physician of Portland's boxing commission. Yet, on June 18, even though New York was aware of the suspension, Pacheco was allowed to fight in Madison Square Garden. Only forty-three days had elapsed since Pacheco's knockout in Portland, and this was even in violation of New York's own forty-five-day rule. Pacheco took another beating before being knocked out in the ninth round.

"This is the sort of thing, if allowed to go on, that creates your so-called punch-drunk fighter," Dr. Battaglia said. "There's just no reason for having that type of situation."

Pacheco's record, at the time, was a thing of sadness. He was a loser in ten of his last thirteen bouts, six by knockout. Thus the question: Should Pacheco be fighting at all? If not, who's to stop him? And who's to make it stick? "I think as an absolute minimum there's got to be federal uniformity," Florio said. "There's got to be a higher degree of accountability. We shouldn't have this business conducted one way in one state and a totally different way in another state. Just to focus on safety for a minute. There are some states that do a fairly good job in terms of spelling out requirements. Other states do virtually nothing."

I noted that Colorado, where regular fight cards are held, was a good example of the latter. Its boxing commission was abolished in 1978. State Representative Richard Castro was pushing for Colorado to supervise boxing once again. "There are some unscrupulous promoters who are setting up . . . a lot of mismatches," Castro said. "We have the real potential of getting some young people hurt. We have a racing commission that watches over dogs and horses in the state of Colorado to make sure they're not drugged or run excessively. I think the least that we can do is make sure we have some safeguards for human beings. And that by and large are the people we see in the boxing rings."

On the other hand, I reported, California's commission was widely regarded as the strongest in the country, but State Senator Ollie Speraw favored abolition of boxing and believed the state should not sanction or supervise any such activity. "What we're concerned about is that all the most recent medical reports and studies show that there is permanent brain damage every time somebody is hit on the head," Speraw said. "So here we have a state agency regulating people being in the ring and pounding each other on the head. . . . There's an incongruity there."

". . . the experience of trying to ban activities that have a great amount of support in some circles has not been good," Florio said. "But certainly it would be considered if that was the recommendation, and the Congress would take the appropriate measures."

I then delivered the following commentary: ". . . through all the years that I was calling fights, I was afflicted by an inner doubt about the conduct of the boxing business. This troubled me to the point where in the seventies, on four different occasions, I testified before appropriate congressional committees in favor of a federal sports or boxing commission.

"It has been my conviction that only through such a commission and through federal legislation could nationwide uniformity be achieved, uniformity with regard to licensing procedures for promoters, managers, trainers, fighters, and ring officials; in the establishment and maintenance of records and the exchange of information; and above all, medical standards and safeguards, all of those steps necessary for the ultimate protection of the fighter himself.

"The easy solution would be to say 'Ban boxing.' But in the context and attitude of our society today, this is not, in my opinion, a practical solution. So reform must be the answer. As this program has demonstrated, the sickness of boxing is apparent to every responsible person and group in this country. But reform from within has been resisted decade upon decade. Indeed, we have deliberately excluded from this program the promoters, who have only their own ax to grind, and many managers and officials of the same ilk. Nor have we presented fighters because, tragically, they have no control over the conditions under which they perform.

"As for the TV networks, it is not my intention to exonerate them for some of the bouts they have carried. But this must be said: Every network will heartily subscribe to boxing reform. The only answer remains in what I have steadfastly advocated in the past before these cameras—federal regulation and control."

Several days later, I went over the same ground at greater length before Florio's House subcommittee hearings. Their purpose: to sponsor a bill that would establish a congressional advisory commission on boxing, which in turn, based on its studies, would make legislative recommendations to the Congress with respect to uniform federal standards for professional boxing.

It was Florio's hope that these hearings would enable him to garner $2 million to fund such an advisory commission. I had doubt about his ultimate success: It seemed to me that the Congress would be hesitant to provide that amount of funding in the uncertain economic climate of the time. But I felt an obligation to make an appearance. And so, after delivering my opening remarks, which catalogued boxing's unseemly troubles—including sleazy promoters, falsified records, and the lack of uniform standards among the states—I fielded questions from the various members of the subcommittee.

Time and again, under questioning, I called for a federal boxing commission. Representative Bill Richardson of New Mexico, who was particularly inquisitive, asked, "Do you give, for instance, this commission the power to intercede if, say, Floyd Patterson or Muhammad Ali want to deretire and fight again?"

I said, "They would not be granted a license under the licensing procedure of the Federal Sports Commission. . . ."

Richardson wondered if the commissioner—or czar—of such a body would have powers similar to Pete Rozelle in football or Bowie Kuhn in baseball.

". . . I would give the chairman of the Federal Sports Commission complete control over boxing. I think it needs it."

Richardson then wanted to know what would happen to boxing's current governing bodies, the World Boxing Council and the World Boxing Association.

". . . you would find in short order that if we had our own national rating system and if we paid no attention to them and created our own system for the development of world champions . . . that the WBC and the WBA would shortly perish.

"The WBA is a joke to begin with, with the WBC not much above it. There are ten Korean fighters who are rated all over the place in the WBA, and Duk Koo Kim was. And yet he was not even rated by the WBC. They have their favorite sons. If you want a South African to get a rating, look to the WBA."

During the course of my testimony, I had the chance to cite the sorry case of Mark Pacheco, whose career was first chronicled on *SportsBeat*. Pacheco was fast becoming a symbol of boxing's quagmire, as evidenced by his inclusion in a March 12, 1983, editorial in *The New York Times*. The editorial bore the headline "Put the Feds in the Ring," and it was inspired by my *SportsBeat* show from the month before.

The Pacheco case was prominently mentioned, setting up this conclusion: "Reasonable Federal regulation could curb such self-destructive careers. The Department of Labor could write safety rules for the sport much as it does for other kinds of work. It could require health standards, accurate record-keeping, fair matchups and qualified handlers and referees. Supervision would be national: a Pacheco suspended in Oregon could not so easily slip into the ring in New York.

"People may have a right to watch a contest of pain and endurance. But civilized society also has a duty to keep it from becoming wanton."

Pacheco's name then popped up again, this time in *Sports Illustrated*. In an excellent article written and reported by Robert H. Boyle and Wilmer Ames, *Sports Illustrated* explored the new research on brain damage in experienced fighters. I give the magazine credit for taking my lead and convincing Pacheco to undergo a CAT scan. The result: evidence of some brain damage.

Pacheco was only twenty-three at the time, and soon thereafter he quit the ring—but the jury was still out on just how much cerebral atrophy he might yet suffer in the years ahead.

A small victory like Pacheco's retirement gave me added incentive to continue my war against the darker forces within boxing. To that end I devoted a lengthy segment on *SportsBeat* to the abolition of professional boxing in Sweden and Norway, two countries with a long and proud tradition in the sport. Even though former heavyweight champion Ingemar Johansson was a national hero in his country, a man named Stednso Sjoholm, a member of the Swedish Parliament, mobilized the necessary support to push through a law that banned professional boxing. That was in 1970, and·on *SportsBeat*, Sjoholm expressed the same strong sentiments. "I began my campaign against boxing because I hate violence and I love sports," he said. "I still hate boxing. The deaths and the injuries are in its roots. That is not the way it is in real and sound sports, which reward excellence, not brutality."

Twelve years later, Norway also banned professional boxing. Both countries, however, allowed amateur boxing to survive. But if a man wished to pursue a professional career, he had to leave his homeland, and *SportsBeat* carried interviews with several such fighters, as well as interviews with prominent citizens from each country. The inescapable conclusion: Neither Sweden nor Norway had suffered any noticeable deterioration in their respective civilizations because of boxing's abolition.

In closing the show, I noted that both Sweden and Norway had vastly different cultures than the United States. ". . . Sweden is a socialistic democracy, and unlike ours, has no ethnic diversity, no big-city ghettos, no abject poverty. So, while the abolition of boxing may be right for Sweden and Norway, the abolition of boxing in the United States at this time is unrealistic. But clearly the time has long since come for boxing reform, and the forces of government, medicine, law, education, and reason will no longer be still.

"It's a sham to cry, as some boxing writers do, for a national commission. Out of fifty states, it is impossible to achieve agreement on such a commission or a national commissioner or uniform governing rules, regulations, and standards. Indeed, the states themselves are suspect. Witness this demand by State Assemblyman Buddy Fortunato of New Jersey: that the State attorney general and the State Athletic Commission immediately investigate last Sunday's Leon Spinks-Carlos De Leon fight nationally televised from Atlantic City. Fortunato based his demand on what he called a flagrant conflict of interest, since both fighters had the same manager, Carl King, the son of boxing promoter Don King. Astoundingly, the establishment of boxing writers have all but ignored the story.

"As I stated three weeks ago, for professional boxing the only answer is federal regulation and control."

If there were any remaining doubts about the desperate need for boxing reform, then the tragic plight of Sugar Ray Seales should have wiped them away once and for all.

At the 1972 Olympic Games in Munich, Seales was the sole U.S. gold medal winner in boxing. He then embarked on a pro career with high hopes. Fighting as a middleweight, he reeled off twenty straight victories before a 1974 defeat at the hands of an up-and-coming prospect named Marvin Hagler.

Seales continued to fight with mixed success, a title shot eluding him. Another loss to Hagler in 1979, this time by a knockout in the first round, seemed to end his championship dreams. But two years later, Seales won a North American title by knocking out Sammy Nesmith in Indianapolis. Persisting, despite managerial and financial problems, Seales was reduced from a world-class contender to a mere journeyman.

All the while, Seales was battling an unseen opponent. Finally, broke and nearly blind, unable to see even his mother's face clearly, he checked into Good Samaritan Hospital in Portland, Oregon, where a famed ophthalmologist named Dr. Richard Chenoweth performed two operations on him to repair detached retinas.

Seales's hospitalization hardly caused a ripple in the newspapers—until I was able to arrange an interview with the fighter and Dr. Chenoweth for *SportsBeat.* What was revealed was an obscenity, to use *JAMA* editor Dr. Lundberg's word to describe the current state of professional boxing.

The interview took place at Good Samaritan Hospital just a few days after Seales's retinal surgery. Dr. Chenoweth's prognosis: Seales might end up with reading vision in one eye, nothing more. The cause: repeated blows to the eyes.

Dr. Chenoweth unequivocally placed the blame on the boxing commissions in the states where Seales had had his most recent fights. "Obviously there were inadequate medical standards," he said, "and inadequate conditions to enforce those standards."

"What should the tests have been?" I asked.

"A simple vision test, just reading a vision test card . . . to see if he has the ability to read."

"What if he memorized the test cards?"

"Well, that wouldn't be possible if the appropriate test cards were used. We can project the letters just one at a time. There's any number of ways to simply ensure that the person being tested can indeed read the cards."

Seales first underwent retinal surgery in February 1982, and yet the following month he was granted permission to fight in New York. I asked Dr. Chenoweth how that was possible. He replied: "Again, I think it reflects inadequate testing standards, which are certainly not uniform among the various boxing commissions throughout the United States. . . . It's very simple to detect if an individual has an extensive retinal detachment like Ray had. That eye doesn't see."

Turning to Seales, I wondered what had impelled him to keep fighting when he knew he couldn't see. "We were so close to a shot at the world title," he said. ". . . we were getting ready to sign contracts and I was running out of money. All the time I was fighting, I was being passed by these commissions, so I was able to continue."

"Did you think these commissions would pass you? What made you believe that they would?"

"I didn't believe they would pass me. I wanted to take the chance . . . to see if they would give me the final word to get out of boxing, but they never did."

I asked, "Weren't you afraid when you couldn't even see your mother's face clearly that you were going blind?"

"Well, I knew that, but nobody ever stopped me. They never told me that they saw anything in my eyes that wouldn't keep me going. I passed quite a few exams. I passed New York. I passed New Jersey. I went through California, which is a tough one. I passed all those. I had the permission to keep on going."

"And Nevada, too, I might add."

"Yes."

"Presumably the four toughest states all passed you. California, Nevada, New Jersey, and New York."

"Exactly, Howard."

Wrapping up the story, I called on "decency to prevail, and the forces of reason to prevail. Put the feds in the ring."

But by the summer, nothing had changed. Oh, sure, the

WBC had reduced championship fights from fifteen to twelve rounds, but that was merely cosmetic. What about fighters who used aliases to keep getting bouts? And shoddy medical examinations? And the lack of uniform standards among the states? And the ongoing and dangerous travesty of frequent mismatches?

Too many people were paying lip service to boxing reform, but hardly anybody was making significant progress. Representative Florio's hearings flopped; he was unable to persuade the Congress to allocate the $2 million to fund an advisory commission. Representative Richardson, however, fought on. He and Representative Pat Williams of Montana sponsored a new bill that would have provided $1 million to fund a study group for a possible federal boxing commission. It, too, was defeated handily.

And the death toll continued to mount.

On September 1, in Los Angeles, a twenty-two-year-old bantamweight named Kiko Bejines was pummeled into a stupor—and died several days later. That same week, blind and unyielding to the woe that enveloped them, the people who run professional boxing pitted heavyweight champion Larry Holmes against somebody named Scott Frank. The fight figured to be—and indeed it was—a mismatch of such pathetic dimensions that *Ring* magazine, often an apologist for the sport, refused to cover it.

Violence and danger are inherent in professional boxing, and even the most stringent safeguards don't guarantee absolute protection against death in the ring. Only abolition can accomplish that. I knew that, of course, but I was firm in my conviction that a ban on boxing remained unlikely in our contemporary society.

Thus I pressed on for reform. Amid the scandals, my new targets were a faded fighter launching a comeback—and a twenty-year-old American Indian who was fighting with a pacemaker. That's right, a pacemaker!

Combining both stories into one *SportsBeat* segment, I first dealt with Jerry Quarry's return to the ring. The popular former heavyweight contender was thirty-eight and hadn't fought in almost six years, but on August 31, in Albuquerque, New Mexico, he stepped into a ring and knocked out a nonentity named Lupe Guerra in the first round. The fight was a farce. Guerra had been knocked out four times the year before and once suffered five straight KO's. But with a flurry of publicity, Quarry was booked for a December 28 fight in Scranton, Pennsylvania.

I asked Jimmy Binns, the chairman of that state's athletic commission, to justify Quarry's receiving a license to fight in Pennsylvania. "I ordered certain medical tests to be performed," Binns said. "He has had a CAT scan, and he has had his heart tested, his eyes tested, and he has had a general physical examination in a Scranton hospital. However, in addition to those tests, he is going to have to demonstrate to me, during a workout of ten rounds, that he is able to go ten rounds."

Quarry was ultimately denied permission to fight in Pennsylvania, and he blamed me and the negative publicity generated by my show for influencing Binns and the athletic commission. But, wouldn't you know it, he got a license to fight three months later in Bakersfield, California. His opponent was a journeyman named Jimmy Williams, and Quarry looked awful in winning a highly questionable decision.

And by the way, because it bears repeating, California is reputed to have one of the stricter athletic commissions in terms of licensing and protecting fighters.

The state of Oklahoma has no such pretensions. It doesn't even have an athletic commission. The result: A half-Creek, half-Seminole middleweight named Benny Harjo was able to get matches. Harjo's record in September 1983 was hardly newsworthy. He had won one bout and survived two knockouts. What made Harjo unique—and his story all the more bizarre and troubling—was that the April before, after suffering a broken jaw in a fight, it was discovered that Harjo had arrhythmia, an irregular heartbeat. A dual-chamber pacemaker was implanted in his upper right chest, and incredibly, he had at least one fight after the operation.

Harjo lost in the first round.

His manager, Mike Helderman, exploited his fighter by billing him as "Bionic Benny." He contended that Harjo took no abnormal physical risks by entering the ring, and he planned future matches. ". . . it is not a life-threatening situation," Helderman said. "This is called an on-demand pacemaker. If his heart skips a beat, the pacemaker will make it up. If Benny's pacemaker was completely dislodged and unplugged, if he was cut and his pacemaker was exposed, there still wouldn't be any life-threatening situation."

Harjo also played down the bodily harm he might be exposing himself to. "I'm not in it to make boxing look like a freak show," he said. "Me and my doctors alone know what's going on. . . ."

The medical director of the New York State Athletic Commission, however, was flabbergasted by the Harjo case. His name: Dr. Edward Campbell. "I think it's horrendous," he said. "Anyone who's got an arrhythmia so severe that he needs a pacemaker should not be boxing in the ring. He could never, never, get a license to fight in this state."

One of the most egregious examples of boxing's slimy devotion to the almighty dollar and its unwillingness to police itself occurred on the Friday night after Thanksgiving Day—a full year after the Holmes-Cobb disgrace. That night in Las Vegas, before a national television audience, Holmes promptly disposed of young Marvis Frazier, the son of former heavyweight champion Joe Frazier, in the first round with a potentially lethal right-hand punch.

Frazier's defeat brought into focus all the sordid elements that prompted my departure from professional boxing. The bout screamed mismatch from the beginning: Young Frazier was simply too small and too inexperienced to offer Holmes much of a challenge. Again, I went on the attack, doing my best to alert the public as to what was likely to transpire. And then after the fight, I expressed my feelings in no uncertain terms. There was plenty of blame to go around. That fight was made possible by:

1. The greedy promoters, Murad Muhammad and Robert Andreoli, who, in a touch of poetic justice, were reported to have lost $1 million promoting the fight.

2. Marvis's father, Joe Frazier, who should have known better—and who let his hopes and aspirations for his son blind him to the realities of his own business.

3. Larry Holmes, who for the past year had stuffed his pride in his back pocket and fought a succession of patsies.

4. The NBC Television Network, which put up the money and agreed to televise it, even though it had on its staff a so-called boxing expert named Dr. Ferdie Pacheco, who's billed as the "Fight Doctor."

5. The Nevada State Boxing Commission, which approved the fight.

6. The International Boxing Federation, a new organization comprised of various state boxing commissions, which stepped in at the last minute to give the fight its blessing—even though both the WBC and the WBA refused to sanction the bout as a championship fight.

7. Veteran boxing writers, such as syndicated columnists Dick Young of the *New York Post* and the *New York Daily News*'s Phil Pepe, who helped create the hype that cloaked the fight in seeming respectability by picking Frazier to pull off an upset.

A couple of days after the fight, Pepe had the gall to use his column to blame NBC for "brainwashing" him into giving Frazier a chance to win. I took care of him on *SportsBeat* by closing a commentary on the fight with these words: "One wonders how the nation's largest-circulation tabloid can entrust a column to a man who can't control his own mind.

"I'm not saying," I continued, "that I was alone in branding this fight a mismatch before it took place. I am saying that there were too few of us and far too many of them . . . people who should have known better . . . people who could have prevented this near tragic fight from ever taking place. But, alas, I realize that in the year that has transpired since I said my farewell to boxing, nothing has really changed at all. More's the pity."

The pity of it all eventually reached across an ocean and into the Vatican. On December 11, an Italian bantamweight named Salvatore LaSerra beat Maurizio Lupino in Milan. Ironically, though, it was the winner—LaSerra—who collapsed after the fight and had to undergo a brain operation. LaSerra's plight received attention in an editorial in the Vatican newspaper *L'Osservatore Romano*. Translated from the Italian, it read in part:

. . . As in other occasions, the case of LaSerra, too, has provoked reactions from public opinion and the mass media. The basic argument is a moral one, the question always the same: Is it legitimate to continue to accept a sport whose fundamental aim it is "to inflict corporal damage to the adversary," as the World Medical Assembly held in Venice some months ago defined it?

Physicians are in their majority of one mind in responding that it is neither legitimate nor moral. But opposition is manifold. . . . Nonetheless, boxing remains a violent sport, if not in the intentions of the contestants at least in its form of expression. The ring is a stage of confrontation, said to be reliable and regulated but always brutal and sometimes savage. . . .

No sporting discipline nor any kind of "show" can be accepted by a civic conscience if it endangers human life. Much worthier causes call for putting lives at stake.

LaSerra died a couple of weeks after that editorial was published.

Just before Christmas, Mike Marley of my *SportsBeat* staff told me that promoter Don King intended to introduce a resolution at the annual WBC convention in Las Vegas. To wit: Boxing needs Howard Cosell and let's urge him to return.

My reaction was to tell Marley, "You make sure King knows I want no part of his ludicrous resolution. I don't approve of what he intends to do, and I'll never call another professional fight and that's final."

King got the message but chose to ignore it. He gave an interview to a writer with the *USA Today* newspaper, saying that even though I had kicked his butt many times, he would lead the hue and cry for my return to the ring. In the interview, King somehow managed to invoke my stand against the injustice of apartheid, adding, "Boxing needs Howard's genius, personality, and magic voice to tell it like it is, and help us in a time of crisis. I love what he stands for and how he stands for it.

"Howard has left an unfillable void in our sport. Every friend of boxing, whether they like Howard or not, whether they like me or not, must join the cry in unison: 'Howard, come back. Say what you want, but come back. We need you.'"

The public-relations arm of my company asked me if I wished to issue a reply to King's statements. I declined. Whether King was aware of it or not, I had spent the last year saying precisely what I wanted to say about boxing on my *SportsBeat* show and in my daily radio reports.

During the next several months, the debate over boxing seemed to recede. New pieces of legislation were proposed for consideration, but they got nowhere. It was business as usual once again, and I turned my attention to other subjects.

Then, just like that, boxing found itself at the center of a new storm of controversy. First, in May of 1984, *JAMA* published yet another study on the hazards of the sport and used its editorial pages for yet another call for abolition.

Within weeks, the British Medical Association followed suit, resolving to "organize a campaign to influence political opinion ultimately to ban boxing."

The lull had ended, and the ban-boxing movement suddenly received a groundswell of impressive support. Medical societies representing Canada, New York, and California urged that steps be taken toward the goal of total prohibition of the sport. Joining those forces were the American Academy of Pediatrics and the American Academy of Neurology, and the attack began to broaden to include boxing at the amateur and interscholastic levels.

A lightning rod for the abolitionists was none other than Muhammad Ali.

Ali's extensively reported stay at Columbia-Presbyterian Hospital in New York, where he was diagnosed as suffering from Parkinson's syndrome, sparked outrage as well as sadness among the millions who had come to revere him. One of those was Dr. Nelson Richards, the president of the American Academy of Neurology.

Originally, Dr. Richards was of the opinion that even though boxing was a hazardous sport, it was practically impossible to outlaw it. Thus, Dr. Richards concluded, the best policy was to strive for reform. Then he heard Ali speak while the champ was in the hospital. "I was struck that this man, who previously was known for his glibness, was almost unintelligible," Dr. Richards said. "I changed my mind. Boxing should be banned."

On October 27, in view of this sudden new attack on boxing, I covered the controversy on *SportsBeat*. In addition to the impact of Ali's illness, were there other reasons why the hue and cry to ban boxing was reaching a fever pitch? Dr. George Lundberg, the editor of *JAMA*, provided an answer: "The scientific articles that we have published in our journal, plus those in other journals, have become general medical knowledge now, and these articles indicate that chronic brain damage is a very frequent occurrence among fighters who've had a significant number of fights. So once the medical knowledge gets out there, physicians' attitudes change, and they're changing now. And you can expect more change in the future, which just might alter the way the general public feels about boxing."

Dr. Lundberg went a step farther, putting the heat on amateur boxing as well. He is one of a growing number of physicians, lawyers, sociologists, and other experts who contend that younger boxers face a greater risk—and this might legally constitute child abuse. "It is abuse, pure and simple," Dr. Lundberg said. "It is predictable damage, and it involves children. And if adults promote, for their own pleasure, children bashing each other, hurting each other, then this makes a pretty good case for child abuse."

The focal point of the show was my interviews with two eminent physicians, each of whom possessed radically different philosophical attitudes toward boxing. One was Dr. Dominick Purpura, the dean of the Albert Einstein College of Medicine in New York and a professor of brain sciences; the other was Dr. Mortimer Shapiro, a psychiatrist and neurologist who sits on the medical advisory board of the New York State Athletic Commission.

Dr. Purpura demonstrated how boxers' brains are damaged by a blow to the head, noting that repeated blows to the head of a young man can stunt the development of his brain. "I must point out," Dr. Purpura stressed, "that the brain continues to develop into the fourth decade of life, and a boxer may interrupt that process by fighting while in his teens."

Dr. Shapiro, on the other hand, defended boxing, disagreeing with his colleagues who favor abolition. Although Dr. Shapiro agreed that boxing was harmful, he believed that the best course of action was to stay involved in the sport and work for reform. "The problem is not the dangers of boxing," Dr. Shapiro contended. "What we must wrestle with is, what does boxing serve in the community? And I think it serves a genuine purpose. It does permit the vicarious expression of a tremendous amount of hostility, anger, rage, frustration, and so forth that's built up in various cultures. One can discharge some of this vicariously in the observation of a boxing bout on television.

"Secondly, one can say that it does afford an economic opportunity for a certain number of people who are disenfranchised by the culture—let's say because of educational deficits—and boxing provides them with a way out."

Dr. Purpura took objection to that theory, saying, "I believe the notion that boxing is a route to social and economic success is a very deviant notion. I believe that society has to worry about [the underprivileged] and provide access to the structure of the economy of this country without sacrificing the human brain."

But Dr. Shapiro contended that it would be futile to abolish boxing. "If an institution has a psychological value to the culture, that institution continues," he said. "At various times, boxing has been outlawed by various cultures, but it occurred despite the outlawing."

"I believe that could happen to a limited extent," Dr. Purpura countered. "It would be hard, however, to conceal the roar of three thousand fans, unless they put them within the deepest caves under the Rockies. If that's where they're to be, then those people will gravitate there. But I have a little more optimism about the dignity of the human soul, and I believe such dignity will not allow that to happen."

In closing, these two physicians succinctly summed up their opposing positions.

Dr. Purpura: "Boxing is a strictly nonhuman endeavor. It shouldn't be."

Dr. Shapiro: "Do we need better regulation of boxing? Absolutely . . . however, should we abolish boxing? That is not a medical problem. That is a moral problem, and it is a sociological problem. It has nothing to do with medicine."

The American Medical Association did not agree with Dr. Shapiro. Several weeks after my interview with him, on December 5, the AMA overwhelmingly adopted a resolution calling for the abolition of professional boxing—and amateur boxing as well. It marked the first such formal action taken by the AMA's 365-member House of Delegates, although the sport had been condemned previously in official AMA publications.

"It has been increasingly evident from scientific evidence that there is both acute and long-term brain injury to people who are involved in boxing," AMA President Dr. Joseph Boyle said. "Evaluation of that evidence indicates that people are seriously disabled even after short exposure to boxing, even in relatively minor settings. Amateur boxing is the farm team for professional boxing.

"It seems to us an extraordinarily incongruous thing that we have a sport in which two people are literally paid to get into a ring and try to beat one another to death, or at least beat them into a state of senselessness, which will then leave them permanently brain-damaged."

"It seems a little bit strange," Dr. Boyle added, that there are laws against pitting dogs and chickens while "putting two human beings in the ring is perfectly legal."

Over the past two years, I had produced no fewer than ten segments on *SportsBeat* that dealt with professional boxing, delineating the dangers inherent in the sport, its abuses, and the growing opposition of the medical community. On December 8, the following was my last boxing commentary of 1984:

"On both medical and moral grounds, Dr. Boyle's position and that of the AMA would appear to be unassailable. And around the world, remember, Sweden and Norway have already abolished boxing, and by every account, the United Kingdom and Canada may shortly do so. For myself, my position has been well known. On moral grounds, I had to give up calling professional boxing matches, and I did so more than two years ago in the wake of a chain of intolerable events that had beset the professional boxing scene.

"I've had different feelings about amateur boxing. I have made those feelings clear—because watching kids working in programs such as the PAL, knowing the amateur boxing people and their care and concern for the youngsters, it was still within me to support amateur boxing. But now, in the face of the AMA recommendation and mounting medical evidence ... I must wrestle with myself again, look into my own conscience about whether or not there should be a future for amateur boxing."

It was hardly surprising that boxing's apologists quickly rose in indignation at the AMA's resolution. Of all publications, *The New York Times* ran a sophomoric piece by the former editor of *Ring* magazine, Bert Sugar, who attacked the AMA for picking on boxing and not paying closer attention to rising medical costs, caring for the aged, and finding a cure for the common cold. How the AMA's position on those matters impacts on its call for the abolition of boxing is beyond me, but Sugar used issues such as those to tell the AMA to keep its opinions about boxing to itself. Brilliant.

Then there was José Sulaiman, the president of that upright and sanctified organization called the World Boxing Association, who termed the AMA's resolution "irresponsible and demagogic." I know Sulaiman fairly well, and I can't say I was shocked by his intemperate reaction to the AMA's resolution. Sulaiman said that the AMA had produced not a shred of evidence—can you imagine?—of the medical threat that boxing supposedly poses to a fighter. "Where are the legions of punch-drunk boxers?" he asked.

My God! And this is a man whom the professional boxing people look to for executive guidance!

Joining Sugar and Sulaiman in sidestepping the issue, promoter Bob Arum had this to say: "There'll be more fatalities in Harlem in one day because of inadequate medical care than there are in twenty years of boxing."

With men such as these, is it any wonder that professional boxing is under such heavy attack?

The Thanksgiving weekend of 1984 marked the second anniversary of my decision to quit professional boxing. In that time, I had come to possess serious doubts about the reformation of the sport. Only when a fighter dies in the ring is the public scandalized, and the editorial writers and the legislators moved to rage against the contemporary condition of the sport. And then, a few months later, when the rage is stilled, what is left?

Professional boxing survives and sometimes thrives as it always has, brutally, wantonly, thoughtlessly, and it is foolhardy to expect that it will change for the better. There will always be with us too many Mark Pachecos and Sugar Ray Sealeses and Benny Harjos, wounded and perhaps even senseless, roaming the earth, wondering where the money went and why nobody seems to care.

I was firm in these feelings when, on the night of January 24, 1985, quite unexpectedly, I got a call at my apartment from Bob Arum, the boxing promoter. It took me by surprise because I hadn't talked to Arum in many, many months. He insisted that he had to see me, that it was urgent.

"What about, Bob?"

"The Hagler-Hearns fight, but we have to talk in person."

Since we lived in the same neighborhood, I told Bob he could stop by my apartment on the following Saturday afternoon. I had a pretty good idea what he wanted. He was in the midst of promoting a match between the junior middleweight champion, Tommy Hearns, and the middleweight champion, Marvelous Marvin Hagler. Scheduled for April 15 in Las Vegas, it was the biggest fight in a long time, and Arum intended to show it on closed-circuit television in theaters across the country. Sure enough, he wanted me to call the fight.

"This is one of the greatest matches in boxing history," he told me at my apartment. "You're the only one who can bring it the distinction it deserves. You can name your price."

"You know my position, Bob. What makes you think I'd make an exception in this case?"

"Look, Howard, we can release a joint statement. Your stand against boxing had to do with mismatches and the deplorable administration of the sport. But you never said you'd never do a truly great match like Hagler-Hearns. This is not a mismatch. These are two skilled boxers. This is what's right with the sport."

"Come on, Bob. I said very clearly that I'd never call another professional boxing match as long as I live. It's as simple as that. I'll never return to the sport on moral and medical grounds." Then I painstakingly reviewed what the most respected medical minds had taught me about brain damage in fighters and why I thought that boxing was destined to enrage an ever-increasing number of people in our society. In closing, I said, "I'm through with the sport, Bob. It's another closed chapter in my life."

Before Arum left, he said, "If you change your mind, Howard, you know where to find me."

"Don't count on it, Bob."

The Hagler-Hearns fight went off on schedule. Several days before, in a television interview with Jack Cafferty of NBC's local news program in New York, I predicted that Hagler would knock out Hearns—as I had several times on my daily radio reports. My prediction was based on what I perceived as a fatal flaw in Hearns and all fighters trained by Manny Steward in his Kronk Gym in Detroit: They carry their left hand perilously low and thus are easy targets for opponents who can effectively deliver righthand blows.

And so, it was hardly surprising to me when Hagler tagged Hearns in the third round with a succession of rights, dropped him, and retained his middleweight crown. Of far more interest to me, however, was the reaction of the media. Hagler-Hearns was hailed as one of the greatest fights in boxing history! Granted, the first round was an exceptionally furious piece of business, but how can you call a fight that lasted only two and a half rounds one of the greatest of all time?

This wave of ecstasy that swept over the media was merely the latest attempt to rescue boxing from the clutches of its critics. At this point in time, I can't say for sure whether the sport's apologists will prevail, but using the Hagler-Hearns fight to glorify boxing won't work in the long run. Boxing is on the ropes, and there are too few fighters of the Hagler and Hearns variety who can make a fight that is capable of seducing the public into forgetting about boxing's ills and thinking the sport deserves to survive and prosper.

In the weeks before Arum came to visit me, I had already reached the only conclusion that was left to me: The Swedes and Norwegians have the right idea—let's abolish professional boxing in America.

9

Sugar Ray Redux

It is not strength, but art, obtains the prize.
—Homer, *The Iliad*

When Sugar Ray Leonard announced his return to the ring after a two-year layoff, I was asked to cover the fight. I declined, regarding my decision to quit professional boxing an irrevocable one.

Being made of flesh and blood like everyone else, I'll not deny that it wasn't tempting to be with Leonard again. We had traveled a long road together. I truly admired his craftmanship in the ring, and I liked him on a personal level. He had provided me with an enormous amount of excitement and a mother lode of good stories, and I always felt we shared a mutuality of respect.

Sugar Ray Leonard was a fine man.

He wasn't Muhammad Ali.

Up front, that distinction must be made. Ali was far and away the most fascinating personality in sports, and other than Jackie Robinson, perhaps the most important. Ali was the symbol for a whole generation, and in the 1960s and even the early 1970s, if you had asked a person how he or she felt about Ali, you'd get a pretty accurate fix on that person's political, sociological, and religious view of the world.

It may seem hard to imagine today, but when the young Cassius Clay bragged about his pretty black face and his superiority over white men, people gasped in horror. And when he changed his religion and his name and told the world, "I don't have to be what you want me to be," he signaled the so-called Athletic Revolution and the coming changes in the behavior of athletes.

Ali's life touched the civil rights movement. He became a hero to the anti-Vietnam War movement when he refused to serve in the army and endured an unjust three-year exile from the ring. He changed the financial structure of sports, demanding multimillion-dollar paydays and getting them. And what other athlete could have saddened millions around the world as Ali did when he was admitted to a New York hospital for blurred speech and thought?

Ali was always larger than the ring in which he floated.

The same cannot be said of Leonard. He was simply a marvelous athlete, and I am certain that he will one day win recognition as one of the greatest fighters in history.

It is in that spirit that I want to remember my association with him.

• • •

I first met Sugar Ray Leonard in July of 1976 at the University of Vermont in Burlington. It was two weeks before the start of the Olympic Games in Montreal, and I was there to cover what is called the Olympic box-offs, the final round of bouts to determine the U.S. Olympic boxing team.

Leonard seemed a cocky kid, outgoing and self-possessed. And I was assured by the late Tom (Sarge) Johnson, the assistant coach of the U.S. team, that Leonard was an extraordinary fighter, perhaps the best amateur this country had to offer. But Johnson also informed me that Leonard had a bad left hand— the knuckles were terribly swollen. It seemed to me that he would experience a lot of difficulty winning his match in the box-offs. And even if he did win, how was he to survive the rigors of the competition in Montreal?

The day before his fight, Leonard accompanied me on a walk to the top of one of the hills on the edge of the Vermont campus. From there, without realizing it at first, we could see the sparkling city of Montreal in the distance, and Leonard took it as an augury of great things to come.

I wasn't so sure. That left hand of his was hurting him, which he frankly admitted, but he refused to dwell on it. "Don't worry about me, Howard," he said. "Two hands, one hand, no hands ... I'll make it work."

And then he winked and flashed that big, beautiful smile at me and ... well, he made it work. He devastated his opponent, Bruce Curry, a tough, slick fighter who later turned pro and won the WBC superlightweight championship. He shut Curry out, winning all three rounds—and securing a spot on the Olympic team.

That afternoon, watching Leonard fight, my mind flashed back across a dozen years, and memories of a youthful Muhammad Ali swirled in my gut and caught in my throat. It was a visceral experience. Leonard's speed and balance, his jab and lateral movement—my Lord, I thought, this kid is blessed with the kind of talent that only the great ones have. That's how impressive Leonard was, even at first glance.

I had become a believer.

Since I was assigned to cover boxing—and a story about U.S. team member Howard Davis was breaking—the moment I arrived in Montreal I grabbed a ride to the Olympic Village, where the team was lodged. In two rooms. The whole team. Coach Pat Nappi, Assistant Coach Johnson, and thirteen fighters. And it seemed a disgrace that they should be jammed in those two rooms, packed together, sleeping on cots, one cot lined up against the next, as in an army barracks.

But observing Nappi and Johnson and those kids, I came to realize how much they loved it. They were as one. They had a very special togetherness, and that closeness found its expression in the way they comforted and supported teammate Davis, whose mother had died just before the Games were to begin.

I wanted to interview Davis, but first thought it wise to consult with Johnson, a man for whom I had the utmost respect. It was a sad, sad day in American sport when, on March 14, 1980, Johnson was killed in a plane crash, along with several of this country's most promising amateur fighters, en route to Poland for a tournament.

Johnson was an Ohioan, a military man to the core, but his real passion was boxing. His was a rallying spirit, and those kids in those two rooms loved him, absorbed his lessons on boxing fundamentals like so many pieces of sponge absorb water. And, as was always the case, he knew his fighters inside out—their educational backgrounds and their religious convictions, their girlfriends' names and their favorite desserts, everything.

Johnson filled me in on young Davis and his relationship with his mother. As it happened, he had already had a long talk with Davis about whether he should continue to fight or return to his home in Glen Cove, New York, for the funeral services.

Davis had decided to stay in Montreal and fight.

I asked Johnson if I could interview Davis about his decision. He said he'd ask Davis but couldn't promise anything.

While waiting for Davis's reply, I walked over to where Leonard was resting, and we talked about Davis. Leonard graciously volunteered to join Johnson in convincing Davis to go on the air with me. He thought that the interview might act as a catharsis for Davis, enable him to get his feelings out into the open and deal with them. And it would also help him cope with the barrage of similar questions that other reporters were sure to be asking during the course of the competition.

Thanks to Johnson and Leonard, Davis agreed to the interview. He was upset and depressed, but he expressed himself eloquently, telling me about his love for his mother and his attachment to his father. He would stay and fight, he said, because he knew how much his winning a gold medal meant to his mother, and his father had given him his full support and blessings.

Davis proved himself a valiant man in the grip of tragedy, giving a hint of the character he would display in his upcoming fights. As for Leonard, he showed me that he was emerging as the leader of that gifted team, the shining example of confidence and composure that was destined to influence each and every one of his teammates.

That night, while in attendance at an ABC party, I was paged to the phone. It was Roone Arledge, the president of ABC Sports, calling from the Control Center. He was preparing to produce a pre-Olympic special at Cartier Square for airing live the next morning, and he needed a star.

"Neither Olga Korbut nor Nadia Comaneci can speak English well enough," he said. "You got anybody?"

"I've got the guy who'll be the Olga Korbut of '76," I said. "Who?"

"A kid named Ray Leonard," I replied. "They call him Sugar. He's a light-welterweight, fights in the one-hundred-thirty-nine-pound category, and he reminds me of Ali when Ali was young and green."

"That good? You serious?"

"Absolutely. I really believe in him."

"Will he come across on air?"

I said, "He's a good-looking kid, and he's uninhibited. He talks a streak. And he does the Ali Shuffle like he invented it."

"Sounds terrific," Roone said, and I could hear the excitement creeping into his voice.

I was even starting to pump myself up. "And get this—he wears his girlfriend's picture taped to his sock when he fights. He's got all the color in the world. He'll be a sensation!"

"We need him as soon as possible. Can you get him over to Cartier Square?"

"I'll call Sarge Johnson, the assistant coach. He'll bring him."

"And bring the Juice with you. We'll use him with some of the track athletes so we've got protection."

Arledge was referring to O. J. Simpson, then an active NFL player, a bona fide celebrity whom Arledge understandably wanted around in case Leonard didn't live up to my expectations.

He needn't have worried.

Cartier Square was packed with spectators, and when Leonard arrived, he was sky-high, not a hint of nervousness within him. He couldn't wait to take the air, to let the world know just how good he really was and just how confident he really was about winning the gold medal.

Leonard stole the show. Dancing the Ali Shuffle and flicking punches to describe how he would achieve ultimate victory, he dazzled the crowd and lit up the screen. A star was born!

What I recall most vividly about that evening, however, was the discovery I made about Leonard's hands. I knew that Leonard's left hand still wasn't in the best of shape, though Leonard again pooh-poohed it when I broached the subject with him. But after the taping, when I shook his hand to thank him for the interview, he winced ever so slightly. It was enough, however, to catch the change in his expression, and I quickly observed that the knuckles of his right hand were swollen, too.

Leonard insisted that his right hand was fine, and nobody would know about that additional handicap until after the Games, when he finally talked about it.

Leonard's magnificent performance belied the pain he endured as he buzzed through the most difficult draw I had ever seen in all my years of covering Olympic boxing—six fights in thirteen days, and every opponent was a tough customer. He used his jab with splendid effectiveness, and he threw his right with ferocious abandon when the situation warranted it, never giving any hint of concern for the welfare of his hands. In fact, he seemed far more concerned in securing tickets to his fights and other events for his parents, who had traveled from Maryland to Montreal in a camper to be near their son.

Leonard's most troublesome fight in Montreal was probably his first. It was against an unorthodox Swede named Ulf Carlson, who bobbed and weaved in a crouch and was deceptively hard to hit. But Leonard figured him out in about a round and a half and swiftly piled up the necessary points.

His most memorable fight was his last, a beautiful piece of work against a gifted Cuban named Andres Aldama, who had won all his previous fights in these Games by knockout. The decision went to Leonard—and so did the gold medal.

Leonard was one of five American boxers to win gold medals in Montreal. The others were Leo Randolph (flyweight), Davis (lightweight), Michael Spinks (middleweight), and his brother Leon (light-heavyweight). What a joy it was being around those kids! They charmed and they sparkled, capturing the hearts of millions of Americans; youthful heroes who gave boxing a bracing new image, wiping away age-old notions of punch-drunk pugs, slimy managers, and cigar-chomping mobsters.

When it was all over, Davis was named the outstanding boxer of the Montreal Olympics. In light of his personal quest to honor the memory of his mother, it would have been, at the time, mean-spirited to quarrel with Davis's selection. But being objective, Davis had serious flaws, which still manifest themselves today—among others, his inability to take a punch.

No, Leonard was the outstanding fighter in Montreal, both

in terms of the quality of his performance and his potential for greatness. And, indeed, within five short years after turning pro, he had not only emerged as the most skilled craftsman in boxing, but he had also become its most popular and colorful citizen. He single-handedly manipulated the sport to his own advantage, thumbing his nose at powerful promoters such as Don King and Robert Arum and making more money in a shorter period of time than any other fighter in history.

As the welterweight champion of the world, Leonard stole the thunder from that traditional ruler of the ring, the heavyweight champ, and he did it with consummate style and grace and courage. Look at his record, and consider this: In twenty-two months—from November 30, 1979, through September 16, 1981—Leonard fought Wilfred Benitez, Roberto Duran twice, Ayub Kalule, and Tommy Hearns. All were champions, and they had a combined record of 177–1–1 going in against him. Hearns and Kalule had never been knocked down, but Leonard knocked them down. Neither had ever been beaten, but Leonard beat them. He knocked out Kalule, the WBA junior middleweight champ, in the ninth round in Houston, and he stopped Hearns, the WBA welterweight champ, in the fourteenth round in Las Vegas.

Damn few champions had ever fought such a withering assortment of opponents in so short a period of time. And thus, as 1982 dawned, Leonard was poised to establish for himself a place alongside legends such as Ali, Willie Pep, and Sugar Ray Robinson, and Leonard's star was ascending far beyond the ring.

In the spring of that year, however, an eye injury cut the twenty-six-year-old champion down in his prime, but I applauded his decision to quit boxing and enjoy the $30 million to $40 million he had earned with his fists. When he returned after a two-year layoff to fight an undistinguished Philadelphian named Kevin Howard, I was disappointed in Leonard, and said so publicly. Quite frankly, it caught me by surprise when, immediately after stopping Howard, Leonard retired again, though few were happier than I for the fighter himself and his family. This time, I hoped, his retirement was for real and everlasting.

During World War II, Cicero Leonard was a boxer in the Navy. When he got out, he never even considered turning pro.

He went home to Wilmington, North Carolina, got a job in a soft-drink plant, and married a strikingly attractive young woman named Gertha, whose good looks and infectious smile were inherited by her son Ray. She named him after the blues singer Ray Charles, whom she admired.

When Ray, the fifth of his seven children, was three, Cicero packed his family into a '57 Mercury and headed for Washington, D.C., where he worked as a night manager in a supermarket. He later bought a house in Palmer Park, a predominantly black, lower-middle-class community in suburban Maryland.

Leonard's childhood was uneventful. He kept to himself, staying home, reading comic books, and playing with his German shepherd.

Never much interested in team sports—he was too small to excel in basketball or football—he preferred wrestling and gymnastics and took up boxing only because his brother Roger goaded him into it. Roger, a year older than Ray, had begun winning boxing trophies and waved them in Ray's face, chiding him for hiding out at home with his mama.

And so, in 1969, when he was thirteen, Ray walked into the recreation center in Palmer Park and laced on a pair of gloves. There he came under the tutelage of two men who would start him out on his journey to fame and fortune. They were Janks Morton, an insurance salesman who would become Leonard's closest friend and adviser, and Dave Jacobs, who worked for a pharmacy and in his spare time guided the center's boxing team.

For reasons Leonard always found hard to explain, he knew almost instantly that he was meant to be a boxer, that this was the road he must take to achieve self-fulfillment. He was an outstanding pupil, absorbing every lesson that Jacobs and Morton taught him. Victories came in bunches, and in 1972, he lied about his age so he could try out for the Olympic team at the trials in Cincinnati. He was sixteen. The minimum age was seventeen. During one fight, Johnson, a coach then, too, turned to Jacobs and said, "That kid you got is sweeter than sugar."

From then on, he was Sugar Ray to amateur fight fans, and with his marvelously quick hands and feet, he did indeed conjure up memories of the fabled Sugar Ray Robinson. The pressure of wearing that nickname never seemed to bother Leonard, and by

1973, he had won his first major title—the National Golden Gloves championship in the 132-pound class. The next year, he was the national AAU champ, and the next, the Pan American champ.

By the time the 1976 Olympic Games rolled around, the toll of his long and grueling amateur career was evident in the condition of his hands. Both were badly swollen, and he tried all sorts of remedies—epsom salts, rubbing alcohol, even Ben-Gay. The pain persisted, and he couldn't work out as intensely as he wanted to. Whatever he did, though, was enough—and in the 150th and final amateur fight of his career, on his way to his 145th victory, he methodically took apart the crafty Cuban Aldama and won the gold medal.

"This is my last fight," Leonard said. "My journey has ended. My dream has been fulfilled."

Leonard hoped to trade on his Olympic fame, making enough money on commercial contracts to attend the University of Maryland and become the first college graduate in his family. He hired an attorney named Mike Trainer, a friend of Morton's, to handle legal work, and PR man Charles Brotman to screen requests from the media, schools, shopping centers, and other outfits that wanted a piece of his time.

And then he waited.

And waited.

Bruce Jenner, the winner of the decathlon, got all the endorsements. For one reason, aside from his handsome features and athletic prowess—which, of course, Leonard could match— he was white. For another, Leonard's clean-cut image went into a tailspin.

Shortly after the Olympics, to qualify for welfare, Leonard's girlfriend, Juanita, had to make a formal identification of her two-year-old son's father. His name was Little Ray. His father was Leonard. And even though Leonard had time and again told the world about his son and girlfriend in Maryland—remember, he wore her picture on his sock—the press reacted as if it had unearthed a scandal. Some reports got the story all wrong, calling Juanita's action a "paternity suit."

Bye-bye, Madison Avenue.

Leonard would eventually marry Juanita, that was always his intention, but he was deeply hurt and embarrassed by this turn of events. There he was, no longer an Olympic hero but just another black kid, penniless and with a child out of wedlock, cruelly stereotyped.

Those were the worst days of Leonard's young life. Depressed and unable to decide about his future, he began to lean toward a career in professional boxing. It could win him back his self-respect. It could put money in his pocket. And then there was this encouraging sign: After a couple of months of inactivity, his hands healed and no longer pained him.

When I next saw him, in September, at Yankee Stadium for the heavyweight championship fight between Ali and Ken Norton, Leonard had yet to make up his mind. In fact, before the fight, he had visited Ali in his dressing room, and the champ asked him: "Are you going to turn pro?"

"I don't know," Leonard replied.

"If you do," Ali said, "don't sell yourself out. Keep all the money for yourself—and get a good manager."

Leonard looked at Angelo Dundee, Ali's longtime trainer, then back at Ali. The champ smiled and winked.

"Call me when you make up your mind," Ali told Leonard.

Several weeks later I got a call from Brotman, and he told me that Leonard had made up his mind to turn pro. This didn't come as too much of a surprise. I had heard that his father had contracted meningitis. At about the same time, his mother had suffered two mild heart attacks. And it was the illness of his parents, neither of whom could now work, that ultimately forced Leonard's decision.

During the course of my conversation with Brotman, he told me that Trainer had already incorporated Leonard, and it would soon be announced that the fighter was president and sole stockholder in Sugar Ray Leonard, Inc. He also told me that Leonard had hired Jacobs and Morton as his trainers but was still undecided about a manager.

Being neophytes in pro boxing, the team of Trainer, Morton, and Jacobs were looking for someone who could take control of the corner during a fight and who could pick the right opponents. Brotman said they were talking to three candidates: Eddie Futch, who handled heavyweight champ Joe Frazier; Gil Clancy, who was welterweight and middleweight champ Emile Griffith's man; and Angelo Dundee, who was always with Ali, one of nine fighters he had either managed or trained to a world championship.

"What do you think?" Brotman asked.

"I like Angelo," I said. "Not to take anything away from the other two guys, but Angelo's a quick thinker in the corner, he's got the knowledge and the contacts, and his association with Ali through the years has got to help. And besides, he's warm people. I think Ray will respond to him."

"Well, to be honest, Howard, that's the way Ray's leaning. He feels a compatibility with Angelo, and then there's the Ali thing. Ray thinks, hell, if he's good enough for Ali, he's good enough for me."

Dundee got the nod. His arrangement with the Leonard group worked splendidly, though bitterness between him and the Leonard group would eventually set in. Whatever their differences, however, the best interests of the fighter were never sacrificed.

The deal went like this: Jacobs and Morton would handle the daily training regimen, while Dundee arrived at camp a week or two before the fight to touch Leonard up and discuss tactics. And once the fight started, Dundee was in total control of the corner. No noise. He did all the talking.

His most important job, however, was picking Leonard's opponents. Promoters would call him with a list of fighters, and Dundee checked them out. Maybe he had seen them in action. If he hadn't, he'd look up their records, size up their opponents, even call a friend.

And Dundee's got friends all over the world. A promoter in Manila, a trainer in Italy, a manager in Rio de Janeiro. When he needed an opinion, he was almost certain to get a reliable response. Is the guy a banger? Is he strong inside? Which way does he prefer to slide? Does he take the play to you? Does he grab in close? Is he a goat (a fighter who butts)? Is he a bleeder? Does he have stamina? Does he start slow or fast? Is he prone to getting knocked down early?

Dundee brought Leonard along brilliantly. He never missed a trick, always reminding himself that no fighter was a sure thing. To paraphrase Ernest Hemingway, never fall in love with a fighter because he's sure to break your heart, and Dundee has suffered plenty of broken hearts. And so, from the outset, he was cautious.

When it was announced that Dundee would manage Leonard, I called him to arrange an interview. "Congratulations, Angie," I said. "Ray can't miss. You've got another Ali."

Dundee moaned. "Don't say that, Howard. You know I got that Italian superstition."

"C'mon, Angie, you saw him in Montreal."

"On television, yeah. And he was pretty as a picture. The kid lit up my living room. When they asked me to manage him, I immediately thought, *marone*, here we go again, bright lights and applause. I know the networks got to love him. He's show biz."

"And he's got the ability to go with it," I said. "I'm sure of it."

Dundee said: "I've got good feelings about him, too, Howard. Even on TV, I could see a lot of what he was doing because he throws everything from the outside. And he was throwing everything in the book. But, hell, you know how many great amateurs buckled when they had to fight for their supper?"

"Too many," I said, showing respect for Dundee's caution.

"You got it. Can he take a punch? Can he adapt? When a guy doesn't do what we expect, can Ray change his tactics?"

"Only the great ones can shift gears like that."

"That's right, Howard. And what about a killer instinct? I can't teach that."

"Angie," I joked, "why the hell did you take this kid?"

Dundee laughed, but I knew he wasn't about to make any predictions, wasn't about to say he had a potential champion in the mold of Ali. "This ain't a crystal-ball business, Howard, but I'll tell you: There ain't another kid around I'd rather have. And I'll take care of him.

"The opponents I pick, I want each of them to give Ray a different problem. Each fight's gotta be a new lesson. And I want guys who fight back. If the kid's gonna learn, I gotta take a small risk here and there, but I won't put him in the ring with a guy I think can beat him. What's the sense of that?

"It'll be rough enough. He's gonna get a real education, from kindergarten to college."

Leonard's course load went something like this:

February 5, 1977. Baltimore. Leonard's first fight as a pro was against Luis (Bull) Vega, providing Lesson No. 1: It's a lot harder trading punches with a pug who fights for a living. Vega was sturdy and low-slung. No finesse, but he kept coming, and nobody had ever knocked him out.

Late in the fight, Dundee wanted to test his pupil and told him: "Let me see you back him up."

Leonard obliged, bouncing horrific punches off the Puerto Rican's head—and winning a unanimous, six-round decision.

Unwilling—or unable—to acknowledge what Dundee was trying to accomplish with this fight, most boxing writers pooh-poohed Leonard's victory. "Big deal," they said. "Vega's a bum," they said. You'd think they'd have learned a thing or two about developing a fighter, turning a raw prospect into a mature pro. What did they expect? A fight against a contender his first time out?

A lot of old-time ringsiders were also upset about the money that Leonard received. He took home $40,000 ($30,000 from the gate and $10,000 from CBS), and they figured he hadn't paid his dues to earn that much for his first pro fight. But CBS scored in the ratings, and Leonard drew a live gate of 10,170, a record, at the Baltimore Civic Center. Believe me, he earned it.

The attorney Trainer was ready to capitalize on those numbers. All three networks tried to sign Leonard to a multi-year contract, but Trainer didn't want to tie himself to one network for an extended period of time. So he signed a six-fight contract with ABC for approximately $400,000, taking a lot less money than he would've made on a longer deal. He was gambling on Leonard's ability to stay undefeated and command even bigger money the next time around.

The ABC deal was made just prior to Leonard's second fight, in which he decisioned Willie Rodriguez in Baltimore. And while the television money was flowing in, Trainer was also making separate deals with arena operators, taking a cut of the live gate and freezing out the promoters.

Justice at last. For decade upon decade, promoters ruled supreme, a sleazy, cutthroat bunch who made millions peddling other men's flesh and never giving a damn for the fighters' welfare. They usually held all the cards, locking up champions and contenders to long-term contracts, dictating who will fight whom, where and when and for how much. And then Leonard came along, and they were dumbfounded. Nobody owned him, and everybody wanted him. He didn't need them. And to get him, the arena operators didn't need the promoters. All they had to do was pay Leonard a percentage of the money that people had paid to see him fight.

Simple.

And the simplicity was refreshing.

I loved it.

Leonard's education continued in Hartford, Connecticut. His third opponent was Vinnie DeBarros, selected because Dundee wanted to see how well Leonard could handle speed. Well enough. The referee mercifully stopped the fight in the third round. It was an impressive performance by Leonard, and nobody was more impressed than a spectator at ringside, a little guy with a flat nose—the great Willie Pep, the former featherweight champion.

"What'd you think?" Dundee asked Pep.

"Too much, Angelo, too much," he said, shaking his head.

"Who does he remind you of?"

"The speed is something else, something else. I dunno. He got the name Sugar Ray, which I don't think he should use outta respect. I can't say he can be another Robinson, but I can't say he can't be, either. Ya know what I mean? Anyways, he's good, real good, and ya gotta like his youth. I gotta keep my eye on him. Definitely."

Dundee was enthusiastic. Everything was falling into place. He could feel it.

"We're going barnstorming now," he said. "Different places, different smells, different crowds. I want him to react to all kinds of situations."

March 1, 1978. Dayton, Ohio. Art McKnight had an awkward, helter-skelter style, and Dundee wanted to see if Leonard could get to him. He did, in the seventh round, in a corner, flailing away at McKnight's ribs, arms, head for a TKO. Leonard's record was now 8–0.

March 19. New Haven, Connecticut. Javier Muniz was supposed to be Leonard's toughest opponent to date. Smart and cute, he once went the distance with the murderous Roberto Duran. In the very first round, however, Leonard separated Muniz from his intellect for the first time in thirty-one pro bouts. Sliding right, he dipped, then threw a sucker right over Muniz's left. It was textbook gorgeous.

May 13. Utica, New York. Randy Milton was a runner, a frustrating opponent because he didn't care how cowardly he looked trying to keep out of harm's way.

"Chase him," Dundee told Leonard.

Leonard finally caught him in the eighth and notched his eleventh victory, on a TKO.

June 3. Baltimore. Could Leonard go the distance? To answer that question, Dundee picked a strong, granite-jawed veteran named Rafael Rodriguez to test his fighter's stamina. Leonard could have gone another ten rounds. Jabs, overhand rights, nightclub footwork—and Leonard won a unanimous decision.

September 9. Providence. Leonard had his hands full with Floyd Mayweather, a hotshot, a clever boxer who knew how to make maximum use of the ring. And it showed. Up to that point, I hadn't seen Leonard look worse. He was devoid of his usual movement and verve, and Mayweather kept tagging him.

"He's outpunching you," Dundee told Leonard late in the fight. "You gotta slug with him. Go get him. Now!"

Leonard finally got him—knocking him out with a barrage of punches in the ninth round.

Later, at the airport, Leonard was still disgusted with himself. "I just couldn't get up for that fight," he told me. "I don't know why, but it won't happen again."

December 9. Springfield, Massachusetts. Armando Muniz never ducked anybody. A good combination puncher, he had a solid left hook and liked working the body. He went the distance with Carlos Palomino when Palomino was the welterweight champ.

In that fight, Leonard surely had the look of future greatness about him, constantly turning Muniz, moving from side to side, and throwing punches from countless angles. And when Muniz tried to retaliate, Leonard simply wasn't there for him to hit.

Leonard stopped Muniz in the sixth round and boosted his record to seventeen victories without a defeat.

The Muniz fight was Leonard's last on the ABC contract. His ratings had been gloriously high on *Wide World of Sports*, and so ABC naturally wanted to sign him to another contract. It got him, in early 1979, this time for a five-fight package worth in excess of $1 million.

Trainer's gamble had paid off.

Surely, television had enhanced Leonard's appeal, but a lot of boxing writers couldn't get beyond his telegenic personality. They showed little respect for his natural ability and swiftly improving skills, instead labeling him merely a television hype. Some went so far as to call him my creation—"Howie's Baby."

Leonard deeply resented those jibes, and I came to wonder if he held me responsible, if he blamed me for the press not giving him his due. In all honesty, if he had started to rip me in print and tried to disavow the friendly relationship between us, I would have understood. That's how sick the whole thing had become.

Wanting to clear the air, just before ABC was to embark on a new series of Leonard fights with me at ringside, I put the question to Leonard: "How do you feel about being called 'Howie's Baby'?"

"I hate it."

"I don't like it much either."

"It's just not fair, Howard. What do I have to do to prove to them that I've got what it takes?"

"Keep winning."

Leonard shrugged, as if doubting that yet another string of knockouts would silence his critics.

I asked: "Do you think that they're saying these things because I like you, because I've been saying all along that you're going to be a great one? Maybe they're just reacting to me, and if that's so, I'm sorry."

"I don't blame you for one second, Howard. It's them. It's their problem. I think they resent all the money I'm making and I'm not even a champ. Am I supposed to give it back? Am I supposed to say, 'Hey, please, don't give me all this money 'cause I like being poor'?"

"I'll be champ someday, Howard, and I'll be a great champ. Then let's see what they say."

"They'll think of something, my friend. Just be ready."

And the education continued:

January 18, 1979. Landover, Maryland. Dundee kept getting badgered about matching Leonard against Johnny Gant, a popular fighter from the same area as Leonard. Gant was a dangerous welterweight, a ranked contender. His reputation was that he could lick any fighter on any given night, and he was coming off five straight victories.

Gant didn't get the sixth. Leonard dropped him in the second round with a series of rights. Then, in the eighth round, he peppered Gant with a fourteen-punch flurry, finishing him off with a left-right combination.

March 24. Tucson, Arizona. Leonard never looked more awesome than against Danny Gonzales, another ranked contender, scoring his quickest knockout as a pro—two minutes, three seconds of the first round.

Moments before the fight, Dundee visited Gonzales's dressing room and saw that he was talking to friends and relatives rather than warming up. There wasn't a bead of sweat on his body.

Dundee rushed back to Leonard's dressing room and switched gloves—from Everlast to Reyes, a Mexican brand that contains less padding around the knuckles and is designed for punchers.

"This guy's cold as ice," Dundee told Leonard. "Nail him."

"I thought I broke his jaw," Leonard said after the fight.

April 21. Las Vegas. The book on Adolfo Viruet was this: Spoiler. Counterpuncher. Difficult to move around. Licks good fighters. Gave Duran fits.

Viruet was also a southpaw, the first Leonard would face as a pro. A new lesson, another test.

Leonard had faced a lot of lefties in the amateurs, mainly fighters from Cuba and the Eastern Bloc countries. He already knew of one way to beat them—right-hand leads—and he was pretty good at it. Against a seasoned pro such as Viruet, however, he would have to be better. And to complement his right-hand leads, he'd have to be aggressive, keeping his jab in Viruet's face and throwing left hooks over Viruet's right jab.

No chance of that, according to the renowned matchmaker Teddy Brenner. A lot of boxing people think Brenner's got the best opinions in the business, and I'll admit he's knowledgeable. But when it came to Leonard, he was often dead wrong.

Before the Viruet fight, Brenner worked the phones, talking to his friends in the press, influencing their copy.

"Your boy's got no shot against Viruet," he said when he got around to calling me.

"Now, Teddy, you know I like you and I don't want to hurt you, but . . . you're full of shit."

"Oh, yeah? Viruet's got too many weapons. His left hook alone will kill Leonard."

"Why do you hate Leonard and other American blacks of his ilk?" I said, goading Brenner on.

"I don't hate blacks, Howard. That's not fair. I just think Leonard's a hype. You guys in television made him, and now Viruet'll break him."

Leonard broke Viruet, decking him in the fourth round with a right to his head. Then he took Viruet apart, piece by piece, in a thoroughly professional manner, and gained victory No. 21 on a decision.

May 20. New Orleans. Leonard's fight with Marcos Geraldo was perhaps his most significant test on his way to the title. He was in college now, looking to graduate with honors.

Geraldo was a no-nonsense middleweight, and Dundee wanted to see how Leonard would react to hitting a bigger man who could take it, then keep coming, and hit you back. Hard. A fight with Geraldo had the aura of inevitability about it.

In the third round, Leonard took a solid left hook to the head, and he was on queer street, seeing shadows. Trying to clear his head, he backed off, moving continuously, giving himself time. Then—*pow!*—another left hook, and moments later he staggered to his corner.

"I'm seeing three guys out there," he told Dundee.

"Go for the one in the middle," Dundee advised him.

At the bell, Leonard was still a little shaky, but he pulled himself together, dominated the fight from then on, and won a unanimous decision.

"I learned survival in that fight, Howard," he said. "That's something you can't learn in a gym."

"Were you scared?" I asked.

"I was too spaced out to be scared. All I know is that somehow I was able to reach down inside me, deep down inside me, and bring everything up."

"It looked like you were using every trick and every tactic you knew to get away from him."

"And some I didn't know," Leonard said, laughing.

Leonard's victory over Geraldo told Dundee exactly what he

needed to know. His fighter had passed his last test: character. Fancy footwork and mesmerizing combinations do not a fighter make. If he doesn't have the will to overcome adversity—i.e., take a punch—then he's got nothing.

That fight contributed mightily to Leonard's maturity in the ring, but as so often happens in boxing, not everybody in Leonard's camp viewed the fight in a similar light—and the ensuing clash of egos caused a split between Trainer and Dundee that never really healed.

Trainer, in fact, almost fired Dundee, claiming that the venerable manager had made a terrible mistake in matching Leonard against Geraldo and placed too heavy a burden on the fighter's shoulders. A loss to Geraldo, he felt, could have destroyed Leonard's career.

Dundee's opinion: At that point in his education, Leonard needed the fight to test his fortitude and purpose. Win or lose—and Dundee firmly believed that Leonard would prevail—a fight with a bruiser such as Geraldo provided an invaluable learning experience.

The way I saw it, Dundee was right, and Trainer had overreacted. I think that Leonard learned a lot about himself in that fight, and if one had faith in Leonard's innate talent, then a loss to Geraldo would not have had the devastating impact that Trainer feared.

At any rate, the damage was done. Trainer and Dundee were forever locked in a cold war of long silences and petty misunderstandings. Trainer grew to resent Dundee's popularity with the media, and Dundee, for his part, regarded Trainer as a "cold fish."

Their mutuality of interest, however, preserved the image of a united front in Leonard's camp. Trainer was well aware of Dundee's immeasurable value in the corner, and Dundee wanted the glitter and recognition of working with yet another champion. A fighter of Leonard's charisma and prestige, both inside and outside the ring, comes along once, maybe twice in a generation, and neither man could afford to spoil his association with him.

And so the pugilistic juggernaut rolled on.

Leonard plastered two more ranked contenders in quick succession, both in the fourth round—Tony Chiaverini, another lefty, and Pete Ranzany, who was left-hooked into submission. Then he challenged a very tough customer out of California who was supposed to give him trouble. His name was Andy Price. "Bye-bye, Sugar Ray," they sang. Only it was the wrong song. Leonard ambushed Price in the first round, driving him against the ropes and dropping him with twenty unanswered blows.

"Now," said Dundee. "Right," said Trainer. And Leonard signed to fight Wilfred Benitez, the WBC welterweight champion of the world.

Some people are never satisfied. Give them a star, and they want the moon. A lot of so-called boxing experts still doubted Leonard's skills. They questioned the caliber of his opponents, even though on many occasions they had picked those same opponents to win. Why hadn't he fought former welterweight champ Carlos Palomino? Or Duran, who had moved up into the 147-pound class? Or the lethal-looking Tommy Hearns? And what about the knockout artist Pipino Cuevas, who held the WBA slice of the welterweight crown? Safer going after Benitez, huh?

Uncharacteristically, Dundee found it increasingly hard to hide his annoyance with his fighter's critics. "They weren't part of the plan," he said. "I think I know something about bringing along a fighter. They'll all get their chance. You can't keep everybody happy."

Then, with a shrug and a smile, Dundee said, "Hey, there's some people that don't like linguini and white clam sauce."

No matter what Leonard's critics said, however, they could not dispute the fact that he was on the verge of making boxing history.

Though undefeated in thirty-eight fights and twice a champion—he was the junior welterweight champ before winning the welterweight title—Benitez had never earned more than $150,000 for a fight. Thanks to Leonard, he was to get $1.2 million, while the challenger would bring home $1 million. And because of Leonard's drawing power, both on television and in the arena, they would become the first fighters outside the heavyweight division to earn at least $1 million each for a bout.

The harping of Leonard's critics reminded me of the early days with Muhammad Ali when he was Cassius Clay. Nobody thought much of the caliber of his opponents either, and thus he was a 7–1 underdog against the allegedly invincible heavyweight champ Charles (Sonny) Liston.

And, indeed, the parallels between Leonard and Ali were most evident inside the ring, where each, in his own way, transformed the financial structure of the sport and accumulated a vast fortune. While plying his trade, Leonard imitated Ali's shuffle and bolo punch, and he'd annoy opponents with arrogant gestures, like sticking his chin in their face and daring them to hit him—and running his glove through their hair after the bell had rung.

Both Leonard and Ali were blessed with left jabs that stung and cut and demoralized opponents, and their combinations were like poems of doom. Early in their careers, they felt safer as moving targets, jabbing, circling, always hunting for the head. As the years went by, though, they were more amenable to moving in close and punishing an opponent's body, risking shots to their pretty heads. And each had a killer's instinct, always ready to stalk an opponent if he smelled a kill.

Most significantly, however, these two fighters possessed amazing reserves of courage and will. They could take the best anybody had to offer, and when the moment was darkest, dig down deep and find enough strength to fight on.

They had it all. Body and soul.

Beyond the ring, the differences between Ali and Leonard were apparent to longtime observers of both fighters. Though each was a product of his generation and responded to the temper of his time, certain knowledgeable judgments, I think, can be made about the magnetism and magnitude of their personas and how their personas shaped them as men.

On several occasions, when Ali was the object of eager, jostling crowds, whether on the street or in the gym, he'd say to me, breathlessly, "Ever see a crowd like this, Cosell? But you can't just look at the size. Look at the faces!"

And that's as good a place as any to start when comparing these two great champions, because the crowds reflected their images.

The faces in Leonard's crowds looked on respectfully, perhaps even admiringly, but there was little if any astonishment in their eyes. They knew exactly how they should feel about him.

Personable and intelligent, a man of simple virtues, Leonard rarely challenged the people's belief in him. He worked hard and provided for his entire family, not only his wife and son but also his parents and brothers and sisters. He was businesslike in appearance and demeanor, untainted by the sharks in the smoky back rooms of boxing, and he surrounded himself with a small group of dignified, unassuming advisers, not a large, unruly entourage of sycophants looking to make a quick buck or score a handout.

Also, Leonard was unfailingly gracious toward his fans, who instantly warmed to his handsome face and his shy, childlike smile. A creature of the 1970s, he understood the realities of television. The camera loved him, and he used it to his own advantage. And when the Madison Avenue hucksters finally took notice of what was happening, they commercialized his personality, capitalizing on Leonard's almost universal affection among whites as well as blacks.

Leonard treasured every dollar and cherished every moment in the spotlight. "You see, I don't consider myself a fighter," he said. "I'm a personality."

Like Michael Jackson in concert. Or Burt Reynolds in a movie. Or Johnny Carson on TV.

Ali always believed that he was bigger than everybody else, and it was impossible to dispute him. He'd take anybody on. He constantly amused or outraged the media and the public by switching roles—clown and martyr, preacher and poet, philosopher and savior—and he gradually fused all those roles into a single persona that was as complex as it was cosmic.

The faces of Ali's crowds wore expressions of anticipation, and there was wonder in their eyes. He was the guru of the unpredictable, and he dazzled them with new contradictions and mischief. He drew energy from the crowds, and he positively reveled in their admiration. He went so far as to search out strangers, holding sidewalk seminars, kissing babies, teasing beautiful women, sparring with street-corner winos, even granting lengthy interviews to high-school editors.

And it didn't matter where he was—in London or Manila or Kinshasa, Zaire—they gathered around him like moths to a naked, glowing ball of light, reaffirming his own profound conviction that he was indeed the most famous person on the face of the earth.

Ali was easy to love and easy to hate, and many people felt

both ways about him. Loud and brash, he told the world he didn't have to be what everybody wanted him to be, and he bragged about his pretty black face and his beautiful black body. Unwavering in his convictions, he lost his title and endured an unlawful exile from the ring when he refused to serve in the military on religious grounds, and besides, he said, "Them Viet Cong ain't never called me nigger."

When Ali returned to the ring, he commanded the attention of countless millions, strutting on a stage that was grand and global in scale. His skills had dimmed with age, but it hardly mattered. The man himself was so endlessly fascinating. He used to tell reporters to take out their notebooks and he'd fill 'em up. He could be mysterious and elusive, but sometimes he'd let you ride the sharp curves and walk the dark alleys of his psyche. He'd babble and fake you, then surprise you with flashes of witty insight and wildly entertaining ad libs.

Leonard was another kind of cat. When the cameras stopped rolling, he was more introverted than people ever suspected, and he guarded his privacy. Though he was articulate and smooth, his interviews were rarely spiced with revelations. His mood was almost always on an even keel, and he shuffled away with his secrets and his dreams virtually intact. You knew that he'd never sully his carefully polished image by uttering an angry sentence or dancing to a different drummer.

This is not to say that there wasn't anger in him, and hurt also, but you had to get close to him to draw out his emotions. It wasn't always easy, but it became less difficult as his stature as a champion helped him grow as a man.

The fight between Leonard and Benitez for the welterweight championship of the world was scheduled for November 30, 1979, in Las Vegas.

Leonard was twenty-three, with only twenty-five professional fights behind him, but he had proved himself a keen student and displayed tremendous improvement with each succeeding victory. As his opponents grew tougher, he emerged ever more dominant. And he had fought them all—righties and lefties, runners and bulls, dancers and sluggers, jabbers and hookers and counterpunchers.

And there were these gifts to contend with: A quick thinker, Leonard was superb at feinting and putting together combinations, throwing a variety of punches with speed and strength. He could jab and hook, maybe follow up with another hook, then throw his right and hook again. Or perhaps somewhere in there he'd throw a left uppercut, bewildering his opponent, then pouncing on him with a flurry of punches if he sensed a knockout.

And yet . . .

Though Benitez was almost two years younger than Leonard, he was a more experienced fighter and hardened to the pressures of a title, having won the junior welterweight championship when he was a mere lad of seventeen. He was tricky and shrewd and could use either hand with equal dexterity.

On January 14, 1979, in San Juan, when Benitez fought welterweight champ Carlos Palomino for his title, I worked the bout, and it was one of the most beautifully executed fights that I had ever witnessed. In the seventh round, Palomino went for it, pinning Benitez against the ropes and flailing away at him. Then, suddenly, Benitez unleashed an awesome counterpunching attack, ripping the heart out of Palomino—and ultimately winning the title on a decision.

Benitez loomed as Leonard's toughest opponent thus far, no doubt about it in my mind, and as great as I thought Leonard was and would be, I seriously questioned whether he could take the champion.

"He slips a punch better than any fighter in the ring today," I told Leonard.

"I'll get to him," Leonard said. "I'm not worried about that. It's his counterpunches that I'm training for."

"The way I see it, Ray, speaking candidly, I think you'll get hit more than you've ever been hit before. There's no getting around it. And to win, you're going to have to do more, in a technical sense, than you've ever done before."

"I've been teaching myself the left uppercut all over again, trying to refine it, surprise him with it. I've been studying it in films of Wilfredo Gomez [then the junior featherweight champ], who's a master at it."

"That may not be enough."

Leonard said: "You sound more worried than me, Howard. I'll beat Benitez. He's mine."

The fight was a masterpiece of technical wizardry: Every imaginable punch, feint, and maneuver had come into play—

until Leonard stopped Benitez with a scant six seconds to go in the fifteenth and final round.

And indeed, Benitez took Leonard to places he had never traveled before, places on the jagged edge of physical and emotional stress, and he passed the test with high honors.

At first it appeared that Leonard would have an easier time than expected, as his jab hit home and a left hook rocked Benitez backward. Benitez escaped—but in the third round, Leonard got to him again, this time with a stiff left jab that sent Benitez sprawling on the seat of his pants.

In the fourth round, however, Benitez started to show his superb, ringwise craftsmanship, tagging Leonard with two right-hand leads. He had adjusted to Leonard's style, slipping one punch after another, especially Leonard's right.

"Go downstairs!" Dundee kept telling Leonard between rounds. "Work the body! Forget the right hand."

The fight wasn't easy to score. To the uninitiated, it might have seemed a boring affair. Neither man dominated; each was having a difficult time trying to make the other do what he wanted him to do—like grand masters at opposite ends of a chessboard.

Leonard, though, was landing the more telling blows. In the ninth round, for example, a flurry of punches drove Benitez into the ropes, and in the eleventh round, a jarring left hook caused Benitez's mouthpiece to fly out of his mouth.

Both fighters thought they needed the last round to win, and so they came out swinging, transforming the bout from a chess match into a rumble. Then—bam!—the left uppercut that Leonard had studied so diligently caught Benitez on his chin and down he went. When Benitez got up, Leonard pounced, throwing a deft two-punch combination that prompted the referee to stop the fight.

Later that night, Leonard soaked his aching body in a hot bath, expressing mild concern about the first-time bruises on his face and talking about the fight.

"The man was incredible," he told me. "He slips punches better than any fighter I've ever seen. He's right there in front of you. No problem, I'm saying to myself, 'cause you know how fast my hands are. You throw the punch and he's not there. He moves his head a fraction of an inch and it's just not there."

"Much like Ali," I said. "And much like you yourself, Ray, except for this: Wilfred doesn't fight with his hands down like Ali did, like you do. And you might be doing too much of that."

"Maybe so, Howard, but he's so fast and so accurate that the best defense in the world isn't going to keep you from getting hit."

If Leonard vs. Benitez was confection for the connoisseur, then Leonard vs. Duran was meat for the masses. It was savage and relentless, as both fighters displayed uncommon valor over fifteen rounds, going face-to-face and toe-to-toe, brutalizing each other in the corners and along the ropes. A close fight, certainly. But when the final bell had rung and the decision was awarded to Duran, only the most myopic of partisans would have dared complain too loudly about the verdict.

From the moment the fight was signed, the hype began, and the anticipation intensified with each passing day. Without a doubt, this was the most eagerly awaited fight since the epic battles between Ali and Joe Frazier in the early 1970s. And just as with Ali vs. Frazier, the drama that swirled around Leonard vs. Duran had a lot to do with the contrasting styles of the fighters, both in and out of the ring.

Here was Leonard, the clean-cut Olympic hero, cool and detached, as comfortable in a three-piece suit as in a pair of boxing trunks, the complete boxer, graceful and stylish and undefeated in twenty-seven fights. And there was Duran, off the mean streets of Panama, wild and fiery, with glowing black eyes that reflected his reputation as a lethal brawler, a former lightweight champion who had lost only once in seventy-two fights and had abdicated his 135-pound title early in 1978 to hunt bigger prey in the welterweight division.

Rare is the sporting event that truly lives up to all the hype that surrounds it, but Leonard vs. Duran seemed destined to justify the billing supplied by its French Canadian hosts: *Le Face-à-Face Historique*.

I knew that the moment I landed in Montreal and visited Leonard. He was furious, agitated, and angered in a way I had never witnessed before or since.

"I'm going to kill him, Howard," Leonard said, and he slammed his right fist into the palm of his left hand.

"What the hell's wrong?"

"Duran's an animal. The other day, he saw my wife in the lobby of the hotel and flipped her the finger. I've run into him several times, and he curses me out. I try to ignore him, but he's had it. I swear, I'm going to kill him."

"You're going after him?"

"Yeah, jump on him at the bell, take him out early."

"That would be foolish, Ray. You fight your fight, not his. Otherwise, you're in trouble."

The next day at the weigh-in, Leonard almost came unhinged, aggravated as he was over the reception he got. Waiting in the wings, watching Duran approach the scales, he heard the crowd cheer lustily for his opponent—and some in that crowd were veteran sportswriters who were supposed to be objective men. When Leonard walked in, he was greeted by a stony silence interrupted by sporadic booing, and it was obvious that he was crestfallen by what had transpired.

"I don't believe this," I said to Budd Schulberg, the author of *The Harder They Fall* and *On the Waterfront*, who was standing next to me.

"Neither do I," he said.

"What an atrocity! And those newspaper guys? What the hell were they doing cheering?"

"Don't expect me to defend them, Howard. I'm just as shocked as you are."

"I don't like this crowd, Budd. Something's terribly wrong here."

I admit that I was repelled by Duran, regarded him as a great little fighter but uncivilized and belligerent as a man, while I possessed a long-standing affection for Leonard. That said, however, it is still impossible for me to understand how right-thinking people could react to Duran in such a worshipful manner and at the same time throw stones at a warm and decent man like Leonard. Admire Duran's fistic skills, okay, but don't exalt him as if he had just discovered a cure for cancer. He isn't worthy of it.

Leonard and I talked later in his hotel suite. You could hear the distress in his voice. "There were a lot of Americans at the weigh-in, and they were booing me and cheering Duran," he said, shaking his head. "Why? I won a gold medal for my country. I've lived a clean life, been a good husband and father, never did anything I should be ashamed of. How can they treat me like that?"

I couldn't answer him.

"I'll kill him," Leonard said again. "I'll show them, and I'll show up the sportswriters, too. No fancy stuff. I will not run. I'm going to stand flat-footed, and I'll have his head."

"Nah, no way," Dundee said when I repeated what Leonard had told me.

"He seems serious to me, Angie. I've never seen him in such an emotional state."

Dundee said: "He's too smart to mix it with Duran. You've got to do what got you here, and he knows that. And I'm talking about feinting left and moving right, lateral movement always, don't get caught on the ropes.

"Ray's a boxer, a great one, and a great boxer plays checkers. Side, side, inside. The key is the jab. Everything off the jab. He'll tip-tap Duran silly, then his time will come to knock him stiff."

I've known Dundee a lot of years, and it seemed that he was protesting too much. He was giving me a nice, neat lecture on how a boxer takes apart a brawler, but theories and strategies have a way of evaporating once two fighters step between the ropes and try to knock each other's head off.

Leonard wasn't Ali, who never let any opponent get to him psychologically. Ali didn't care how he looked in the ring or what people would say about him; he'd play a fool or a penitent, run away or absorb punishment, whatever strategy it took to achieve victory. That takes a special kind of courage, and now it was time to see if Leonard had it, too.

The fight was fought on June 20, 1980, in a ring set atop second base in Montreal's Olympic Stadium, and from the opening bell, Duran orchestrated the tempo and pace of the evening.

Duran promptly attacked Leonard, driving him against the ropes, bulling him from corner to corner. Always moving forward, mauling and wrestling Leonard, scoring inside with fists and elbows and knees and whatever else that might hurt his opponent.

Leonard's prefight scars hadn't healed, and they took control of him as he insistently engaged in a slugfest with Duran. Then came the second round, and Leonard paid dearly for his hubris. Duran caught him with a hook and a straight right. Leonard reeled and covered up, unable to hide the pain that had gripped his body.

Leonard told me later that it wasn't until the fifth round that he had felt like himself again, and indeed he did win the sixth round, scoring with his jab and several snappy combinations. The middle rounds were marked by an ugly fury, so ugly and furious in fact that Leonard's wife, Juanita, fainted in her seat. Her husband did not notice. He was trying to keep his own intellect intact. Every now and then, when Leonard broke loose, he fired effective combinations, but always there was Duran, countering, rushing, cutting off the ring.

Through it all, while calling the fight, I could hear Dundee screaming in the corner:

"What the hell are you doing!?! Get off the ropes!"

"Don't fight his fight, Ray!"

"Move, Ray, move. Box him, box him."

"Where's the jab? The jab. Everything off the jab!"

Dundee's words seemed lost on Leonard, intent as he was on waging a barroom brawl with Duran. Finally, in the thirteenth round, Leonard showed how he could handle Duran if only he'd employ more of his boxing skills. And by almost unanimous agreement, the thirteenth round was the most extraordinary round of the fight.

Duran hooked the champion into a corner, but Leonard easily escaped. Duran pursued, landing a hook and a solid right, but Leonard responded by snapping Duran's head with a right of his own. Then they were joined in fierce, unforgiving combat—until near the end of the round when Leonard, digging deep within himself, landed three lefts to the body and a couple of rights to the head.

That round stood as a shining testament to Leonard's bravery, and two of the three judges gave the round to Leonard. The last two rounds were anticlimactic. Leonard got the better of Duran, in my opinion, but the triumph rightly belonged to Duran—as did the welterweight championship that went with it.

Judging a fight is a highly subjective matter. Most ringsiders held to the opinion that Duran had forced Leonard to fight his kind of fight, depriving him of his most valuable tool—his foot and hand speed. By cutting off the ring and applying unyielding pressure, Duran had stifled Leonard's jab, which is the punch that is used to set up all the others.

I didn't agree then, and I still don't. What goes on inside a fighter's head and heart, I believe, is of paramount importance. Leonard's heart overruled his head, and he was determined to prove that he could take a punch as well as give one. He wanted to avenge the insults to his wife and to himself by beating Duran at his own game, and he was unwise to take that course of action.

This is not said to take anything away from Duran's gritty performance, but he was not, on that night, unbeatable. There was at least one welterweight in the world who could have beaten him, and that was Sugar Ray Leonard. It didn't work out that way, and the fault, as I saw it, was Leonard's.

After the fight, I worked both dressing rooms. Duran was utterly graceless, calling Leonard an amateur and boasting that he would beat him even more easily the second time around. "Then, you will see, I will knock him out," Duran said, unwilling to praise a gallant opponent who had given him hell for fifteen rounds.

The mood, as you can imagine, was somewhat more subdued down the hall. Dundee was uncharacteristically glum. He had already faced the sportswriters in a mass press conference and had ended it with a wry smile when somebody asked him, "Will you admit now that Leonard was an overrated fighter?"

"That's it, gentlemen," Dundee answered and walked away.

Now, several minutes later, Dundee was trying to explain to me what had happened. "Ray tried to outstrong the guy. Duran was throwing everything, from every angle, fists, elbows, knees, even his head, and he was taking Ray to places he shouldn't have gone. But he went and ... what can I tell you, Howard? He rushes, he pushes, he wings, and you're supposed to move. Counter and move, but Ray didn't. I tried to get him to, but he didn't."

Dundee sighed and shrugged his shoulders wearily, saying, this time with a dash of enthusiasm in his voice, "Ray is a great fighter, and I'm certain he will prove it. And that is that, my friend."

Then I spoke with Leonard, who was crying openly. "I salute Duran," he said. "I fought as best I could, and I want to fight him again."

Leonard was so distraught that I had to cut the interview short. The following week, however, having regained his composure, Leonard was his eager, confident self again, and he winked at me and said, "I will definitely fight Duran again, and this time I'll fight as Sugar Ray Leonard."

The fight was scheduled for November 25 in New Orleans, and when I got there, there was little doubt in my mind that Leonard would win. A lot of people were picking Duran on the theory that his brawling style was too much for Leonard to handle. I liked Leonard because: (a) I didn't believe that Duran was capable of reaching the same heights of fury; (b) Leonard was still growing as a fighter, and the experience of weathering Duran's savage attack was of enormous benefit to him; and (c) the day before the fight Leonard said to me, "It will be no contest, Howard. You will see the real Sugar Ray Leonard in that ring."

And I believed him.

Leonard had prepared himself assiduously—mentally, physically, and tactically. He wanted Duran so badly that it caused, among other reasons, a falling out with Dave Jacobs, his trainer since his amateur days. Jacobs wanted Leonard to take a couple of tune-up fights before meeting Duran again, but Leonard wanted the Panamanian right away. They argued—and Jacobs quit.

So single-minded was Leonard's pursuit of Duran that he shrugged off his long-time trainer's absence and called Dundee into camp earlier than usual. Discussions of strategy went deep into the night, and this time Dundee had Leonard's undivided attention. Every lecture had sunk in.

Duran, meanwhile, was riding high as the new welterweight champion, flaunting his churlish, swaggering behavior, and my disapproval of him had come full circle the previous month at Ali's return fight against Larry Holmes in Las Vegas. After the fight, I bumped into Duran, who stepped back and started winging punches in my direction. My first inclination was that he was being playful, but looking into those smoldering eyes of his, I wasn't so sure.

And then Duran caught me a glancing blow on my shoulder, and I was dumbfounded. My wife, Emmy, was with me, and bless her, she stepped into the fray and screamed, "How dare you do that, you thug!!"

I never felt safer in my life.

And I never felt more certain of a champion's downfall as I

did that night in New Orleans. Don't get me wrong, though: I never expected this fight to provide perhaps the most bizarre and controversial conclusion in the history of the sport.

It happened with sixteen seconds left to go in the eighth round, and the scene is always with me in my memory. Duran threw up his arms and surrendered. Quit. Though unhurt, he turned his back on Leonard and said to referee Octavio Meyran, "*No más, no más.*"

Meyran was incredulous. "*¿Por qué?*" he asked.

"*No más,*" Duran said again.

That was it!

In a few swift moments, Duran went from champion to bum. Worse than a bum, actually—a disgrace. It seemed impossible, but it had happened, leaving everybody groping for answers. And for all he was for all the years—hands of stone, *macho* gladiator, lethal mongoose—Duran had assured himself a terrible stigma, forever to be remembered, first and foremost, as the champ who quit against Sugar Ray Leonard.

To this day, it still irritates Leonard when people suggest that his victory was tarnished because Duran surrendered in such an ignoble fashion. As Leonard himself put it: "What I did, people thought was impossible. I *made* him quit. To make a man like Roberto Duran quit was awesome, more awesome than knocking him out."

I agreed wholeheartedly with Leonard's assessment of his victory, and his use of the word "awesome" was proper and to the point.

Leonard's performance that night in New Orleans was a fistic *tour de force.* Constantly on the move, he made a weapon of his jab, snapping Duran's head back again and again. When Duran tried to bull him into the ropes, he'd pivot, spin, and befuddle his opponent with rights to the head or uppercuts to the body. And while Duran had scored well in the third and fifth rounds, he was never able to take control as he had done in Montreal.

Leonard slipped most of Duran's punches, danced, mugged, posed, taunted, and embarrassed him. For Duran, perhaps the most humiliating moment of all came late in the seventh round. Winding up his right hand and looking like he was ready to launch a bolo punch, Leonard suddenly snapped out a left jab that landed squarely against Duran's nose.

Leonard had made a fool of Duran, and he wouldn't let up. He was merciless, sticking out his chin and inviting Duran to hit it, then scoring with rights and hooks and combinations.

Some purists at ringside clucked their tongues over Leonard's outrageous posturing, but he had achieved a tremendous psychological advantage. He now owned Duran. Nobody had ever treated the *macho* Duran with such contempt and disdain and escaped to tell about it. He had turned Duran into a laughing-stock, and Duran couldn't recover. Later, Leonard told me: "He was totally mine, Howard. I knew it, and you knew it. I could actually hear your voice at one point"—and he mimicked me—" 'Duran is completely bewildered!' "

And then came the ignominious eighth round, and *"No más, no más"* reverberated through the cavernous Superdome and echoes still in the corridors of sports history.

After the fight, Leonard was composed and even gentle-manly. He didn't lay into Duran as wickedly as he might've been expected to. Instead, he was more intent on focusing his thoughts on how people would ultimately regard this strange species of a championship fight. He believed that somehow he'd come up short.

Leonard said, "They won't give me the credit I deserve, Howard, I just know it. They'll say that Duran quit and he shouldn't have, that I wasn't really put to the test. But I *made* him quit, Howard, and I'm not sure a lot of people will appreciate what that means."

Duran's people had considerably heavier emotional baggage to cope with. Promptly after the fight, Duran claimed he was suffering from severe stomach cramps, felt nauseous and weak, and was unable to continue. Wily old Freddie Brown, his assistant trainer, screwed up his bulldog face and spat out his words: "He just quit. That's it. There's no fancy words for it, and no fancy excuses. He quit. I been with the kid for nine years, and he was an animal. At least he was supposed to be, right? What kind of an animal quits? A pussycat? He just quit. Period."

Ray Arcel was Duran's trainer, an honest, hardworking man who was almost too distraught to speak—but he had kind words for Leonard. He said: "No question, from the opening bell, Howard, it was Leonard's fight. It was no contest at all, and I hope the people will recognize what a truly great fighter Leonard is."

At eighty-one, Arcel had been associated with a long list of great champions, including Benny Leonard, Barney Ross, and Ezzard Charles. Arcel had grown very attached to Duran, like a father, and bragged about the Panamanian as every inch the fighter as his other champions. Nothing could possibly prepare him for that awful moment in the eighth round.

Arcel said: "This is it for me, the worst thing that's ever happened in all my years. Believe me, Duran was a fighter of enormous courage and determination. I don't know what happened. Maybe his mind snapped, blew out. I still can't believe it. What can I say? It's time for me to get out."

Duran himself was sticking to his story, as churlish and obstreperous as ever. "He no fighter," he said. "Me not well. He no beat me."

In the days and weeks after the bout, the sportwriters and the TV commentators and the fight mob rehashed Duran's stomach cramps and how he had gorged himself on too many steaks and too much orange juice prior to stepping into the ring. There were also theories about the complicated precepts of the Latin *machismo* culture—how it's more acceptable to walk away from a fight that you can't win than endure a humiliating defeat—and there were even widespread rumors about Duran's heavy use of cocaine.

Maybe there was a scintilla of truth in all of that, but I still hold to another theory. A bully, once exposed, quits, and Duran was a bully. That's what happened in the first Ali-Sonny Liston fight, when the supposedly invincible big, bad bear, unable to attack his younger and quicker opponent, refused to come out for the eighth round, blaming an injured shoulder.

In my opinion, you didn't have to be a Rhodes scholar to explain Duran's surrender. It was as simple as that—the bully exposed. And it was confirmed forever in my mind when it was verified that the allegedly sick Duran had spent the hours after the fight partying with his wife and friends in his hotel room.

A postscript: Freddie Brown, upset and disgusted, walked away from boxing, as did the venerable Arcel, though he appeared as an adviser of sorts in Larry Holmes's corner at the Holmes-Gerry Cooney heavyweight title fight.

As for Duran, his career was revived by promoter Bob Arum, who maneuvered Duran into a title fight with a youthful and inexperienced junior middleweight champion named Davey

Moore. Duran won. He later lost a decision to middleweight champion Marvin Hagler—and then, on June 15, 1984, got knocked out in the second round by Thomas Hearns, which ended, finally, Duran's career in the ring.

In a way, the coincidence—or irony or whatever you want to call it—of Hearns laying Duran to rest pleased me. For it was Hearns, the feared Hit Man from Detroit, who played the unwitting accomplice in securing Leonard's reputation as a champion among champions.

The temperature hovered above ninety degrees that night of September 16, 1981, in Las Vegas, and the desert air was thick with excitement, tension, and anticipation. There's nothing in sports like the atmosphere that surrounds a great championship fight, and this one had all the ingredients that usually come to a boil only when heavyweights clash.

Three months previously, Leonard had won the WBA junior middleweight title by knocking out the Ugandan Ayub Kalule, but that was viewed by many as merely a day at the beach. What everybody wanted was Leonard vs. Hearns, boxer vs. puncher, WBC champ vs. WBA champ for the unification of the welterweight title.

It was one of the most ballyhooed fights of all time, and again, the prevailing opinion was squarely in Hearns's corner. At six-one, he was too tall for Leonard, too long of reach, and too powerful, with a devastating right hand that had stopped thirty of thirty-two victims.

Hearns also boasted an umblemished record—until 1:45 of the fourteenth round in a ring that was erected on the tennis courts at Caesar's Palace.

Hearns was lucky to get that far.

That's because Leonard had made several crucial mistakes in the first half of the fight. Which is not to imply that Leonard's performance was not a testament to his greatness. It was.

But let's begin at the beginning.

The strategies were simple enough. Hearns was programmed to keep his long jab in Leonard's face and look for the opportune moment to unload his right hand. Leonard, on the other hand, was to keep Hearns moving, pile up points, test his opponent's stamina, and bide his time until the later rounds. Leonard was also supposed to exploit a chink in Hearns's armor, a chink that is prevalent among fighters who are trained by Emmanuel Steward—they carry their lefts exceedingly low and thus are susceptible to right-hand leads.

Neither fighter followed his script. They improvised as they went along.

As Leonard bounded into the ring, he was the picture of confidence. In fact, just prior to the singing of the national anthem, he danced above me at ringside, winked, and said, "I've got him, Howard."

Hearns was more subdued, seemed even a bit nervous, as he darted around the arena as if in awe of the spectacle that he was about to participate in.

The first two rounds were uneventful, except for this: Just past the two-minute mark of the second round, Hearns unleashed a thundering right to Leonard's head—and nothing happened. Leonard shook it off and laughed at him. That's the sort of thing that unnerves fighters who rely on power, and that's when Leonard achieved his first and perhaps most important advantage. Hearns had to be thinking: "Damn, how am I ever going to hurt him?" And Leonard was probably saying to himself: "He can't hurt me, so I might as well take it to him."

Which Leonard did. In trading punches with Hearns, however, Leonard started to display some puffiness under his left eye. It was nothing serious at first, and Dundee and Morton were able to control the swelling by using a miniature flatiron, which they kept frozen in a bucket of ice and pressed against the puffy area between rounds.

The sixth round was a revelation. Many said that Leonard couldn't punch with Hearns, but here he was on the attack, blasting through Hearns's amateurish defense, landing all sorts of punches from all sorts of angles. Then, with twenty-six seconds to go, Leonard ducked a wild right and countered with a hook that pulverized his opponent's ribs.

It was perhaps the most damaging punch of the evening—and yet Leonard failed to capitalize on it. Instead of pursuing Hearns and knocking him out, Leonard mistakenly played it cautiously, worried about Hearns's heralded right, even though he had already absorbed Hearns's best punch. It wasn't until the last few seconds of the round that Leonard went after Hearns, but by then it was too late.

Hearns had survived, and he survived yet another brutal assault, in the seventh round.

And then Hearns turned into a boxer.

He came out in the eighth round on his toes, flicking his jab, and bicycling in circles. It was a wise decision, I felt, on the part of Hearns's handlers. For one thing, Hearns was primarily a boxer as an amateur, having scored only eleven knockouts in his 163 victories; and for another, because of the pain from the punch he took in the sixth round, Hearns kept his right elbow tucked against his aching side, making it rather difficult for him to employ his potent roundhouse punch.

And so the puncher became a boxer, and the boxer went flat-footed, stalking the fleeing Hearns with patient determination. Too patient, now when I think about it.

Hearns began scoring, aiming his jab at Leonard's bruised left eye, and he was getting to him. The tide was turning as Leonard began losing vision in his swollen left eye. After the twelfth round, in fact, in the corner, Dundee screamed at Leonard: "You're blowing it, kid! You're blowing it! Now go out there and put him away!"

And that's exactly what Leonard did.

He first caught Hearns with a vicious right to the temple, staggering Hearns against the ropes. Then he unloaded almost two dozen unanswered punches, sending Hearns reeling through the ropes.

Incredibly, the referee, Davey Pearl, ruled that Leonard had pushed Hearns rather than knocked him down, and he let Hearns scramble to his feet. But Leonard was all over Hearns again, scoring a three-punch combination and then two rights that returned Hearns to the lowest strand of the ropes.

As the bell for the fourteenth round sounded, Leonard looked like he was coming out of the starting block for a hundred-yard dash. He was across the ring in a flash and staggered Hearns with a mighty right to the head and a hook to the body, driving his opponent against the ropes. Leonard followed, raining blow after blow on all parts of Hearns's anatomy—until Pearl mercifully came to Hearns's rescue and stopped the carnage.

Hearns didn't complain, and neither did anybody in his corner. He was a beaten man, and he knew it.

Too bad the judges didn't.

Believe it or not, if Hearns had managed to survive the fourteenth round and went on to finish the last round, he would've won the fight. No kidding. The three judges were Lou Tabat, Duane Ford, and Chuck Minker, and I still can't figure out what fight they were watching. No matter that Leonard dominated the fight. No matter that Leonard won the only three lopsided rounds—the sixth, seventh, and thirteenth. And no matter that Hearns was the more seriously hurt. Each of these so-called experts had Leonard far enough behind on points that a knockout was his only salvation. Otherwise he was a sure loser!

After the fight Leonard said: "In New Orleans, when Duran quit, they had the fight just about even on the cards. They scored the Kalule fight a lot closer than it actually was, and I had to knock him out, too. Why they treat me like that, I don't know. Am I supposed to be an exception to their rules?"

And about his victory, he said: "I made a mistake, Howard. I should've knocked him out in the sixth round. I don't know what it was, maybe a reaction to what I had done in the first fight against Duran, but this time I went the other way. I played it too conservatively. I had him, and I let him slip away by laying back, being overly cautious.

"But you know, with each fight, I keep learning something new. And this fight was no different. I'm a better fighter right now than when I stepped into that ring tonight."

By some estimates, Leonard earned about $11 million against Hearns, perhaps the biggest payday in the history of sports, let alone boxing. Add that sum to what Leonard had reaped in the two Duran fights—anywhere between $15 million and $18 million—and it doesn't take a C.P.A. to conclude that he was set for life.

Early the following year, Leonard took on an outclassed pug named Bruce Finch. To keep busy, I guess. The fight was held in Reno, Nevada, and the crowd was an unsophisticated bunch of suckers. Finch survived the first round, but in the second, he scored heavily with a flurry of blows against a listless Leonard, who was letting the kid have his way.

When the third round began, the crowd went wild with visions of an upset. Finch, full of himself now, stalked Leonard and landed several blows. The crowd was in an uproar, and I responded on the air: "The crowd just doesn't understand. Finch is not in Ray Leonard's league. And Leonard will, at any moment, take over and destroy this kid. It's a sham, believe me, because when Leonard gets going—"

Just then, Leonard unloaded on poor Finch and knocked him cold. Simple as that. All over.

Moments later, I interviewed Leonard at ringside and asked him some tough questions. Why fight such an overmatched opponent? What good does that do boxing? Weren't you embarrassed? How does it do you any good?

Leonard's replies were predictable enough. "You know, any time a guy steps into the ring against me, it's a dangerous situation. I have to stay in shape. Finch was a lot better than people gave him credit for. He actually hurt me a couple of times."

Apparently that interview did not go over too well with Trainer, who complained to Jim Spence, one of the vice presidents of ABC Sports. When I next ran into Trainer, I asked him directly, "Exactly what got you so upset with the telecast, Mike?"

Trainer said: "First of all, Howard, I felt you were unfair to the people of Reno. They went to great pains to be kind to everybody connected with the promotion, and the city is trying to become another Las Vegas in boxing."

"That's their problem, Mike, not mine."

"But calling Reno a lower-case Las Vegas . . ."

". . . is dead accurate, and you know it."

"Don't you think your interview with Ray after the fight was a little tough?"

I said: "That's how I make my living, Mike. You should know by now what to expect from me. And I don't think you have any right to interfere or complain about what I say on the air. My credentials speak for themselves. All week long on radio, I pooh-poohed that fight, called it a mere workout, predicted Leonard would knock him out in an early round. What the hell kind of questions was I supposed to ask Leonard?

"I love the kid, Mike. I've made no bones about that, but I'm not his flunky and I'm not yours."

It's difficult to relay the tone of my conversation with Trainer on the printed page, but we didn't scream at each other. Rather, we were cordial. He played his cards, and I played mine, and not another discussion was had about the Finch fight.

At the time, of course, I had no way of knowing that I would never call another Leonard fight again.

Leonard was winding down his training in Buffalo, where he was scheduled to fight Roger Stafford, when I put in a call to Leonard's hotel room. I'm not sure who answered the phone, but the person on the other end said, "He's gone back to Baltimore."

"What?" I said. "He's fighting in a couple of days."

"He's gone back to Baltimore," the voice insisted.

I finally tracked down Charlie Brotman, the PR adviser in Leonard's camp. "What's up, Charlie? Where's Ray?"

Brotman hesitated, then said, "In Baltimore."

"I know that, Charlie. Why?"

Again Brotman hesitated, and I knew something was up. "Well, Howard . . ."

"Well, what? C'mon, Charlie. This is me, Cosell."

"Okay, Howard. I can't keep this thing a secret too much longer anyway"—and then he took a breath—"Ray's got a detached retina. He's being operated on at Johns Hopkins Hospital."

While training for Stafford, Leonard began seeing spots out of his left eye. When he first complained about his vision, nobody near him took it seriously. Finally, on his own, he consulted a doctor in Buffalo, and she prescribed eye drops. They didn't work. He then got a second opinion—and was told bluntly that he had suffered a detached retina.

Leonard immediately flew to Baltimore. That was on May 8, and the following morning, he was operated on by Dr. Ronald Michels, one of the country's leading ophthalmologists.

I called the hospital several times, but nobody was being let through. Once I got as far as Leonard's nurse, who politely told me, "I'm sorry, Mr. Cosell, but Ray can't talk to anybody right now. Try again in a couple of days."

Trainer was available, however, and we got together several days later at Pimlico, where I was preparing to cover the Preakness, and taped an interview for *SportsBeat*.

While Trainer explained in depth the nature of Leonard's injury, he wasn't prepared to say whether Leonard would retire. "The operation was a tremendous success," he said, "but no decision on Ray's career will be made until six months from now.

According to Dr. Michels, that's how long it will take to determine if the retina is fully reattached."

Nobody was quite sure—and that is true today—just how or when Leonard hurt his left eye. In the Hearns fight? In sparring for the Hearns fight, when he got clipped by his partner's elbow? While training for the Finch fight? For the Stafford fight?

One thing was certain: Leonard had seriously begun to think about retirement, and I became convinced that he would indeed retire when, several weeks after the operation, we met in Washington for an interview that would appear on ABC's weekly newsmagazine program 20/20.

For quite a while, the two of us talked privately in my hotel suite. Leonard seemed in good spirits and actually looked dashing in his black eye patch. It was a warm and touching conversation, and we spoke of many things—his fear of blindness, his increasing disenchantment with the sacrifice of boxing, his love of family, his potential career as a sportscaster.

"Will you retire, Ray?" I finally asked him.

"I'd like to say yes and get it over with, but I'm still not absolutely sure in my mind. Aside from my physical condition, I worry about being mentally tough. There was Benitez, and the two Duran fights, and then I let Finch get to me."

"Finch?"

"I know you thought that was a nothing fight, and it should've been. But that sucker really hurt me in the second round, and that's ridiculous. I couldn't concentrate, couldn't get up for him, didn't want to be in there with him. There's no more challenges."

I said: "Suppose somebody comes along and offers you a twenty-million-dollar deal to fight Marvin Hagler [the diabolical-looking middleweight champ]?"

Leonard smiled softly, saying, "It's tempting, Howard, very tempting. That's the conflict. That's what's keeping me from saying right now, 'Good-bye, boxing, I retire.' "

As the summer stretched into fall, Leonard came to realize how much he missed a normal life-style. He was covering fights as a color commentator for HBO and CBS, making commercials, attending to his business affairs, and spending more time with his wife and young son. No more early-morning running, no more grueling sparring sessions in the gym. He ate when and what he wanted to, got up when he wanted to, and went to bed when he wanted to.

And the temptation of fighting Hagler for a potential $20 million had subsided sufficiently enough for Leonard to announce his retirement.

That announcement was to be made on November 9, 1982. Several weeks before, I got a call from Trainer, informing me that Ray indeed intended to retire, and then he asked if I would emcee Leonard's gala farewell to boxing. Naturally, I accepted.

I later spoke with Leonard, who thanked me for accepting his invitation. He said: "I'm just not with it mentally, Howard. Dr. Michel's given me a clean bill of health, says my eye's as good as new, and I can fight again if I want to. I just don't want to."

"Are you afraid for your eyesight?"

"A little, maybe. I know that from now on, that whenever I fight, I'll be thinking about the eye. The injury just made my decision easier to make."

"I want you to know, Ray, I think you're doing the right thing."

"So do I, Howard."

And so, on November 9, there I was in the middle of a boxing ring in the Baltimore Civic Center, and thousands of Leonard's friends and fans were there, too. Admission was charged, and the proceeds were turned over to charity. Ali showed up, and so did Hagler, and at one point in the night's festivities, Leonard put his arms around the middleweight champ. "Marvin Hagler is a great man and a great champion," he said. "The two of us in the ring, now that's a helluva fight! A great fight! And we'd make more money than any fighters in history. But, I'm sorry, Marvin, that will never happen. . . ."

A little more than two weeks later, on November 26 in Houston, I also quit professional boxing. That night, I watched heavyweight champ Larry Holmes slaughter Randy Cobb over the length of fifteen rounds, and it sickened me. I had had enough of the sport, and I decided to walk away. My decision was irrevocable.

Just as I thought Leonard's was.

On December 11, 1983, at a press conference in Washington, Leonard announced that he was returning to the ring.

Rumors were flying for weeks about Leonard's impending

comeback, but I didn't nail it down until several days before the official announcement, when I received a call from Brotman. He invited me to attend a six-round exhibition on the night of December 10 at Andrews Air Force Base near Washington. There, Leonard was to box his cousin, Odell Leonard, and the next day, he planned to meet with a select group of columnists and sportswriters.

I couldn't attend either function, but I pressed Brotman: "Clue me in, Charlie. The kid is coming back, isn't he?"

"Yes, he is, Howard, but please don't use it. That's off the record."

"Maybe so, Charlie, but a lot of people are talking about it. And now you're inviting a bunch of guys for a private discussion with Leonard. What the hell am I supposed to think?"

"You're right, of course, Howard, but you didn't hear anything officially, not from me."

Neither Leonard nor Trainer were commenting on the rumors either. Nevertheless, respecting Brotman's wishes, I delivered a commentary on *SportsBeat*, noting that Leonard was going to meet the next day with certain members of the press. "I am not absolutely certain what Leonard will tell them," I said, "but I think I have a pretty good idea. He intends to come out of retirement and eventually challenge Marvin Hagler for the middleweight title."

Mentioning my distress over this apparent turn of events, I went on to say that, in my opinion, Leonard wasn't motivated by money. He was, after all, worth millions. "He loves boxing," I said, "views it as an art form, a means of self-expression that he apparently can't find anywhere else."

There was also another reason, I theorized. Leonard had recently worked the Hagler-Duran fight for HBO and was not impressed with Hagler's plodding, inefficient performance over a faded fighter whom he should've handled easily. I said: "I think Leonard came to realize that Hagler is not the fighter he was cracked up to be—and that the Sugar Ray of two years ago could beat him.

"Even so, the ring is a cruel place. And the business of boxing is a hustler's kingdom. Not only chumps, but the champs are often victims, too. Sugar Ray Leonard is one of the lucky ones. His light shines on, and there are other worlds for him to conquer. I don't want to see him risk his life, but it's his life to live. And I can only pray he knows what he's doing."

On December 11, Leonard admitted he would fight again. Then, the following night, he appeared with me at half time on the *Monday Night Football* game between the Bucs and the Packers in Tampa, Florida. It was a split-screen hookup, with Leonard in Washington and me in the booth, and I was pleased that he had consented to come on with me, for two reasons. One, even though Leonard was under contract to CBS, he chose to grant his first network interview to me on ABC. And two, he came on knowing how I felt about his return to the ring, which I took as an indication of the respect he still had for me.

In a nutshell, his most interesting answer concerned his motivation for returning: ". . . not money, but being content," he said. "I made a hasty decision because of my eye injury. But, thank God, it's been corrected by Dr. Michels. I was sincere about retiring, but I also realized I was denied history. Now, with my youth and my eyesight, I can make history possible, fight them all, show how really great I am. . . . Another reason is that they're talking so bad about boxing now, I want to come back and clean it up."

Leonard also mentioned that he would fight only with thumbless gloves, which he thought would help him avoid another injury to his eye. I closed out the interview by telling him to take care of his eyesight.

"See you at ringside," he said.

"No, you won't," I said, "but I wish you luck. And God bless you, Ray."

Leonard was scheduled to fight somebody named Kevin Howard on February 25, 1984, in Worcester, Massachusetts. There were a lot of questions—about Leonard's reflexes, his hand and foot speed, his punching power, his ability to take a punch. To what degree were Leonard's skills still intact? How long would it take for him to reach the level of the Leonard of old? Could he ever attain such heights again? And most importantly, what were the psychological scars of his eye injury? Would fear of reinjury debilitate him?

The fight was supposed to answer at least some of those questions.

HBO was to carry the fight live, but ABC purchased the

delayed-broadcast network rights. As a matter of courtesy, Dennis Lewin, a senior producer, asked if I wanted to call it. I thanked Lewin for asking, but no, my decision to stay away from professional boxing was for all time.

This is not to suggest that some small part of me didn't want to cover the fight. I'm only human. I had been with Leonard from the beginning, and his fights had provided me with some of the most memorable moments of my career.

But then, on February 13, that small part of me was forever cured of its yearning for the big fight.

That's the day that Leonard visited Dr. Edward Ryan, an ophthalmologist at the prestigious Massachusetts General Hospital, for a routine examination. In simplest terms, Dr. Ryan discovered a loose retina in Leonard's right eye, which was his good eye. He promptly performed preventive surgery, which took only five minutes, and termed the operation a success. But he also said, "I would not recommend that he fight, but if the eye heals properly, I could not prevent him from fighting."

It was confirmed that Leonard's left eye was fine, but Dr. Ryan's statement seemed to put him at odds with Dr. Michels, who had operated on the left eye and given Leonard the green light to fight again. Several days later, however, Dr. Ryan indicated that his differences with Dr. Michels were not of a medical nature but philosophical. "I'm against boxing," Dr. Ryan said. "Not only would I advise Leonard not to fight again, but I would give the same advice to Marvin Hagler or other fighters with perfect retinas. If Leonard's right eye heals properly, there's no reason why he couldn't resume his boxing career."

Well, Leonard's right eye did indeed heal properly, and his fight with Howard was rescheduled for May 11, again in Worcester. Now, I'm no ophthalmologist, but I thought that Leonard was thumbing his nose at Fate. How many warnings does a man need? Retinal detachments are not uncommon in boxing, and they can lead to impaired vision, even blindness. As the primary objective of prizefighting is to knock the other guy out, the eyes will always be potential victims. Why take the risk?

Leonard's determination to make a comeback sorely tried my respect for the man. He was well aware of my feelings, which were oft stated in public, and in the ensuing weeks, we did not have any contact with each other.

In the meantime, of all people to call me and express concern for Leonard was Bob Arum, the promoter. Here and now, let me say that Arum, a Harvard-educated attorney, has a brilliant mind. He's also devious, shrewd, cunning, and an indefatigable manipulator of TV executives, sportswriters, and fighters, playing them against each other like pawns in an elaborate game of chess. He got me at my apartment and said: "What the hell's wrong with Leonard? He's crazy to fight again."

"You know my position on that, Bob."

"It's a disgrace, those people letting him get back into the ring. How can you have any respect for guys like Trainer and Dundee? You can't let this happen."

"What am I supposed to do, Bob? Put a gun to his head?"

Arum's sincerity was quickly wearing thin. If Leonard vs. Howard were his promotion, I thought, he wouldn't be talking to me and doing a fairly good impersonation of St. Francis of Assisi. Our conversation fast approached its end, though, when Arum said, "I implore you, Howard, you must do some stories about the good people in boxing."

"Bob . . ."

"Yes, Howard."

"Where the hell am I going to find them?"

Several days later, another senior producer at ABC asked me if I wanted to call the fight. This time it was Chuck Howard, and again, saying thanks, I reiterated my position in even stronger terms. Not only wouldn't I cover the fight, but also I had no intention of watching it.

And I didn't.

The day of the fight, I sent Leonard a telegram, expressing my fervent hope that he emerge from the fight unharmed. That night, I went out to dinner with my wife and some friends, then headed for the ABC studios on the West Side of Manhattan. I was to appear on *Nightline*. In reaction to the Leonard fight, the producers of the show had booked a fighter named Bobby Czyz, an allegedly bright young man who had forsaken a chance to go to medical school. Why, Ted Koppel and I were supposed to ascertain, would a man choose a career of brutality over one of compassion?

The segment with Czyz went off smoothly if uneventfully, and during the commercial break, Koppel asked me to stick around. Leonard was going to make a surprise appearance on the show from the arena in Worcester.

Before taking the air, I had learned that Leonard was knocked down in the fourth round but rallied to beat Howard on a TKO in the ninth round. That's about all I knew. And neither Koppel nor I knew that at the press conference after the fight, which was not televised by HBO, Leonard said he was retiring again. The wire services were just beginning to run the story.

Leonard's appearance thus was a coup for *Nightline*.

Koppel welcomed Leonard, then said, "You've got a surprise for us, Ray. You've retired again. Why?"

". . . I found out it wasn't there, and I was very apprehensive in the fight tonight. . . . I know fully well that there were a lot of people opposed to my return to the ring. But, Ted, being an athlete like I am, I had to find out for myself. . . . No one could convince me that I couldn't do it. I tried, and it wasn't there. So I told my wife, Juanita, and Little Ray that's it, and that's it for good."

Koppel complimented Kevin Howard, and Leonard agreed, adding, "The people here were somewhat upset. I guess they expected more of me, Ted, and the expectations were just too great, considering my two-year layoff. I'm the first to admit—there's no sense fooling myself or the public."

Koppel mentioned the interview with Czyz, then wondered why a man of Leonard's financial status had resumed his boxing career. "What drove you to return to the ring?" Koppel asked.

"All great athletes are perfectionists. We don't want to retire because of injuries. . . . I just could not accept that an injury knocked me down and not an opponent. . . ."

". . . is this for real?"

"It's for real. . . . When I was knocked down, I went back to the corner and looked over to see if my wife was okay. Thank God, she was. But it's just too much for her. We're expecting our second child, and I want us all to be together. This made her very happy."

Koppel then turned to me, graciously saying, "Howard, I'm sure there are a lot of things I should've been asking Sugar Ray about. Go ahead and fill in the gaps."

"Not true, Ted," I said. "That was a great interview. The only thing I want to say to Ray is . . . well, you're like a son to me,

Ray. You always have been. I went down to emcee your retirement dinner, and I'm glad now that you've made your decision. I happen to believe that could you have spared yourself future eye injury, you could've come back all the way. But I didn't want you to even try.

"I believe from my thirty-two years in boxing, heart and soul, that you're up there with Ali and Sugar Ray Robinson, inch for inch and pound for pound, as great a fighter as I have ever seen. . . .

"God bless you, and stay well."

Trainer later told me how much Leonard appreciated my telegram, and when he heard I was doing *Nightline*, he wanted to come on and show that everything was all right between us.

I finally got to view the fight when it was replayed on ABC, and in my opinion, considering his layoff, Leonard had performed remarkably well. Oh, sure, he got caught by a sucker right, but that's happened to all the great ones. He instantly jumped to his feet, then showed flashes of the old Leonard in handling Howard without undue strain.

If Leonard had continued fighting, could he have eventually beaten Hagler? I think so. At any rate, it would have been hard to bet against a fighter of Leonard's heart and will.

But he's a better man for resisting the siren song of a brutal glory.

And in retirement, he has made me as happy as any athlete ever has, because I can't help but think of the opening lines of John Milton's immortal sonnet "On His Blindness":

When I consider how my light is spent,
Ere half my days in this dark world
And wide . . .

Well, now Sugar Ray Leonard is gone from boxing, and his light is not spent. Personally, I thank God for that.

10

Kuhn's Last Stand

A world torn loose went by me.
Then the rain stopped and the blowing.
And the sun came out to dry me.

—Robert Frost, *One Step Backward Taken*

Other than baseball, a few of Bowie Kuhn's favorite things are poetry, opera, cats, and gardening. He's a devoted father and husband, and he's an incurable romantic. That's right. The same man who was so wrongly portrayed for so many years as being a pompous stuffed shirt is in reality a hopeless lover of underdogs and lost causes.

And while it may be difficult to regard Kuhn as a man blessed with the common touch, take it from me that he possesses great warmth and charm, and he's got a marvelous sense of humor. He may be 6 feet, 5½ inches tall, gray at the temples, and stiff in posture, but he is anything but a starch-ass.

The man has never lived who could outdrink Kuhn. His right leg is utterly hollow. He can devour more martinis and put more people under the table than any man I have ever known. And with each person he puts away, a new glow comes to his face. I have seen many fall prey to his drinking skills, including myself.

I'll never forget a summer day at my home in Westhampton Beach. A friend of mine named Sig Hyman, who runs the NFL players' pension fund, was over, and he boasted to Kuhn, "No man can outdrink me." Kuhn took up the challenge. Both men prefer vodka, and they went at it. At two o'clock in the morning, Hyman said, "I don't feel well. How about one more?"

"No problem," Kuhn said.

That was it for Hyman.

At six o'clock in the morning, Hyman stirred awake. "I think somebody should take me to Southampton Hospital," he said.

Two hours later, Kuhn was back at my home, ready to play several sets of tennis. And when he appeared at the door, Hyman looked at him in shock and screamed.

• • •

Bowie Kuhn and I began our relationship as firm antagonists and ended up as close friends. In the beginning, I found Kuhn stiff and aloof, a man who took himself terribly seriously. For his part, Kuhn thought I was much too harsh on his beloved baseball, and there were deep and pervasive disagreements between us. In Kuhn's favor, however, I'll say this for him: During that time when we were at odds, Kuhn was always accessible; he'd come on the air with me and confront any issue I questioned him about.

Some of my criticism of baseball, in the late 1960s, concerned the game itself. It had become an artistic and aesthetic mess. The balance between offense and defense was pathetically out of whack, and it had turned the national pastime into a national bore. The quintessential excitement of the game—the ability of batters to hit pitchers and score runs—was rapidly eroding. I said so. Kuhn didn't like that. He was even more displeased with my attacks on certain aspects of baseball that transcended strikeouts and home runs.

First, I was a staunch and unrelenting critic of the game's carpetbagging owners. The strong opinions I have about teams deserting cities were formed in 1958, when Walter O'Malley moved the Brooklyn Dodgers and Horace Stoneham moved the New York Giants to the West Coast. I deplored the Braves' removal from Milwaukee to Atlanta and in 1971, I viewed with disdain yet another team abandoning our nation's capital when the born-again Washington Senators became the Texas Rangers.

The second reason I was critical of baseball was because of its long-standing exemption from the federal antitrust laws, which was clearly an anomaly at law—and is still described as such in just about any legal textbook you can find. I watched Kuhn closely in the case of *Curt Flood* v. *Bowie Kuhn et al.* Curt Flood, you'll recall, was the St. Louis Cardinals'-outfielder who refused to be traded to the Philadelphia Phillies, and he tested baseball's reserve clause in the courts as a violation of antitrust laws. The case went to the U.S. Supreme Court. I was very much disturbed when the Court ruled against Flood and sustained baseball's exemption from the antitrust laws. In effect, the ruling meant that while a player was to stay tied to his original team— unless that team wanted to trade him—an owner could hop from one city to another with impunity.

There were numerous times when I called upon the Congress to revoke the exemption. Indeed, in 1972 I testified before the Senate Anti-Trust Subcommittee presided over by the then senator from Kentucky, Marlow Cook, and registered my objections against carpetbagging owners and baseball's antitrust exemption.

As a result, Kuhn did not take too kindly to me, and the ill feeling between us continued until 1976. That's the year that ABC bought the rights to televise baseball on Monday nights. ABC signed veteran Bob Prince to the initial package, then brought up a young broadcaster named Warner Wolf from Washington to join him. The marriage didn't work. ABC's president of sports, Roone Arledge, felt that Wolf wasn't connecting with the viewers, and he wanted the kid off the package.

I knew none of this when, abruptly one morning, Arledge called me. "Howard, kill whatever you're doing," he said. "We've got to meet Bowie Kuhn for lunch. I want you on *Monday Night Baseball,* and I want to resolve it with Kuhn."

I was stunned, and not only because Arledge's determination to have me on baseball had come out of the blue. Apparently Arledge had already told Kuhn of his intentions, and the commissioner was less than sanguine about my presence in the booth.

The three of us met at the "21" Club. I sat against the wall, with Arledge next to me and Kuhn across from us. Kuhn didn't mince any words. "I don't want you on *Monday Night Baseball,*

Howard," he said. "Most of the owners, I'm sure, share my feelings. You have long been very critical of baseball, and I can't imagine you'd be the right man for the job. It's wrong for the package, wrong for ABC, wrong for baseball, and certainly wrong for you."

That was the nub of it. Kuhn had much more to say, and I sat there and listened politely. So did Arledge. Occasionally I made an observation, but Arledge said absolutely nothing. I bided my time, and when Kuhn finished, it was my turn to vent what was on my mind.

I said: "Frankly, Bowie, I don't really know what I'm doing here. I understand and respect your feelings about me and my criticisms of baseball. As far as *Monday Night Baseball* goes, I didn't ask to be assigned to the package. I only learned about it from Roone within the past few hours.

"Now let's get to it. Roone is the only one who tells me where I'm going and what I'm doing. He's my boss, not you, and I do what he tells me. Let's get another thing straight: You're dead wrong if you think my attacks on baseball are unwarranted. They are based on my training as a lawyer and my knowledge of the law. What's more, they are a matter of principle, and nobody knows better than you what it means to stand on principle.

"As for my criticisms of the game itself, much of that is in the past. The game has made impressive strides, though I still find some of the action tedious. But on the whole, I appreciate the nuances within the game, and hell, I grew up in this country on baseball. There's no denying it, Bowie—one of the most important influences in my life was Jackie Robinson, and I can't tell you what joy I got out of Ebbets Field and the Brooklyn Dodgers.

"But under any circumstances, Bowie, you're wrong, and you're wrong because you're trying to dictate who should be on a show and why. In effect, you're seeking to operate as a censor, and that must not be tolerated. You're trying to put shills on the baseball package, and that should not be tolerated either.

"That's all I have to say. I will do what Roone tells me, and I don't see any point to my staying at this luncheon. This matter is between you and Roone, not you and me."

Kuhn was clearly taken aback, but I also believe he was impressed with my candor. And what did I do? I got up and went to my office, leaving Arledge and Kuhn to thrash things out between themselves.

What was said between those two after I left, I never did find out. But several days later, I got my assignment sheets, and there was *Monday Night Baseball* on my schedule. It was as simple as that.

Then an odd situation developed. My wife, Emmy, and I were at our summer home in the Hamptons when I got a call from Kuhn inviting us to dinner with him and his wife, Louisa, at a club on the water. It was one of Kuhn's favorite restaurants, serving excellent seafood, and I accepted his invitation. When we got there and met the Kuhns, Emmy looked Bowie straight in the eye and said, "I don't know why we're here. You don't like us, and we're not particularly fond of you. Why are we having dinner together?"

This is exactly the way she always is with people in sports. She shoots from the hip, fires away, and it's take it or leave it.

Kuhn said, "I don't like the positions your husband has taken on baseball, Emmy, but I've always found him an interesting man, and I enjoy his company."

Fair enough. So we ate and drank and spent a thoroughly enjoyable evening together. There were other good times, but our friendship was actually sealed one night at a restaurant in Westhampton Beach called Casa Basso. It was there that we learned about the romance between Bowie and Louisa, and I was deeply touched by the story of how they had fallen in love and married.

As it turned out, Bowie had proposed to Louisa in that very restaurant. When they were younger, Bowie and Louisa mixed in the same social circles. He fell madly in love with her; but she was married to somebody else, and he kept it to himself. Louisa gave her first husband a son named George. Then tragedy struck. While Louisa was pregnant with her second child, her husband was killed in a car accident on Park Avenue. Bowie rushed to her side, consoled her, cared for her. Louisa had a second son named Paul, and she eventually married Bowie, who adopted both boys and raised them as his sons.

Bowie and Louisa then had two children of their own, Steve and Alexandra. Each Sunday, George and Paul accompany their mother to Episcopalian services, while Bowie attends Catholic mass with Steve and Alexandra. The Kuhns are one of the most loving families I have ever encountered, and Bowie's familial devotion, which is very much like my own toward my wife and children and grandchildren, drew us closer through the years.

As our friendship warmed up, Kuhn conceded that my disdain for carpetbagging owners was justified. In fact, he even revealed that he shared my views on that subject. He also told me that he was dead set against the Milwaukee Braves' removal to Atlanta, but as an attorney for Willkie, Farr & Gallagher, he represented the National League, and he had a duty to his client to smooth the way for the transfer. I wholeheartedly accepted his explanation, knowing full well the responsibilities and obligations of an attorney.

Kuhn was also upset when Washington lost a big-league team for the second time, in 1971. He had rooted for the Senators as a kid, and he vowed that he would do all in his power to prevent other teams from leaving other cities as long as he was commissioner. Kuhn kept his word, while that other commissioner, Pete Rozelle, took the 1970s and made carpetbagging the trademark of the National Football League.

Speaking of Rozelle, I think it's a damn shame how the sportswriters continue to treat that man with downright adoration, while they had a high old time lambasting Kuhn. They play the fool for Rozelle's earthy elegance, his mastery of public relations, and his slick approach to troubling issues. Something is rotten in the state of the NFL, as I have detailed in this book, but leave it to Pete to massage the press and keep it looking the other way.

In contrast, most sportswriters never really took the time to get to know Kuhn and what he was trying to accomplish as commissioner, and thus they rarely dealt with him fairly. It hurt him because he wanted so much to be liked by them. Sometimes, I think, he overreacted to their stories, let them get under his skin, and he'd brood about their perceptions of him.

What difference does it make what Dick Young of the *New York Post* thinks of you? I'd tell him—but he cared because he respected Young's talent. I disagreed with Kuhn on that score, but he was probably right to get angry about his treatment from the late, venerated *New York Times* columnist Red Smith. Kuhn came to despise Smith. He felt that Smith was deliberately carrying on an ugly vendetta against him, and he couldn't figure out why. "Considering his reputation for integrity, Howard, he has shown none toward me," Kuhn once told me. "I talk with him whenever he wants to, answer every question directly, and then he reports what I say in a mocking and derisive way."

But no words ever written enraged Kuhn more than a column by Dave Anderson of *The New York Times*. It appeared in the midst of the 1982 NFL players' strike. At the time, Kuhn was on the ropes, his job in jeopardy, and he was still reeling from the ramifications of a major league baseball players' strike the previous year. So what did Anderson write? He nominated Pete Rozelle to be the new commissioner of baseball! No matter that the football players were on strike. Of course, Kuhn was excoriated in the media for his handling of the baseball players' strike and for failing to devise a miraculous solution to settle it. Not Rozelle. He had vanished during the negotiations, but he was doing just fine. He got pushed for the job of baseball commissioner! Incredible, isn't it?

During his time in office, few men in sports were more misunderstood and less appreciated than Bowie Kuhn.

He is a decent, compassionate man, with a wry sense of humor and a youthful sentimentality for baseball. There is tenacity within him, dignity, and a strength of character that are rarely glimpsed today in sports. He is stubborn, too, and it's a pity that so few sportswriters tried to get beyond the enduring caricature of Kuhn, shivering coatless in the cold, making a stand for his support of night games in the World Series. It was no big deal, but they gleefully promulgated the image and refused to let it die.

Kuhn suffered for his patrician bearing; his cautious, thoughtful approach to problems; and his distaste for self-promotion. He was often portrayed as aloof and arrogant, when in reality he is a gentleman in the finest sense of the word, uncomfortable with comporting himself in a backslapping, glad-handing kind of way.

Hell, that's just the way he is. To use a phrase, Kuhn was to the manor born. His mother named him "Bowie" after a relative, Jim Bowie, a frontiersman famous for inventing a knife and dying at the Alamo. His father made his money in the oil business, and he's also related to two former Maryland governors. He was educated at Princeton and received his law degree from the University of Virginia. It is not surprising, then, that Kuhn possesses a traditionalist's view of the world. He respects institutions, and he believes in sticking to his principles.

Growing up in Tacoma Park, Maryland, Kuhn worked the scoreboard in old Griffith Stadium for a dollar a day, and he worshiped the Washington Senators. One of his biggest disappointments was his ineptitude at playing the game he loved so well. Despite his rather stodgy public persona, Kuhn never stopped admiring the players, even looking upon them almost wistfully. And if he sometimes seemed inconsistent and political in his dealings with them, it's because he was truly convinced that the best interests of baseball—its present and future prosperity— were lodged in the men who spent the money and took the risks. Not always, but often enough.

If that made Kuhn an owners' man, so be it. They plucked him out of Willkie, Farr & Gallagher, where he represented the National League, and they paid his salary. There were times, however, when his actions outraged them. Just as players felt the lash of fines and suspension, so did several owners. He even went so far as to refuse to allow large cash transactions for stars, and once he lifted an owners' lockout of players in the heart of a labor dispute.

Whatever dictums Kuhn laid down, he did in the name of "the best interests of baseball." Long an axiom in the sport, the phrase became Kuhn's motto, and he jealously guarded the image of the national pastime as if he were fighting for his wife's honor. Critics quoted the phrase to skewer him, while supporters invoked it to laud him. But the point is, it was the guiding principle of Kuhn's tenure, and he embraced it so fervently precisely because he is a moral man to the core.

I am the first to admit that Kuhn's sense of righteousness was sometimes cloying, and I understand why his critics were put off by it. But isn't that the way it is with many such idealistic and principled men? And what's so wrong with a little idealism and morality mixing in with the business and pleasure of a professional sports league?

Shortly after Kuhn resigned as commissioner in the summer of 1983, when he realized all hope of being elected to another term was gone, he wrote these words: ". . . most importantly, the new commissioner must be a man of integrity, have a great sense of baseball integrity and have a willingness to die in the trenches on integrity issues. The Hun will be at the gates, demanding the commissioner compromise, give ground, put aside outmoded shibboleths.

"He'll be told, for instance, that legalized gambling and baseball are perfectly compatible and that we can even turn a profit from the relationship. He should tell the compromisers to get lost. They are burglars of our patrimony. They will never understand the threat to baseball posed by such things as legalized gambling, sports betting, drug abuse and undesirable associations. He should use his powers fearlessly to protect the integrity of the game. The critics will call him self-righteous and moralistic. Have courage. Ignore them."

That's Bowie Kuhn, pure and simple.

Kuhn was the fifth commissioner in baseball history, serving more than fifteen years in the job, longer than any other except cantankerous old Judge Kenesaw Mountain Landis. Landis was the first, dispatched from the federal bench to restore the image of baseball in the wake of the "Black Sox" scandal of 1919, and he was given extraordinary powers to rule with an iron hand. The judge's successor was Albert (Happy) Chandler, a good ol' boy politico from Kentucky. He was followed by Ford Frick, a wishy-washy bureaucrat who ran the National League headquarters. Next came General William D. Eckert, a faceless functionary who was derisively dubbed "the unknown soldier."

Kuhn got the job early in 1969, and by then, Judge Landis's days of ruthless supremacy and arbitrary justice were a dim memory. The owners had gradually eroded the commissioner's authority, and the hierarchal structure of the game was beginning to change. Increasingly, old-line families were getting out of baseball, selling their clubs to executives and entrepreneurs from the corporate world, and Kuhn promptly understood that he would have to bring baseball into the twentieth century. He was determined not to let the murky powers of his office get in the way. He would knock heads with this new breed of headstrong owners, and he would end up presiding over the most revolutionary period in the history of the game.

When Kuhn assumed office, baseball had no designated-hitter rule, and there were no night World Series games. A players' strike had never happened, and free agency was not part of base-ball's language. Then, attendance for twenty teams was twenty-three million, a franchise was worth about $5 million, and the average player was making close to $30,000 a year.

In 1983, attendance for twenty-six teams climbed past forty-five million. Players' salaries zoomed toward an average of $300,000 a year, and a pizza magnate bought the Detroit Tigers for more than $50 million.

Finally, network television revenues jumped from $16.5 million a year to a $1.2 billion, six-year deal that began in 1984.

I'm not suggesting that Kuhn is solely responsible for the re-vival of baseball's popularity and good fortune. The circum-stances were doubtlessly right, and baseball went along for the ride. But let's be fair: Kuhn deserves respect for his skills as com-missioner—just as a twenty-game winner receives accolades even though he has a lineup of .300 hitters to support him.

It's not my purpose here to detail the bits and pieces of Kuhn's reign. His demise as commissioner is a far more fascinat-ing story, one that I will devote greater attention to. But there is a necessity, I think, to cover briefly the highlights of Kuhn's career, letting them serve as a backdrop to his leaving baseball. As you will note, despite our friendship, Kuhn and I have had our share of disagreements, and it was my job to say so publicly when they arose.

Kuhn wasn't exactly at the top of his form when he repri-manded Jim Bouton for writing *Ball Four*; it was a puerile book, I thought, and Kuhn's actions only helped to make it a best seller. He carried his integrity-of-the-game philosophy to extremes when he cried to the heavens about the Mike Kekich-Fritz Peterson wife-swapping episode, and he simply should have ignored in-stead of fined silly Bill Lee for joking about sprinkling marijuana on his pancakes.

These were minor incidents, but I bring them up to demon-strate Kuhn's overall consistency in his stubborn fight to safe-guard what he saw as the best interests of the game.

Two of Kuhn's most egregious mistakes, in my opinion, prompted ringing denunciations from me. In the case of *Ludtke* v. *Kuhn*, the commissioner's efforts to keep a woman sportswriter from entering the New York Yankees' locker room were prepos-terous. And I wholeheartedly agreed with the judge, who eventually ruled that Kuhn's position was "clearly too insubstantial to merit serious consideration."

Another mistake was his suspension of Mickey Mantle and Willie Mays from baseball on grounds that they had accepted jobs as glad-handers at casinos in Atlantic City, New Jersey, where gambling is legal. I always regarded Kuhn's steadfast objections to gambling as admirable, but he was totally wrong and hypocritical in the matter of Mays and Mantle. After all, he had permitted the owners of the Pittsburgh Pirates, the Galbreath family, to continue to run racetracks, and he made no public outcry when Yankees owner George Steinbrenner purchased Tampa Downs.

In Kuhn's conversations with me, he tried to differentiate between casinos and racetracks. He once ended up admitting that his position might be tenuous, but he said he was right for adhering to his principles. In his defense, he noted that he had ordered Oakland owner Charles O. Finley and Atlanta owner Bill Bartholomay—both now out of baseball—to dispose of their stock in a company that owned several Las Vegas casinos. To bolster his argument, he also pointed out that racetrack ownership among baseball's hierarchy was a thing of the past; he had looked the other way with Steinbrenner, but no more. And in 1980, he played a leading role in the American League owners' decision to reject a bid to purchase the Chicago White Sox by billionaire Edward DeBartolo, who owned several racetracks around the country.

That was all well and good, I told him, but Mantle and Mays were forfeiting none of their integrity as spring-training batting coaches and goodwill ambassadors of the game by working in Atlantic City. It served no purpose whatsoever—certainly not the best interests of the game—to keep those two great athletes out of baseball.

On the plus side, Kuhn established a drug education program as far back as 1971, and he was at the forefront among commissioners in providing assistance for drug users who sought help and penalizing those who didn't. He was also tireless in pushing the owners to hire a black manager, and later he privately tried to get several teams to make former New York Mets' first baseman Donn Clendenon major-league baseball's first black general manager.

While the sportswriters bitched about Kuhn's preoccupation with television, he was shrewd enough to appreciate its importance as professional sports entered the 1970s. A better marriage between baseball and television, he knew, would bring baseball more fans, more money, and more prestige, just as it had pro football. It rankled Kuhn when critics charged that World Series night games in the middle of October damaged the quality of play. I'm not sure that such criticisms are even true, but Kuhn was right to showcase the World Series in prime time. It gave baseball a huge economic boost and increased exposure. Check out the figures. In 1969, less than thirty million people watched a World Series game. Today the audience is close to seventy million—and the money keeps pouring in.

Kuhn was also right when he blocked Oakland's $2 million sale of Joe Rudi and Rollie Fingers to the Boston Red Sox and the $1.5 million sale of Vida Blue to the Yankees. That was in the spring of 1976, and Kuhn established a precedent, placing a $400,000 maximum cash outlay on any player deal. He believed he was preventing owner Charles O. Finley from destroying the Oakland franchise, and in the process, preventing the stockpiling of talent by the wealthier clubs.

Some accused Kuhn of wanting to get even with Finley, who had led a movement the year before to unseat him. Kuhn's bitterness toward Finley was real enough, but I'm certain that Kuhn acted honestly and forthrightly. He was truly convinced that huge cash transactions for players were a threat to the competitive balance of the sport—and thus, of course, not in the best interests of baseball.

Finley took Kuhn to court and challenged his authority, which was fine with Kuhn, who once and for all wanted to determine just how far the limits of his power went. The owners hired him, and they could fire him. The relationship between the owners and the commissioner was never really very well defined. Was he boss? Or was he servant? The answer came back in 1977. His powers were unlimited, according to the decision in a federal court that ruled against Finley and upheld Kuhn's banning of player sales for exorbitant sums.

That decision, however, was based on the major-league agreement that was in effect when Kuhn voided Finley's sales. As we shall see, the structure of the game was already beginning to change, and Kuhn would be powerless to act in the most crucial crisis of his career.

With the advent of World Series night games and more lucrative television deals, baseball was uneasily becoming an industry, and Kuhn had to wrestle with the same frustrating and complex problems that beset chief executives of large corporations everywhere. For Kuhn, the biggest headache of all was labor unrest.

Coinciding with Kuhn's elevation to commissioner was the arrival of Marvin Miller as the executive director of the players' union. Miller was savvy and tough, a former economist and negotiator for the United Steelworkers of America. Under Miller's guidance, the union started to beat the owners. He solidified the players, rallying them to strike in 1972 for the first time in history, and they came away with more pension money, salary arbitration, and other important concessions. And thanks to Miller, who had negotiated a binding arbitration system to handle grievances, the players won their biggest victory late in 1975—free agency.

The grievance was brought by a couple of pitchers named Andy Messersmith and Dave McNally, who wanted to find out how much they'd be worth on the open market. Traditionally, a player was tied to his original team in perpetuity; if he didn't like the salary he was being offered, the club invoked a "reserve clause" to get his signature on a contract. At that point, a player had two choices. He could sign and take the money his team was offering; or he could refuse to report to work, in which case he was out of a job in baseball because no other club could hire him. It was indentured servitude, archaic and obviously unfair, and arbitrator Peter Seitz ruled that the language in the standard player's contract in no way gave his team the exclusive right to his services as a baseball player for the entirety of his career.

The decision infuriated the owners, and Kuhn shared their outrage. If players were allowed to sell their services to the highest bidder, he said, it would mean economic doom. What's more, the richest clubs in the most glamorous cities would end up with the best players and thus destroy the competitive balance of the game.

Kuhn was wrong on both counts. The game prospered as never before, and a variety of teams were good enough to get into the playoffs and win the World Series. At the time, however, the exaggerated fears of the owners were deposited on Kuhn's doorstep, and he would one day pay the price.

Why didn't Kuhn steer the owners away from their total reliance on the reserve system and push for a compromise with the players? As an attorney, in my opinion, he should have foreseen the inevitability of free agency, or at least the possibility of it. Today, I know, he wishes he had been insightful enough to persuade the owners of what was coming and convince them to work out a modified form of free agency with the union. He didn't, and it was the beginning of the end for Kuhn.

Several months after the players had won free agency, the owners locked them out of spring-training camps, hoping to roll back free agency in a new basic agreement with the union. Kuhn knew the owners were wrong, and he lifted the lockout. He then contributed mightily toward engineering a settlement with the players that incorporated the free agency they had won at the arbitrator's table.

The settlement allowed players with six years in the major leagues to negotiate with several teams if they chose to play out their contracts. In other words, they could put their services on the open market and listen to bids from other teams. No compensation was involved. If a Red Sox outfielder, for example, wanted to accept an offer from the Yankees, the Yankees were under no obligation to compensate the Red Sox with another player—which was a real boon to the players.

(In the NFL, a free agent can make a deal with another team, but his former team must be compensated. That compensation is often prohibitive, usually involving high draft choices, and the free agent finds himself without a team that wants to pay for him. This was best illustrated in the case of Walter Payton, the Chicago Bears' brilliant running back. When he became a free agent, he couldn't find another team to bid for his services. He ended up staying in Chicago, though he was eventually rewarded with a lucrative contract. Other players aren't so lucky.)

"We've been hornswoggled, and we're going to pay for it," fumed St. Louis Cardinals' owner Gussie Busch, who never forgave Kuhn for lifting the lockout.

It took a lot of guts for Kuhn to do what he had done, but union problems would continue to haunt him. And then there was Busch, waiting in the wings, looking for the first opportunity to pounce on Kuhn and lop off his head.

The stage for Kuhn's dismissal was set soon after that 1976 lockout and the settlement with the players' union. I'm not sure if Busch had some long-range Machiavellian scheme in the back of his head, but it was the St. Louis owner who called for a re-structuring of the game. Never again would he allow a commissioner to overrule the owners on labor issues, and the rest of his colleagues agreed with him. Taking their cue from Busch, the owners organized their own Player Relations Committee—and it became the province of that committee to deal with the union. They had effectively tied Kuhn's hands, and he no longer would have any say in labor relations.

Four years passed, and it was time again to negotiate a new basic agreement between the owners and the players' union. To head their negotiating team, the owners had hired Ray Grebey, an experienced executive in labor relations with General Electric, and though Kuhn approved of Grebey, he had no authority in actually hiring him. The ultimate decision was made by the owners, and together with Grebey, they were adamant about getting some form of compensation for lost free agents. It was hardly surprising that the players resisted, and the issue was tabled.

Kuhn had no power to bring about a settlement; but trying to maintain an appearance of leadership and dignity, he made a foolish promise. If the labor situation became desperate, he said, "I'd play my hole card."

Well, the situation got desperate, and Kuhn had no hole card to play. The compensation issue smoldered for a year, the owners dug in, and then the players struck for fifty days in the middle of the 1981 season. Throughout the strike, Kuhn's public posture of staying above the fray and working behind the scenes was futile. He made any number of statements to the effect that the Player Relations Committee had the ultimate responsibility to settle the strike, but the sportswriters wouldn't buy it. They savaged him, accused him of vanishing when baseball needed him most, and some actually blamed him for prolonging the strike. Thus there grew the image of an ineffectual, powerless, and even inept commissioner, and Kuhn never fully recovered.

In my opinion, the real problem during the strike was Grebey, the owners' man. A wisecracking, combative negotiator, he inflamed the players, and even the cool and steady Miller came to dislike him intensely. As for Kuhn, he was duty-bound to support Grebey, but privately he knew that Grebey's personality and tactics had become increasingly detrimental to the negotiations. But there was nothing Kuhn could do about it.

To this day, a tinge of bitterness still creeps into Kuhn's voice when he discusses the events of 1981 and the treatment he got from the press. At the time, he thought it inappropriate to express his true feelings, but he agonized over what was written about him—and, even worse, what was implied. "To suggest that I fomented the strike, or want to break the union, is simply wrong and unfair," he told me during the strike. "They're writing as if I have some vast, godlike power to end this strike, Howard, and I don't."

"Is there nothing you can do?" I asked.

"I'm trying to establish better lines of communications between my office and the Player Relations Committee, but it's difficult. The owners want to beat Miller, and the players don't seem like they want to give an inch."

"Is there any hope of a settlement, or is this season finished for good?"

"I don't know, Howard, I just don't know," Kuhn said. "I'm hopeful, that's my nature. But what really gets me is the perception that I can tell a labor union not to strike. I can't even tell the owners and the players to stay in a room until they solve this thing. I can't tell Miller how to bargain, and the owners think they're following the right course of action. I'm caught in the middle."

It was Kuhn's belief that the union was wrong, that Miller and the players were mistaken in calling the strike. Kuhn claimed that the players had agreed in 1980 to negotiate in good faith for some form of compensation. They were well aware, he said, that the compensation would not be all that grievous. Then the next year, according to Kuhn, they backed off their promise to negotiate, refused to make any concessions—and called a strike when the owners resisted caving in.

Miller had a different story to tell. At no time, he said, were the owners serious about conducting fair and reasonable negotiations. As proof, he pointed to the fifty-day strike-insurance policy with Lloyd's of London that the owners had taken out before-hand. Then, on the fiftieth day, after 713 games had been wiped out, the strike was settled. According to Miller, the owners ended up agreeing to a proposal that he had personally made to them before the strike began.

I have enormous respect for both Miller and Kuhn, and it wasn't easy figuring out who was right and who was wrong. One thing is certain: Both are honest men, and each firmly believed in his assessment of the events that led to the strike. For as long as I have supported the players' union on so many issues, however, my sympathies in 1981 were with Kuhn. Let me make that clear—Kuhn, not the owners. To a large extent, he was unjustly pilloried, and he took the rap when there was plenty of blame to go around.

But it wasn't over. Kuhn got ambushed again. To save the season, Kuhn placed his stamp of approval on a split-season plan that was designed to renew interest in the game and hype the gate. The Cincinnati Reds finished the season with the best record in baseball, but they were denied the playoffs according to the guidelines of the plan.

Sportswriters came down hard on the plan, called it idiotic and shortsighted. Naturally, Kuhn took the heat; again, he was the scapegoat, the whipping boy, even though the plan was supported wholeheartedly by the vast majority of teams and the players' union.

Did the plan result in inequities? Yes, it did. But what were the alternatives? Pick up with a partial season? In my opinion, having first-half leaders play second-half leaders to determine division champions wasn't all that horrible an idea. At least it got people talking about baseball again. And I don't know if I would have done anything differently, considering the peculiar circumstances of that 1981 season.

In the aftermath of the 1981 strike, the Cardinals' Gussie Busch was ready to make his big move against Kuhn. Five years earlier, as I have noted, Busch had spearheaded a drive to restructure baseball and render Kuhn powerless in labor relations—and it worked to the owners' advantage. Unwilling to forget about Kuhn's lifting of the 1976 lockout, he had long wanted the commissioner out of office, and now was his chance.

Discredited, under fire in the media, Kuhn was easy pickings, and Busch didn't waste any time.

At the winter meetings in December, nine owners signed a letter calling for Kuhn to resign. It charged him with lack of leadership. The letter itself was signed by an attorney named Lou Sussman—who just happened to be Busch's general counsel.

Kuhn's departure seemed inevitable. His contract wasn't due to expire until August 1983, but under baseball's rules, the nine signatories of that letter had enough power ultimately to block the commissioner's reelection.

To get reelected, Kuhn would need three-fourths approval of the owners in each league. Only four owners in the American League lined up against Kuhn. For the National League, arrayed against Kuhn were the Williams brothers of Cincinnati, Houston's John McMullen, Atlanta's Ted Turner, Nelson Doubleday of the New York Mets—and, of course, Gussie Busch.

McMullen had a personal grudge against Kuhn, which I will reveal later. For their part, the Williams brothers were still seething over the split-season plan that cost the Reds a spot in the playoffs. But there were other forces at work here. The Williams brothers were getting into cable, as was Doubleday, and Turner's superstation in Atlanta was growing increasingly rich. Kuhn had expressed concern about the spread of cable TV, and he started to push for some form of revenue sharing. All clubs were already sharing network monies, but Kuhn wanted the owners to consider various formulas for the distribution of cable revenues to protect the teams in the weaker markets.

Doubleday wouldn't hear of it, and neither would Turner. They had no intention of sharing their profits with anybody. Doubleday started squawking about baseball's need for a businessman as commissioner, while Busch basically kept his mouth shut and pulled the strings behind the scenes. He was sitting pretty. He owns the biggest brewery in the country, Anheuser-Busch—which spends a lot of money advertising Budweiser beer on television. Those sudsy dollars help men such as Turner and Doubleday turn a profit on their local and cable telecasts. Busch wanted Kuhn out, while Doubleday and Turner wanted more advertising money from Anheuser-Busch—and wanted to keep it.

Talk about teamwork!

See how this plays: Busch tells Turner and Doubleday and the Williams brothers he wants Kuhn out. They tell Busch they want beer advertising for their cable operations. Busch says no problem. They say, great, but we also want to keep the profits. Okay, Busch says, you've got my support in trying to shoot down revenue sharing. Then they confess they don't like Kuhn either and promise to vote against him. Busch smiles contentedly. He waited a long time to get Kuhn.

Shortly after the winter meetings, early in 1982, Kuhn appeared on my *SportsBeat* show. I had reached all but two of the signatories of the December letter, and each declined to voice his specific objections to Kuhn. But Kuhn was forthcoming.

COSELL: "Commissioner, are you going to resign?"
KUHN: "Howard, I have no intention of resigning."
COSELL: "You're well aware that Edward Bennett Williams has stated publicly that you failed to exercise leadership, that you could have averted the baseball strike of the past season. You could have used the general-welfare clause to that effect. Your response."
KUHN: "I disagree with Ed Williams. The general-welfare clause does not permit the commissioner to tell a labor union whether it can strike or not strike. The Players' Association is protected by federal law. I couldn't tell them they can't strike, and I couldn't stop them when they got into it, however much I might have wanted to."

Later in the interview, I asked Kuhn if he thought any of the nine signatories of the December letter might change his vote when the commissioner's reelection came up.

"I don't know, Howard," Kuhn said. "Certainly, if I'm to be reelected, someone will have to change. I think these are decent men. I think they're looking to do the right thing for the long-term good of the game. . . ."

"Do you think these signatories are acting in concert, in a conspiracy?"

"Howard, I really can't answer that question. I don't know the facts for sure. I would like to think that they are working to do the constructive thing for the game. . . ."

Several months later, at the All-Star Game break, Kuhn made another appearance on *SportsBeat* to discuss the state of the baseball nation. We covered numerous topics—the effects of the strike, drug abuse among players, revenue sharing, expansion—and, of course, Kuhn's political situation.

"You remain under attack from some owners, most notably in the National League," I said. "Where do you stand with regard to retention of your job?"

"Howard, I'm not altogether certain about the accuracy of the phrase 'under attack,' " he said. "There have been people [who] felt that you shouldn't reelect Kuhn or elect any other commissioner until certain matters had been straightened out, such as restructuring, such as revenue sharing. It wasn't so much an issue of Kuhn as it was an issue of how do we deal with those other problems. Oh, there might be an isolated case where Kuhn is the issue, but I think that's minimal.

"The majority of clubs have consistently supported me—and are continuing to support me."

I asked: "So you think you're going to keep your job?"

Kuhn replied, "Howard, I'd like to, and one is always optimistic. I'm of that nature."

The ax came on November 1, 1982, in Chicago. Kuhn's hopes for reelection to a third seven-year term were dashed. The same five National League owners who signed that letter the previous December lined up against him again, and that was it for Kuhn. Instead of resigning, however, Kuhn chose to carry out the duties of his office until the owners could find a new commissioner. I felt he should've quit as a matter of pride and self-respect, but he honestly believed that baseball needed his services while the owners searched for a new commissioner.

Kuhn also had other reasons for staying on. He held out the hope that the owners would come up empty in their search and that he would ultimately receive a mandate for another term. He loved the job so deeply, wanted to keep it so badly, that he refused to quit until only days before his contract actually expired.

In the meantime, Kuhn negotiated a record $1.2 billion, six-year deal with ABC and NBC, and there were some who thought that the lucrative new television contract might yet force the owners to reconsider Kuhn for the job. One man who was in Kuhn's corner was Edward Bennett Williams, the prominent trial attorney who had purchased the Orioles in 1979. Originally critical of Kuhn during the strike, he changed his tune. Once he was drawn more intimately into baseball's inner circles and became better acquainted with the system, he turned into one of Kuhn's staunchest allies.

At any rate, I posed this question to Kuhn: "Do you think that this new billion-dollar television contract enhances your chances of remaining on as commissioner?"

"I seriously doubt whether it's going to change the situation very much one way or the other," he replied. "I think it's a very good deal, and I think it's good for our clubs. But frankly, I don't think it's going to have much effect on my situation in the political sense."

"Then why keep fighting for this job? Aren't you forsaking your personal dignity by doing so?"

"I don't think so, Howard. . . . I continue to carry out the duties of the office in what I think is a proper and forceful way by doing the things that are necessary to be done. I don't feel any loss of dignity in that, and nor do I feel that I'm on any sort of will-o'-the-wisp cause here. I think what I'm doing is proper, and I'm not ready to forsake it."

"But why not?" I said. "Why keep fighting these people who wanted you out and apparently still do?"

Kuhn insisted he wasn't fighting to stay on. "I take some pride in the way baseball is going these days," he said. "If, as a result, things come out well for me, let it be so. If it comes out otherwise, let that be so, too. But I made a commitment to stay on this job until my term was completed. It's a necessary transition for baseball, and I'm prepared to keep my word."

"Would it be the ultimate fulfillment of your professional life to be reelected after all you've been through?"

"It would be particularly fulfilling," Kuhn said, "if the commissioner were given greater powers to do what he has to do for baseball. . . ."

As the weeks dragged on, the owners debated the benefits of the new television deal. Some insisted that Kuhn could have done better, that the money was in place for that kind of deal several years before. Others said the deal was too long and didn't take into account the future of pay television in the country. That position was voiced by one of Kuhn's most strident foes, Doubleday of the Mets, who kept drum beating for a businessman in the office of commissioner.

One of Kuhn's supporters, Eddie Einhorn of the Chicago

White Sox, a former television executive who had helped Kuhn shape the new package, took a swipe at Doubleday. "I have forgotten more about the television business than Mr. Doubleday will ever know," Einhorn told me. "When he criticizes the television agreement as far as restricting the future, he's totally wrong. We have taken every means to protect our future, which is the pay television area. I happen to be one of the biggest proponents of pay television in the country."

Doubleday would have none of it. "I think that the survival of Bowie Kuhn has been put to rest," he told me. He then went on to say that he hoped Kuhn would not test baseball's musty rules, which require the commissioner to be liked by a full three fourths of the owners in each league, in the courts. "We the minority have subscribed to that constitution," he said. "We have listened to it. We have operated within it, and I feel strongly that baseball is bigger than one man. . . ."

"There are twenty-six teams in baseball," White Sox owner Einhorn countered. "In the last count, Bowie had about eighteen or nineteen of those. So that's what makes this whole thing a travesty, but I guess we have to live with it. Because it's a tyranny of the minority, a lot of efforts are being made by the majority to convince the minority that they're wrong. They shouldn't do this when the majority of baseball thinks Kuhn is the man for the job."

Using *SportsBeat* as my forum, I then asked two prominent candidates for commissioner—Olympic officials Peter Ueberroth and William Simon—if they were interested in the job. Simon admitted that he had had a long chat with Bud Selig, the owner of the Milwaukee Brewers and the head of the owners' Search Committee, but simply wasn't interested.

Ueberroth also denied any interest in becoming the commissioner of baseball. "I'm not interested now," he said, "and I don't think I will be in the near future. . . . I have not been contacted, and I have no interest in that position."

Oddly enough, though Doubleday and others kept repeating that baseball needed a businessman in the commissioner's office, one name rumored as a possible successor to Kuhn was A. Bartlett Giamatti, the president of Yale University, a brilliant and distinguished academician. Giamatti's passion for the sport was well known, but I don't believe the owners ever really considered him. Every time I tried to call him, he was always away on vacation, and he never did speak publicly about being a candidate or even wanting the job. He simply chose to let the rumors die on their own.

Several days later, on July 19, an extraordinary delegation of five National League owners and presidents assembled at Lambert International Airport in St. Louis. They were Peter O'Malley of Los Angeles, Bob Lurie of San Francisco, Ballard Smith of San Diego, Charles Bronfman of Montreal, and Bill Giles of Philadelphia, and they had come to meet with August A. Busch III, the chairman, president, and chief executive officer of Anheuser-Busch, Inc., which owns the Cardinals and the brewery, among other subsidiaries. It was a last-ditch attempt to save Kuhn's job.

Since Busch's father, Gussie, had inspired the anti-Kuhn movement and since he remained adamant in his opposition, these men hoped to persuade the son to reason with the father. Their pleas did not move the son, who so much as told them they'd have to deal with the father. Old Gussie wasn't going to budge, they knew that, and so the saving of Kuhn's job seemed to be a dead issue. Not only did the gang of five have the necessary votes to block Kuhn's reelection, but also it was rumored that the Chicago Cubs would join them at an owners' meeting in early August.

Kuhn's contract was to expire on August 12, and as the owners gathered in Boston, the intensity of feelings was running high. Some owners were predicting a "blood bath" if the pro-Kuhn forces insisted on taking one more vote in hopes of getting Kuhn reelected. It never happened.

On August 3, realizing that his refusal to step aside was creating much bitterness and divisiveness among the owners, Kuhn resigned as commissioner of baseball. Another vote was never taken, but Kuhn knew it was all over.

Before resigning, Kuhn tried to reach me at my office in New York to tell me about it. I was tracked down at Wesleyan University in Connecticut, where I was conducting a seminar on sports in our society. Kuhn and I made contact, and he said he wanted me to know he intended to resign within the hour. I wished him well and told him I thought he was doing the right thing.

Not long afterward, I got word that Arledge was trying to reach me. It was urgent. I got back to him, and he said: "You've got to come on *Nightline* tonight, and see if you can get Kuhn for us exclusively."

"Well, Roone, he's already held his press conference and announced his resignation."

"That's just a formality as far as I'm concerned. It doesn't matter. On *Nightline* we can get into it in more depth."

I reached Kuhn in Boston, and he consented to appear on *Nightline* along with two American League owners, Einhorn and George Argyros of the Seattle Mariners. Einhorn was a Kuhn supporter, Argyros a critic. Though a coterie of National League owners was primarily responsible for Kuhn's ouster, it was impossible to nail one of them down for an appearance that night.

It turned out to be a helluva show, very dramatic, and it pulled in a big rating.

The host of *Nightline*, Ted Koppel, threw a few perfunctory questions at Kuhn, then turned to me. "Howard," Koppel asked, "what was it that Commissioner Kuhn's opponents held against him?"

"The reasons are varied," I answered, "but basically, laying it on the line, the swingman was Gussie Busch, who owns Anheuser-Busch brewery. In effect, a brewery owner had the control to dispossess Bowie from his job."

"All right, but what are the issues?"

I told Koppel about Kuhn's desire for revenue sharing from cable and how owners such as Turner and Doubleday would have none of it. And as a corollary issue, such owners receive millions in advertising dollars from Busch's brewery, and thus Busch could exert great influence over them.

Then I disclosed the genesis of the personal animus between Kuhn and John McMullen of Houston. Kuhn wasn't even aware that I knew the story. McMullen had fired Tal Smith as his general manager and wanted to hire Al Rosen—but there was a hitch. A former outstanding player and an experienced baseball executive, Rosen had come under investigation because of previous connections as an employee of an Atlantic City casino that was under scrutiny. McMullen wanted Kuhn to clear the way for him to hire Rosen as quickly as possible. Kuhn resisted, refusing to supersede the investigation. An upstanding man, Rosen was eventually cleared and signed with Houston, but McMullen never forgave Kuhn for his stance in the matter.

"These are the kinds of things," I said, "that happen behind the scenes, that the commissioner had to live with and couldn't possibly disclose himself. Now, Bowie, are you surprised that I've now told McMullen's story?"

"No, Howard, I'm not surprised. I thought John was wrong in the way he handled that, in the way he reacted to the situation. Your description of it is a fair one."

Kuhn had agreed to stay in office until the end of the year, serving the game while the owners looked for a new commissioner. I asked him, "Why not go out now?"

He said that baseball needed a commissioner to carry out the functions of the office, adding, "I will not turn my back on the people who've supported me through this whole thing. . . . The game needs me more in a sense than it's ever needed me. I will not let it down."

At his press conference, Kuhn had said that under no circumstances did he want to be considered a candidate for the job, and he was through with trying to seek another term. I pursued that point, saying, "What if they turn to you? Isn't there a last lingering hope inside you. . . ?"

Absolutely not, Kuhn said, calling his decision "irrevocable."

Einhorn and Argyros then joined Kuhn, and Koppel asked Argyros exactly what was the rap on the outgoing commissioner. Argyros said, in part, "It's time for a change, and I think that's in effect what happened."

Koppel wanted Argyros to be more specific. Argyros was not, and Koppel kept after him. Argyros talked about baseball needing a new structure, and the right kind of management to take it to "new heights."

Somewhat befuddled, Koppel turned to Einhorn, noting that the majority wanted to retain Kuhn. "Is the majority going to pick the kind of man that Argyros is talking about?" Koppel asked.

"I don't know what the majority is going to do," Einhorn replied, "because right now the majority is a little angry. In the American League, Mr. Argyros was one of three who voted against Mr. Kuhn. That leaves eleven who were for him. In the National League, it was six to six;"—indeed, the Cubs had joined the gang of five—"that adds up to a minority, but those are our rules. . . . That's what really irks me about today, besides losing a fine man."

This time, Koppel asked Einhorn what the rap against Kuhn was.

"I have to tell you," Einhorn said, "this is a classic power struggle. It is not insignificant that the votes against Kuhn were from people who were basically not involved in the executive structure of baseball, not on major committees. A number of them in the National League, as Howard so aptly pointed out, have interests other than baseball—like cable interests and sponsorship interests. And they finally figured out that they could make their power felt by voting in a bloc. . . ."

Koppel then turned the questioning over to me, and things started to heat up.

"Let's lay it on the table, Eddie," I said. "Recently, did the Williams brothers, the owners in Cincinnati, make a big deal for cable sponsorship with Anheuser-Busch?"

"Correct," Einhorn said.

"Okay. Similarly, haven't the Chicago Cubs made a big deal for television sponsorship with Anheuser-Busch?"

"Over eight million dollars a year," Einhorn said.

Argyros jumped in and said I was missing the point. Einhorn laughed, telling Argyros, "You'd better explain it."

Argyros uttered more generalities about leadership and the need for a restructuring of baseball.

"The restructuring you keep talking about, sir," I asked. "What do you mean? Do you want to wipe out the commissioner's present powers? Do you want an executive council of owners to run baseball?"

Believe it or not, Argyros talked about voting procedures. "The minority has been able to direct the game, and that needs to be changed. . . ."

I shot back, "Doesn't that mean that Bowie would have been reelected if what you just suggested were true?"

"Possibly," Argyros said.

I asked Einhorn if the owners had any serious candidates to succeed Kuhn. That was the province of the Search Committee, he said, and he wasn't sure. He hadn't heard of any, but he gave a warning to all potential candidates. "Why anyone would want to work for twenty-six characters like Argyros and myself is beyond me," he said.

The day after that show, I got a call from a man named Jerry Solomon, a former ABC salesman who was in charge of dispensing millions of dollars in Budweiser advertising to the networks. I had always regarded Solomon in a friendly way—but he was decidedly unfriendly on the phone.

"I'm calling, Howard, to register my complaint about *Nightline* last night," Solomon said. "I thought you were unfair in your characterization of what happened to Kuhn, and Mike Roarty feels the same way."

Roarty is a key executive with Anheuser-Busch, Inc. I liked Roarty. In fact, I was on good terms with a lot of people in that company and had recently accepted an invitation to speak at a dinner in St. Louis that Budweiser was sponsoring to promote soccer in the area.

At the start, I was cordial with Solomon. "I'm sorry you and Mike feel that way," I said. "But perhaps you can be more specific, Jerry. Exactly what was I unfair about?"

"First of all," he said, "Budweiser and the St. Louis Cardinals are two separate corporations. Gussie runs the Cardinals, and he doesn't exert the kind of control over Budweiser advertising as you suggested. As for his involvement in Kuhn's dismissal, I think you overstated the case."

"Look, Jerry, it's my business to know these things," I said. "I stand on what I said. And furthermore, please don't give me that crap about two separate corporations. The old man still has all the power in the world."

"Howard, you're simply wrong, and we don't like it. This isn't pleasant for me, but I think we're going to have to go above your head on this one. . . ."

I cut him off, my blood rising. "What are you saying, Jerry? Are you trying to scare me? You think you can censor me? I don't give a shit about your company's advertising! I'm a newsman, and I will not tolerate any of your veiled threats, and neither will ABC!"

"We bring ABC a lot of dollars, Howard, and I think we deserve better treatment."

"You little pip-squeak," I screamed, "don't you ever call me again and try to censor me! Who the hell do you think you are to tell me how to do my job?!? You talk with anybody you want to, you hear! Talk to the chairman of the board, talk to the president, go ahead and threaten them if you can, but I will not back off on what I said. It's the truth, and that's that!"

Later on in the day, Roarty called me. He wanted to fly in

from St. Louis and have a meeting with me. I told him I'd be glad to meet with him at any time, but perhaps he should go through channels first and talk with the ABC president, Fred Pierce. It was distasteful and just plain wrong that I should discuss what I said on the air with one of my company's biggest advertisers. In my opinion, such a meeting would compromise my position as a journalist.

Roarty agreed with me, saying he would indeed make an appointment with Pierce and fly into New York.

In the meantime, one night at dinner with one of my *Sports-Beat* staffers, Pete Bonventre, the former president of the New York Mets, M. Donald Grant, approached our table. I invited him to join us for cocktails, which he did, and then he brought up the subject of Kuhn's resignation.

"If you only knew the real story about that one," Grant said rather imperiously.

"Did you see *Nightline* the other night?" I asked.

Grant dismissed my question with a wave of his hand. He hadn't seen the show, but he repeated his contention that nobody had gotten the inside scoop on Kuhn's departure.

"Well, Donald," I asked, "what is the real story?"

"It all has to do with a man named Lou Sussman. You know who he is?"

I kicked Bonventre under the table, gave him a sly wink, then said to Grant, "No, who is he?"

"Sussman is Gussie Busch's lawyer," Grant said, "and he wants Kuhn's job. Now, he knew the old man hated Kuhn, and he was Gussie's guy behind the scenes who was getting those National League owners to vote against Kuhn."

I kicked Bonventre again. "Is there anything to the fact," I asked, "that those owners have big cable interests and superstations?"

"Now you're thinking, Howard," Grant said condescendingly, but I let him get away with it to draw him out. "Don't you think that beer advertising means a lot to those men? Of course it does. That was Sussman's trump card, and Gussie let him use it. Nice and neat, huh? And Sussman was able to keep fellows like Turner and Doubleday in line."

"Really, Donald, thanks for telling me," I said, dripping with gratitude. "What a fascinating story."

Several days later, I got a call from Pierce, who said that

Roarty was flying into town to meet with him and Tony Thomopoulos, the president of ABC's broadcast group. Pierce wanted me to talk with them about the *Nightline* show before Roarty arrived.

It was a quick meeting. I told them that my information was correct. I stood on it, and I didn't like the idea of a sponsor, no matter how important, implicitly threatening to get back at my company for what I had said. I had given the public information it basically wasn't getting anywhere else, and there was no way that an advertiser should seek to controvert what was said on a news program.

Pierce and Thomopoulos agreed with me, and I received their support.

After Roarty had met with those two men, he stopped by my office. We shook hands, exchanged pleasantries, and then he handed me a letter in which was stated Budweiser's position: that Anheuser-Busch and the St. Louis Cardinals were two separate and distinct corporations and that Busch wasn't involved in mobilizing National League owners against Kuhn.

The way it turned out, I honored my commitment to speak at the Budweiser-sponsored dinner in St. Louis, and ABC executives never said a word to me about Anheuser-Busch's complaints. I had gotten the story right, my company knew it, and it backed me.

A curious thing happened several months after Roarty paid his visit to ABC. Dodgers' owner Peter O'Malley, an unwavering Kuhn supporter, ordered the cancellation of all sales of Budweiser beer in Dodger Stadium. People in the concessions business refer to Dodger Stadium as "the world's largest saloon." Considering the Dodgers' attendance, gross sales of Budweiser beer in that park probably amounts to between $8 million and $10 million a year.

O'Malley's action stung Busch, who then turned around and canceled all Budweiser advertising on the Dodgers' radio and TV.

Not long after, another Kuhn ally, Ballard Smith of San Diego, also canceled the sale of Busch's beer in his stadium. I had to chuckle to myself as I wondered what Roarty and Solomon were thinking. My story was accurate, as I'd always known, and it was satisfying to know that now it was forever confirmed in the starkest terms.

At about the same time, baseball was conducting its winter meetings in Nashville, Tennessee, and Kuhn delivered what appeared to be his farewell address. But several days later, he announced that he would stay on as commissioner until March of 1984, continuing to serve the game while the owners searched for a new commissioner. I disagreed with Kuhn. I thought he owed the owners nothing and that he was harming his self-respect by sticking around. I questioned him in that regard on *SportsBeat* and also brought up O'Malley's refusal to sell Budweiser beer in Dodger Stadium.

"Did you, sir, instigate this action by Peter O'Malley?" I asked Kuhn.

"I did not instigate it," Kuhn replied. "I'm certainly aware of what Peter did. Whether that will be a good thing for the future of the game remains to be seen. But I had nothing to do with instigating it."

I then asked Kuhn if he recollected the *Nightline* show the previous summer in which it was brought out that Gussie Busch, the beer baron, was the guiding hand behind Kuhn's dismissal.

"I recollect," Kuhn said. "Certainly the Cardinals played an important role. How important I think only time will tell. But I think much of this is still cloaked in murky uncertainties. . . ."

Kuhn, of course, was being diplomatic, but privately he was pleased with what O'Malley had done. Hell, he's only human. He knew that O'Malley's action wasn't going to break Busch, and he knew, too, that the good of baseball hardly depended on whose beer was sold in major-league stadiums. It was the gesture that counted—and it was no small gesture at that. O'Malley had graphically showed his loyalty, and Kuhn was gratified still to have powerful friends in baseball.

Kuhn also stressed that while he stayed on he had full and thorough powers to carry out the duties of his office. Otherwise, he said, he would not have remained on the job. I believed him, and he conducted himself as commissioner as he always had—staunchly, with an upright posture, both eyes cocked on matters that might damage the integrity of the game. He fined and suspended players for drug abuse, kept a tight rein on the owners—

and continued to push for some form of revenue sharing among the clubs in the cable television area.

Then, on March 3, 1984, the owners finally found their man—Peter Ueberroth, the president of the Los Angeles Olympic Organizing Committee. I had gotten to know Ueberroth well, having done several *SportsBeat* shows regarding his efforts to stage the 1984 Summer Olympics. He was doubtlessly the best man for the job, a personable, forceful man with enormous administrative and organizational talents.

The owners were holding a meeting in Tampa, Florida, and it was there that Ueberroth was officially confirmed as the new commissioner. I was the first to have Ueberroth—along with Kuhn—on network television to discuss his taking of the baseball commissioner's job.

My first question to Ueberroth concerned his appearance on *SportsBeat* the previous July, when he claimed that he had no interest in the job. In response, Ueberroth praised Kuhn, then said, "I wasn't a candidate as long as Bowie was one. We're friends, and we both understood that."

Ueberroth also revealed that Kuhn would stay on until September 30, at which time his obligations as head of the LAOOC would have been completed. Before taking the job, he said, he had made sure that the owners were willing to enhance the authority of the commissioner's office. For example, he had gotten the owners to change their archaic voting procedures; no longer would a commissioner need three-fourths approval from each league to retain his job, but a simple majority.

"I would not have taken the job," Ueberroth said, "if Bowie weren't permitted to stay on."

Turning to Kuhn, I asked him why he had consented to remain in light of the way he had been treated by the owners.

". . . Peter said he simply would not take the job unless I stayed on. He's the man I felt should have the job. I told Bud Selig, the head of the Search Committee, this man was the man for the job."

"Were there any other choices, Bowie?"

"Other men were considered, but I think this was the best-qualified man."

"Then he got the only offer?"

"He got the only offer."

One last time, I asked Kuhn if there were any great personal regrets.

"Looking back over the last couple of years, Howard, of course there are. I would like to have continued. But at a certain point, I said to myself, 'Look, Bowie, you ought to get out of here. Open the door, and let some new air come in.' The new air is sitting here on my right, and he's going to be a great commissioner of baseball."

Ueberroth ended up making a smashing success of the Summer Olympics, and the LAOOC was able to turn a profit of $215 million—an unheard-of achievement in the annals of the Olympics. When it came time for him to assume the commissionership, he invited Kuhn to attend the playoffs and the World Series with him. Kuhn discussed the invitation with me, and he decided, rightly so, to decline. He felt that Ueberroth should be alone on center stage, and he didn't want in any way to dampen the events by his presence. Instead, he made a goodwill tour of Korea and its baseball facilities, then accompanied the Orioles on their trip to Japan.

Before he left office, however, Kuhn made one more big splash. As the Chicago Cubs drove toward the National League playoffs, he realized that baseball was facing a huge problem. The home of the Cubs, Wrigley Field, has no lights, and day games had become a way of life for Cubs' fans. Privately, Kuhn wanted to order lights into Wrigley Field, but pressure was mounting. Cubs' rooters were clamoring for the preservation of day games, and they were supported by columnists everywhere, exhorting Kuhn to honor the traditions of baseball and ignore the wishes of network executives who wanted prime-time telecasts.

Kuhn was justifiably concerned about the economics of the game. Should the Cubs make the playoffs and then the World Series, the playing of day games would cost each team more than $750,000 in television revenues. It would also mean that millions of baseball fans who work during the day would miss the games.

There was another problem. The governor of Illinois, James R. Thompson, a self-professed lifelong Cubs' fan, had signed a noise-pollution bill in 1982 that, in effect, forbids night games in Wrigley Field.

Naturally, the owners wanted night games—and that included the owners of the Cubs, who are owned by the Chicago

Tribune Company. That's right, the same corporation that owns the *Chicago Tribune* newspaper. While the newspaper's columnists were drumbeating for day games, their own management was working behind the scenes, trying to get Kuhn to order lights in Wrigley Field so it could save face with a coterie of diehard fans who don't work but sit in the bleachers in the afternoons to watch their team in action. In the process, the Chicago Tribune Company also wanted Kuhn to defy the governor and take the heat for dragging baseball through the courts on the issue.

Kuhn resolved the dilemma as best he could. He left the schedule of playoff games intact. But if the Cubs were to get into the World Series, then games three, four, and five would be played in Wrigley Field, rather than games one, two, six, and seven, as originally planned. The American League would get the home-field advantage—an edge that historically hasn't amounted to much—but the switch in the schedule meant that weekend games, which are always played in the day, would take place in Wrigley Field. (The Cubs made the playoffs but not the World Series.)

Kuhn was hailed by the press for standing up for the rights of the Cubs, the traditions of day baseball, and the interests of the fans of the long-suffering Cubs. Nobody found this more amusing than Kuhn, who had thought all along that lights should be installed. In fact, if he had not been a lame-duck commissioner, and if he had had enough time to fight the noise-pollution bill, he probably would have ordered lights into Wrigley Field. As it happened, he simply did the best he could with an impossible situation.

We both agreed on one thing: Sooner or later, considering its heavy interests in cable television, the Chicago Tribune Company will indeed put lights into Wrigley Field.

Sure enough, less than two months after the World Series, the Chicago Tribune Company tried to pull a fast one, making it seem as if the matter of lights in Wrigley Field had slipped beyond its control.

First there was this statement released by the commissioner's office: "If we cannot play our normal League Championship Series at night, baseball will be delinquent in its obligation to the fans across the country who are available in the greatest numbers at those times. In addition, baseball's revenues will be seriously impaired.

"The commissioner has told the Cubs the solution to the problem lies with them and has urged them to address it now, while there is time to work out appropriate solutions."

The Cubs promptly filed a lawsuit against the city of Chicago and Governor James Thompson, asking a state court to block enforcement of the noise-pollution bill—and thus allow them to put lights in Wrigley Field. Considering the commissioner's directive, they said, they had no choice.

The people who run the *Chicago Tribune* must have been smiling like Cheshire cats. They could try to get lights into Wrigley Field, and they could place the blame squarely on Ueberroth's shoulders. Hey, fans, it wasn't our fault. Ueberroth made us do it.

That wasn't quite the truth. When the Cubs went to court, Ueberroth was on a boat, heading toward Mexico for a vacation. He had no idea what the Cubs were up to, and there was hardly any opportunity to find him for a statement.

When Ueberroth returned from vacation, however, he found himself on the cover of *Time* magazine, hailed as its Man of the Year, and I got him to appear on *SportsBeat.* Here's what he said when I mentioned that he had ordered the Cubs to take legal action and install lights in Wrigley Field: "Definitely not true. Without question, it's not true."

Ueberroth insisted that he had never ordered the Cubs to file any kind of suit. "I told them there is a problem they need to solve and suggested half a dozen ways to solve it," he said. "I never ordered anything. . . . It might be as simple as temporary lights for a few games."

As of this writing, the Cubs were still pressing ahead with their suit. Why not? Maybe they are a bunch of wimps for trying to misguide their fans and let Ueberroth take the heat. I hardly respect them for that, but the fact is, the Chicago Tribune Company is in the business of increasing its profits and satisfying its stockholders. And how silly were all those columnists and commentators bleating over day baseball games. Come on, guys, this is the twentieth century.

By the way, in that same interview, Ueberroth said he was going to take a long, hard look at Kuhn's decision to ban Mays and Mantle from baseball for working for Atlantic City casinos. Privately, he told me that he was leaning toward lifting the ban, believing that both players were the victims of a double standard and that they were practically national institutions. A couple of months later, on March 18, Ueberroth did indeed reinstate Mantle and Mays, enabling them once again to hold salaried jobs in the game they so magnificently graced.

When Kuhn left baseball, he went back to his old law firm, Willkie, Farr & Gallagher, and he got a deal with a public-relations firm as a special counsel. He also signed to write a book about his tenure as commissioner.

One thing I was certain of, and Kuhn tended to agree with me: He'd never be completely happy as a practicing lawyer. I'm a former attorney myself, and the relative anonymity of the law does not make it a satisfying refuge, not after you've experienced the spotlight for so long. Kuhn knew that, and in the months following his departure from baseball, he was still beset with uncertainties, trying to cope with and figure out exactly what he wanted to do with the rest of his life.

Kuhn missed baseball terribly and probably always will. He loves the game, and it hurt him to watch a new commissioner come in and take over. Ueberroth was granted the kind of respect Kuhn had wanted, the kind of respect that enabled him to settle the umpires' strike before the 1984 World Series and that gave him the freedom to push forcefully for revenue sharing of cable television revenues and risk the wrath of the owners.

Bowie and I once discussed the possibility that Ueberroth might not remain in the job for more than a couple of years. Ueberroth, in our opinion, seemed destined to take over a major corporation or perhaps run for public office in his home state of California. And as we talked about Ueberroth, I got the uneasy feeling Kuhn was thinking that maybe the owners would ask him back—and he'd go.

I hoped he wasn't thinking that. He's too fine a man to let baseball have that kind of hold on him. He should let go. He's got the capacity to move on and find happiness beyond baseball. He deserves it.

11

The Beat Goes On

*Knowledge is of two kinds. We know a subject ourselves,
or we know where we can find information upon it.*

—Samuel Johnson, *Life of Johnson*

On January 3, 1985, Senator Arlen Specter of Pennsylvania
honored my *SportsBeat* show in a manner unparalleled in the
sports television industry. That day marked the opening of the
Ninety-ninth Congress, and Specter was prepared to introduce
his Professional Football Stabilization Act, a bill designed to
control the movements of sports franchises from one city to another.

The previous month, on December 15, Specter had appeared on *SportsBeat* to express his views on the threatened
shift of the Philadelphia Eagles to Phoenix and discuss his proposed legislation. The first fifteen minutes of that show were devoted to a history of franchise carpetbagging dating back to the
Brooklyn Dodgers and their move to Los Angeles in 1958 and
containing many of the events that I have detailed in previous
chapters. So impressed was Specter that when it came time for
him to introduce his bill, he proceeded with these words: "An
excellent analysis of the unfairness of sports franchise moves,
the unfair pressure on cities, a discussion of certain legal issues,
and Philadelphia's problem with the Eagles was eloquently
articulated by Mr. Howard Cosell in his *SportsBeat* program on

ABC-TV on December 15, 1984. Since that program was and is so instructive on this issue, I ask unanimous consent that the transcript of that program be included in the record at this point."

Specter got unanimous consent, and the entire transcript of that program was read into the Congressional Record.

In addition, that program ended up being nominated for a Peabody and a George Polk award, two of the most distinguished honors in broadcast journalism. I couldn't be prouder of the show—the only half-hour show in television that is devoted exclusively to sports journalism—and if I had to choose one show that I'd like to stand as my legacy in this business, *Sports-Beat* would be it.

• • •

On August 30, 1981, the show called *ABC SportsBeat* was officially born.

SportsBeat might never have taken the air, oddly enough, if it weren't for a man named Van Gordon Sauter. When Sauter assumed the presidency of CBS Sports, he promptly coined the slogan "sports journalism," then launched a one-man PR campaign about investigating the seamy side of fun and games. He was going to unleash a horde of righteous reporters against the sports Establishment, and they would unearth all manner of scandals, drug abuse, racism, forged transcripts, strikes, fixed fights, gambling, violence, shamateurism. . . .

You name it, you'd get it. Just the facts, ma'am.

And so the battle cry was raised—and it reached near-hysterical proportions. You would have thought that "sports journalism" had never existed on the air.

What nonsense!

The fact was that my whole life as a broadcaster had been dedicated to what Sauter called "sports journalism," and everybody in the industry knew it. The historic evidence was rife. And yet Sauter's public statements had the effect of making CBS look like the only network in pursuit of truth and beauty in sports.

This is not to imply that Sauter did not have some valid arguments to make. For too long, CBS, NBC, and ABC had confined their sports journalistic efforts to an engaging and diverting mix of features, interviews, and scores on their various pregame shows. Some shows were more ambitious than others, such as ABC's *Wide World of Sports* and CBS's *Sports Saturday-Sunday* with Brent Musburger, but in the main, these shows could hardly be classified as hard-hitting forays into journalism.

The plain, unvarnished truth is this: What passes for sports journalism on television, both on the local and network levels, too often comprises a cursory sideline interview with an athlete, or a critical comment here and there about a manager's pitching change or some such nonsense, or reading from a piece of wire copy about a trade or another drug arrest, or even a montage of action shots played to the strains of Sinatra singing "Here's to the Winners."

There were exceptions, of course. One, I am proud to say, was my daughter Hilary, who at the time was producing the Emmy-nominated "Sports Journal," a segment within an NBC anthology called *SportsWorld.*

The other exception was Hilary's father. As Don Ohlmeyer, then executive producer of NBC Sports, said in an interview with a Chicago writer, "Whether you like it or not, sports journalism on television was begun in this country by Howard Cosell, and nobody else. And he still practices it."

The attention paid to Sauter's remarks finally prompted a lunch between Roone Arledge and me. In addition to being president of ABC Sports, Arledge was also running ABC News, and we decided to create a show that the other networks did not have—and one we knew that Sauter had no intention of creating. It was to be a half hour in length and devoted exclusively to sports journalism.

As suggested by Arledge, the show was called *SportsBeat.*

Actually, Arledge and I were simply extending a fifteen-minute show I had done for a number of years. It was first entitled *Howard Cosell's Sports Magazine,* then later, *The ABC Sports Magazine.*

The premiere of *SportsBeat* contained three stories, each designed to give the show pace, topicality, and mood variety. John McEnroe was enormously controversial because of his churlish behavior on the court, but it seemed to me that far more important than McEnroe's unsportsmanlike conduct was the plus side of his personality. To that end, I got McEnroe to reveal on *SportsBeat* that he had rejected a $1 million guarantee to play Bjorn Borg in South Africa, the land of apartheid. Borg, by the way, had accepted.

The second story was an example of the kind of reportage that I foresaw as the staple of future *SportsBeat* shows, hitting the big issues in sports long before anybody else. Thus I mobilized my staff for an in-depth report on labor relations in professional football. We examined the increasingly rebellious spirit of the NFL players' union, canvassed all the points of contention, and raised the likelihood of a players' strike during the 1982 season—which proved correct.

The first *SportsBeat* ended with a short, humorous look at Darryl Dawkins, then with the Philadelphia 76ers, trying to shatter a prototype of the National Basketball Association's new, unshatterable backboard.

The show was well received and well reviewed, and it continued on a once-a-month basis. Other shows included a no-nonsense profile of New York Yankees' owner George Steinbrenner and a touching exploration of former Minnesota Vikings' defensive end Carl Eller's despairing battle with drugs.

At the start of the new year, Arledge gave *SportsBeat* a regular schedule—or as regular as was possible. Sometimes the show appeared on Saturday, sometimes on Sunday, and always there were differing time periods, making it difficult to establish viewer habit. At least, however, *SportsBeat* was alive, and I was happy for that.

In preparation for the new season, I sent a memo to Arledge, copying Jim Spence, a senior vice president of ABC Sports. In it, I listed a variety of subjects I planned to deal with on the show. These included:

1. An exclusive interview with Polish tennis star Wojtek Fibak, who couldn't continue playing tennis because of his constant concern for his father. Unable to contact him, Fibak revealed that he planned to take whatever steps necessary, regardless of martial law, to get into Poland and find his father.

2. A story entitled "Foreign Invasion," which detailed the often underhanded manner in which some colleges and universities were fighting to get foreign athletes, particularly in the Southwest Conference's track and field program. The focus of the story was a Kenyan half miler named Sammy Koskei, who gave his age as twenty-three when he enrolled at New Mexico Junior College in 1980. Then, when he transferred to SMU, Koskei claimed to be nineteen, which enabled him to eke out a couple of more years of eligibility.

3. A visit with Mike Burke, the former president of the New York Yankees, Knicks, and Rangers, who had renounced his U.S. citizenship and settled on an estate in the town of Aughrim in County Wicklaw, Ireland, where he planned to write his autobiography.

Unbeknownst to me, Arledge dropped a remark to Spence. In effect, he said, "Let's make sure that all these shows are as newsworthy as possible."

Apparently, Spence had taken Arledge's word to mean that he should exert a greater authority over the show than was otherwise intended.

About a week before the first show, I got a call from John Martin, then the other senior vice president of ABC Sports, and he asked me to come up to Spence's office.

"He wants to see you right away," Martin said.

"What for?"

"It's about SportsBeat, Howard. Please come up."

When I got to Spence's office, he informed me that he had read my memo, adding, "Your shows have to be on top of the news, Howard, and you've got to get ratings."

Then Spence proceeded to tear apart almost every story idea that I had outlined in the memo.

"Nobody cares about a Polish tennis player," he said. "Strike that one. Foreign athletes in the colleges? So what? Strike that. And who cares about Mike Burke? He's yesterday's news. Strike that one, too."

Spence is normally a well-intentioned man, but he dotes on authority. His demeanor was outrageous. As for his opinions, they simply were of no consequence to me. Where and when had Spence acquired his journalistic expertise? His experience in the field was severely limited, whereas I had been hustling stories from one end of the country to the other for twenty-five years and more in broadcasting.

In an angry voice, I told Spence exactly how I felt about what had just transpired. Then I turned to Martin and said, "After all my years in this business, I will not be told what stories to play on my show!"

I walked out, went downstairs to my office, and called Elton Rule, then the president of the network. Even though it was early evening, I told Rule, "I must see you right away, Elton. I've made a decision and I will only talk to you about it."

Rule told me to come right up, and when I got there, he said, "Before you say anything, Howard, let's have a drink."

He then poured two vodkas on the rocks, settled back in his chair, and took a few sips of his drink. "Now, what's up?"

"I've just had an intolerable meeting with Jim Spence, and I've had it! I've been through this too many times for too many years, and I want out of here!"

After hearing a blow-by-blow account of the meeting, Rule called Fred Pierce, who was then his chief aide and later succeeded him as president of the network. "Fred, I want you to come in here right away," he said. "I've been talking with Howard, and I want you to hear what he's got to say."

Within seconds, Pierce was in Rule's office, and I was repeating what I had told Rule. I also detailed the brief history of *SportsBeat*, the critical acclaim it had received, and how the show had consistently made news even on a once-a-month schedule.

"I'm sorry, Fred, but after being with this company for as long as I have, it's just too much to bear," I said. "I've endured enough interference from Spence on other shows, and I won't take it with *SportsBeat*. I'm not going to suffer any more. It's that simple."

"You're happy with the material you have for the first show?" Pierce asked.

"Happy? I'm ecstatic! The Fibak story and the foreign-invasion story will be picked up across the country. Nobody else has them!

"Fibak met with me secretly at the Plaza Hotel, and then we went to his home in Connecticut, where he's got one of the most fabulous art collections you'd ever want to see. And we've un-earthed a scam at SMU that will make headlines.

"These stories are an indication of the dimension of sports in the world today. It would take an imbecile not to under—stand that. Yet that man told me to strike them, and I won't tol-erate it."

"It seems clear to me that Howard's right," Rule said to Pierce. "What do you propose we do about it?"

"I'd like to get into it," Pierce said. "But let's not forget that it's Roone's department, and I can only operate through him."

"I understand, Fred," I said.

"Give me time to get to Roone," Pierce said, "and you'll hear from either one of us as soon as possible."

"Please, Fred, because I'm not going through this anymore. There's no sense to it. I'm tired of it, and quite frankly, I don't need it anymore."

On the way home that night, I thought, well, this can't go on much longer. Every six months now, you're telling them that you're leaving, that you're not happy. If they say, finally, get the hell out, we're sick of you, you'd have to appreciate their point of view—because you're becoming a pain in the ass to all of them, Cosell.

And yet, I was sure, they all liked me and respected me. We had been together for so many years, and the contretemps with Spence over *SportsBeat* were just too important to let slide. I had to take my chances.

The next morning, Arledge called me. We met for lunch, and Arledge was as direct with me as he had ever been.

"I want to make it perfectly clear, Howard," he said. "This is your show. You do it your way. No interference."

"Under those conditions, Roone, I have no problem," I said. "But be firm with Spence. I'm willing to forget about his posture at yesterday's meeting as long as he stays out of my way."

I went ahead with the Fibak and foreign-invasion stories. Im-mediately after the show had aired, the phone rang in the studio. It was Arledge. "That was a helluva show, Howard," he said. "Congratulations, and congratulate your staff for me."

Then Arledge said something to me that I will never forget, something that genuinely moved me and made me feel proud of my association with ABC for so many years.

"Howard," he said, "this show will be our legacy."

We had sent transcripts of the show to the wire services and newspapers around the country, and the next day, both stories made headlines—as I knew they would.

SportsBeat was off and running. *The New York Times* followed our Mike Burke profile with one of its own. Unlike no other show, *SportsBeat* stayed on top of the NFL-Al Davis antitrust trial, NBA franchise problems, college scandals, and Olympic woes.

Other stories included: a moving interview with former St. Louis baseball star Ken Boyer just before he died of cancer; a report on the suicide of pro basketball player Bill Robinzine, highlighted with an exclusive interview with his widow; American basketball players who had converted to Judaism to play in Israel; San Francisco wide receiver and hurdling world record-holder Renaldo Nehemiah's battle for Olympic eligibility; and beset by disgruntled owners, the baseball commissioner, Bowie Kuhn, said, "I won't resign."

The reviews were extraordinary, and *SportsBeat* was hailed as the *60 Minutes* of sports. As an example, this from *The Washington Post*: ". . . 'ABC SportsBeat' may be the best thing to happen to sports TV this year." And this from *The New York Times*: "Cosell's 'SportsBeat' towered in a journalistic class by itself, the only genuine investigative sports program on the air."

SportsBeat went on to win two Emmys in as many years—and Van Gordon Sauter ended up leaving CBS Sports to become president of CBS News. Ironically, Sauter's highly publicized pronouncements about "sports journalism" had their greatest impact at ABC, for the fact is nothing much had changed in this area at either CBS or NBC.

SportsBeat is the most important show I've done. There have been more dramatic moments in my broadcasting career, but *SportsBeat* represents what I truly believe in—fair, honest, probative, enlightening journalism.

No television executive in his right mind puts a show like *SportsBeat* on the air to get ratings or to make money. It will achieve neither. You put *SportsBeat* on the air for the same reason that you make *This Week with David Brinkley* part of your network schedule—because it's right and because it's a public responsibility.

Sports is a multibillion-dollar industry, and as I have made clear throughout this book, it pervades almost every facet of contemporary society—the media, the courts, the Congress, medicine, education, the arts, you name it. And as such, the obligation exists to throw a searchlight on the owners, coaches, players, officials, and agents, much as the network news departments and newspapers probe politicians, businessmen, lawyers, and doctors.

By my professional precepts, anybody who would call himself or herself a journalist has the duty to act as a watchdog, protecting the public interest against the increasingly arrogant and powerful sports Establishment. That philosophy governs *SportsBeat*. Time and again, as an example, I have explored the ramifications of franchise removals and how professional team owners go so far as to use the threat of abandoning a city to win utility, rent, parking, concessions, and real-estate benefits—often at the direct expense of the taxpayer.

The questions, then, are these: If a show like *SportsBeat* is necessary and deserving of air time, and if it imparts an image of integrity to a network, why does *SportsBeat* stand alone? Why aren't there more shows like it? And why are there so precious few bona fide journalists plying their trade in the sports departments of the networks?

Through the years, *SportsBeat* has found itself buffeted by forces beyond my control. The show has appeared on both Saturday and Sunday and in various time slots. Unless interested viewers had religiously consulted their local listings, they probably missed many opportunities to catch it. Thus, it has been difficult to maintain the kind of ratings *SportsBeat* is capable of getting. *SportsBeat* has performed very well in big-city markets, often outpointing golf and tennis events and sometimes even horse racing and college basketball. Mix in the rest of the country, however, and *SportsBeat* has endured a seesaw existence, scoring as high as a 5 rating and as low as a 1.5. With greater regularity of scheduling and more support from ABC's affiliate stations, *SportsBeat* could indeed reach a larger audience.

I'm not fooling myself, though. In reality, there is simply no way *SportsBeat* can compete against the popular pro sports—football, baseball, basketball, and boxing. Which means, of course, that a network can make a helluva lot more money showcasing a live event rather than a serious, journalistic program.

Networks survive and prosper by delivering the largest possible audience to their advertisers. The overwhelming majority of sports fans wants games. And besides, through the years, thanks largely to sportswriters, they have been conditioned to regard stadiums as cathedrals and players and coaches as deities. No wonder, then, that they don't want ugly stories about racism, slush funds, courtroom battles, and other hard issues intruding into their fantasy world. It doesn't play in Peoria.

As I have indicated, considering the multiple problems and the legitimate commercial concerns of a network in constructing its programming schedule, a show like *SportsBeat* is allowed to exist only because an executive with the strength and conviction of a Roone Arledge believes in it. When he said that *SportsBeat* will be "our legacy," that statement will forever be true in principle—even if its shaky financial viability one day forces its cancellation. As of this writing, *SportsBeat* is well into its fifth full season, which in itself indicates a measure of success. Not many half-hour network shows survive that long, especially one that must constantly struggle to attract an audience with its seriousness of purpose, its changing time periods, and the consequent difficulty in obtaining broad clearances from network affiliates.

Nevertheless, considering the vast number of hours devoted to games and the millions made on them, wouldn't you think that the people at CBS and NBC could devote a half hour to sports journalism? Why do they resist? What's their problem?

As it turns out, ratings and income are only part of the answer. And here's where one of the more startling about-faces in network history enters the picture.

Sauter was succeeded as president of CBS Sports by a former lawyer with the William Morris Agency by the name of Neal Pilson. No sooner had Pilson assumed command than he went about discouraging journalism in his division. His position seemed so drastic that it went beyond a mere repudiation of Sauter's original goals; it was as if Sauter had never even raised the battle cry of "sports journalism" in the first place.

In the summer of 1982, in a speech to television writers, editors, and critics, Pilson fired from the hip:

1. CBS Sports did not have the necessary resources to produce "*60 Minutes*-style" reporting. Whereas *60 Minutes*

employed more than two dozen producers, he said, CBS Sports had three.

2. All three network sports departments are in bed with the various leagues and franchises because they pay dearly for their games; thus they can't be expected to provide detached news coverage both on and off the field.

3. Serious sports journalism is best left to the network news divisions.

That speech by Pilson sparked as much debate as had his predecessor Sauter's manifesto about sports journalism. In a story in *Sports Illustrated*, the man who gave me the go-ahead to launch *SportsBeat*, Arledge, had this to say about the implications of the new CBS philosophy: "Baloney . . . It's naïve and almost cynical to say that sports is just entertainment. If it were just entertainment, people wouldn't be lobbying Congress all the time, and there wouldn't be all these multimillion-dollar lawsuits."

Curiously, several sports TV critics seemed to agree with Pilson. (You can't win with these guys. They knock you when you attempt serious journalism, then they knock you when you don't.) Take, for example, Ron Powers, who is a recipient of the Pulitzer Prize for his radio and television commentary. In a column in *Inside Sports* magazine, Powers wrote: "Network TV would be doing itself a big favor if it got out of the sports journalism business as soon, and as quietly, as possible."

Later in the column, Powers boldly stated: "Big Television and Big Sports are interlocked in a common interest. TV's mission is to make sports as attractive a package as possible—so as to catch an audience for delivery to advertisers. By what perversion of human nature should those same Big Sports Departments be expected to turn around and act as adversary watchdogs upon the activities of their business partners?"

In fairness to Powers, he had praised *SportsBeat* in that same column—but he had also given legitimacy to Pilson's new approach to sports at CBS. With that kind of support, Pilson pressed his views in *The New York Times:* "When you are sponsoring sports events and generating profits, you can create conflicts and problems. In CBS Sports, we have major business relationships that are worth in the billions of dollars and are renewable. You cannot use the people associated with CBS Sports to investigate the morals of the people you do business with."

And this: "We can cover breaking stories like the use of drugs at the Pan Am Games. But basically we are event-oriented. Maybe we shouldn't be, and people will say it's a copout, but that's the business. It doesn't mean, though, that we are not journalists."

What the hell else does it mean? Of course it means they're not journalists, and of course it's a copout. Why pretend otherwise?

And sometimes this philosophy is taken to absurd extremes. Take, for example, CBS's telecast of the 1985 NCAA basketball tournament. Several days before the Final Four in Lexington, Kentucky, a point-shaving scandal broke at Tulane University. Along with three students and a bookie, three Tulane basketball players were arrested and charged with violating Louisiana's sports bribery law. Oddly enough, the Final Four was being staged at an arena named after Adolph Rupp, the late Kentucky coach whose team was deeply involved in the 1951 fixing scandals that rocked college basketball. And yet, nowhere in CBS's telecast was this major news story covered in any way, shape, or form. At least it deserved a mention. This is the kind of ostrich-like approach to sports that I find intolerable.

Let me say that I like Pilson personally. He is a bright, energetic man, and I respect him for his basic honesty and candor. The fact is, however, that he's overlooked what my broadcasting career has been all about, and he's tended to ignore the impact of *SportsBeat* by consistently noting that it's not a ratings winner.

Arledge had the guts to turn me loose—to let me speak my mind and to let me investigate the people that ABC does business with. Time and again, *SportsBeat* examined the recruiting scandals that plague big-time college sports, exposed the corruption in professional boxing—and received a lot of credit for taking on the NFL and hurting its chances to gain an antitrust exemption in the Congress.

The last time I checked, ABC was still doing business with the NCAA, the NFL, and boxing promoters like Don King and Bob Arum, which illustrates a basic flaw in Pilson's argument. By paying billions of dollars for the rights to televise various events, the networks are the chief financial supporters of sports in America today. Thus, since the networks in effect support the sports operators, I see no reason in the world why they must also cater to them.

Quite the contrary. The best interests of the networks are served by putting a searchlight on the sports operators and trying to keep them clean. That's a huge endeavor—and perhaps I'm being idealistic—but it seems to me to make good business sense. Air the issues, root out the scandals, that's constructive. In my opinion, that benefits both the networks and the sports operators. In the long run, it doesn't do anybody any good to suppress what's sordid about sports and let it fester.

For the moment, however, let's put idealism and good business sense aside. The reality is that the networks have little to fear from the NFL, the NBA, the NCAA, and the rest of them. Until pay television takes hold in this country—and that's a long way off—who else but the networks are going to fill the sports operators' coffers with multibillion-dollar rights fees? The networks are in control, and if they chose to, they could hire genuine sports journalists and get on with their responsibility to the public.

Will the sponsors object? Yes, some will. They want their products associated with athletes who are pure and heroic and games that are unendingly exciting and dramatic. That's not always possible, and the sponsors must be stood up to. On more than a few occasions, sponsors have complained about my on-air comments, but I never backed down, and neither did my network. The fact is, the sponsors need us as much as we need them. Where else are they going to find as large an audience with the right demographics to push their beer, sneakers, and tractors?

As I explained in Chapter 6, the ascendancy of "the Jockocracy" in my business is yet another facet of sports television with which I am not comfortable. The limitations of most ex-jocks in the booth are glaring, but what concerns me here is the chilling effect they've had on the pursuit of stories away from the playing fields.

My three main reservations are these:

First, former athletes are hired on the basis of expediency: Of utmost importance is the recognition value of their names, both with the viewing public and the sponsors who invest in televising the games. They are not hired because they have been trained in journalism.

Second, they are utterly inhibited by past allegiances and loyalties to former teammates, teams, and the leagues they're supposed to be covering.

An example: Several years ago, when then Raiders' quarterback Kenny Stabler was enmeshed in a bizarre scam that involved setting up a sportswriter on a cocaine bust, my daughter Hilary went to Stabler's off-season residence in Gulf Shores, Alabama, to cover the story. When she had finished producing the segment for "Sports Journal" at NBC, her next step was to get somebody for the voice-over narration.

Hilary's boss at the time was Don Ohlmeyer, and he wanted her to use one of NBC's ex-jocks. Hilary turned to Merlin Olsen, who flatly refused her request. Olsen would not put himself in the position of reporting negatively on another player. In the end, the assignment went to Dick Schapp, who, of course, is a veteran newsman.

Such an attitude is prevalent in the industry, and nothing will change unless the networks alter their hiring practices. Unfortunately, at the moment, I see little chance of that happening. Just recently, as soon as they announced their retirements, Steelers' quarterback Terry Bradshaw and Cowboys' defensive lineman Harvey Martin were both employed by CBS. Can you ever imagine these two ex-jocks casting a critical eye on the men who once paid them and the men whom they played with? Can you ever imagine these two ex-jocks reporting on sensitive, complex issues such as drug abuse, antitrust legislation, and racial discrimination?

They are simply not equipped to handle the job. And with the plethora of ex-jocks now populating the sports departments at the networks, is there any wonder that journalism is in such disrepute?

Which leads to my third, and surely most strenuous, objection to the mass hiring of ex-jocks. From my experiences lecturing and speaking at Yale and other great universities, I know there are literally scores of bright, ambitious young people who are majoring in the arts of communications and journalism. They should be hired and nurtured. They are serious and dedicated, willing to work endless hours for far less money than the untrained and unprepared ex-jocks to acquire the experience and expertise. All they are looking for is the opportunity—but they are increasingly hindered and frozen out because of the system created by "the Jockocracy."

A final note: When I started out in broadcasting, I had great pride in my profession. After all, before me there were Ted Husing, an articulate, accurate, and fearless reporter; Bill Stern, though not a journalist, a remarkable communicator who had a mesmerizing delivery and could hold a whole nation spellbound with his *Colgate Radio Hour*; Graham McNamee, the true father of sports broadcasters, who developed his skills in hard news and approached each assignment as a journalist; and Clem McCarthy, who was lively, colorful, and informative and never tried to transform an event into anything more or less than it was.

These were the men I admired, and I believe their brand of professionalism is sorely lacking today. What we have now are broadcasters who prove each and every day that they can't use the language. They defy grammar and mangle speech. As I have already stated, they are not on familiar terms with the truth because they belong to teams, to leagues, to sports in general. Most of them are on the air because they played the game or coached it. The really sad part of all this is the ringing endorsement they receive from almost every alleged sports television critic and many sportswriters who seem to get a cheaply fulfilled feeling of being on the inside from these ex-jocks.

The networks' time and money would be better spent scouting the colleges rather than the playing fields for the next generation of broadcasters and journalists.

Getting back to Pilson and his much-publicized opinions, I take exception to this argument that serious sports journalism should be the province of the network news divisions. That is simply not practical. The network news divisions have the whole world to deal with—wars, politics, the economy, medicine, justice, education, *ad infinitum*—and it's foolhardy to expect them to give ample coverage to the important issues in sports.

What's more, when the network news divisions do venture into sports, they tend to treat their subjects much too whimsically. Either that or much too reverentially. Take, for example, *60 Minutes*. If the folks over there had covered G. Gordon Liddy, Yassir Arafat, and Henry Kissinger in the same manner as they presented Bobby Knight, Martina Navratilova, and Joe Paterno, they'd be the laughingstocks of the business.

As for Pilson's complaint that CBS Sports is not equipped to tackle the hard issues and investigate scandals consistently, that excuse won't wash. For one thing, CBS Sports has enough money to hire more than the three producers that Pilson claimed are assigned to his department; for another, a large staff with a huge budget isn't a vital prerequisite for maintaining lofty standards of journalism.

On *SportsBeat*, I have had as many as fourteen staffers and as few as seven—and that includes secretaries and production assistants. Our budget is meticulously scrutinized by the powers at ABC, but that's never really bothered nor handicapped us. We simply work a little harder to fulfill our goals: to be enterprising and creative, to inform and educate.

As senior producer of *SportsBeat*, it is my responsibility to initiate or approve all story ideas, assign the producers and directors, jump on the interviews myself or use a correspondent in the field, and exert final authority over the script and the finished segment itself.

A half-hour show such as *SportsBeat* requires careful attention to rhythm and pace and mood, which is best accomplished by covering a variety of subjects—for example, a human-interest feature with dramatic production value alongside a story that's on top of the news. Insert a short piece that captures the lighter side of sports, or an interview with a guest in the studio, or perhaps even a commentary, and you have the balance that *SportsBeat* continually strives for.

Exceptions must sometimes be made, necessarily. Of utmost importance is topicality, and *SportsBeat* is at heart an issues-oriented show. Thus, because of the complexity of certain issues and the time required to cover them fully and clearly, a show may contain only two segments. On occasion, I have even devoted the entire half hour to a single subject: pay television; the city of Oakland's eminent-domain suit against the Raiders; the departure of the Colts from Baltimore; and an exclusive interview with former baseball star Roger Maris as he faced his battle against cancer.

Another single-issue show revolved around the point-shaving scandal at Tulane University in March of 1985. Disturbed by the escalating media hype, fan frenzy, and two-fisted betting associated with the NCAA basketball tournament, I wanted to present a cautionary tale, examining the potential danger of another gambling scandal similar to the ones that were exposed in 1951, 1961, and 1981. My staff went to work, and we sought out close observers of the scene to see if they thought it could happen again. Amazingly, less than forty-eight hours after we started the project, three Tulane basketball players were arrested and charged with fixing at least two games—and we were prepared to produce what I now consider a landmark show. Some of the college coaches and administrators and law enforcement officials whom we had already interviewed called my office and wondered if I had been tipped to the story. I hadn't been. It's just that we at *SportsBeat* have developed a keen sense of anticipation to stay one step ahead of everybody else, and it sometimes pays off in spades. As the late Brooklyn Dodgers' general manager Branch Rickey once said, "Luck is the residue of design."

In producing *SportsBeat*, I have counted on all my years of experience, the sources I have cultivated, and the trust I have built as a fair and intelligent journalist. Access is my strong suit. When it comes to *SportsBeat*, the simple truth is that I can produce people no one else can at the moment of maximum impact. And when I've got them, you can bet I'll make news with the kind of bold and incisive questioning that is my trademark.

SportsBeat constitutes my best work and makes the best use of my talents, and I am so proud to say so. I am doubly proud of the people I have surrounded myself with, people of energy, imagination, and a keen awareness and appreciation of sociopolitical issues.

SportsBeat is a team effort, and we have combined our efforts to scrutinize a wide range of subjects and issues. Viewers of *SportsBeat* were the first to learn that Georgia running back Herschel Walker was playing fast and loose with the truth when he insisted at a press conference that he had not signed a contract with the New Jersey Generals of the USFL; and they were the first to find out that middleweight Sugar Ray Seales, a former Olympic gold medal winner, was allowed to fight with detached retinas in New York, New Jersey, California, and Nevada, presumably the four states with the most rigid medical standards.

One of our most enterprising segments dealt with the ambitions of the city of Indianapolis to become "the amateur sports capital of America." First we outlined the city's grandiose plans;

then, as is typical in *SportsBeat*'s angle on such a story, we analyzed how sports madness can infect a city—and detailed the multimillion-dollar burden on taxpayers to finance new stadiums, tracks, and swimming pools, putting the whole scheme in a socio-political perspective, wondering whether Indianapolis's dream was foolish or worthwhile.

An outstanding example of *SportsBeat*'s unique place in the industry was our coverage of the city of Oakland's eminent-domain suit against the Raiders. It is a terribly complex case but one that has tremendous implications for other cities and other teams that may want to leave their present locations. And though the maze of legal opinions made it difficult to predict the outcome, we at *SportsBeat* were determined to tackle the issue in a clear, crisp manner, making it comprehensible to the layman.

To achieve that, I made the decision to devote an entire show to the subject, realizing that a report on an eminent-domain suit in sports would be our most ambitious undertaking to date. The newspapers had failed to cover the case adequately—and in many instances had not covered it at all—and I knew that nobody in television would touch it because of its inherent complexity.

The show aired on February 25, 1984.

It was one of my proudest moments in television. What is eminent domain? An NYU law professor named John Costonis, a national authority on the subject, explained: "Eminent domain is the power of government to take private property for some kind of public use. For example, if it had to run a highway through your farm, it would acquire the land through that power. It's particularly important when the owner doesn't want to sell the land. . . . In that case, the government could force the transfer of the property to it at a fair price."

We then gave a brief history of eminent domain, noting that today it is frequently used for purposes of urban renewal. Seizing a football team for public use, however, seemed so unusual that the Raiders figured they had nothing to fear. But thanks to some clever arguments by the city's attorney, David Self, the Supreme Court of California reluctantly ruled that Oakland should have its days in court.

The case went to trial in May of 1983. In simplest terms,

Judge Nat Agliano of the Monterey County Superior Court ruled in favor of the Raiders. Seven months later, however, the State Court of Appeal ruled in favor of Oakland, remanding the case to the lower court for a clearer ruling on public use. The bottom line: The case seemed destined for the California Supreme Court—and maybe even the Supreme Court of the United States.

The California Supreme Court had already ruled that there was no difference between intangible property, such as a team, and tangible property, such as a building. No matter what kind of property was at stake, however, it could not be seized by the government except for public use. Thus, according to the best legal minds, public use was the key issue in the case.

Professor Costonis explained: "Public use is any legitimate governmental purpose. There are some examples of public use that are obvious—like highways, post offices, urban renewal. In those instances, government clearly can take property. But when government starts taking property in very unconventional contexts, the question whether those contexts provide a public use or not is sometimes very difficult to establish."

Does the seizing of the Raiders by Oakland constitute a public use?

Costonis said yes, adding, "The Raiders are very important to the image and stability of the city of Oakland. And if you look at other cases . . . our government has been allowed a pretty broad scope with respect to these kinds of matters."

Naturally, Oakland attorney Self agreed with Costonis. So did George Will, the nationally syndicated columnist and ABC commentator.

Self cited the social, cultural, and racial benefits that accrued to Oakland from its indentification with the Raiders, and Will noted that a city like Oakland derived what little glamor it had from the team, which made the Raiders "very unlike a shoe factory."

The Raiders' attorney, Moses Lasky, was indignant. "What's the justification?" he asked, fuming. "During our trial, the city's attorney said that people dance in the streets when the Raiders win. Well, that's mobocracy, isn't it? That's your Roman bread and circuses. To provide circuses for the people, a man's property is to be taken away?

"If you don't feel in your bowels that there is something obscene about that, then you're a different kind of man than I am on my outlook of American democracy."

Lasky had a formidable ally in Julius Sachman, the author of an eleven-volume text on eminent domain, who predicted that the Raiders "have to win as a matter of law."

The baseball commissioner, Bowie Kuhn, and the NBA commisioner, David Stern, both attorneys, also sided with Lasky. If Oakland should win, Kuhn wondered, where would you find new owners? How could you expect an owner to pour millions into a team that a city might condemn and seize by eminent domain?

Stern argued that Oakland was misusing its power of eminent domain, stretching the statute to an absurd point. "As a resident of New York," he said, tongue firmly planted in cheek, "I'm offended that Mayor Koch hasn't sought to condemn Tom Seaver's contract and bring him back to New York. Where does it stop?"

Should Oakland win, the city would have to pay full, fair, market value for the Raiders, as determined by a jury at a later trial. In the years ahead, according to some people, the Raiders might be worth as much as $100 million.

At the time, Oakland's annual budget was only $200 million. Almost half of that was committed to police protection and fire services. Another $25 million went to community and economic development, and $18 million more went for public works.

Lasky questioned Oakland's ability to pay $100 million for the Raiders. And what would happen if Oakland couldn't find a buyer in the private sector to operate the team? "That's another reason I think it's a joke," Lasky said. "I think that at the end of the line, the city would have to realize that there are more important things to spend money on—like police, firemen, teachers—than on a football team."

Lasky raised yet another question: "If this goes through, what's to prevent Oakland from taking over Kaiser Industries?"

To this, Self replied: "What we're talking about here is condemning property for recreational use, and recreational use has always been a proper public use."

Would the eminent-domain case in Oakland have meaning in New York, which had just lost the Jets to New Jersey?

Mayor Koch didn't think so. Though Koch considered the seizing of a football team to be a valid public use, he had no intention of invoking eminent domain to try to keep the Jets in New York. "Can you imagine what the taxpayers of this town would do to me," he said, "if I paid one of our employees—who happened to be on the team—a million dollars a year?"

What were Oakland's chances of winning?

Pretty good, said Costonis. He predicted that the California Supreme Court would eventually rule in Oakland's favor—provided that the case was decided strictly on grounds of public use.

But . . .

Costonis warned that the court could find other grounds on which to rule. "For example," he said, "the property must be located specifically within Oakland. Where are the Raiders really located? They're just a bunch of contractual relationships. Perhaps the court will say, hey, the property isn't located in Oakland, and therefore the city doesn't have the power to acquire it."

A technicality, to be sure, but Costonis said he wouldn't bet against it—or others like it. "This is an uncomfortable situation," he said. "I don't think the California Supreme Court will be happy in saying that [seizing the Raiders] is a public use. It wouldn't be the first time that a court might use some other grounds to avoid a case that it's not too happy with."

I closed the show with a commentary, which said, in part: "What is needed is a federal law that would protect both team and city. A law based on the rule of reason. It would provide that after good-faith negotiations between a city and a franchise, the franchise could remove itself from that city [if] it had suffered undue financial distress over a prescribed period of time, or upon abridgement of the lease by the landlord.

"Such a law would be consistent with the principles of free enterprise and the implied obligations of municipalities and sports operators.

"One other note: We extended an invitation to the NFL to express its views on the eminent-domain suit. But because it is not party to the suit, the NFL declined, and understandably so."

At *SportsBeat*, as often as not, we consider ourselves the adversaries of the sports Establishment in the finest tradition of journalism, and I see no inconsistencies in the show's guiding philosophy. If ABC can air a show such as *SportsBeat* without any deleterious effect on its business relationships, so can CBS and NBC. After all, take a look at the newspapers and magazines: They run cigarette and liquor advertising while publishing stories about lung cancer and drunken driving.

I'll give this to CBS's Pilson: He has confirmed that he would never pull a story, and that CBS will continue to cover pertinent issues within its main weekend shows. That's commendable, but neither CBS nor NBC has yet to match the breadth and scope of what *SportsBeat* has achieved in its pursuit of journalistic excellence.

As evidenced throughout this book, *SportsBeat* speaks for itself.

CARL ELLER, the former Minnesota Vikings' defensive end, talking about his drug problem (November 22, 1981): "I really had everything I wanted, but I was using drugs. The thing that hurt me probably more than anything else was when I'd be asked for autographs by little kids, people that I knew looked up to me. They didn't have any idea what I did at night when I'd go home."

KEN BOYER, the former St. Louis Cardinals' All-Star, when asked if he was bitter about his cancer (March 7, 1982): "No, I think that's the one thing I really have to combat. I don't feel victimized by anyone or anything—except probably my own living habits. I have to clean out my system if I am going to whip this thing. That's the first thing a lot of people have to accept— that we're probably victims of our own living habits."

BILLY MARTIN, talking about his return as manager to the New York Yankees (February 5, 1983): "Believe me, I'm going to work harder this year than I've ever worked in my whole life. I have a reason for that. I really want to show them again that I can come back and do the job. You know, I never complained when I got fired in Oakland. I never said one word to the press. I let them do all the talking. They had me not going to Hawaii [for the winter meetings] because I would mess up the trades, like I didn't even know what was going on. I didn't say a word, and now I just want them to eat their words. It's going to be a pleasure to come in there [Oakland] when we're in first place, and I'm going to enjoy every bit of it."

RON FRANKLIN, the jockey on Spectacular Bid, concerning his cocaine habit (June 4, 1983): "I had a lot of pressure on me when I was riding Bid, and I would just run to drugs to get away from it. I took some counseling—that's not the thing to do. Thing is, stand up if you're a man and face the facts. If you can't do that, you might as well get out of the business."

REGGIE JACKSON, the California Angels' outfielder, on whether he plans to marry and have children (March 17, 1984): "I hope so. I was pretty close for a while, but then I hit a little storm and things got rough. I'd like to get married, I'd like to have some kids, desperately. I really want to do that. I don't mean harm to anybody, but right now my family is here [holding up his bat]. This is what I'm concerned about. I'm concerned about hitting the baseball and nothing else. Everything else has to wait."

JOHN THOMPSON, the Georgetown basketball coach, imparting some personal philosophy (April 2, 1983): "I'm sick of people running up to me and telling me that kids should stay in college to fulfill their education. I was taught all my life that a person had to have money in order to get an education. I think that an NBA player can get an education if he's committed toward getting that education. I think you can stay in college and play for four years and never get an education. It's been proven.

"But, by the same token, I think there's several things that have to be weighed when you're making that kind of decision. You have to look and see whether the kid is able to deal with some of the psychological and emotional effects of the National Basketball Association. Nobody can pay you a million dollars to destroy your life emotionally and physically."

BOBBY KNIGHT, the Indiana basketball coach, giving his opinion on the printing of gambling information (September 29, 1984): "I think a newspaper that publishes point spreads should also publish the names and services rendered of prostitutes—because prostitution and gambling have approximately the same legality in almost every one of our states, and I can't see why one is any better than the other."

ANGEL CORDERO, JR., the jockey, regarding his innermost fears (June 2, 1984): "I have had fourteen major accidents. I've broken mostly every bone in my body, and it hurts some nights when the weather gets bad. I only pray to God that I never become paralyzed. I don't care if I get killed. That sounds rough, but we got to die sometime. I don't care about that because you don't feel any pain when you're gone. I just don't want to be around to see me in pain, that's all. But I don't think about it when I ride."

TED WILLIAMS, the Hall of Famer, recalling his playing days (June 18, 1983): "If [Stan] Musial was hitting more than Ted Williams, I was going to hit more than Musial. Or if [Joe] DiMaggio was hitting more than me, I was going to be hitting more than DiMaggio. Or it could have been somebody else. Whoever was on top was my target."

CLAUDIA ROBINZINE, the wife of the late NBA player Bill Robinzine, talking about her husband's suicide when he realized his career had come to an end (November 7, 1982): "I think it's important for people to realize the pressures and problems that caused Bill's death. For too long in professional sports, the pressures have not really been publicized. There's a lot of talk about the dollars that are paid to professional athletes, but there's very little emphasis put on the life-style and the anxieties it causes. . . . The pressures are so great, and they're constant pressures. From the minute you sign the first professional contract, your life is determined by coaches and general managers and organizations that I feel don't look at the players as individuals."

PAUL HORNUNG, the former Green Bay Packers' halfback, regarding his and the Detroit Lions' Alex Karras's one-year, 1963 suspension from the NFL for gambling on their own teams

(July 16, 1983): "I don't remember anybody ever betting serious money. Do you really believe that the people in the United States are so gullible to think that Karras and I were the only two betting on professional football? But I never held it against anybody that Karras and I were singled out."

DONALD TRUMP, the New York real-estate impresario, concerning his plans for the New Jersey Generals and the USFL (January 7, 1984): "I know what it takes to be successful, and my idea of success is confrontation with the NFL, challenging them to games, challenging them in the fall, challenging them to the television money. I see challenge."

HANK AARON, career record-holder with 755 home runs, in an interview just prior to his Hall of Fame induction (August 1, 1982): "In my talking to a lot of black kids around this country, they thought the lowest thing that ever happened was when Jackie Robinson was traded. They thought it was the lowest thing when Willie Mays got traded. This kind of thing just doesn't happen. I don't mean to be sounding like I'm bitter, but the truth is the truth. Ted Williams never was traded. Joe Di-Maggio never was traded. Mickey Mantle never was traded. When you think about Jackie Robinson, you think about all the things he'd done for the Brooklyn Dodgers. When you think about Willie Mays, you think about the New York Giants and him playing stickball in the middle of the street with the kids. What is the price? I think when you trade players like that, you're telling people, 'Well, I've gotten everything I could from you and now it's time for you to go elsewhere.' It leaves scars."

EDWIN MOSES, two-time Olympic gold medalist in the four-hundred-meter hurdles, commenting on the problem of anabolic steroids in American sports (August 27, 1983): "In my six or seven years as a competitor, I've seen the use of anabolic steroids first mostly confined to people in the weight events, but now it's moved into track and field. It's very widespread. It's proliferating all over the place. I'd say about fifty percent of all American world-class athletes are taking these drugs. I know that I'm correct, and other athletes from around the world know that

I am correct. They're really glad that someone is able to speak up. I have a lot of support, believe me."

MIKE TROPE, agent, in response to critics claiming his fees for representing players are exorbitant (January 28, 1984): "I'm not a charitable organization. I'm not the community chest. I'm not the Red Cross. I'm not a nonprofit organization. All these ultrapurists around the country that claim they'd do it for free . . . yeah, they'd do it for free until they get some clients. Then, when they make some money, you'll see more newcomers on the block criticizing their fees so they can get a foot in the door."

BOB ARUM, boxing promoter, defending his promoting of matches in South Africa, where there is a codified system of racial segregation known as apartheid (April 30, 1983): "In order, short of revolution, for that system to change, it's going to take people like myself dealing with the situation by example. By example! Because once boxing became a truly integrated sport over there—as far as facilities were concerned, as far as the corners were concerned, as far as everything was concerned—the same thing occurred as far as rugby. The same thing occurred as far as soccer. Okay, now maybe that's cosmetic, and maybe we're talking about games and that's not important. But real progress is being made in South Africa. Maybe the problem is, it's not being made fast enough."

JOHN McENROE, tennis champion, who refused $1 million to play Bjorn Borg in South Africa, when asked what he was proudest of in his life (August 30, 1981): "I think I've always stood up for what I thought was right. I'm not a phony person. I'm there. I'm out in the open. People can either like me or not like me. Just give me a chance."

JACK NICKLAUS, golfer extraordinaire, talking about whether he was losing his edge of greatness (April 4, 1982): "In many ways, maybe yes. Many ways, no. I think in an athlete's career, it's very difficult for him to know when his time is past. In my case, my ability to play and my ability to think are far better than they ever were. But then I keep asking myself, 'Why in the world am I not winning to the extent that I was before? Is it the competition?'

"No, not really. I think it's very simply that I've played golf for a long time, and I've done well for a long time. It's very difficult to continue to build myself to that level, and at age forty-two, it's even more difficult—even though I still think that my time [to quit] hasn't come yet."

GEORGE ALLEN, former Washington Redskins' coach, on taking over the USFL's Chicago Blitz (February 26, 1983): "I got back again because I'm a part owner. That was always one of my goals in life, to be an owner of a team. I had an option to buy five percent of the Redskins and that was taken out of my contract when they offered me a new deal. I think that a coach has to be able to make decisions that affect what takes place on the field, and if someone else is making those decisions, then he doesn't have the authority to control his own destiny."

WILLIE STARGELL, former Pittsburgh Pirate, talking about the pressure of playing in the major leagues (August 29, 1982): "In the minors, when I was going to the ball park in Plainview, Texas, a guy put a shotgun to my head and said, 'Nigger, if you play tonight, I'm going to blow your brains out.' So when people yell things today like, 'You bum, you struck out,' you really can't think it's too important."

STEVE CAUTHEN, rider of Triple Crown winner Affirmed, on the verge of capturing the British jockey championship after five years of racing in England (October 13, 1984): "I suppose I've matured. I'm not trying to prove anything. I know my own capabilities, and believe me, I know I'm not the greatest. I have chinks in my armor just like anybody else. But I'm not worried about it. I'll keep working. The way the cards are stacked, they're in my favor now. I think, if anything, I'll keep improving, and things will get better instead of worse."

GEORGE STEINBRENNER, New York Yankees' owner, speaking out about critical books written by former Yankees Reggie Jackson and Graig Nettles (April 28, 1984): "I always thought there was an unwritten code that you kept things within yourself. People say to me, 'Why don't you write a book?' Geez, you can't believe the offers I have had to write books, and I mean totaling seven figures. I don't believe that, at this time, I have any interest in doing it because that might be embarrassing to some of the players who've taken shots at me, the Yankees, and other players."

ALISON GORDON, *Toronto Star* reporter, concerning her problems as a female sportswriter (May 30, 1982): "I certainly get very specific remarks of a sexist nature when I enter some locker rooms. I think the dear old Detroit Tigers always have been and always will be the most childish. Whenever I go into their locker room, it's now reached the point where they say, 'Look out, here comes the whore.' "

DWIGHT SLAUGHTER, former Cal State—L.A. basketball player, discussing the courses that coach Bob Miller had signed him up for in his freshman year (April 23, 1983): "The first day of school, I went to Miller's office, and he handed me a registration card. I had eighteen units of PE courses: backpacking, theory of movement, archery, how to climb a mountain, how to swim, beginning football. And I asked him that day, 'Are these the classes I'm supposed to have?' He said, 'Yes, you're on the freshman basketball squad, and these are your classes.' "

ISAAC ASIMOV, prolific author of science fiction, commenting on the future of sports (February 9, 1985): "I doubt somehow we'll come to the age, though, when we'll have actual robots competing. It's hard to care much about robots, especially in boxing. I think that boxing robots are not reasonable, in addition, because robots are too expensive. You wouldn't want them damaged. I hate to say this, but men are easily replaced, not robots."

BILL TALBERT, former tennis great and longtime executive director of the U.S. Open, expressing his opinion of the on-court behavior of some of today's players (August 13, 1983): "I remember the elegance of a Fred Perry or a Don Budge or a Jack

Kramer. I like to see a player go out and play, and I don't think it helps them to do the things they do. Now, there are those that contend that some players play better when they get mad and shout and scream. To me, I don't like to see it."

DOUG FLUTIE, Heisman Trophy winner from Boston College, commenting in an exclusive interview after he had signed with the USFL's New Jersey Generals (January 27, 1985): "I never heard from the NFL. I would have liked to have known what they were thinking. I guess we'll never know what their thoughts really were. I would have liked to have gotten some feedback. It might not have made a difference, but I wanted to know. . . . I was a little disappointed. I wanted to find out how they perceived Doug Flutie. Am I, in their eyes, a first-round draft choice? If I'm not, I'm not. I would have liked to have found out."

12

Monkey Business

Six days shalt thou labor and do all thou art able,
And on the seventh—holystone the decks and scrape the
cable.

—Richard Henry Dana, *Two Years Before the Mast*

Without question, the most important influence upon me in sports was Jack Roosevelt Robinson. After Jackie joined the Brooklyn Dodgers, sports was never the same again. It had become part of the mainstream of a changing civilization, and Jackie stood as a symbol of a brave new era.

Jackie and I were close friends and neighbors. I still feel warm all over when I remember our Saturday gin rummy games. Jackie played gin rummy the way he played baseball—all out. Lose a hand, and he'd slam the cards on the table in disgust. Win a hand, and he was the greatest card sharp who'd ever lived. To this day, his widow, Rachel, is very dear to my wife and me, and I'm a member of the board of directors of the Jackie Robinson Foundation. My dedication to that organization is an everlasting tribute to a man of intellect and emotion, dignity and fire; a man with an ethical and moral code given to few; a man who possessed a sense of history, who endured, who surmounted the worst kind of adversity—except the diabetes that eventually killed him.

Without question, Muhammad Ali was a critical factor in my professional life. Like Jackie, he transcended sports, and he too came to symbolize the winds of change that were blowing through our society. I never had the personal relationship with Ali that I had with Jackie, but Ali endeared himself to me. He was a superb athlete, and I knew just how deeply he believed in his adopted religion. I admired and respected the way he stood tall in the 1960s and never buckled, despite the fact that he had been denied two constitutional guarantees—due process of law and equal protection under the law.

I supported Ali as vigorously and vehemently as I could in the firm conviction that the Supreme Court of the United States in the last analysis would vindicate him. Thus it was the greatest thrill of my life to receive a letter from the late William O. Douglas, an associate justice of the U.S. Supreme Court, complimenting me and urging me to keep up the good fight for Ali's rights under the Constitution.

* * *

All of my professional life I've been called a nigger-loving Jew bastard. Then, in one night—boom!—I'm called a racist.

It was September 5, 1983, and the Dallas Cowboys were playing the Washington Redskins at RFK Stadium in the first game of a new *Monday Night Football* season. The Redskins had surged to a 23-3 half-time lead. Leading that surge was the brilliant play of a smallish, black wide receiver named Alvin Garrett. Pleased by Garrett's unexpected success—he had previously failed to last with the San Diego Chargers and the Giants—I went out of my way to extol his performance.

First, I observed that Redskins' head coach Joe Gibbs, while an assistant at San Diego, had come to appreciate Garrett's talents, and when Gibbs got the chance, he brought Garrett to Washington. Then I said, ". . . that little monkey gets loose, doesn't he?"

That single, innocent crack caused a national furor, sparked headlines across the country, and thinking about it today, it's still hard for me to accept what actually transpired. America was reeling over Korean Air Lines Flight 007, fighting in Beirut, and death squads in El Salvador, and yet there I was, thrust into the midst of a controversy that had reached grotesque and absurd proportions.

Why? Two reasons, I believe. Upon hearing the remark, the president of the Southern Christian Leadership Conference, the Reverend Joseph E. Lowery, promptly dashed off a telegram to me and then foolishly copied it to the wire services—as if he had no more important matters to occupy his time and energy. And then the sportswriters and the so-called TV critics got into the act and kept fanning the flames with story after story about what was essentially a nonevent, the most egregious offender being Leonard Shapiro of *The Washington Post.*

At the time, I thought absolutely nothing of the remark. In fact, I didn't even know I had said it—because in the course of ad-libbing for three and a half hours, it is simply not humanly possible to remember every word you've uttered. And so my reaction was one of shock when, during the second half, I got a call from the truck, what we call our control room. It was Bob Goodrich, the game's producer, on the line. "Some reporters just tried to get into the truck," Goodrich told me. "They said that a guy named Lowery, the head of the Southern Christian Leadership Conference in Atlanta, called the wire services and denounced you for making a racist remark."

"What the hell's he talking about?"

"He said you called Garrett a monkey on the air."

"I can't believe that," I said.

"Neither can I," Goodrich said, and I turned my attention back to the game.

At the next commercial break, I asked Frank Gifford, "Did I call Garrett a little monkey?"

"Good Lord, Howard, you had him playing in the Pro Bowl in the first quarter."

"Well, they're saying I made a racist remark."

"Oh, Jesus, Howard, forget about it," Don Meredith said. "What do these people want? There are a lot of nuts out there. Come on, let's get on with the game."

When the game resumed, I denied making the remark, saying, "According to the reporters, they were told that I called Garrett a 'little monkey.' Nothing of the sort and you fellows know it. No man respects Alvin Garrett more than I do. I talked about that man's ability to be so elusive despite the smallness of his size."

Gifford backed me up. "I don't know who they were listening to," he said on the air.

We were wrong, of course. What we had recalled was my praise of Garrett and it simply never entered our minds that anything that could be interpreted as racist was said by me.

After the game, I left the booth with my two security guards and the anchorman of ABC's *Nightly News*, Peter Jennings, whom I had interviewed on the air at half time. As is usually the case, a large group of people had gathered outside the booth, and as the guards were clearing a path for Jennings and me, I spotted Shapiro of *The Washington Post*. Before the game, Shapiro and his editor, George Solomon, had joined me at an ABC cocktail party and buffet. I had always liked Shapiro. Indeed, he was once a guest on my radio show, *Speaking of Everything*, to plug his book *Athletes for Sale*, which he had coauthored with a *Washington Post* colleague named Ken Denlinger.

I asked the guards to stop for a second. "What's up, Leonard?" I said.

"They're trying to make an issue out of this remark you made," he said. "The Reverend Lowery called the wire services and he said—"

I cut Shapiro off. "Let's stop right there, Lenny. First of all, I'm not even sure I made that remark. I haven't had a chance to find out definitely."

"You did, Howard."

"You're sure."

Shapiro nodded his head. "Okay, Leonard, but if anybody writes about me negatively with regard to black athletes, they've got to be out of their minds, and they're in for trouble. Because nobody, but nobody, in the history of sports in this country has served the cause of black athletes as I have, and you know it."

"I know, Howard," Shapiro said. "It's ridiculous."

Jennings and I shared a limo from the stadium to the hotel. He noticed how perturbed I was by the evening's events, and he said, "You really expect trouble, don't you?"

"Yes, I do. The sportswriters will blow this thing up beyond all proportion."

"Don't worry about it," Jennings said. "Everybody knows where you stand."

"You just watch, Peter."

Sure enough, on the plane ride home the next morning, I read *The Washington Post*'s account of the story, which ran under this headline: "Cosell's Remark Raises Ire." It was written by Shapiro, a reporter I had trusted. The first line of his story read, in part, "A furor developed last night . . ."

A furor? Shapiro went on to report that his own newspaper received "about 20 calls," AP "about a dozen" and UPI "a complaint." Considering the fact that forty million people or more watched that telecast, do those numbers add up to a "furor"? Obviously not, but Shapiro had blown up the story. He also got a quote from Lowery, who wanted me to issue an apology. But the cheapest shot of all was Shapiro's reporting of Garrett's comments: "It doesn't offend me because Howard is always shooting off his mouth. Half the time he doesn't know what he's talking about. I think he looks like a monkey. I guess it would bother me if I heard it in person, but that's Howard."

There was little doubt in my mind that Garrett was not informed of the context in which I had uttered the remark, and I would soon be proven correct.

By the time I reached my New York office, my assistant had already received dozens of phone calls, most of them from reporters who wanted a comment. My first concern, however, was to get in touch with Roone Arledge, the president of ABC News and Sports. I tried repeatedly but was unsuccessful. I was able, however, to contact Tony Thomopoulos, the president of the ABC Broadcasting Group, who said, "Come on, Howard, calm down. Don't worry about it, it's a lot of crap."

"No, it isn't, Tony. Print is out to get me."

"They can't touch you on this one."

"They'll try, Tony, believe me."

Thomopoulos told me to sit tight, that he knew where to reach Arledge. Within minutes, Arledge called. "What a bunch of shit," he said. "I didn't even give the remark a second thought."

"It's going to be in all the newspapers."

"Fred Williamson tried that crap, remember, Howard? And he paid the piper." (Williamson was a former pro football player whom Arledge fired off *Monday Night Football* in 1974 after only several games. Williamson blamed it on me, calling me antiblack. Arledge told him, "For your sake, Fred, don't take that tack with Howard, not with his record. You'll be hurt by it." Williamson later admitted he was wrong, but not before some newspapers actually had given credence to his charge.

"I know what I'm talking about, Roone. The phone hasn't stopped ringing. Everybody wants a statement."

"For you to defend yourself against a charge of racism is absurd. Lowery's an old fool who's going to pay the piper just like Williamson did. But okay . . ."

Arledge agreed to make a statement, which would serve as ABC's position as well as my own. He dictated it to me. I jotted it down in pencil, then had my assistant type it and deliver it to our people in public relations. "As far as I'm concerned," Arledge said, "that's the end of it. If you think you should say something on your radio show, that's up to you."

Arledge's statement was concise and to the point. It noted that the use of the word "monkey" was "unfortunate," but it also praised my "superlative and continuing record of promoting harmonious race relations"—and ended with the conviction that the comment was "intended as an expression of affection."

Shortly after I spoke with Arledge, Rachel Robinson, the wife of the late Jackie Robinson, called me to render her support. As one of the founders of the Jackie Robinson Foundation, I was touched and gratified by Rachel's reaction. "It's a shame that people can carry on so over an incident like this, instead of concentrating on the real problems. Nobody has your record, Howard, and I'm going to have my board issue a statement to the press."

Herewith the press release: "Too often decent men and women are accused of wrongdoing based on misinterpretation of the words they speak, rather than being judged by their deeds. Howard Cosell has been an ardent supporter of JRF since its inception in 1972. As a Vice Chairman, he has given unstintingly of his time and resources. He has actively demonstrated his commitment to the struggle for human rights and equal opportunity for minorities. In the most difficult times Howard Cosell has been a loyal and supportive friend and has used his professional position to speak out in favor of justice and fair play."

Other words of encouragement in the form of phone calls, telegrams, and letters started pouring in. Most significant was a call from Bobby Beathard, the general manager of the Redskins. "Alvin is really upset by what's happened," Beathard said. "He wasn't aware of the why and how you referred to him last night. But now that he knows, he wants to set the record straight."

Then Beathard read to me a release that the Redskins' front office had prepared for Garrett with the player's wholehearted approval. It went thusly: "I, Alvin Garrett, think Howard Cosell is just great. And I did not, and do not, take exception to anything he said about me in the broadcast last night. Matter of fact, I am pleased he singled me out for such favorable attention."

Those words hardly jibed with Shapiro's quotes from the night before. Even the Redskins' president, Jack Kent Cook, felt compelled to make his feelings known, saying he was "flabbergasted" over the reaction to my words, which, he felt, were uttered "in a manner that can be described, at least, as affectionate."

I had never received such overwhelming support in my life, but as the afternoon wore on, I was increasingly troubled by the fact that I had not yet spoken out on the incident. Arledge's words kept spinning in my head—"If you think you should say something on your radio show . . ." I finally decided to follow that course.

Almost always, I deliver my radio reports without a script, but I carefully organized my words on a typewriter for that night's commentary. It read as follows:

"Ever since last night's *Monday Night Football* telecast, based upon remarks I made about Alvin Garrett, the wide receiver of the Washington Redskins, many of you have undoubtedly read or heard that I uttered a racial slur in his direction. I think the time has come to tell you about me. For thirty-two years I have been in public life; my career a matter of public record; my positions well known and documented. I have often taken stands that were not popular but which I believed were right. Those stands have very often concerned the black athlete. Throughout the turbulence of the sixties and into the seventies I supported Muhammad Ali and fought for his constitutional rights. The greatest influence of my life was Jackie Roosevelt Robinson and certainly one of my closest friends. We worked together in the black ghettos of New York. I helped start the Jackie Robinson Foundation and am a member of the board of directors thereof. My relationships with Curt Flood and Willie Stargell and Joe Green and Sugar Ray Leonard are all matters of public notice. I have fought against fights held in apartheid South Africa. I have fought constantly for black managers in baseball and black front-office people and for the same thing in football. In short, my entire professional life has been predicated upon making the good fights—the fights that I believe in. And much of the time it was centered around the black athlete. Now about last night. I respect and admire Alvin Garrett and coach Joe Gibbs, who waited a long time to get this fine player and fine man. When I talked of him I was bragging on him with affection and I used a word that I use endearingly with my own grandchildren when I play with them. The word was never, in the context in which it was used, remotely related to a racial slur or anything resembling. It's as simple as that. Alvin Garrett himself said so in a statement issued today."

After rendering my commentary, I headed out to the U.S. Open tennis tournament with my wife, Emmy, and baseball commissioner Bowie Kuhn and his wife, Louisa. We had been invited as guests of Bill Talbert, the director of the tournament. Arthur Ashe was there, and he told me that he had been interviewed by Shapiro. "Why the hell is that man keeping this story alive?"

"You'll have to ask him, Howard," Ashe said. "All I know is what I told him—that you were anything in the world but a racist and the issue was absurd." Then Ashe related some disturbing news. "Lowery intends to have people picket next week's Monday night game, and all subsequent games, unless you make a public apology."

"The man is insane, Arthur." I was shocked. "This will rebound against him in the black political hierarchy. Doesn't he know that?"

"I've told him that, Howard, but he's determined. Maybe it's best that you call Lowery and apologize."

"I think Arthur makes sense, Howard," Kuhn chimed in.

I was frankly outraged. "I've got nothing to apologize for, and my company agrees with me."

After several heated exchanges, I calmed down and took Ashe with me to Talbert's office, where I could use a phone. I called Thomopoulos, told him what Ashe had told me, and asked for his opinion. He said: "First of all, Howard, I heard your radio show tonight, and it was wonderful. The company is behind you a hundred percent, and nobody here wants you to apologize. We stand on Arledge's statement. If you want to call Lowery, that's your business, but I see no need for you to apologize. If they want to picket, let them picket."

I thanked Thomopoulos for putting me at ease, then figured, what the hell, and I put in a call to Lowery. I wanted to deal with him man-to-man on this matter and persuade him to be reasonable. I was convinced he'd hurt himself politically if he carried out his threat, and there was simply no need for it.

Lowery wasn't in, however, and so I returned to my box with Ashe. Kuhn held to his original thinking. "Keep trying to get ahold of Lowery," he said. "I'm very troubled by what can happen."

"How can a man of your integrity say that to me, Bowie? You know the stands I've taken. I shouldn't have to apologize to anybody."

"Howard, I know the situation, and it's an impossible one."

"I don't think it is. I don't think my whole life can be overturned by falsity."

"Heaven knows what print will do," Kuhn said.

"Let them do what they want to do. They'll be exposed in the long run if they go against me on this one."

As for Ashe, he waffled. "The political militants will go after you," he said. "If they picket, it'll be terrible."

I said, "That's not the issue, Arthur. What about the rightness or wrongness of his position? My record speaks for itself."

"That's true, Howard," Jeanne Ashe said. She is Arthur's wife. Then, turning to her husband, Jeanne said, "Howard's right."

That's all she said. But it was the first time I had ever heard Jeanne disagree with her husband on a matter of this weight. She loves him deeply, and I knew what it took for Jeanne to give me her support.

Ashe's posture, however, deeply disturbed me. While I think Kuhn spoke out of a genuine concern for my company and me, Ashe was hypocritical. He had no greater ally in his battle against apartheid in South Africa than Howard Cosell, and he should have been a stand-up guy when I was up against the wall. But Ashe wants to be friendly with everybody and yet maintain the image of being a fearless leader in the black movement. Other black leaders would soon come to my defense, making Ashe's posture regrettable on the face of it.

Later that night, at my apartment, I was finally able to reach Lowery.

"I'm calling, Reverend, because I want to speak personally with you," I said. "I want you to know that Roone Arledge issued a statement today, which I heartily endorse."

I read Arledge's statement to Lowery, then told him, "I don't think any more need be said about this matter."

"I tried to reach you earlier this evening," Lowery said. "I was hoping we could reach a conciliation."

"Reverend, you don't know me. You don't know my background."

"I'm beginning to find out," Lowery said. Then he told me about talking with Shapiro, and Shapiro said he was in the Reverend's corner and he'd carry the ball for him.

"You listen to him, Reverend, and you're making a big mistake."

I thought that was the end of it—but the next morning, there was Lowery on a television news show in Atlanta claiming that I had called him to apologize. And, of course, the story was being picked up around the country.

That was the least of it. When I got into the office, I read another story by Shapiro under this headline: COME ON, HOWARD, SAY YOU'RE SORRY. Shapiro used extensive quotes from Ashe and O. J. Simpson, who used nothing but laudatory words for me. But after quoting them, Shapiro wrote, "Clearly, not everyone agrees."

Shapiro quoted only one other person—Reverend Lowery—who clearly did not agree. Everybody else in the story—including Garrett himself—was most gracious to me. Shapiro also excoriated me for denying "the undeniable." My God! Did Shapiro really believe that I thought I could get away with deliberately lying on the air? Did he really think that I had no idea of inventions such as instant replays and video recording machines? I denied making the remark because I honestly believed that I had not. But I got no benefit of the doubt from Shapiro. He was more interested in milking a story for all it was worth. He even went so far as to label my remark "one of the worst" moments in the history of *Monday Night Football.*

I ask you: Is that fair and objective journalism?

And here's another question: Why had Lowery, with the help

of Shapiro and others in the press, turned this rather innocuous event into a story of national proportions? According to my sources, many of whom were—and still are—leaders of the black community, Lowery's political clout within the Southern Christian Leadership Conference was on the wane, and he wanted to prove that he still had enough power to bring somebody like me to my knees. Why didn't the sportswriters investigate that aspect of the story, which certainly carried greater significance?

I'll tell you why. They were too busy getting their jollies by zeroing in on me and the hell with the responsibilities of journalism. Oh, sure, just about everybody in that fraternity came to my defense—they had no choice based on my record—but most of them used the opportunity to throw a few bricks my way. Such stories and columns had a familiar ring: "I've never liked Howard Cosell because blah, blah, blah—but how can anybody call him a racist?" That sort of thing. As Leonard Harris, media critic for *Entertainment Tonight*, put it, "With supporters like these, Cosell doesn't need enemies."

I am no stranger to controversy, of course, but the "little monkey" chapter of my professional career reached new heights of absurdity. Two daily newspapers, representing two of this country's great cities, went so far as to deal with the incident in editorials.

On September 7, the *Los Angeles Herald-Examiner* stepped forward with a vicious, slanderous attack, calling me "an embarrassment to journalism . . . an embarrassment to his own network." Two days later, the *Miami Herald* praised me as "a champion of minority athletes and equal opportunity," then went on to accuse Lowery of hitting me "below the belt" and hurting the cause of equality rather than helping it.

Throughout that week, the mail and phone calls I received were extraordinary. The Reverend Ralph Abernathy, Bill Cosby, Willie Mays, and numerous NFL owners, coaches, and players contacted me to extend their best wishes. In particular, however, I was most appreciative of the response I got from four men who have never wavered in their commitment to their people's civil rights.

Two of those men—Georgetown head basketball coach John Thompson and CORE head Roy Innis—sent telegrams. Dr. Harry Edwards, a former athlete who helped organize the black protest at the 1968 Olympic Games in Mexico City and now an associate professor of sociology at Cal-Berkeley, sent me the following letter:

September 9, 1983

Mr. Howard Cosell
ABC Sports
7 West 66th Street
New York, N.Y. 10023

Dear Mr. Cosell:

I believe it is important that I register my disagreement with the tack taken by the Rev. Joseph Lowery relative to your "monkey" reference made during the September 5th N.F.L. "Monday Night" football game. I think that the reference was clearly unfortunate given the racial sensibilities of Black society, particularly relative to "monkey," "ape," and other lower primate characterizations. Thus, I understand Rev. Lowery's concern, especially since others in White society might take *your* statement as encouragement to so characterize Blacks themselves—not out of exuberant, affectionate praise, but rather out of racist prejudice and animosity. Nonetheless, it was a human error and under the circumstance I believe that your record on issues of racial justice more than exonerates your sentiments and intent—if not your judgement.

I believe that Rev. Lowery was quite right in attacking the persistence of racial segregation in the press boxes and broadcast booths of American sport. But that issue should have been addressed—not in reference to your remark—but, as I have done over the years, as the abominable state of affairs that it constitutes in and of itself. If millions of Blacks in the viewing audience did not prevent the utterance of that unfortunate remark or its being allowed by ABC onto the airwaves, then a Black sports journalist or color commentator in the broadcast booth probably would not have prevented what was essentially a human error in judgement.

So, for what it's worth, I think you've gotten a *very bad*

rap; and I want you to know that there are those of us who are not buying it—on the basis of your record.

Sincerely,

Harry Edwards
Associate Professor

cc: Rev. Joseph Lowery
President of S.C.L.C.

I also received the following telegram: "Please call me at your earliest convenience. We need to talk. Yours in Peace and Freedom, Reverend Jesse L. Jackson."

It wasn't until the day after I received Jackson's telegram that we were able to talk. He was about to depart for Wiesbaden, West Germany, and he finally tracked me down at the Vikings' training camp in Minneapolis, where I was on hand for a *Thursday Night Football* game. No sooner had I picked up the phone than I heard Jackson's mellifluous tones. "Howard Cosell, you are no racist!"

"If I am, Jesse, you've got a helluva scoop."

On Sunday, in an act rare, if not unprecedented, in network television, Dick Enberg of NBC went on the air and said, in part, "I don't always agree with his style or his self-appraisal, but I do admire his talent and considerable contribution to the sportscasting profession. And Cosell a racist!?! That's absurd. His record and support of blacks and black athletes is to be admired and applauded."

Several days later, I was in Washington to emcee a dinner for the United Cerebral Palsy Association honoring Redskins' quarterback Joe Theismann. "The whole thing was a joke," he told me. "Alvin was never troubled by it, but Shapiro kept pumping it."

He sure had. One week after that Monday night game, Shapiro was at it again, this time with a story headlined: ALVIN GARRETT: COSELL'S WORDS STILL CARRY STING. Again, I was exhorted to make an apology—on national television, no less—as if this whole crazy affair hadn't received enough unwarranted attention.

During this time, Garrett and I never spoke. We missed each other's calls on a couple of occasions, and once the brouhaha died down, we never did get around to talking to each other. It wasn't until the night of October 30 in San Diego that we came face-to-face.

I was preparing for another Monday night game—Washington vs. San Diego—when Redskins' general manager Bobby Beathard visited me in my hotel suite. We were discussing various topics that would aid me in the telecast when I asked Beathard, "By the way, how's Alvin?"

"Oh, he's fine," Bearthard said with a chuckle. "You know, Howard, none of that stuff really fazed him at all. In fact, he kind of got a kick out of it. Now everybody knows who he is."

"Just as long as he understands what happened, how he was used by that kid on *The Washington Post*."

Beathard then leaped for the phone. "Hello, Alvin, this is Bobby. Come on over to room sixteen-oh-two. It's important. There's somebody I want you to see."

A few minutes later, Garrett walked in wearing a tight black T-shirt and black warm-up pants. His face lit up, and he shook his head. "Oh, nooooo, Howard! Fix me up again! I'm not big enough yet."

Garrett and I shook hands. "How does it feel shaking hands with a racist?" I asked, laughing.

"C'mon, Howard, you were just fixing me up."

"Yeah, but you can't believe the shit I went through."

"When the guy on the *Post* came over and told me what you said, I couldn't believe it. You were always fixing me up when I was in New York. I thought the whole thing didn't make sense, really."

"You didn't know I was praising you?"

"Not until the next day, when Bobby here told me about it."

"I was using the most laudatory language. Then, with great affection, I slipped in that 'little monkey.' I call my grandchildren that."

"Well, it's over now," Garrett said. "Nobody asks me about it anymore."

"I'll mention you tomorrow night."

"Fix me up, Howard. Tell 'em about me again."

"Catch some passes, and I'll tell the world how great you are.

That's all you have to do. Catch some goddamned passes and I'll say plenty."

"First I gotta get in the game."

"No excuses, you little monkey."

Garrett left my room in the same manner he had entered it—laughing. He never did get in the game.

There are a couple of footnotes to this story, and I think they speak volumes about the responsibilities of journalism and my relationship with the print medium.

On October 20, in spite of the controversy that my remark sparked, Will McDonough wrote a story in the prestigious *Boston Globe*. The headline: THE GREEN NEEDS A GORILLA. The story was accompanied by a cartoon that took up more than half the page, depicting a couple of black players in Celtics' uniforms seated next to a fearsome-looking gorilla—which was also dressed in a Celtics' uniform.

The gist of McDonough's story had to do with the Celtics' need for a big, strong player under the boards. It prompted the following letter:

The Reverend Doctor Joseph E. Lowery
President, Southern Christian Leadership Conference
334 Auburn Avenue, Northeast
Atlanta, Georgia 30312

Dear Reverend Lowery,

Enclosed you will find an article that appeared in the *Boston Globe* on October 20. The headline is offensive enough, but I think you'll agree with me that the cartoon accompanying the article achieves new heights of bad taste.

I bring this article to your attention for several reasons. Why is it, sir, that I have yet to hear one word of protest regarding this matter? Your indignation over a remark I made about Alvin Garrett on a Monday Night football telecast was well documented. My words were ad-libbed, innocently and affectionately chosen in the midst of a tribute to Mr. Garrett's abundant talent. And even though my record on race relations is exemplary, I was made to feel, by you, somewhat unsavory and insensitive.

Now here we have Will McDonough's article in the *Boston Globe*, a daily newspaper with a glittering reputation far beyond its city's borders. I think it is important to note that in contrast to my ad-libbing during a football telecast, this article—and the cartoon accompanying it—took hours to prepare and reflect on. And in the wake of the national furor that my remark ignited, isn't it curious that the editors over at the *Globe* would consider printing it? What is one to think of Mr. McDonough's opinion that the Celtics need a "gorilla" like Milwaukee's Harvey Catchings. By the way, sir, Catchings is black.

Mr. McDonough is a writer with whom I am well acquainted. I respect him as a perceptive and tenacious reporter, especially on the pro football beat, and if he's a racist, it's news to me. And yet I wonder, sir, is Mr. McDonough judged by a different set of standards than I? Is the *Boston Globe* untouchable? Why can I not hear the outrage?

I gratefully await your reply.

Respectfully yours,

Howard Cosell

I never received a reply.

On November 8, Stan Isaacs, the sports TV critic for *Newsday*, a suburban Long Island newspaper with a large circulation, wrote a column about John Brodie, a former San Francisco quarterback who is today a color commentator for NBC. The previous Sunday, Isaacs actually sat in the booth with Brodie and was obviously impressed with Brodie's work. The first line of Isaacs' column read, "John Brodie is a lively, insouciant television football analyst."

In the course of the game Brodie was covering—the New York Jets vs. the Baltimore Colts—he referred to Jets' defensive end Mark Gastineau and his leaping, arm-pumping histrionics as somebody who looks like he has palsy. An insensitive remark in the extreme. Some might even call it cruel. Nowhere was Brodie's crack mentioned in Isaacs' effusive column. One week later, Isaacs scrambled to recover. In a one-paragraph note at the end of a column, he finally wrote that NBC had received numerous calls as a result of Brodie's "dumb" comment. He quoted Brodie: "It was a mistake and I would be happy to apologize, but how can we do it without making it worse?"

Isaacs apparently agreed.

I had thought that last line would end this chapter. Every now and then, a reminder of the so-called monkey incident would pop up, but I was convinced that it was behind me.

I was wrong.

Exactly a year and a half later, on March 2, 1985, an interview with Lowery was carried on the Associated Press wire, marking the twentieth anniversary of the historic civil rights march from Selma to Montgomery in Alabama. Lowery noted the persistence of discrimination in this country, adding, "Without agitation there is no change. Without agitation the issues will not be raised."

Then Lowery made a remarkable statement. Recalling how he had made a national issue out of my "little monkey" reference to Garrett, he said, "In the end, I used that as an opportunity to say [to ABC] that if we had more black producers, more black directors, if we had blacks on this end of the camera in proportion to blacks on the other end of the camera providing entertainment down there on the field, we probably wouldn't have had this problem."

In effect, Lowery admitted that he had made me a scapegoat for racial troubles in America. Despite all my battles for the black athlete, he figured he was perfectly justified to paint me as a bigot, to cause me personal travail and heartache, to get publicity for his message. I guess Lowery believes in the ends justifying the means. That's a helluva way to do business, especially when you're asking for an even break and fair play from others.

Considering Lowery's comments, you can imagine my surprise when, less than three weeks later, the reverend himself called my office. My secretary had taken the call and in amazement relayed Lowery's message to me. He had requested that I join a special committee to help underprivileged black children and attend a fund-raising tennis tournament in Atlanta. As the tournament was scheduled for early June, there was no way I could make it. I was taking my family to Israel for the dedication of the Howard Cosell Center for Physical Education at the Hebrew University in Jerusalem.

That night I debated whether I would personally return Lowery's call in the morning or assign the task to my secretary. I decided to call Lowery myself. His cause was a worthy one, and I wanted to tell him I'd gladly serve on his committee but couldn't attend the tennis benefit. I had no intention of resurrecting the monkey incident or ascertaining why he had used me as he had, but I must admit to a certain curiosity as to whether he'd broach the subject with me. He didn't. We had a brief, pleasant chat, and he thanked me for wanting to get involved with his committee. Our past contretemps never came up.

And that was that—with a whimper rather than a bang.

13

Going My Way

Whatsoever things are true, whatsoever things are honest, whatsoever things are just, whatsoever things are pure, whatsoever things are lovely, whatsoever things are of good report; if there be any virtue, and if there be any praise, think on these things.

—The Epistle of Paul the Apostle to the Philippians 4:8

My family means everything to me. My wife, Emmy, my two daughters, Jill and Hilary, and my four grandchildren, Justin, Jared, Caitlen, and little Colin, are my reasons for living. I will grow old with them at my side. No man can ask for more.

And I will have my memories, too. I've logged more than thirty years in broadcasting, a profession I love with all my heart and soul. Oh, sure, there are far too many instances of maddening incompetency, distressing hypocrisy, and sometimes frightening abuses of power. In the long run, though, I don't think I could have achieved what I did if I didn't care more than I can say for the medium.

Like many men who ponder their mortality as they approach retirement, I often wonder what I might have accomplished in another profession. Might I have found more satisfaction had I stayed in law? I thoroughly enjoyed my teaching experience at Yale in the late 1970s and early 1980s. Might I have made a great educator and inspired tomorrow's leaders? I was once urged to run for U.S. senator from New York, and I gave it serious thought, though the personal fears of my wife and daughters over a virulent press caused me to decide against it. Might I have made an effective legislator and effected real change in this country?

I will live with these questions until the day I die, but deep within me there will always be a blunt, burning passion for television, and I take comfort in the fact that I told it like it is and remained faithful to my precepts of fair and honest journalism. I would have liked to have tested my skills and tackled the larger issues in hard news. How might I have covered Vietnam, or Watergate, or a political convention? I'll never know, but at least I was able to demonstrate my ability to communicate to a mass audience and to realize an impact that very few in television have ever matched.

I paid a price, of course, and that is the price of fame. I have endured unending scorn in print. And for what? Standing up for what I believed in? Fighting and taking on the press when I felt I was unjustly criticized? The bigger I got, the worse the attacks. I represented the rise of the television superstar over the sportswriter superstar, and the newspaper guys were jealous of me. I became rich and famous and passed them by, and they envied me. They couldn't beat me, and it only added to their frustration. I was pilloried and excoriated for doing my job and getting ahead and making a reputation beyond my wildest dreams. What did they want from me? An apology?

The plain fact is, on almost every important issue in sports in my lifetime, the record stands: The overwhelming majority of sportswriters was wrong, and I was right. Quick examples include Muhammad Ali and the denial of his constitutional rights and Curt Flood and his fight for free agency. Most sportswriters also failed to grasp the sociological, political, and economic ramifications of franchise shifts, the moral bankruptcy of condoning the participation of U.S. athletes in sporting events held in apartheid South Africa and the affrontery to human dignity and civilized behavior in supporting and glorifying professional boxing in the face of mounting medical evidence that clearly established the link between fighting and brain damage.

The amazing thing is that I survived and prospered despite the press's venomous attitude toward me, and I am proud of that. And I am proud that I have never let anyone rob me of the pleasures of my work—and the people and the places and the events that have combined to fill my life with such a marvelous tapestry of gladness and remembrance.

How many men can say they came to know the likes of a Joe DiMaggio and a Walter Cronkite, a Frank Sinatra and a Henry Kissinger, a Woody Allen and a Lee Iacocca? I've traveled to every corner of the globe, and I've had a front-row seat at some of the greatest spectacles ever staged. Telling it like it is, I've had a remarkable life.

And so, to all of my friends and all my foes, let me say it's been a helluva ride. And to you, my readers, let me leave you with a few parting tales since last I shared my experiences in a book.

• • •

I can't pinpoint the day or even the year exactly, but something tells me that the first time I met Roone Arledge had to be in 1962 or 1963. He was walking toward the ABC studios on West Sixty-sixth Street in Manhattan as I was leaving the building, and we bumped into each other. We had never been formally introduced, but each of us knew who the other was, and we exchanged hellos.

"Hey, you're doing good work," Arledge said to me. "We've got to get together. I'd like to talk with you."

"Sure, no problem," I said. "I'd like that."

Arledge was several years away from becoming the official president of ABC Sports, but he was already making his mark as an innovative new force in television. No doubt about it. Arledge was going places—fast—in the hierarchy of the network, and I welcomed the chance to meet with him in the future. At the time, I was still working on the local level, both in radio and television, receiving stiff resistance from the ABC brass in my attempts to get network exposure. In effect, I was being blackballed by my own company.

Arledge had obviously been watching me on the local station and appreciated what I was doing. It's now part of sports television folklore how Arledge adopted me and gave me the opportunity to become ... well, Howard Cosell. He defied his own superiors and fought for me. He got me on *Wide World of Sports* because he believed that nobody could call a fight better than I, that nobody was a more probing and provocative interviewer than I—especially when paired with a young heavyweight champion who was then named Cassius Clay—and nobody in television, even then, had the kind of access to the athletes that I had. They were only a phone call away, and I could produce them at a moment's notice for *Wide World of Sports*.

Those were exhilarating and rewarding years for Arledge and me. Working for Arledge, I glowed with the knowledge that I was part of a wonderful enterprise, that I, too, was making a mighty contribution toward establishing ABC as the standard of excellence in sports programming. And then came *Monday Night Football*. Arledge put me on the package and stuck with me in the face of a broadside attack on me in print. He knew we'd both prevail. His intuitive genius, that sixth sense that told him what would or wouldn't play on television, was never more apparent than when we first worked together in the 1960s.

As a result of the attention and nourishment he lavished on my career, Roone and I forged a close friendship. Unfortunately, sadly, it didn't last.

Today, as you probably suspect from reading previous chapters, I have decidedly mixed emotions about Roone, and I am certain that he also blows hot and cold about me. I guess some might say that we enjoy a love-hate relationship, though there's really not much to enjoy about it. Some of our differences are too petty to mention, but others concern personal and professional matters that I simply cannot ignore.

Essentially there are two characteristics that define Roone Arledge. For one thing, he is obsessed with power. He is also a very private man who's uncomfortable about displaying his emotions and revealing his innermost thoughts. Indeed, in social settings, he is almost benign, unfailingly cordial and attentive, which makes him ingratiating company. Thus, it is often hard to get a fix on the man behind the legend, even when you've known him and worked for him as long as I have.

Arledge's obsession with power is perhaps most glaringly evident in his persistence in retaining the presidency of ABC Sports while devoting most of his energy and resources to ABC News. He should remove himself from sports because he's outgrown it, and I think it's tacky for the head of news to have his name appear as the executive producer of a prizefight or a body-building contest.

What about the question of conflict of interest? As I explained in Chapter 11, Arledge has never interfered with me or others in pursuing stories that have cast an unseemly light on the people and the leagues he does business with as chief of sports. But let's face it: Appearances count. Why should the president of news even put himself in a position where critics might suspect that he either suppressed information or failed adequately to cover a story to protect his financial arrangement with major-league baseball, the NCAA, and the NFL?

Why? Because Arledge can't bear to let go. He takes the title of executive producer of telecasts he has little or nothing to do with. He likes to see his name in lights. Nobody appreciates that urge more than I do, but I wouldn't take credit for a program I wasn't personally involved in. This is not to suggest that Arledge doesn't make the final decision on matters of major importance to ABC Sports. Of course he does. It's just that I believe he cares more about news than sports—who can blame him?—and he ought to step aside and give somebody else a chance to take charge of the division. He won't—not yet, anyway. The more people Arledge controls, the better he feels about himself and his life.

What a shame. Since Arledge assumed the presidency of news in 1977, ABC Sports has suffered. There's a dearth of leadership. Arledge has delegated authority to a coterie of loyal, long-time associates, but it's a joke. He tolerates only yes-men who rarely voice opinions and contradict the boss. This has produced a stifling atmosphere within ABC Sports and smothered the free flow of ideas and the creativity that once were our hallmarks. I can only hope that Roone will one day come to realize that he has more power than he needs. Give up ABC Sports, Roone. It's beneath you. With news, you've got the whole world at your fingertips. Forget about corporate politics. You've won. Devote yourself with renewed vigor to the skills that took you to the top in the first place.

In the beginning, Arledge's quest for power was a positive force. To get it, he had to think more progressively and work harder than anybody else. He gathered creative people around him, especially engineers and other technical types, then listened to their ideas, inspired them, and pushed them to perform marvels that brought a new visual intimacy to sports on television. He also demanded that his announcers humanize the athletes and broadcast a contest as if they were telling a story. He always had a knack for knowing how to capture the imagination of an audience, getting people involved in what they were watching.

To this day, Arledge still has a sense of sweep about him, which is reflected in ABC's telecasts of the Winter and Summer Olympic Games. He absolutely dazzled me with his brilliance at the 1968 Mexico Olympics and the 1972 Munich Olympics, where he masterminded the coverage of the black-power protest and the Arab massacre of eleven Israeli athletes. He was bold and unafraid, thumbing his nose at Olympic officials and giving me free rein to cover every controversy that popped up. And there's no doubt that his telecasts of the 1984 Los Angeles Olympics had a profound impact on the American public.

If I had to guess, I'd say it was the huge success of *Monday Night Football* that started to alter our friendship. *Monday Night Football* had boosted me to superstardom, and I think Arledge came to resent my celebrity. The bigger I got, the less control he had over me. I was always an independent person with a healthy ego, but I became even more fearless in disagreeing with him and telling him when I thought he was wrong. It rankled him. Nobody talked to him like I did—and still do—and I know that Arledge privately fumed when I wouldn't knuckle under.

But Arledge is a clever, calculating man. Machiavellian in nature—but gifted with uncommon intelligence. It's a combination of traits he knows how to use with maximum effect. He understands that the flip side of my ego is the insecurity within me because of my background and my need for acceptance and financial security. He always did. And he'd try to keep me in my place by making snide comments about me in the press. As the years went by, it was rare to get a compliment from Arledge. He kept playing games with me, but I wouldn't crack and become his or anybody else's patsy.

Early on, my wife, Emmy, recognized that Machiavellian streak within Arledge and how he'd try to break my independence. On the night of our thirtieth wedding anniversary, in 1974, we gave a big party at our home in the New York suburb of Pound Ridge. As is his wont, Roone stayed later than anybody else, drinking and talking with us until the small hours of the morning. At one point in the conversation, as Arledge was fishing for a compliment, Emmy handled him the way he'd try to handle me, delivering a line that would become a running gag between the two of them for years. "Roone," she said, "the jury is still out on you."

My friendship with Roone seriously deteriorated in the autumn of 1975, when we joined forces on a prime-time variety show. It was called *Saturday Night Live with Howard Cosell*, and it lasted only twenty-two weeks. Neither one of us believed that we could possibly flop. Neither one of us were emotionally and intellectually equipped to accept defeat. But it happened, and there was enough blame to go around.

The show failed for any number of reasons, some less complex than others. Basically, I don't think the public was ready to accept me, a sportscaster, as the host of a variety show, regardless of how well known I had become. Also, the television critics and other ladies and gentlemen of the press were relentless in their attacks on me and the show. As Bob Hope told me later, "The newspaper guys got you this time."

As for Arledge, after the first several weeks of the show, he got frightened by the adverse press. He quickly lost faith in the endeavor, in me—and probably even in himself. The ratings were going nowhere, and he didn't know which way to turn. For the first time in his professional career, he was a failure—and he couldn't cope.

It wasn't easy for me either, and sometimes I wondered how I could go on.

As I remember it, Roone and I had jointly hit on the idea of a variety show. On the surface, the idea seemed to have everything going for it. A couple of years before, Arledge had produced a live prime-time special with Frank Sinatra. Called "The Main Event," it originated from Madison Square Garden, and I introduced Sinatra as he climbed into a boxing ring to begin his concert. The show received a lot of attention, and the album that was later released, which included my introduction of Sinatra, was a smash.

That was a heady experience for Arledge and me, and I think it whetted Roone's appetite to expand his talent beyond sports. In the meantime, I got red-hot. My first book became a best seller, and I started to appear with frequency on some of television's most popular sitcoms—such as *The Odd Couple, Laugh-In, The Partridge Family,* and *Nanny and the Professor.* In addition, Woody Allen had used me in two of his movies, *Bananas* and *Sleeper*, and I was practically a regular on the Dean Martin roasts.

The timing seemed perfect for Roone and me to team up for a variety show.

ABC gave us the green light to proceed, and we threw ourselves into the project. It's impossible to describe how excited and enthusiastic I was. We hired King-Hitzig Productions—producer Rupert Hitzig and comedian Alan King—for day-to-day advice and assistance. We signed Don Misher, one of the finest directors in television. We rented office space on the tenth floor of the Rolex Building on Fifth Avenue. We were going to bring live television back to America! We'd book the biggest acts in show business. We'd use the Ed Sullivan Theater and revive memories of television's glory days. We'd scale new heights! We'd last for decades!

The first show was a sensation. Among others we had Frank Sinatra, Paul Anka, Shirley Bassey, Jimmy Connors, and John Denver. The truth is, we weren't able to sustain the momentum. As soon as Arledge realized the show was doomed, he quit on me. He became remote and inaccessible. Chaos set in. Arledge wouldn't arrive until Friday morning to review the show; then he'd rip everything apart and demand changes at the last minute. Once, I happened to bump into Lionel Hampton on the morning of a show—and persuaded him to appear with me that night. That's how crazy it got. I was running a variety show like a news operation.

Of all the differences we had, Roone and I argued most vehemently over a group of kids who called themselves the "Prime Time Players." In this group were Christopher Guest, Billy Murray, and Brian Doyle-Murray—all of whom went on to star on NBC's *Saturday Night Live*. Today, of course, Billy Murray is a huge box-office attraction in Hollywood.

Roone hated their skits. Hardly a week went by that he didn't severely criticize their stuff—and replace them with a juggler or an animal act or some other such nonsense. I thought they were brilliant, and I fought for them. But I couldn't convince Arledge that these kids were funny and original and destined to revolutionize comedy in this country. While talking to Christopher Guest not long ago, he reminded me of a skit that he and the Murray brothers were particularly fond of. It involved a contest among Chinese stand-up comics, and there was an interpreter to translate the jokes into English. It was wild and wacky. I roared. Arledge didn't crack a smile.

"You really think that's funny?" Arledge asked me.

"It's hysterical."

"You've got to be kidding."

"Roone, I'm telling you. These kids are terrific."

"You're wrong, Howard. They're not right for the show, and I don't think they'll ever make it in television."

Afterward, I gave the kids a pep talk. "I want you to know I'm in your corner, and I'll continue to support you," I told them. "Don't change a thing. Keep doing what you believe in, and I'll handle Arledge."

"What's the use, Howard?" Billy Murray said. "He doesn't think we're funny, and I don't think we can change his opinion."

"I don't think he understands what we're trying to do," Guest said. "He just doesn't get it."

"Look," I warned them, "the worst thing you can do is lay down and die. Don't give up. Remain true to yourselves."

Obviously, when it came to comedy, Arledge and I had radically different tastes. In addition, Arledge clung to the conviction that only superstar guests could make the show fly. I wasn't averse to experimenting a little, but Arledge resisted. And he was the boss.

None of this is said to blame Arledge for the failure of the show. I was equally at fault. But the demise of the show served only to magnify the differences between us, and it caused a split in our friendship. As far as the show is concerned, that's my biggest single regret. Oh, sure, I wish we had made it, but I emerged from the experience with a lot of new friends.

Several days before Thanksgiving Day weekend, when it was announced that we would be canceled, I got calls from Sinatra, Hope, Andy Williams, Tony Bennett, and many others, offering to appear with me in a last-ditch effort to save the show. I thanked them but told them it wasn't necessary. I didn't want to use them like that. There was no sense kidding myself. The show was dead.

Several weeks later, at a Christmas party thrown by Bob Shanks, the creator of *Good Morning America*, I found out that

Arledge was to be named the president of ABC News. The man who told me was Fred Pierce, then the executive vice-president of the network and who today is the president of ABC. He had arrived late. His face was like a storm. He had just come from a meeting where the top executives in the company were gathered around a conference call from Arledge, who was in London. It wasn't a pleasant experience. Arledge had let loose, accusing the group of blowing the Moscow Olympics to NBC and not backing him fully in his negotiations with the International Olympic Committee.

Pierce was furious. As I was sharing a drink with him and our wives, he said, "Tell me, Howard. Is your friend Arledge a genius or a hoax?"

"I won't discuss it with you," I said. "Everything I say about the man seems to get back to him, and I'd rather keep my opinions to myself."

"Well, I've made up my mind. I'm going to bite the bullet and make him president of News."

The next morning, I related the story to Elton Rule, then the president of ABC. "If I ever write another book," I told Rule, "I'm going to use that story."

"It's true," Rule said. "Write it."

When Arledge got back from London, we had a miniconfrontation. He had heard rumors that I was knocking him. "Howard," he said, "I hear you are blaming me for the loss of the Moscow Olympics. After what we've been through lately, wouldn't it be better if you just left the company?"

"Roone, no matter what you've heard, it's other people who are blaming you, not me. In fact, I'm going to tell you of an incident that occurred at a party at Bob Shanks's house."

I then told Roone of Pierce's remark. He smiled. "Freddy's my friend," he said. "I'm sure it was said in a moment's pique."

I must admit, that was Arledge at his best—unflappable, secure in the knowledge of what he had done for the company, of how much the company needed him, and of how indispensable he really was. We made a peace of sorts, and he never again suggested that we both might be happier if I left the company.

Of course, Arledge and I continued to work with each other on various sports telecasts and at the 1976 Olympic Games in Montreal. But it wasn't like the old days. We slowly drifted apart. And once he took over ABC News, we saw even less of each other. He was struggling. I recall a night in Los Angeles when Herb Granath and I ran into Roone in the bar at the Beverly Wilshire Hotel, and he stayed to have a drink with us.

"I don't need news," Arledge said, and it wasn't hard to see that the pressure was getting to him. "I'm on top in sports. Why do I want to knock my head against a wall with news?"

"Why?" I said. "Because you'll find a lot more satisfaction, Roone."

Arledge sighed, then said, "All I need is a breakthrough. One big story and we'll take off."

"That's not going to do it, Roone, not in the long run," I said. "What you need is the proper staff, and you need great correspondents out in the field. That's the way to go."

After another drink, I told Arledge, "Why don't you end your troubles? Make Jim McKay and me coanchormen, and your ratings problems will be over."

I was damn serious. I had always wanted to switch to hard news, but I stayed in sports because I had become famous, and I was very proud of my impact on the American public. Still, within me there was the desire to cover national and world events, and Arledge knew it.

"Don't think I haven't thought of that, Howard," Arledge said. "I'm not through with that idea yet."

In subsequent conversations, whenever the topic of my switching to news came up, Arledge would say, "We're going to get to that, Howard. We'll show those bastards a thing or two about journalism."

We never did. I'm sure that Arledge was afraid of the beating he'd take in print if he used me on network news. It's too bad. I would have busted a gut for him, just as I had in sports, and I think we would have won.

For several years, I resented Roone for not bringing me to news. And considering what had already happened between us on the variety show, I sometimes wondered aloud what the hell I ever saw in the man. I was wrong, just as he's been wrong for making statements to the press that denigrate me, like, "People don't like Howard" and "Howard's insecurity makes it hard to deal with him."

Remarks such as those hurt. I guess we're the kind of men

who don't want to give an inch. Our egos get in the way. And I'm sure for as long as we live, we'll probably continue to follow an adversarial course. We've lost a lot of trust in each other, and maybe the wounds will never heal. I just don't know.

At least we were able to begin 1985 on a high note. At a party honoring an ABC executive named Julie Barnathan at Tavern on the Green, Roone joined Emmy and me at the bar, and we stayed together for almost three hours. As he usually does, Roone asked my wife, "Well, Emmy, how am I doing?"

Emmy looked him squarely in the eyes and smiled. "I've made my decision, Roone," she said. "The jury's no longer out. I'm accepting you."

"Finally!" Roone said and squeezed her hand.

Listening to the two of them laugh, I must admit it moved me. We hadn't shared a moment like that in a long time. Later on, after Roone dropped Emmy and me off at our apartment, I thought deeply about our relationship. "You know, Emmy," I said, "there's no denying it. I'll always respect the man for his brilliance. And let's face it: Without his help and support, I could not have made my mark in broadcasting."

"I've never thought otherwise, Howard."

On March 18, 1985, Arledge was in New York City, ordered back by Pierce from South Africa, where he was making broadcast news history, for a momentous announcement.

That same day, Leonard Goldenson, the chairman of the board, announced that ABC would merge with Capital Cities Communications, Inc., a highly successful broadcast and publishing group. It was termed a merger, but was in fact a friendly takeover by the smaller company for a reported price of $3.7 billion.

Most of us in the company were aware that a shakeup was imminent, and I personally knew that Goldenson was desperately afraid of a hostile takeover. Old friends of Goldenson's like Tom Murphy, the chairman of CCCI, and Dan Burke, the president, provided the ideal way out for a company that was languishing terribly on the entertainment side and had clearly declined radically where once it had reigned supreme in sports.

There is no way I can write about this except from the heart. As I watched Goldenson on closed-circuit television talking to all the employees about the growth and development of the company over a span of thirty-two years—the precise amount of time I had been with ABC—all of the memories flooded over me like a tidal wave and tears came into my eyes. Somebody once wrote that I wore ABC like a brand, and I will fully admit to that. No man has ever been more supportive and more caring in my direction than Goldenson. And as he supported me through the years when I adopted positions that I personally believed in but were contradictory to the best interests of the company, I came to view Goldenson as a father. He was due to retire to an advisory capacity, and it is hard for me to imagine ABC without him. Unlike CBS and NBC, we were called a family network, and aptly so because all our triumphs and disasters had made us feel like one. Frankly, I can't conceive of it ever being that way again.

It will probably take about a year to unravel the mind-boggling technical problems of the takeover, all of which will have to be approved by the FCC, but when that happens, there will surely be sweeping changes in the conduct of the company's business. The Capital Cities people are highly efficient, and they are brilliant managers. But whatever happens at ABC in the years ahead, I can't imagine Arledge not continuing as a signal figure within the company. On the very week of the takeover, he was capturing the world with a week-long series of telecasts conducted by Ted Koppel on *Nightline* from South Africa and proving all over again that he could do brilliantly in news what he had once done in sports. No company in its right mind would tamper with that kind of talent.

On December 8, 1980, John Lennon was mortally wounded by an assassin's bullet outside his New York apartment. That night, I was in Miami for a *Monday Night Football* game, and in the midst of the telecast, I got word of the tragedy. It was my task to inform an audience of some fifty million people of Lennon's death. I delivered what amounted to a eulogy of the man, noting that Lennon was no ordinary rock star, but as the driving force of the Beatles had had a tremendous cultural impact on the youth of the world.

I couldn't help but recall how we had briefly crossed paths several years earlier.

In the summer of 1975, when I was busily preparing for the debut of my prime-time variety show, I had given an interview in which I said that I wanted to get Lennon to appear with me. I had never met the man. Then, quite unexpectedly, I got this letter:

Dear Howard:

Someone told me that you mentioned me in a newspaper in regard to your new show. For personal reasons I must decline any commitments until next year. I might add that the equally weird and wonderful monsieur Ringo Starr might well be available for your variety show! (and perhaps more suited.)
I wish you all the best,
I'm sure it's going to be a big hit!
love and dressed fishes,
yer old pal,
what's his name?

The letter was signed "John L."

I was more determined than ever. In fact, I eventually decided to go all the way—I'd try to reunite the Beatles!

The Beatles hadn't sung together in five years. Reuniting them was practically an impossibility, but I just had to take my best shot. I called Rick Sklar, the program director who had helped create "music radio" and turned WABC into the most listened-to station in the country.

"Ricky," I said, "get me the Beatles!"

Sklar couldn't believe what I was asking of him. I pressed on, telling him how the show was going to originate from the Ed Sullivan Theater and that I wanted to re-create the night that the Beatles first appeared on American television. We'd do it from the same theater, on the same stage.

"I'll make some calls," Sklar said with a sigh. "John is in New York."

The following week, Sklar and I joined producer Rupert Hitzig at the "21" Club, and we waited for Lennon. He showed up wearing a black velvet jacket with a large diamond-studded pin that spelled "Elvis."

Sklar handled the introductions, and we ordered drinks. Lennon had no idea what I was really up to. He thought I simply wanted to meet him as a result of his letter. First we talked about *Monday Night Football.* Then I brought up my variety show and said, "John, I want you guys on my show."

"What do you mean 'you guys'?" Lennon said.

"You, George, Paul, and Ringo."

After a long pause, Lennon said, "I don't know." He shook his head. "After what's gone down, I don't know. I thought you wanted me."

"Of course I do. But let's be realistic. This is bigger than both of us."

Hitzig jumped in with a suggestion about reuniting the Beatles electronically with a four-way split screen. They wouldn't even have to be in the same city.

Lennon mulled it over. He was doubtful. "Sure, we've thought about getting together again," he said. "But we'll probably never do it. What would the people expect? We might leave them disappointed. It's better to let them have their memories, have them remember us as we were."

I tried again to persuade him. "Think of it, John," I concluded. "Imagine restaging the most electrifying moment in American television! It will be fantastic!"

Lennon listened, but it was no use. In the unlikely event that the Beatles ever did get together again, he said, they'd go for a huge financial bonanza and hold a concert on closed-circuit TV so they could reach countless indoor arenas and theaters all over the world. Tickets would be sold at a premium, and a deal for an album and a motion picture would be thrown in. A reunion on network television didn't make much sense to him. He was right.

When Lennon got up to leave, he shook my hand and said he'd love to visit with me in the booth at half time of a *Monday Night Football* telecast. As for the variety show and reuniting the Beatles, that was out of the question.

Lennon left the "21" Club sooner than he had expected and headed straight for a Man Ray exhibition that had just opened at the Huntington Hartford Gallery of Modern Art. There he spotted Yoko Ono standing in front of a painting. They had been separated for quite some time. They began to talk—and ended up leaving the gallery hand in hand. They stayed together until the day he died.

Not long after his reconciliation with Yoko, John told Sklar that he might not have gone to the Man Ray exhibition that day if his meeting with me hadn't ended when it did. "He brought us back together, Howard did," Lennon said.

Peter Ueberroth is perhaps the most remarkable figure in sports. I truly believe he is destined for greatness. In my opinion, he'll one day find the office of baseball commissioner too confining for his vast skills. Look for him to run for political office, or perhaps become a captain of industry in the mold of Lee Iacocca of Chrysler.

Once Ueberroth puts his brains and energy to a task, anything is possible. I was astounded by his spectacular success as the president of the Los Angeles Olympic Organizing Committee. A lot of cynics were predicting the death of the Olympics, but Ueberroth believed that they could be saved and that he could save them. In the end, the Olympic Games worked, and worked brilliantly—even turning an amazing, it-couldn't-be-done $215 million profit!

I watched Ueberroth closely before, during, and after the Olympics and spent many hours with him. I've never seen a man with so much of the crusader in him. He relishes problems, and he sets what seems like impossible goals for himself. He was a whirling dervish at the Olympics. He scrutinized practically every detail and never missed a thing—well, almost.

Several days before the opening ceremonies, I went to the Los Angeles Memorial Coliseum to report a story on the former American gold-medal winners who'd be carrying the Olympic flag into the stadium. The athletes were chosen to represent the ethnic diversity of the country, and they included Dr. Sammy Lee, Bruce Jenner, Wyomia Tyus, and others.

When I got there, I dropped by David Wolper's trailer to have breakfast. Wolper is the Hollywood producer who was in charge of staging the opening and closing ceremonies. He was excited as hell.

"Howard," Wolper said, "what great athletes we've got for flag bearers! Here, read the list."

Scanning the names, I noticed a glaring omission. "You've got trouble, David," I said.

"What?!?"

"You don't have an Hispanic among the athletes," I said.

"You can't do this. There's something like seven hundred fifty thousand Hispanics in this city, maybe more. You're crazy."

A look of horror spread across Wolper's face. "Oh, my God," he said, "you're right."

Wolper promptly reached for his walkie-talkie to contact Ueberroth, who came running to the trailer.

"Peter," I said, "if you don't have an Hispanic along with the others, you're going to get a lot of heat. And besides, it's not right."

"I couldn't agree more," Ueberroth said. Then, turning to Wolper and without cracking a smile, he said, "David, why have you failed me like this?"

"What're we going to do?" Wolper said.

"What do you suggest, Howard?"

"Richard Sandoval," I said. "I think he lives right here in L.A., and he's the bantamweight champ. The kid's perfect. He made the 1980 boxing team, and he can also represent all the athletes who weren't able to compete in Moscow because of the boycott."

"I like it, Howard," Ueberroth said.

"How can we get him?" Wolper asked.

"I'll take care of it through my office," Ueberroth said.

Ueberroth dispatched his executive aide, David Israel, to find Sandoval, which he did. But I later found out a problem still existed that might have prohibited Sandoval from appearing as a flag bearer.

The former decathlon champion, Rafer Johnson, was secretly scheduled to carry the Olympic torch into the Coliseum, run a lap around the track, then climb the steps to the rim of the stadium and light the flame. Johnson, however, developed a muscle pull in his leg, and there was considerable doubt whether he could climb the steps after running his lap. The decision was made to use one of the flag bearers—Gina Hemphill, a granddaughter of the late Jesse Owens—to carry the torch around the track. Gina would then hand it to Johnson, who was fit enough to ascend the steps and light the flame.

If Johnson hadn't experienced leg trouble, Gina would have remained a flag bearer—and there would have been no place for Sandoval.

Luckily for Ueberroth, everything worked out perfectly, and I chided him, "No more, Peter. From here on in, you run your own damned Olympic Games."

Through all the years, from the days when he was baseball's preeminent hitter to his life in retirement as a passionate fisherman, Ted Williams hasn't changed one bit. I was with Ted in June 1983 as he approached his sixty-fifth birthday. Imagine: The Splendid Splinter on Social Security! We met in Westport, Connecticut, where Ted was attending a baseball card collectors' convention. After I had interviewed him, we had drinks in the bar of the motel where he was staying, and the conversation turned to politics. As always, Ted was tough as leather, fervid and combative.

"Tell me, Howard," he asked, "what the hell do you think we ought to do about what's going on in Central America?"

"It's a difficult, complex problem," I said. "We must proceed cautiously. Otherwise, I fear, we could get involved in another Vietnam."

"I'll tell you what we ought to do," he said, pounding a fist into his palm. "We ought to bomb the hell out of 'em. All of 'em, wherever there's trouble, get 'em now!"

"Now, wait, Ted, it isn't so simple. . . ."

"What're we going to do? Wait till those Commie sunsuvbitches are crawling all over Miami Beach? We've got to stop them somewhere! I say, bomb the hell out of 'em!"

The U.S. amateur boxing team was facing the Cubans in Havana in February 1978, and I was there to call the fights for *Wide World of Sports*. At the time, there was serious talk about the Cubans playing a major-league baseball team in an exhibition game. In fact, the then general manager of the Cleveland Indians, Gabe Paul, had already visited Cuba to try to set it up. Also, the State Department was in the midst of exploring avenues to ease tensions between the United States and Cuba.

ABC Sports hardly lent a helping hand to either venture, and I was an unwitting accomplice in an international fiasco that I still can't believe really happened.

In attendance at the fights was Fidel Castro, and I was lucky enough to get him for his first live appearance via satellite on American television. Castro had an interpreter with him, and naturally we talked about baseball and the possibility of the Cubans playing a big-league team. He instantly warmed to the subject, colorfully expressing Cuba's love for baseball and how kids play the game on every vacant lot across the country.

All of a sudden, while Castro was talking, I heard in my earphones the voice of Ned Steckel, the producer in the truck. Steckel was screaming, "You've got to throw it to Jim McKay and speed skating in Lake Placid. Hurry up!"

I thought, What, is he insane? I can't do that. It's ridiculous. I've got the leader of Cuba, and he's telling me to cut him off for speed skating!

I had no intention of doing what Steckel wanted, but he kept yelling in my ears. I was rapidly losing my concentration. Then an engineer named Sandy Sandberg got into the act, crawling on the floor and pulling at my microphone wire. "You've got to give it to McKay," Sandberg said with a hiss. "Come on, Howard, throw it to McKay right now!"

I was going absolutely nuts! Finally, out of despair, I said, "I'm sorry, El Comandante, but I must now throw it to Jim McKay for speed skating from Lake Placid. I'm terribly sorry."

The interpreter looked horrified. When he told his leader that I had ended the interview, Castro was outraged. At first I didn't realize just how furious he was. I was with Emmy and then ABC senior producer John Martin and his girlfriend, and when we later arrived at the airport to fly home, we were not allowed to board our private plane and take off.

As we later found out, Castro thought that President Carter had ordered him off the air, and he was giving us a hard time. Martin tried to explain what had actually happened to an intermediary at the airport, but I guess it made no sense to him. Hell, it made no sense to *me*.

After five hours or so, they finally let us go. Castro had come to understand the circumstances surrounding his aborted interview, and he even sent me a box of cigars with his good wishes.

The whole crazy affair wasn't over, not yet. During the telecast, ABC ran a feature on life in Cuba and how time had seemed to stand still since the revolution. Hotels were decaying, theaters were showing old movies, and everybody was driving around in American cars from the 1950s. As part of the feature, I was seen in a decrepit nightclub where the chorus girls wore battered shoes, and there were shots of Emmy with a Soviet official, who had asked her to dance.

The next morning, I read in Dick Young's column in the New York *Daily News* that I had shown my Commie traits by consorting with Cubans in a posh nightclub and referring to Castro as "El Comandante." Now I was a Communist!

At the same time, an official in the State Department contacted Roone Arledge and demanded to know why Castro was yanked off the air. What an unholy mess! And all because a producer who had lived his professional life in a thimble thought that speed skating was more significant than an interview with a world leader.

A little more than a year before the 1984 Summer Olympics, I did an interview with Bobby Knight, the fiery and outspoken basketball coach at Indiana University. The thrust of the interview concerned Knight's fitness to coach the U.S. men's squad in Los Angeles. It was a hot topic because of Knight's behavior at the Pan American Games in 1979, when he was arrested in San Juan for getting into a fight with a Puerto Rican policeman. The incident surfaced again after Knight was named the Olympic coach, and there were those who were openly critical of his selection.

Knight faced my questions squarely, and I thought he had handled himself rather well. Several days later, I got a letter from him, thanking me for dealing with him in a fair and objective manner. In his letter, Knight recalled when we first met, which I had totally forgotten. He was then the head coach at West Point. "The Holiday Festival of 1965 was the first time you ever talked to me and it was in John Goldner's office in the Garden. You concluded the interview by saying, 'A college coach has just referred to me as "Mr. Cosell,"' and I said to you that it was an indication of respect, not difference in age. I thought in 1965 that no one in your profession could approach your honesty and integrity and have never varied in that opinion."

Thank you, Bobby.

In my long career, as you doubtlessly can imagine, I've received untold thousands of letters from people I don't know. The senders run the gamut from admirers and critics to sports freaks and scary kooks. Few have moved me as much as a letter I got in February 1985 from a New Jersey woman who identified herself as a widow. She was writing to apologize, she said, for an incident that had occurred in the distant past.

In part, her letter read: "I phoned your office some years ago regarding Ali, never dreaming you would answer the phone. My five brothers and sisters had enlisted in the Navy. My seventeen-year-old cousin had been killed in World War II. I resented Ali for not serving his country.

"When you answered—being Irish—I really lit into you. I was shocked when you remained a gentleman and spoke quietly and in a charming voice. You told me I was entitled to my opinion.

"Mr. Cosell, I hung up ashamed for having screamed at you. I realized that one day I must apologize, and ever since, I've been an ardent supporter of yours. . . ."

After all these years, it's still gratifying to know that my defense of Ali, based on the laws of the land, touched so many people in so many different ways—and won't soon be forgotten.

Mike Wallace and I have known each other since the days when we were both struggling to make a name for ourselves. When ABC dropped him from an interview show in the late 1950s, Wallace hooked up with Channel 13, then a local station in New York, for a nightly news program, and I'd frequently appear as a guest without a fee because I liked and respected him. He liked and respected me, too, and we still feel the same way about each other. We will always be good friends. Every now and then, though, even good friends get into a scrap, and in our case, it was monitored in the press.

Mike started it. Late in the summer of 1984, while sitting for an interview on ABC's *20/20*, he told Barbara Walters that *60 Minutes* had scrapped a 1976 segment on me because I turned out to be a "marshmallow."

Naturally, I couldn't let Wallace go unanswered. A week later, at a convention in Los Angeles, the National Radio Broadcasters' Association presented me with its first Radio Award, and I had to make an acceptance speech. After expressing my gratitude and my love for the industry, I let Mike have it between the eyes. While acknowledging our friendship, I said, "I was not a marshmallow. The interview with me was never aired because I beat Mike Wallace's ass."

What had happened was this:

Mike's questions were neither searching nor penetrating. Instead of painting a personal portrait of me, he seemed bent on strutting his stuff by trying to get me into an argument and put me down. I wouldn't let him get away with it. He'd constantly refer to a file of press clippings, quoting sportswriters and sports television critics who were critical of me and then asking me to reply. It was ludicrous, like asking a guy if he still beats his wife. It was beneath Mike, and I told him so. I had no intention of sitting still for a blustering, confrontational interview that was all ambush and no substance. He could go ask the critics why they wrote what they did. I was there to answer thoughtful, probing questions, not to defend myself against vitriolic attacks in the press.

Then, inexplicably, Wallace brought up the Bobby Riggs–Billie Jean King tennis match, which ABC had carried several years earlier and which I had called. "Now, Howard, you will admit that you know nothing about tennis?" he asked.

It should be noted that the interview was conducted in the living room of my apartment, and Billy Talbert, the former tennis star, the executive director of the U.S. Open and a close friend, was there as an interested observer. When Mike questioned my knowledge of tennis, I paused to glance at Talbert. He was smiling, shaking his head, and rolling his eyes. What the hell was Wallace up to?

"You want to talk about tennis, Mike?" I said. "Okay, then, let's talk about the scandal over at CBS and the winner-take-all matches your network televised."

"Hold it, hold it!" the producer with Wallace suddenly yelled. "We can't use that!"

I had obviously touched a raw nerve. I was referring to a series of matches between top-ranked players that CBS had falsely promoted. The loser got paid as well as the winner, but you'd never know it if you had listened to CBS's hype of the matches as winner-take-all contests. The Federal Communications Commission, which is a stickler about truth in advertising, roundly reprimanded CBS. Even the Congress looked into it.

From then on, whenever Mike quoted yet another sportswriter's opinion of me, I let him have it. "I'll tell you what, Mike," I'd say. "I'll respond to that if you'll talk about CBS's fraudulent tennis matches."

Does that sound like a "marshmallow"?

At any rate, a couple of days after the convention in Los Angeles, Wallace was quoted in the newspapers as saying, "Although I admire Howard Cosell as a sportscaster, the reason the segment was cut was because Cosell was an uncharacteristic bore."

Well, I thought, if Mike wants to keep this up, I'll give him more than he can handle. But before this little feud could escalate into a battle, I got a call from Mike. "This is getting silly," he said.

"I agree," I said. "I'm not looking to get into a hassle with you."

"You just weren't yourself the day I interviewed you. That can happen. I understand."

"That's nonsense, Mike. I was fine. You couldn't stand up to me and you know it."

Mike snickered. "Okay, Howard. I know how we can settle this. I'd like to profile you in the future. You game?"

"Of course I am, Mike. I've got a book coming out in September a year from now. It's a good peg for the segment, and you can have me first."

"That's a deal."

In early 1984, I got a call from Vince McMahon, the marketing and merchandising wizard who's responsible for the boom in professional wrestling. I had never heard of him, but after a quick and precise introduction, he promptly got down to business. He wanted me to be the primary announcer on his wrestling telecasts.

"You can't be serious," I said, laughing.

"I'm dead serious," McMahon said.

"Come on. Boxing was bad enough, and now you want me to end my career by calling phony wrestling matches. Good Lord, you must be crazy."

"I am not crazy," he said, and I could hear anger creeping into his voice. "You really should think about it."

"I don't have to think about it, Vince. I don't want any part of it."

"Well, fuck you, Howard!" he said. "Wrestling's going to be the biggest sport in this country, and I don't need you anyway!"

I couldn't believe my ears. Just like that, the guy turned on me. "I wish you all the luck in the world, Vince," I said, keeping my cool.

"Wrestling will be king, Howard! You're making the biggest mistake of your life!"

"That may be, Vince, but I'm not going to do it."

After I hung up, I thought McMahon was a real kook. I still do—but he's an incredibly successful one. And I meant what I had said. I wish him all the luck in the world.

Remember the announcerless game? Believe it or not, it was a significant moment in recent broadcasting history, revealing the gullibility of certain segments of the print medium and how what they write can have a broad impact on the viewing public, especially sports fans.

In December 1980, NBC had scheduled a national telecast of a game between the Jets and the Dolphins in Miami. It was a meaningless game, and NBC figured it might get a 10 rating. It got a 16—thanks to a gimmick conceived by a young man who had spent his early years in television working with me at ABC.

At the time, Don Ohlmeyer was the executive producer of NBC Sports. He had a nothing game on his hands, and he was looking to do something dramatic, something that would get attention. There was then a lot of criticism in the press about announcers talking too much. Ohlmeyer decided to take advantage of it—and ordained a silent game. No announcers.

Ohlmeyer had another reason for carrying out his scheme. NBC had the rights to the Super Bowl that season, and he wanted to give his audio engineers a chance to experiment with new techniques in sound—to find out just how sharply they could pick up various kinds of noise in the heat of a game. He never intended to make a statement about the irrelevancy of announcers, but a lot of sportswriters and sports television critics turned Ohlmeyer's ruse into the burning issue of the day. The game suddenly took on a life of its own. Could this mean the end of announcers?

Ohlmeyer couldn't believe what was happening. While chuckling to himself, he kept a straight face and watched the newspaper guys make fools of themselves. Nobody knew better than Ohlmeyer that the announcerless game wouldn't prove a thing. No matter how well or how poorly the game performed in the ratings, no matter what anybody wrote, announcers were here to stay. It was ludicrous even to speculate otherwise. But the press swallowed the hook, and the Jets-Dolphins game got more publicity than Ohlmeyer dreamed possible.

In the wake of the game, headlines such as this one were typical: "Announcerless Game Doesn't Work." No kidding. But Ohlmeyer had done his job superbly, which was to generate an audience.

A couple of weeks later, I appeared on Tom Snyder's now defunct *Tomorrow* show and afterward had a drink with Fred Silverman, who was then that network's president. People were still talking and writing about the game. "It's the funniest damn thing," Silverman said. "Ohlmeyer did it as a gag. It was the most boring telecast in history, and all those boobs took it seriously. We even got some raves. We got more attention and better ratings on a game nobody would've watched. I still can't believe it."

On January 18, 1980, at the weekly foreign-policy breakfast in the White House, the Soviet invasion of Afghanistan dominated the conversation. At one point, Secretary of State Cyrus Vance brought up President Carter's decision to withdraw from the upcoming Moscow Olympics. At the time, this was a closely guarded secret. Carter had yet to announce the U.S. boycott, waiting to reveal his plans in a couple of days on *Meet the Press*.

According to Hamilton Jordan, the President's chief adviser, Carter said, "It's the toughest question of all for me. I don't want the onus for the failure of the Olympics to fall exclusively on the United States. It must be seen as a legitimate worldwide political reaction to what the Russians are doing in Afghanistan. After the grain embargo, the farmers raised hell." Then Carter smiled slyly. "But after I announce our Olympics boycott, we'll have to face the wrath of an even more powerful force—Howard Cosell, telling the sports fans that Jimmy Carter killed the Olympics."

Smiling slyly right back at the President, I'd like to take some credit for making his decision a little less of a burden to bear. I ended up supporting the boycott wholeheartedly and repeatedly said so on the air. It was the right thing to do. The Olympics had become an instrument for any group or any country seeking to make a political statement. The precedents were rife. Why then shouldn't we use them in the same vein? I harbored no illusions about the sanctity of the Olympics, and besides, the Soviets had violated every tenet of civilized behavior in their plunder of Afghanistan. It seemed absolutely wrong to me to let them use our athletes and our technological capabilities to broadcast their perverse propaganda to every corner of the globe—and I'll always admire President Carter for having the guts to spoil their party.

Even though he is a rabid sports fan, I never had any contact with Richard M. Nixon until several years after he had resigned the presidency in the wake of the Watergate scandal. Here's how it happened:

Frank Gifford was visiting his son at New York Hospital, where the teenager was recuperating from injuries sustained in an automobile accident. There Gifford bumped into Nixon, and the two stopped to chat. During the course of their conversation, Gifford mentioned that he was on his way to join Emmy and me for a drink.

When Gifford got to our apartment, he said, "I've got a gift for you from the President."

"The President?"

"Yes, Richard Nixon."

"You're kidding?"

When Nixon had heard Gifford was coming to see me, he reached into his pocket and handed Frank a cigar. "I know Howard smokes cigars," Nixon told him. "Please give him this with my compliments. I hope he enjoys it."

There are few people in politics I respect more than Bill Bradley, the U.S. senator from New Jersey. Perhaps not surprisingly, Bill is the most intellectual athlete I've ever known. He's also the biggest eater.

One night in 1973, when the New York Knicks were on their way to another NBA championship, Bradley appeared with me on ABC's local nightly news show. Afterward I invited him to my apartment for dinner. Emmy had cooked a huge roast beef, and we stared in amazement as Bill devoured practically the whole thing. He just kept eating and eating, never shy about asking for third and fourth helpings.

In between stuffing himself with meat, Bradley told Emmy

and me about his extensive travels during each and every off-season, and Emmy asked him to name the most interesting country he had visited.

"Afghanistan," he said, and then he delivered a fascinating discourse on that country's culture—its art, politics, economics, and whatever else we wanted to know about it. At one point, Bill made a prediction that I'll never forget. "They are a proud and fierce people," he said, "and they're extremely independent. It will one day be the source of a terrible conflict with the Soviet Union. If the Soviets think they can make Afghanistan knuckle under, they've got another think coming. Those people will fight to the death."

Under normal circumstances, I am not in the habit of responding to attacks on me in print, even though few people have endured as steady a stream of personal vilification as I have. But in March 1983, I felt compelled to write James Wieghart, then the editor of the New York *Daily News*, concerning one of his columnists. In part, my letter read: "I refer you to George Maksian's 'TV Scene' column of March 4. In reporting on who won what Emmy awards, Mr. Maksian concludes with the comment: 'No, Howard Cosell wasn't chosen Clown of the Year.' I don't know Mr. Maksian, never met the man, and I won't presume to even guess why he chose to take such a cheap shot at me. . . .

"Mr. Maksian's unfortunate crack did not wound me personally, but it hurt nonetheless—hurt because nowhere did he mention the fact that my show, *SportsBeat*, received an Emmy for outstanding programming; hurt because my staff, which is composed of many young people who work long, hard hours, didn't get the credit it so richly deserves. What do I tell these young people, who are deeply committed to journalism? Why shouldn't they receive, at the very least, fair and objective treatment from a member of their own profession, the same kind of fair and objective treatment they strive to give others each week? Instead, from a columnist of a great newspaper in the greatest city in the world, they get the back of Mr. Maksian's hand through his slander of me. That's what really hurts, Mr. Wieghart. . . ."

Several weeks later, Wieghart replied. His letter elated me. It reflected a just and compassionate man, two virtues I have the utmost respect for in a journalist. Wieghart had passed along my letter to Maksian, then talked to him about it. "George said he neglected to mention the award to *SportsBeat* because he felt it was less newsworthy than the awards that he did mention," Wieghart wrote. "And he expressed sorrow that his aside that 'Howard Cosell wasn't chosen Clown of the Year' caused you pain because he meant it as a 'jest.'

"I want you to know, Howard, that I was dissatisfied with Maksian's response on both counts and I told him so. I simply can't understand why columnists today think that calling someone a derogatory name is humorous. I don't find it so and obviously the person on the receiving end doesn't either. I wonder who does?

"I want to apologize to you personally for the gratuitous insult. . . ."

My hat's off to Wieghart. Here's a newspaperman who doesn't confuse liberty and license. If there were more editors like him, I'd feel a lot better about the First Amendment today.

In the winter of 1976, a research editor at *Playboy* magazine named Tom Passavant was trying to put together an article that was intended to be a rip job of me. Apparently, he had taken the time to contact various personalities for negative comments. The following is a letter that Mr. Passavant received from a celebrated criminal attorney:

Dear Mr. Passavant:

I am sorry I cannot contribute to your effort but after racking my brain, I am unable to think of anything that I dislike about Howard Cosell. As a matter of fact, I like him very much and consider him to be a good friend. Sorry.

Very truly yours,

F. Lee Bailey

As you shall see, *Playboy* didn't give up.

David Halberstam won the Pulitzer Prize based on his reporting from Vietnam for *The New York Times*. Later he achieved literary fame as the best-selling author of two books in particular, *The Best and the Brightest* and *The Powers That Be.* We first met in the early 1970s but never really had much contact. Then one day, while talking business with Roone Arledge, he said to me, "By the way, what the hell does David Halberstam have against you?"

"Beats me," I said. "I hardly even know the man."

"Well, I met him at a party the other night, and he was all over me. He's got a real bug up his ass about you."

I shrugged. "What can I tell you, Roone? He's obviously got a problem. I know he has a childlike devotion to the Knicks. He's very immature about it. I've heard from Mike Burke [then the president of Madison Square Garden] that he bothers him with phone calls, telling him who should start, who should sit on the bench. The guy's a nut."

A couple of years later, in December 1982, Halberstam authored a vicious attack on me in *Playboy* magazine. Apparently, he couldn't contain himself any longer. In the article he called me, among other things, a bully and a monster, and went so far as to say I was merciless and violent. This from a man I had only a passing acquaintance with. It was the worst kind of cheap shot I had ever read. He ended the article with a ludicrous attempt at psychoanalysis, trying to get inside my head and figure out my various neuroses. He never even bothered to call and talk to me! So much for the fair and objective journalism he supposedly learned at *The New York Times.*

Naturally, I had no idea that Halberstam was writing the article. I was made aware of it through a phone call from Gary Fencik, a football player who had taken a course I taught at Yale and went on to star at defensive back for the Chicago Bears.

"Do you know anything about an article that's coming out about you in *Playboy*?" Fencik asked me.

"No. Why?"

"It's just vicious, Howard. It's full of lies and distortions. It's terrible. And I can't believe who wrote it: David Halberstam! I always had such respect for the man. How could he write such garbage?"

"Gary, I've been through this more times than I care to recall. There's nothing I can do about it. By the way, how did you find out about the article?"

"My girlfriend is the centerfold for December, and she got an advance copy of the magazine."

I had to laugh. What a way to find out you've just been vilified in *Playboy*.

"I'm glad you can laugh, Howard," Fencik said. "I'd like to get the sonuvabitch and strangle him!"

Despite Halberstam's attack on me, generally speaking I've received even-handed and even praiseworthy treatment from the newspaper and magazine writers who don't cover sports. A recent example came on the night of January 16, 1985, when the *Washington Journalism Review* honored me as the "Best National Television Sports Reporter." Other honorees included George Will, Ted Koppel, David Broder, Dan Rather, and Roger Mudd. We were all selected as the result of a *WJR* readers poll—and most of the respondents worked in print journalism.

As for the sportswriting fraternity, there's no question that I have been the victim of a long and abiding absence of responsibility. Some have even waged what can only be described as a literary pogrom against me. Now, let me make this clear: I don't mean to paint all sportswriters and columnists with the same brush; certainly I've had my share of complimentary articles. The so-called sports television critics, however, are in a class by themselves. I simply have no use for just about all of them. Don Freeman of the *San Diego Union* is an exception. And I'd like to mention a young writer on *The Washington Post* named David Remnick, who no longer writes sports television criticism but displayed a commendable grasp of the industry.

Unlike Freeman and Remnick, sports television critics as a group simply have no understanding of my medium—its technological complexities and idiosyncrasies, its performing talent and executive hierarchy. In most cases, sports editors couldn't care less about television criticism and wind up assigning the column to a former baseball, hockey, or soccer reporter who is several cuts below the better writers in their departments. These columnists are steeped in sports, not television, and their idea of covering my industry is writing clichéd column after clichéd column about announcers and who got off the best line.

Of course, they are almost fawning in their admiration of ex-jocks, who are now covering the same events as they are and they

feel a kinship with them. They have duped the public into believing that only ex-jocks can provide real insights into the game.
Rarely if ever do they try to come to grips with the essence of
what it means to work behind a microphone, which is simply the
ability to communicate—to move the viewers and have an impact on them.

When was the last time any of these critics wrote a serious
essay on television? Why don't they grapple with larger questions? For example: How have sports on television influenced our
language, economy, and politics? Does sports on television promote violence in any way, shape, or form? What impact have
sports on television had on the way Madison Avenue does business?

Don't bother to look. You won't find those kinds of television
columns in the sports pages. And the sad thing is, these critics
wield more power than you can imagine in the power structure of
the network sports divisions. It's one of the terrible failings of my
industry that our executives actually take these critics seriously
and try to curry favor with them. And since the three networks
are headquartered in New York, you'll find that critics such as
Stan Isaacs of *Newsday*, Phil Mushnick of the *New York Post*,
and Rudy Martzke of *USA Today* are the most powerful. These
people know as much about television as the paper in this book.
And why would anybody take *The New York Times* seriously? In
the past several years, that newspaper has used no fewer than six
different writers to produce its television sports column. Way to
cover the territory, guys.

For my money, the best television critic in the land is Tom
Shales of *The Washington Post*. He couldn't care less about
sports. Hardly knows a thing about it. What sets him apart is that
he understands the medium. He appreciates it. He's got perspective, having taken the time to watch and study programs from
television's earliest days. He knows what works and what doesn't
and why. What's more, he covers the medium as a journalist.
And he writes like a dream, wittily and incisively.

When a television personality gets a rave from Shales, believe
me, it *means* something, and the people in my industry know it.
One column Shales wrote about me in late 1978 spoke volumes.
In several hundred words, he was able to get to the core of my
success on television. He wrote the column in my voice, a clever

technique, and I took a punch here and there. In essence, though, he captured Howard Cosell:

"How-word Co-sell—you heard the bell and you came out talking. You bounced off the wall. You covered left field. You went out on a limb. And in the end, there wasn't only one champ, there were two. What a performer! What a man! What a mouth!

" 'Ali!' you exclaimed during round 10. 'So purposeful! So sure of himself! What an extraordinary career, and what an extraordinary man he has been in every way!' You could have been talking about yourself, Howard—your courage in contending with constant, corrosive criticism; your intransigent declination to moderate your immutable and inscrutable modus operandi; your refusal to play the Pollyanna in an industry that encourages diffidence—and, if you will, your pugnacious perspicacity and audacious imperturbability in the face of a chorus of the world's cruel boos. . . .

"Maybe you mangle the language hither and yon; maybe you make an art form of overstatement and maybe you threaten at times to rewrite *Roget's Thesaurus* off the proverbial cuff. What matters is not the words you use but the way you use them—like punches, like jabs, like body blows. We weren't watching the Ali-Spinks fight, Howard. We were watching you watch the Ali-Spinks fight. The sound of your voice was virtually visual—the sensory equal to the picture itself—and more than that, it was a transmogrification into a personal and intimate form, a manageable, living-room form, of the roaring crowd that filled the Super Dome in New Orleans."

Now, to the sportswriters and sports columnists. Gentlemen, keep taking your best shots. I don't care. I've won. And in the end, I'll take solace in the fact that the most decent and talented and cultured members of your fraternity have always been on my side. They've written glowing words about me, and I'm forever grateful. I'm referring to the likes of Pete Axthelm of *Newsweek*; Tony Kornheiser of *The Washington Post*; Mike Lupica of the New York *Daily News*; Diane Shah of the *Los Angeles Herald-Examiner*; David Kindred of the *Atlanta Constitution*; Billy Reed of the Louisville *Courier-Journal*; Jim Murray of the *Los Angeles Times*; David Israel, formerly of the *Chicago Tribune* and the *Los Angeles Herald-Examiner*, who was Ueberroth's executive aide at the 1984 Olympic Games; and Robert Lipsyte of CBS, who once wrote for *The New York Times* and was the best sports columnist in my lifetime.

If I may, I'd like to single out *Sports Illustrated*'s Frank Deford, a writer who has earned enormous respect within his profession. He was the author of a cover story about me, and I shall always cherish the last paragraph in particular:

". . . first and foremost, Howard Cosell is sports. There are all these people, these fans, who claim that when Cosell does a game on television, they turn off the sound on TV and listen to the radio broadcast. Oh, sure. You probably know critics in your neighborhood who vow the same thing. Well, too bad for them. Don't they understand? Cosell isn't television. He's not audio. Howard Cosell is sports in our time. Feel sorry for the people who turn off the sound. The poor bastards missed the game."

"MANAGEMENT
MUST MANAGE!"*

MANAGING　　　　69986-9/$3.95US/$4.95Can
Harold Geneen with Alvin Moscow

"Sensible advice from the legendary practitioner of superior management, ITT Chairman of the Board Emeritus, Harold Geneen."*　　　　　—*Publishers Weekly*

THEORY Z　How American Business Can Meet the Japanese Challenge
William G. Ouchi　　　　59451-X/$3.95US/$4.95Can

"Powerful answers for American firms struggling with high employee turnover, low morale, and falling productivity."
　　　　　—*Dallas Times Herald*

HYPERGROWTH　The Rise and Fall of Osborne Computer Corporation
　　　　　　　　69960-5/$5.95US/$7.75Can
Adam Osborne and John Dvorak

The personal account of the Silicon Valley megabuck bust that stunned the business world.

An Avon Trade Paperback

THE AVON A★L★L-S★T★A★R★S

THE ARTFUL DODGER   70085-9/$3.95 US/$4.95 Can
Tommy Lasorda and David Fisher
"Absolutely irresistible...an uninterrupted lode of anecdotes from
an American original."   L.A. Times

AARON TO ZUVERINK   68445-4/$4.50 US
Rich Marazzi/Len Fiorito   /$4.50 Can
For those who want to relive baseball's golden decade, the 1950's,
Marazzi and Fiorito offer profiles of more than 1,000 major league
players—their records, their moments of glory, and their life after
baseball. Illustrated.

AARON TO ZIPFEL   89694-X/$4.95 US
Rich Marazzi/Len Fiorito   /$5.95 Can
From rookies to Hall-of-Famers, Marazzi and Fiorito tell you what the
players of the 1960's are doing now. They're all here—the men you
cheered and jeered through baseball's sensational sixties.
Illustrated.

THE "ALL-STARS'" ALL-STAR BASEBALL BOOK
Nick Acocella and Donald Dewey   89879-9/$3.95 US/$4.95 Can
For the first time ever—the best rate the best! Major leaguers from
every era cast their votes for their all-time favorite dream teams.

THE ALL-TIME ALL-STAR BASEBALL BOOK   89530-7/$3.95 US
Bart Acocella, Nick Acocella and Donald Dewey   /$4.95 Can
A baseball book that has everything. A comprehensive collection of
team lineups containing baseball facts and opinions with not just
the same old stats: 400 lists of baseball lineups including players
with the most RBI's, doubles, triples, homers, runs scored, worst
goofs, most controversial calls and much more.

DOLLAR SIGN ON THE MUSCLE   69934-6/$3.95 US
Kevin Kerrane   /$4.95 Can
A rare behind-the-scenes look at the inside world of scouting; how
they shape the game, make—or break—careers.

TOUGH CALLS   86777-X/$6.95 US
Zach Rebackoff   /$6.95 Can
Veteran umpire Zach Rebackoff calls 'em like he's seen 'em in this
illustrated book of official baseball rules.   Avon Trade

AVON Paperbacks
Buy these books at your local bookstore or use this coupon for ordering:

Avon Books. Dept BP. Box 767. Rte 2. Dresden. TN 38225

Please send me the book(s) I have checked above. I am enclosing $_____
(please add $1.00 to cover postage and handling for each book ordered to a maximum of
three dollars). Send check or money order—no cash or C.O.D.'s please. Prices and numbers are subject to change without notice. Please allow six to eight weeks for delivery.

Name _____

Address _____

City _____ State/Zip _____

ALL-STAR 4/86